AUDI 100 1969–72 AUTOBOOK

Workshop Manual for
Auto Union Audi 100 1969–72
Auto Union Audi 100S 1969–72
Auto Union Audi 100LS 1969–72
Auto Union Audi 100GL 1971–72
Auto Union Audi 100 Coupé S 1971–72

by

Kenneth Ball G I Mech E
and the
Autopress team of Technical Writers

AUTOPRESS LTD   GOLDEN LANE   BRIGHTON   BN1 2QJ   ENGLAND

The AUTOBOOK series of Workshop Manuals is the largest in the world and covers the majority of British and Continental motor cars, as well as all major Japanese and Australian models. For a full list see the back of this manual.

CONTENTS

Introduction

Acknowledgement

Chapter 1	The Engine	9
Chapter 2	The Fuel System	25
Chapter 3	The Ignition System	43
Chapter 4	The Cooling System	49
Chapter 5	The Clutch	55
Chapter 6	Manual Transmission	59
Chapter 7	Automatic Transmission	81
Chapter 8	The Differential Assembly	93
Chapter 9	Drive Shafts and Suspension	97
Chapter 10	The Steering Gear	113
Chapter 11	The Braking System	121
Chapter 12	The Electrical System	131
Chapter 13	The Bodywork	141

Appendix

ISBN 0 85147 332 6

First Edition   1972
Second Edition, fully revised   1972

© Autopress Ltd 1972

Printed and bound in Brighton England for Autopress Ltd by G Beard & Son Ltd

ACKNOWLEDGEMENT

My thanks are due to Auto Union (G.B.) Ltd. for their unstinted co-operation and also for supplying data and illustrations.

I am also grateful to a considerable number of owners who have discussed their cars at length and many of whose suggestions have been included in this manual.

Kenneth Ball G I Mech E
Associate Member Guild of Motoring Writers

Ditchling Sussex England.

INTRODUCTION

This do-it-yourself Workshop Manual has been specially written for the owner who wishes to maintain his car in first class condition and to carry out his own servicing and repairs. Considerable savings on garage charges can be made, and one can drive in safety and confidence knowing the work has been done properly.

Comprehensive step-by-step instructions and illustrations are given on all dismantling, overhauling and assembling operations. Certain assemblies require the use of expensive special tools, the purchase of which would be unjustified. In these cases information is included but the reader is recommended to hand the unit to the agent for attention.

Throughout the Manual hints and tips are included which will be found invaluable, and there is an easy to follow fault diagnosis at the end of each chapter.

Whilst every care has been taken to ensure correctness of information it is obviously not possible to guarantee complete freedom from errors or to accept liability arising from such errors or omissions.

Instructions may refer to the righthand or lefthand sides of the vehicle or the components. These are the same as the righthand or lefthand of an observer standing behind the car and looking forward.

CHAPTER 1

THE ENGINE

1 : 1 Description
1 : 2 Removing and refitting the engine
1 : 3 Removing and refitting cylinder head
1 : 4 Servicing the head and valves
1 : 5 Valve clearance adjustment
1 : 6 Dismantling the engine

1 : 7 Pistons and connecting rods
1 : 8 Crankshaft and bearings
1 : 9 Reassembling and timing the engine
1 : 10 Oil filter
1 : 11 Engine, USA version
1 : 12 Fault diagnosis

1 : 1 Description

The engine fitted to the cars covered in this manual is available in two sizes ie. 1760 cc and 1871 cc. The stroke in each case is 84.4 mm but the bore is 81.5 mm on the smaller engine and 84.0 mm on the larger. The engine, an in-line four cylinder unit, is installed at an angle of 40 deg. to the left to allow a lower bonnet line, being mounted in the car frame by means of rubber-insulated carriers bolted to the engine block and supports on the transmission. The cylinder block and integral crankcase are of cast iron.

The crankshaft is a tempered steel forging incorporating eight counterweights to ensure perfect balance and runs in five main bearings in the crankcase. Axial thrust is accommodated at the centre main bearing position. The flywheel is fastened to the crankshaft by means of six screws and is secured against turning. The camshaft drive sprocket is mounted at the front of the shaft and secured by means of a Woodruff key.

The I-section connecting rods are tempered steel forgings, having tri-metal big-end bearing shells and lead-bronze coated steel small-end bushes. Pistons are light alloy castings with steel inserts to reduce thermal expansion. They are fitted with two compression rings and one oil control ring each. Pistons for the 90 and 100 bhp engines are similar, pistons for the 80 bhp engines having larger recessed combustion areas to provide a lower compression ratio.

The cylinder head is a light-alloy casting in which the overhead valve gear is mounted, the valve seat inserts and valve guides being shrunk into position. The inlet and exhaust manifolds are bolted to the cylinder head.

The high-mounted camshaft runs in babbit metal shell bearings and is driven from the crankshaft sprocket by means of a duplex roller chain, the chain being controlled by a hydraulic tensioner. The valves are operated via cams, followers, pushrods and rockers.

The engine is lubricated by a pressure feed system. The oil is drawn from the sump through a filter screen and a gear type oil pump passes it to a fullflow filter, cleaned oil then being forced to the oil passages in the cylinder block and thence to the lubrication points in the engine.

1 : 2 Removing and refitting engine

The usual operations of decarbonizing and top overhaul can be carried out without removing the engine. The pistons and connecting rods can be removed with the engine in position, after the cylinder head and oil sump have been removed.

If the operator is not a skilled motor engineer it is suggested that he will find much useful information in **Hints on Maintenance and Overhaul** at the end of this Manual and that he should read this before starting

FIG 1:1   Removing the front apron

FIG 1:2   The throttle shaft and hydraulic brake line

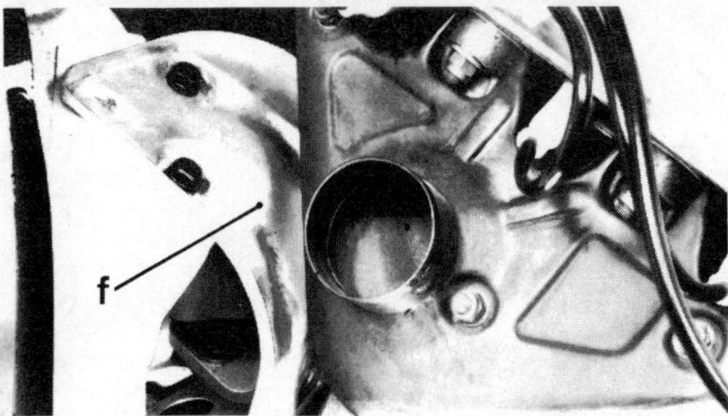

FIG 1:3   Removing the guard plate from the right side engine mounting

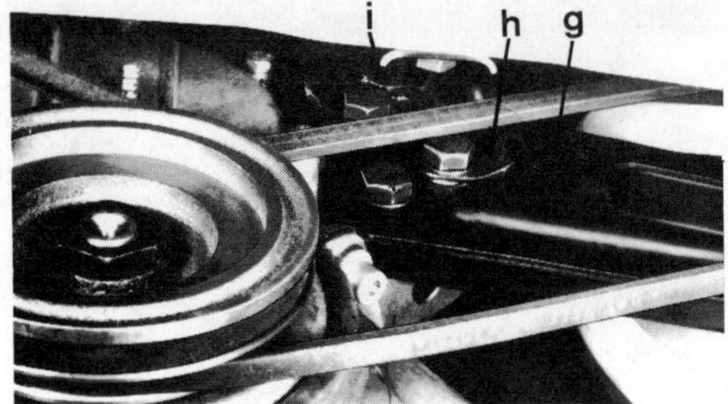

FIG 1:4   Removing the fan assembly or the stop according to the clearance available

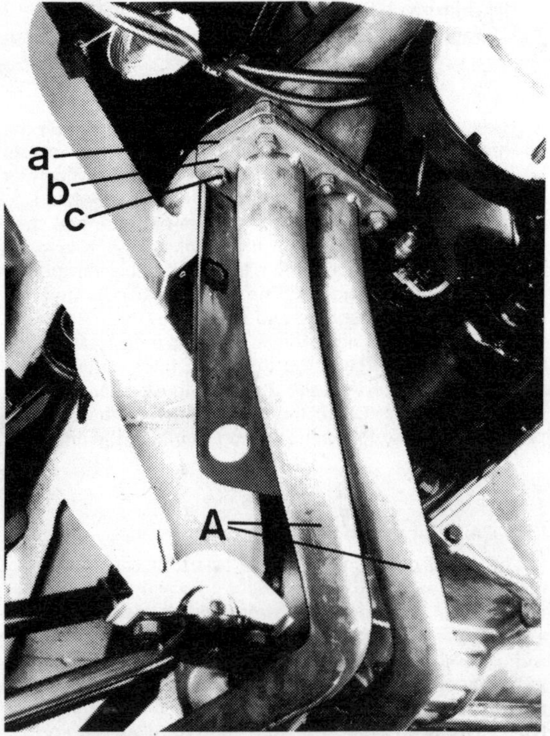

FIG 1:5   Removing the front exhaust pipe

FIG 1:6   Disconnecting the drive shaft flange at the brake disc

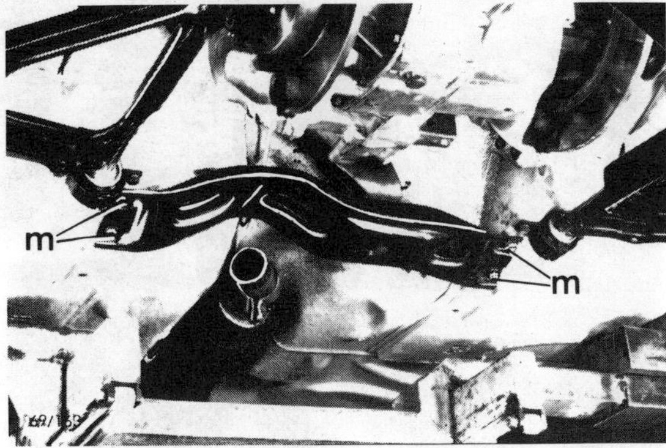

FIG 1:7 Detaching the rear crossmember

FIG 1:8 Detaching the right side engine and transmission mountings

work. It must be stressed that any supports used must be firmly based and not likely to collapse during the operation or serious injury could result. The engine must be removed in unit with the transmission, the assembly being lowered out of position and removed from beneath the car. For this reason, a frame contact type hoist or a pit, as well as an engine hoist or suitably adapted trolley jack will be necessary.

Removal:

1 Remove the bonnet if working with block and tackle or hoist equipment, this not being necessary if the engine is to be lowered with a trolley jack. Disconnect the battery negative connection, the battery being located under the rear seat. Remove the front apron **S** shown in **FIG 1:1**. Drain the engine oil from the sump.

2 Remove the air cleaner as described in **Chapter 2** and use a piece of clean rag to cover the carburetter air intake to prevent the entry of dirt. Refer to **Chapter 4** and drain the cooling system, then disconnect all coolant hoses between the radiator and engine and between the heater and engine.

3 Remove the fuel hose from the fuel pump by pulling it from the connection or by careful levering with a screwdriver. Plug the end of the hose to prevent fuel leakage, using a suitable bolt screwed into the pipe for this purpose. Disconnect the brake servo vacuum hose from the inlet manifold, if fitted.

4 Disconnect the speedometer cable at the transmission, disconnect the clutch cable at the mounting and the gearchange connections at the transmission. Disconnect the throttle linkage at the carburetter and connecting rod as described in **Chapter 2,** then remove the throttle control shaft shown at **d** in **FIG 1:2.** Separate the brake line shown at **e** in **FIG 1:2** at the mounting and plug the pipe to prevent fluid loss.

5 Refer to **FIG 1:3** and remove the guard plate **f** from the right engine mounting. Disconnect the following electrical wiring from the engine and transmission: Ignition leads, idle cut-off valve if fitted, thermostat, regulator four-pole plug, oil pressure switch, starter connections, reversing light switch and the earth leads. Refer to **Chapter 4** and remove the radiator.

6 If there is insufficient clearance with the equipment being used to lower the engine unit complete with the fan assembly, refer to **FIG 1:4** and unscrew the fan support **g** together with the fan and stop pad **h.** This operation is not necessary if sufficient clearance exists, instead just unscrew the stop **i** from the front crossmember.

7 Refer to **FIG 1:5** and remove the front exhaust pipe **A** at the exhaust manifold and primary silencer.

8 Refer to **FIG 1:6** and unscrew the drive shaft flange at the brake discs. Note the thin insulator between the flange and brake disc for correct refitting. Turn the drive shaft flange towards the wheel and tie the drive shafts to the upper wishbones with wire. Refer to **Chapter 9** and remove the anti-roll bar from the front suspension.

9 Position the trolley jack and adaptor beneath the engine unit or attach the overhead lifting gear, whichever is being used, then take the weight of the engine and transmission unit to unload the mountings. Unscrew the four screws **m** shown in **FIG 1:7** which attach the rear crossmember to the car body. Unscrew the retaining nut shown at **n** in **FIG 1:8. When lowering the engine, note the locations of the washers and sleeve on this mounting.** Unscrew the retaining nut shown at **o** in **FIG 1:9,** taking care not to alter the position of counter nut **p** when doing so.

10 Carefully lower the engine and transmission unit and remove it from beneath the car. If necessary, remove the transmission from the engine unit, taking care not to damage the clutch unit when sliding the transmission clear.

Refitting:

Refitting the engine to the car is a reversal of the removal instructions. However, the unit must be aligned in position according to the following instructions to ensure a stress-free installation, otherwise the engine may well be noisy in operation due to strain on the components.

1 Guide the engine and transmission unit into the car body from below. Raise into position on the mountings and install the right and left mounting nuts finger tight. Install the rear crossmember and tighten the fixing screws finger tight.

2 The engine and transmission unit must now be centred and aligned so that the mountings are under

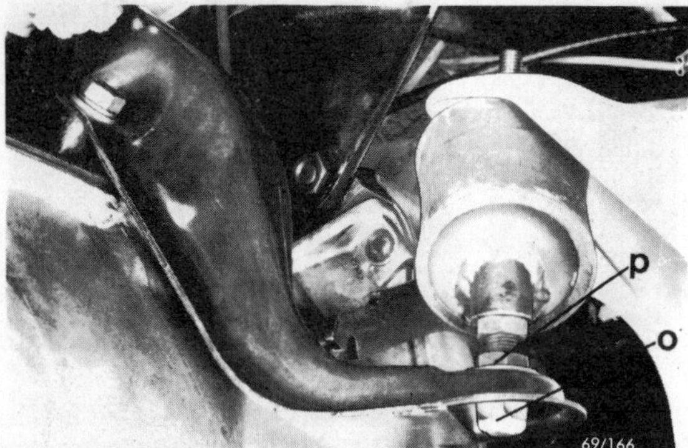

FIG 1:9 Detaching the left side engine and transmission mountings

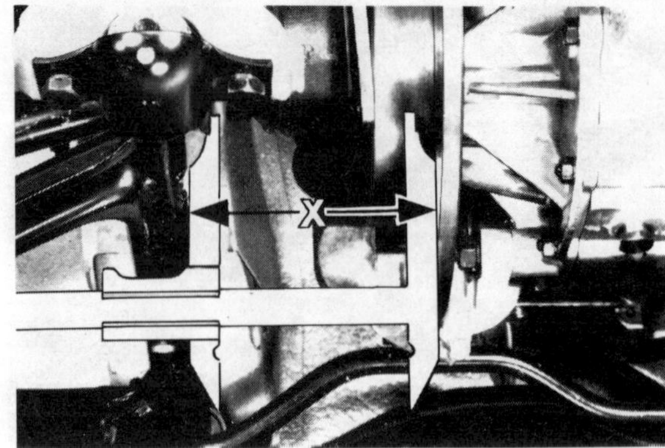

FIG 1:10 Checking engine alignment at the rear

no torsional load, that is, any deviation must be taken up by the slots in the rear crossmember and the engine carriers. Refer to **FIGS 1:10** and **1:11** and align the engine so that the measurements **X** between the brake discs and wishbones are equal on both sides. Further ensure that the measurements **Y** shown in **FIGS 1:12** and **1:13** between the pulley and the front of the sidemembers are equal. Maximum allowable deviation from equality in each measuring operation is 2 mm (.08 inch).

3 Install the rear crossmember mounting screws and screw the engine and transmission unit mounting to the rear crossmember.

4 The engine and transmission must be aligned vertically in such a manner that stop **i** shown in **FIG 1:14** can be screwed to the front crossmember without tension when the engine and transmission unit rests in its mountings. Note that in the case of new engine and transmission unit mountings the stop **i** must be pulled down approximately 3 to 5 mm (.12 to .2 inch) and then screwed in position, in order to ensure tension-free installation after the mountings have settled.

5 The side location of the unit must be aligned simultaneously with the vertical location just described. The distances measured between the castings on the transmission and a straightedge (tool SM-5) as

shown in **FIGS 1:15** and **1:16** must not differ from each other by more than 4 mm (.16 inch). If this alignment is incorrect, act on nuts **o** and **p** shown in **FIG 1:9** to adjust. If necessary, a different spacer (5, 7 or 9 mm) can be installed on the right engine and transmission mounting, but the original washers must be retained.

6 Tighten all the engine and transmission unit mounting screws, the correct torque wrench settings being as follows: Stop to front crossmember 18 lb ft, engine mount to console 22 lb ft, engine carrier to cylinder block 30 lb ft, engine carrier to engine mounting 43.5 lb ft, counter nut to engine mount 69 lb ft, rear engine mount to transmission 22 lb ft, rear crossmember to rear engine mounting 30 lb ft, rear crossmember to body 18 lb ft.

1:3 Removing and refitting cylinder head

Removal:

1 Disconnect the battery negative cable. Refer to **Chapter 2** and remove the air cleaner and carburetter. Drain the cooling system as described in **Chapter 4** and disconnect all coolant hoses between the radiator and cylinder head and between the heater and cylinder head. Disconnect the brake servo vacuum hose from the inlet manifold, if fitted.

FIG 1:11 Checking engine alignment at the rear

FIG 1:12 Checking engine alignment at the front

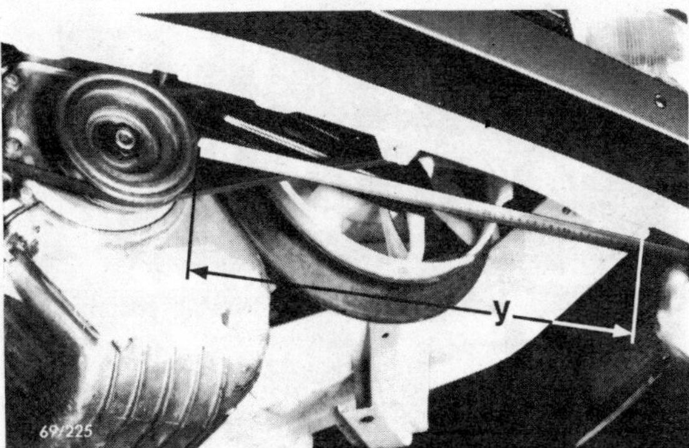

FIG 1:13   Checking engine alignment at the front

2 Disconnect the front exhaust pipe from the exhaust manifold as shown in **FIG 1:5**. Disconnect the spark plug leads from the spark plugs and disconnect all electric wiring from the cylinder head. Remove the rocker cover from the cylinder head.

3 Refer to **FIG 1:17** and remove the exhaust manifold end plate **a** by unscrewing the nuts **b**. Unscrew the eight exhaust manifold securing nuts shown in **FIG 1:18** and remove the exhaust manifold, noting the arrangement of the manifold gaskets.

4 Detach the inlet manifold by unscrewing the nuts **f** and removing the manifold support **A** shown in **FIG 1:19**. Loosen the adjusting nuts **g** shown in **FIG 1:20** until it is possible to move the rockers sideways to expose the pushrods. Lift out the eight pushrods and mark them or store them in the correct order for refitting in the positions from which they were removed.

5 Loosen the cylinder head nuts a little at a time in the order shown in **FIG 1:21**, then remove the nuts and lift off the cylinder head. Use extreme care when removing the head to avoid damage to the light-alloy casting. When the head is off, remove the head gasket and discard. If it is necessary to remove the valve tappets from the bottom of the pushrod bores, use tool M-1 or other suitable tool to slide them out of the block. Store the tappets in the correct order so that each will be refitted to its original position.

Refitting:

This is a reversal of the removal procedure, using new gaskets and seals throughout. Clean off all traces of old gasket material before refitting the cylinder head, taking care not to damage the light-alloy joint face. Place a new gasket into position and refit the head. Tighten the cylinder head mounting bolts in three stages, to 29, 43 then finally to 58 lb ft, following the sequence shown in **FIG 1:21**. Fit the new exhaust manifold gaskets correctly as shown at **e** and **d** in **FIG 1:22**. Refit the remaining components and adjust the valve clearances as described in **Section 1:5** so that the engine can be started and run. When the engine is at normal operating temperature, switch off and remove the rocker cover then tighten the cylinder head bolts to a torque of 65 lb ft, again following the correct sequence. After this tightening, adjust the valve clearances to the correct final settings as described in **Section 1:5**.

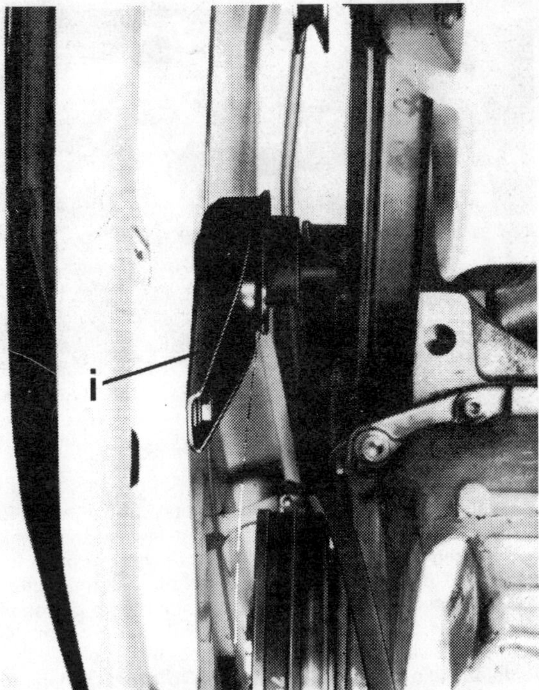

FIG 1:14   Engine height adjustment

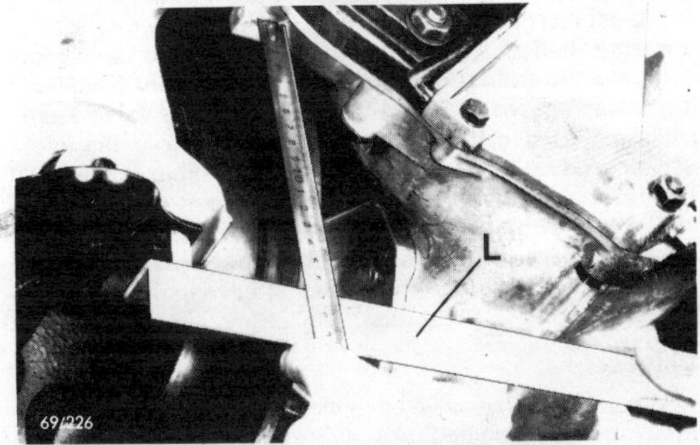

FIG 1:15   Engine side location

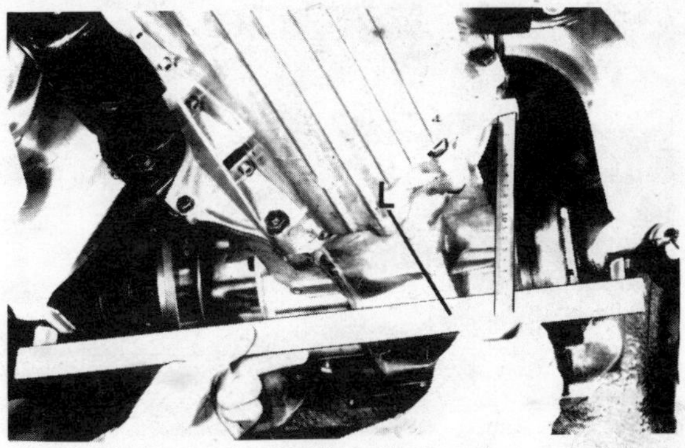

FIG 1:16   Engine side location

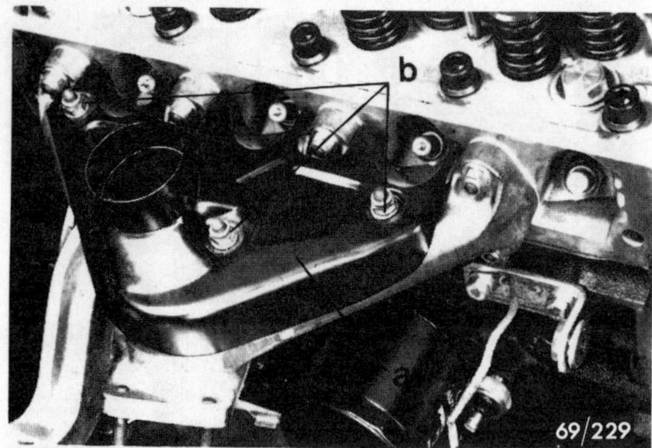

FIG 1:17 Removing the exhaust manifold end plate

FIG 1:18 Removing the exhaust manifold

1:4 Servicing the head and valves

Dismantling:

Unscrew the rocker adjusting nuts shown at **g** in **FIG 1:20** and remove the rocker levers and their bearing segments, storing the parts in the correct order for refitting. If decarbonizing is intended, plug all the waterways in the top face of the cylinder block with pieces of rag. Scrape the carbon from the combustion chambers before removing the valves to prevent damage to the valve seats, using a blunt tool for scraping to avoid damage to the light-alloy surfaces.

Use a spring compressor to remove the valves. With the spring compressed remove the split taper collets, release the compressor and remove the cap and springs. Place the inner and outer springs together with the caps and collets in the correct order for refitting. Using two screwdrivers as shown in **FIG 1:23**, lever off the valve stem seals **g**. Remove the valve spring discs **h** from the inlet valves and the rotocaps **i** from the exhaust valves. **Do not remove the rocker lever mountings screws k and pushrod guides 1 unless damaged, otherwise realignment will be necessary as described later.** Remove the valves after marking them to ensure refitting in their original locations.

Valves:

When the valves have been cleaned of carbon deposits they must be inspected for serviceability. Valves with bent stems or badly burned heads must be renewed. Valves that are too pitted to clean up on grinding to their seats may be refaced at a garage, but the amount of metal that can be removed in this operation is limited and new valves will be required if refacing cannot be successfully carried out. The valve seat angle between opposite faces is 90 deg. plus 30 min. in all cases.

Valve springs:

Test the valve springs by comparison with a new spring. Insert both the old and new spring end to end with a metal plate between them into the jaws of a vice. If the old spring is weakened it will close up first when pressure is applied. Renew any spring if it is shorter or weaker than standard.

Valve guides:

Clean carbon deposits from the inside of the guides with a suitable brush. If the inside surface is worn, scored or damaged a new guide must be fitted. Due to the need for precision measuring equipment and special tools, this operation should be entrusted to a service station.

Valve seat inserts:

Valve seat inserts that are too pitted to clean up on grinding to the valves may be refaced at a garage. If they are too far gone to be refaced in this manner they must be renewed. Due to the need for precision measuring equipment and special tools, this work must be carried out by a service station.

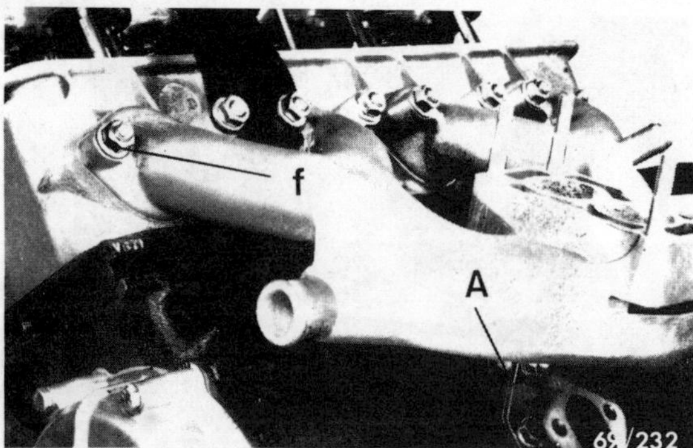

FIG 1:19 Removing the inlet manifold

FIG 1:20 Loosening the rocker adjusting nuts

FIG 1:21   Cylinder head bolt tightening sequence

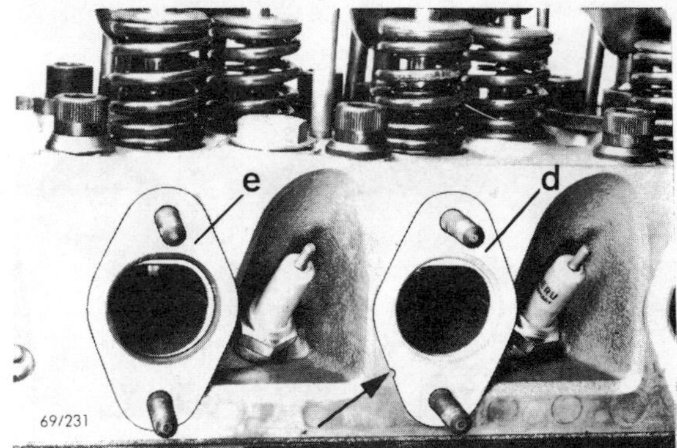

FIG 1:22   Fitting exhaust manifold gaskets

Decarbonizing and valve grinding:

Avoid the use of sharp tools which could damage the light-alloy surfaces. Remove all traces of carbon deposits from the combustion chambers, inlet and exhaust ports and joint faces.

Clean the carbon from the piston crowns, turning the engine over to bring two pistons at a time to the top of their bores. Wipe away all dust and lightly oil the cylinder bore surfaces.

Grind the valves to their seats. using a suction type valve grinding tool. Use medium grade carborundum paste at first, finishing with fine grade paste. When the seats of both valve and valve seat insert have a smooth, matt grey appearance, grinding is complete. Afterwards, ensure that all traces of grinding paste are removed from the cylinder head and valves.

Reassembly:

This is the reverse of the dismantling procedure. Lubricate the valve stems with engine oil before refitting. Use new valve stem seals unless the originals are in perfect condition and take care not to damage the seals

FIG 1:23   Removing valve stem seals

FIG 1:25   Adjusting valve clearances

FIG 1:24   Pushrod guide alignment

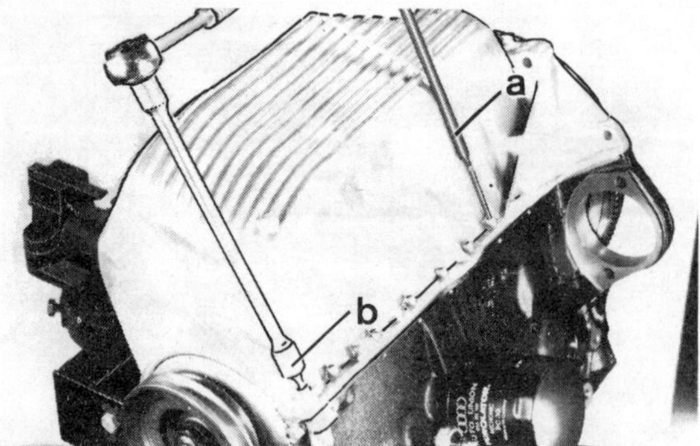

FIG 1:26 Removing the sump

FIG 1:27 Removing the crankshaft pulley

FIG 1:28 The timing gear cover and mounting screws

FIG 1:29 The timing chain tensioner and guide rail

FIG 1:30 Locking the chain tensioner plunger

FIG 1:31   Removing the flywheel

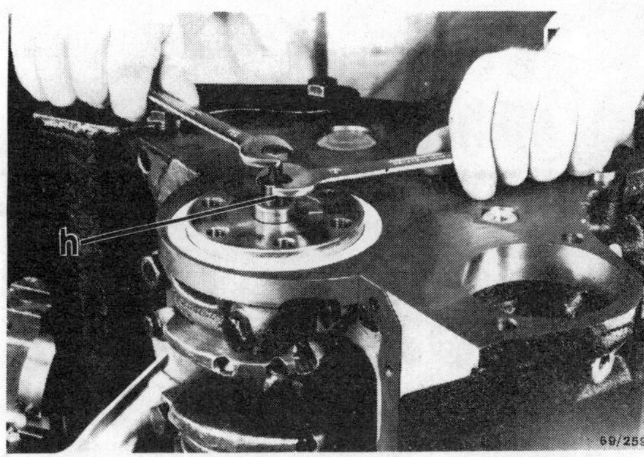

FIG 1:32 Extracting the pilot bearing from the crankshaft

FIG 1:33   Removing the oil pump

FIG 1:34   Removing the connecting rod bearing caps

when fitting over the valves. Use a suitable piece of metal tube to press the seals over the valve guide ends, noting that the seals must be driven on up to the valve guide stop. Oil the rocker lever bearing segments before installation.

Pushrod guide alignment:

This operation is only necessary if the pushrod guides and rocker lever mounting screws have been disturbed. The cylinder head must be refitted as described previously, the guide plates and mounting screws installed finger tight and the pushrods fitted. Install the rocker assemblies and tighten the adjuster nuts until the rockers apply light pressure to both valves and pushrods. Rotate the push-rods to ensure that they are correctly seated in the tappets and rockers. Now align the pushrod guide in such a manner that equal clearance exists on each side of the pushrods as shown in **FIG 1:24**, then tighten the rocker mounting screws securely.

1:5 Valve clearance adjustment

Valve clearances should be checked and adjusted if necessary, at regular intervals. If the clearance is too small or if no clearance exists at all, the valve will not operate properly. This will cause loss of power and possible burning of the valve and seat. If the clearance is too large the valve will open late and close early, causing loss of power. If the engine has just been reassembled after a servicing operation involving head removal, it will be necessary to set the clearances as follows with the engine cold so that it can be started and run. The engine must then be brought to normal running temperature and the clearances reset.

Remove the air cleaner and the rocker cover. The engine will be easier to turn over if the spark plugs are also removed. To turn the engine, make sure that the car is on a flat surface so that it will not move when the brake is released, then select top gear and release the hand-brake. The car can then be pushed backwards or forwards to turn the engine. If the car is raised on a hoist, either remove the front apron and turn the engine in neutral with a spanner on the crankshaft pulley nut, or engage top gear and hold one front wheel tight and turn the other front wheel to rotate the engine.

The valve clearances of inlet and exhaust valves on cylinder No. 1 must be adjusted when the valves of cylinder No. 4 are on the overlap. Turn the engine until both valves are open (springs compressed), then turn the engine backwards or forwards as necessary until the valves are equally depressed. Now check the clearances between the valves and rocker tips at No. 1 cylinder, using feeler gauges as shown in **FIG 1:25**.

Correct clearances are .006 inch for inlet valves, .015 inch for exhaust valves with the engine at normal running temperature. Clearances when the engine is cold,

FIG 1:35 Removing the main bearing caps

FIG 1:36 Lifting out the crankshaft

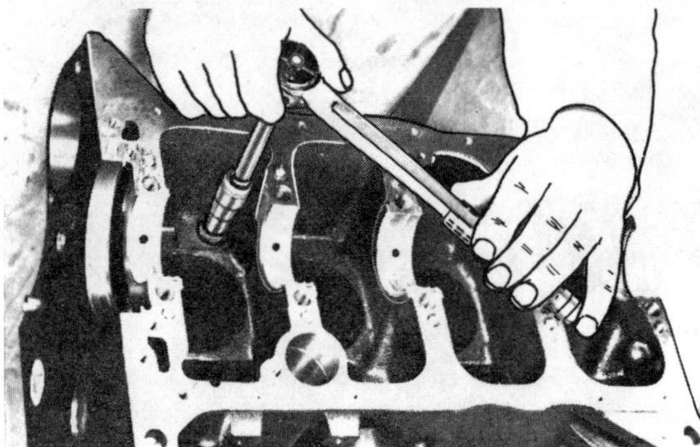

FIG 1:37 Removing the oil pressure valve

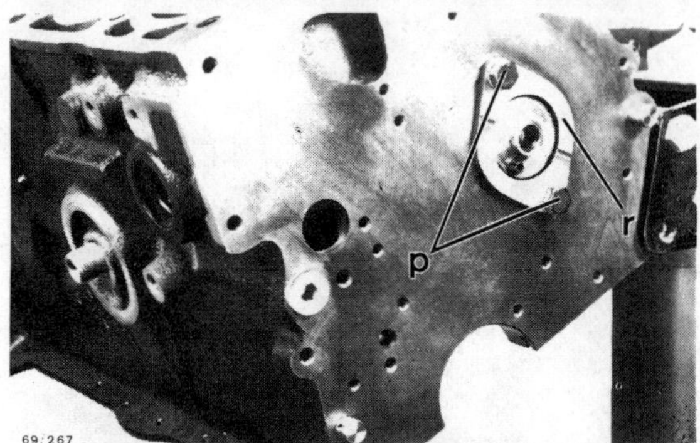

FIG 1:38 Removing the camshaft guide flange

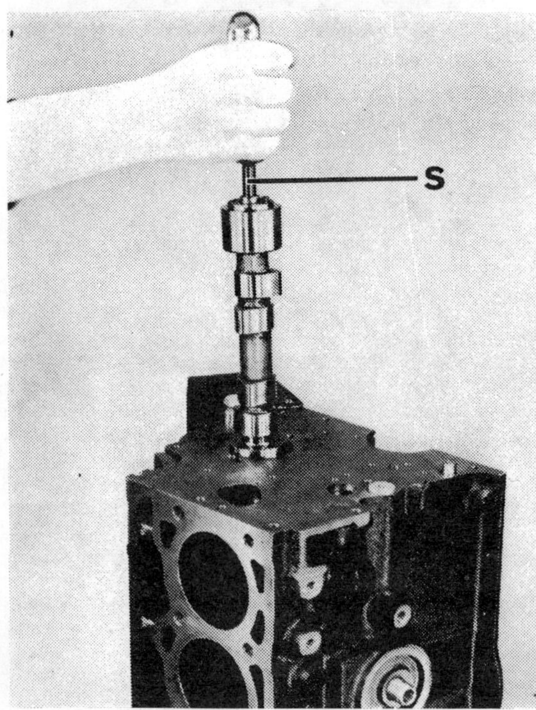

FIG 1:39 Removing the camshaft

for setting after engine reassembly are .004 inlet, .014 exhaust. Set to these figures then warm up the engine before repeating the operation to achieve the previously stated figures on the warm engine. The line of valves nearest the bottom of **FIG 1:25** are the inlets, the upper line the exhausts.

Turn the rocker adjusting nut until the feeler moves in the gap with a slight drag, being neither tight nor loose. If any of the self-locking adjuster nuts are loose they must be renewed, otherwise they could work loose in service. The nuts should require a minimum of 11 lb ft of torque to rotate them if they are in good condition.

Repeat the checking and adjusting procedure on the other cylinders, checking the clearances at No. 3 cylinder with the valves at No. 2 cylinder on the overlap; No. 4 with No. 1 on overlap and No. 2 with No. 3 on overlap. On completion, refit the rocker cover and air cleaner and the spark plugs if removed.

1:6 Dismantling the engine

Remove the engine as described in **Section 1:2**. Remove the alternator, distributor, carburetter, fuel pump, water pump and clutch as described in later chapters. Remove the cylinder head as described in **Section 1:3**. The engine should be dismantled in accordance with the following sequence of instructions and faulty components serviced as described later.

1 Refer to **FIG 1:26** and remove the sump by taking out 15 socket head screws with special tool M-4 shown at **a** and four screws with a socket wrench **b**,

then taking off the sump. Remove the sump gaskets. If the sump is being removed with the engine installed, the left engine mount must be removed and the exhaust pipe and bottom hose disconnected.

2 Remove the crankshaft pulley shown in **FIG 1:27** by undoing the nut **c**. Counterhold the flywheel to prevent the crankshaft from turning during this operation in the manner shown in **FIG 1:31**. If necessary, tap the pulley gently with a soft-faced hammer to assist removal.

3 Unscrew the timing cover mounting screws and remove the cover (see **FIG 1:28**. Bend open the lock tab and unscrew the chain tensioner plug shown at **e** in **FIG 1:29**. Use a $\frac{1}{8}$ inch allen key to lock the tensioner plunger by turning to the left as shown in **FIG 1:30**. This will prevent the plunger from flying out when the tensioner is removed. Unscrew the guide rail **f**. Unscrew the camshaft sprocket mounting screw and remove the sprocket together with the timing chain.

4 Mark the flywheel position in relation to the crankshaft as shown in **FIG 1:31**, this being necessary to ensure correct refitting as the flywheel and shaft are balanced as an assembly. Take out the flywheel mounting screws and remove the flywheel, using tool M-18 as shown at **g** or other similar means to counterhold the flywheel. If necessary, use tool M-5 to extract the transmission mainshaft guide bearing from the end of the crankshaft, as shown in **FIG 1:32**.

5 Refer to **FIG 1:33** and disconnect the oil line **i** at the oil pump and engine block. Remove the screw **c** and pull the oil pump **k** out of the engine block, collecting the spacer **l**.

6 Remove the connecting rod bearing caps shown at **m** in **FIG 1:34** and push the rods clear of the crankshaft. Remove the bearing shells from the caps and rods and store caps, upper and lower bearing shells for refitting in their original positions if they are not to be renewed. Press out the connecting rods and pistons through the top of the cylinder bores and lay

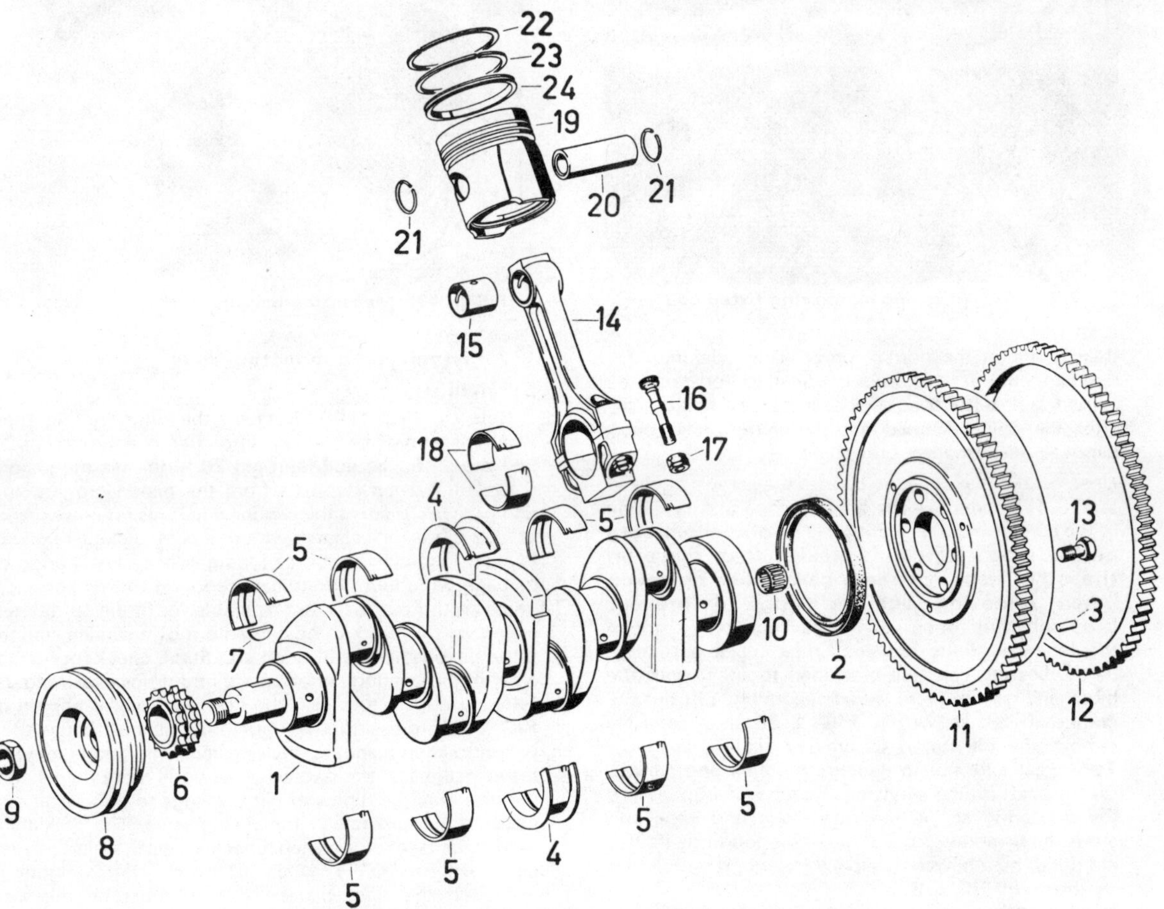

FIG 1:40   Crankshaft, pistons and connecting rod details

Key to Fig 1:40   1 Crankshaft complete   2 Sealing ring   3 Dowel   4 Centre main bearing   5 Outer main bearing
6 Crankshaft pinion   7 Woodruff key   8 Pulley   9 Pulley nut   10 Needle bearing   11 Flywheel complete
12 Starter gear ring   13 Expansion screw   14 Connecting rod complete   15 Small-end bush   16 Screw for big-end cap
17 Nut   18 Connecting rod shells   19 Piston complete   20 Gudgeon pin   21 Circlip   22 Top compression ring
23 Lower compression ring   24 Oil control ring

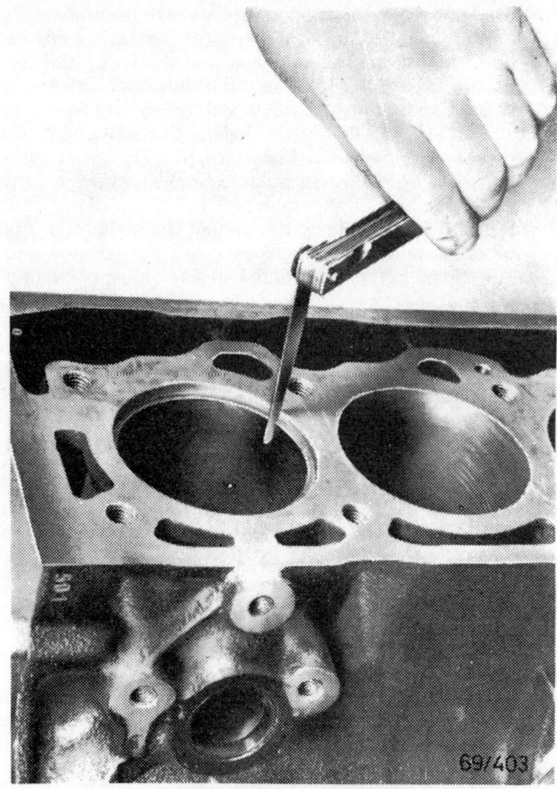

FIG 1:41 Checking piston ring fitted gap

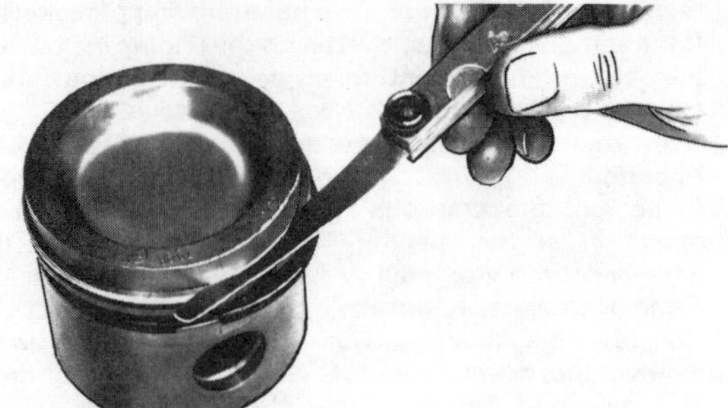

FIG 1:42 Checking piston ring clearance in piston groove

FIG 1:43 Measuring pistons to check for wear

them aside in the correct order. This operation for removing the pistons and connecting rods can be carried out with the engine installed in the car, after the cylinder head and oil sump have been removed as described previosuly.

7 Unscrew the main bearing caps at the screws arrowed in **FIG 1:35,** remove the bearing caps and lay aside in the correct order for refitting. **The dowel pin boss on No. 4 bearing cap is weaker than those on the other caps. Extreme care must be taken when removing and refitting to prevent breaking this boss.** Such breakage would mean the renewal of the entire cylinder block assembly, as the bearing caps are machined together with the block and cannot be renewed separately. Lift out the crankshaft as shown in **FIG 1:36** and carefully remove the oil seal **n** to prevent seal lip damage. Take great care not to damage the seal ring surface on the shaft during servicing. Remove the upper and lower bearing shells from the block and caps and store them in the correct order for refitting, if they are not to be renewed. Unscrew the oil pressure valve as shown in **FIG 1:37.**

8 Refer to **FIG 1:38** and detach the camshaft guide plate **r** by removing the screws **p**. Screw tool M-20 or the crankshaft sprocket screw into the camshaft and remove the camshaft as shown in **FIG 1:39,** taking care not to damage the bearings by knocking the shaft against them or by pulling out at an angle.

1:7 Pistons and connecting rods

Servicing:

Refer to **FIG 1:40.** Remove the rings, noting their locations, and wash them in petrol. Remove the circlips 21 and press out the gudgeon pin 20 to release the piston. Clean off carbon deposits from the piston crowns and ring grooves. Inspect the pistons and rings for score marks or any signs of seizure, which would dictate renewal. Examine the cylinder bores for signs of heavy scoring or damage which would indicate reboring to be necessary. Three piston oversizes are available for fitting to rebored cylinders, this work to be carried out by a service station. If the pistons appear in good condition, check for normal wear of the bearing surfaces and ring grooves as follows. Fit each ring in turn into the cylinder bore as shown in **FIG 1:41,** pressing the ring into this position with a piston to keep it square, then measure the fitted gap with feeler gauges. If the gap on any ring is more than 1 mm the ring must be renewed. Fit the rings to the piston and check the clearance in the ring groove. The maximum allowable clearance when checked with feeler gauges as shown in **FIG 1:42** is .015 mm. If this figure is exceeded the ring, piston or both must be renewed according to the location of the wear. Measure each piston as shown in **FIG 1:43,** using a micrometer between opposite sides 16 mm from the lower edge of the piston skirt, at 90 deg. to the gudgeon pin bore. Pistons that are more than .00158 inch less in diameter than the cylinder bore diameter must be renewed.

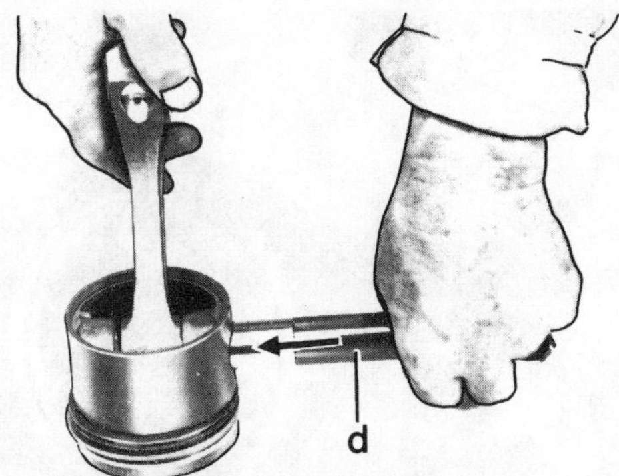

FIG 1:44 Fitting the pistons to the connecting rods

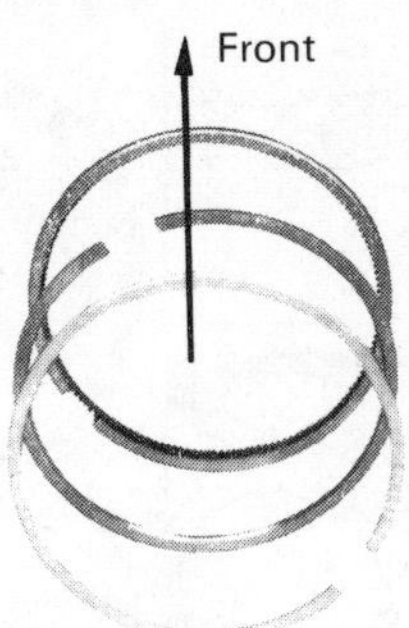

FIG 1:45 Spacing the ring gaps around the piston

FIG 1:46 Fitting the main bearing shells

FIG 1:47 Refitting the camshaft sprocket and chain with the timing marks aligned

Big-end bearing clearance on the crankpins can be checked with the aid of Plastigage as described in the **Appendix**. Maximum permissible wear is .00118 inch. Check the small end bushes for signs of scoring or seizure and, if necessary, have new bushes fitted and reamed by a service station.

Heat the pistons and gudgeon pins to approximately 60°C (140°F) to facilitate refitting, then slide the pin into position as shown in **FIG 1:44**, using tool M-15 if available. Fit the retaining circlips. Refit the rings to the pistons with the TOP mark on each ring uppermost. Space the ring gaps around the piston as shown in **FIG 1:45**, the arrow in the figure pointing towards the front of the engine.

1:8 Crankshaft and bearings

Servicing:

Thoroughly inspect the crankshaft for scoring, cracks and other damage. Big-end and main bearing clearance can be checked by the use of Plastigage as described in the **Appendix**. Maximum permissible wear is .00118 inch. If the crankshaft journals are worn, damaged or out of round the crankshaft should be specialist reground to accept suitable undersize bearing shells, these being available in three sizes. If a bearing failure has occurred, the oilway in the crankshaft should be checked for obstructions, which must be removed before refitting.

1:9 Reassembling and timing the engine

Reassembly of the engine is a reversal of the dismantling procedure. Use new seals, gaskets and lock plates at all necessary locations. Lubricate bearings and all moving parts with engine oil during reassembly.

1 Refit the oil pressure valve to the crankcase. Carefully lower the camshaft into position and fit the camshaft guide plate, tightening the fixing screws to 18.28 lb ft. Check the camshaft for easy turning and check the camshaft end float, preferably with a dial gauge. If the end float exceeds .004 inch a new guide plate should be installed.

2 Place the main and thrust bearing shell halves in the crankcase as shown in **FIG 1:46**, noting the alignment of the oil holes and the end projection arrowed. Oil the shells and main bearing journals, then carefully place the crankshaft into position. Fit the upper shells into the main bearing caps and fit the caps into position according to the noted order and tighten the fixing bolts slightly. Place the shaft seal on the crankshaft and slide it into position with the seal lip towards the shaft. Press the seal home, keeping it square. Tighten the bearing cap fixing screws evenly to a torque of 29 lb ft, then finally to $57\frac{1}{2}$ lb ft. Tighten the socket head screws of bearing cap No. 5 to 23 lb ft.

3 The pistons and connecting rods must be refitted to their original locations, through the top of the cylinder bores. Use a ring clamp when entering the

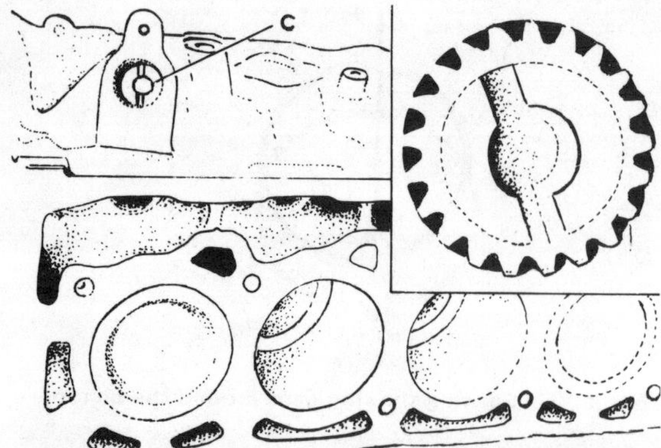

FIG 1:48   Aligning the oil pump drive shaft

FIG 1:49   Refitting the chain tensioner

piston rings into the cylinder, then press the piston down and guide the big-end onto the crankpin. Fit the bearing shells and the big-end bearing caps, using new cap bolts and nuts tightened to a torque of 25 to 31 lb ft. Make sure that all parts are fitted in the original order. The groove in the connecting rod must face towards the camshaft.

4 This part deals with the timing of the engine camshaft and valve mechanism and must be carried out carefully to ensure correct operation of these components. Fit the chain guide rail, tighten the fixing screws and secure with the lock plate. Refer to **FIG 1:47**, fit the camshaft sprocket and turn the sprocket and shaft until the mark on the sprocket aligns with the notch in the guide rail as shown. Now remove the sprocket without turning the camshaft. Turn the crankshaft until the piston in No. 1 (front) cylinder is at top dead centre. With the camshaft and crankshaft set in this manner, refit the camshaft sprocket together with the timing chain so that the timing marks are correctly aligned as before. **Do not rotate the camshaft or crankshaft from their set positions during this operation.** Fit the camshaft sprocket screw and tighten to 58 lb ft.

5 Refer to **FIG 1:48**. Turn the oil pump shaft until the wide segment **c** on the shaft faces towards the front of the engine, with piston No. 1 in the top dead centre position and the timing marks aligned as previously described. Now turn the pump shaft about 15 deg. anticlockwise as shown in the inset in **FIG 1:48** to

allow for the turning of the shaft as it slides into position. After installation the wide segment must face forward, so ensure that this is so.

6 Refer to **FIG 1:33**. Place the spacer 1 in position and fasten the oil pump **k** with the screw and washer, tightening the screw only slightly. Fit the oil pressure line **i** without strain, placing one or more seals as necessary on each side to ensure a stress-free fit and turning the pump to correctly locate the flange. Tighten the oil pump screws to 19 lb ft oil pressure line screws to 7.2 lb ft.

7 Refit the distributor as described in **Chapter 3** and the cylinder head as described in **Section 1:3**.

8 Fit the chain tensioner baseplate and the tensioner with plunger. Refer to **FIG 1:49** and unscrew the plunger with a $\frac{1}{8}$ inch allen key. Press against the chain as shown and turn the plunger anticlockwise until it can be felt to move freely against its internal spring. Fit the cover plug when operation is satisfactory.

9 Using special tool M-8 and working from the inside press a new pulley shaft seal **g** against the stop in the timing housing cover **i**, as shown in **FIG 1:50**.

10 Refer to **FIG 1:51**. Place new cork gaskets **i** in the front and rear grooves of the sump, lubricating them with grease to assist installation. Refer to **FIG 1:52** and fit new gaskets **k** to the engine block, using a small amount of adhesive such as Epple 22 to retain them. Stick the self-adhesive gasket **d** on the block. Apply a thin string of adhesive to the four corners as

68/337a

FIG 1:50   Fitting the timing case oil seal

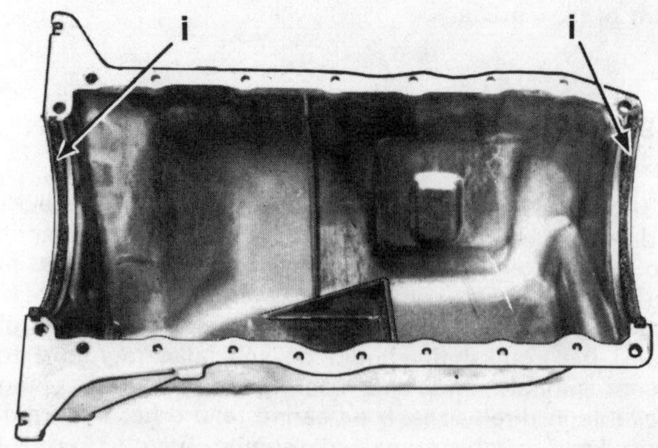

FIG 1:51   Fitting the oil sump and gaskets

indicated by the arrows. Fit the sump in position
and tighten the smaller retaining screws to 5.8 lb ft,
the larger screws to 10.8 lb ft. Fit the sump drain plug,
using a new seal if necessary.

11 Screw flywheel guide pins tool M-16 into the crankshaft flange. Heat the flywheel to approximately 80°C
(176°F) evenly, then slide it into position, indexing
the alignment marks made when removing. Tighten the
mounting screws slightly and allow the flywheel to
cool. **Note that if the flywheel has been heated
in hot oil it must be throughly cleaned in
solvents afterwards.** When the flywheel is cool,
tighten the fixing screws to 65 lb ft. Place the transmission drive pin in needle bearing in position so that
the flat side with the lettering is visible, that is, facing
towards the outside. Slide the pulley over the
Woodruff key and tighten the retaining nut to 180 lb ft.

12 Complete the engine reassembly in the reverse order
of dismantling. On completion, refill the sump with the
correct grade of oil and refill the cooling system.
Adjust the valve clearances as described in
Section 1:5.

1:10 Oil filter

The fullflow oil filter is contained in a steel canister
mounted at the side of the engine block. The filter element
must be renewed at each oil change. To remove the filter
element, unscrew the canister from its mounting, using a
clamp tool such as that shown in **FIG 1:53,** then remove
the filter element from the canister. Have a container
ready to catch the oil which will be released as the canister
is removed.

After a general engine overhaul or after cylinder
reboring and the fitting of new pistons, rings, main and
big-end bearings it is essential to use the special running
in oil filter element which is available, in conjunction with
special running in oil which is supplied under Part No.
AOE.011.000. If this special oil is unobtainable for any
reason, use a good quality HD/SAE.10.W engine oil.

After approximately 300 to 400 miles has been covered,
the special oil must be drained and the special filter
element removed. A standard filter element must then be
fitted and the sump filled with the appropriate grade of oil
for the time of year.

1:11 Engine, USA version

The USA version of the Audi 100LS engine is basically
similar to the standard versions and all maintenance and
overhaul instructions contained in this Chapter will apply.
In order to achieve the necessary low levels of carbon
monoxide in the exhaust gases, a special carburetter,
distributor and cooling system are fitted, these being
covered in later Chapters.

A modified inlet manifold having triple ports is fitted to
the engine, this component being shown in **FIG 1:54.**
A separate duct is included in the casting to allow engine
coolant to circulate through the manifold to preheat the
incoming fuel/air mixture.

Note that the stage 1 gas port **a** is not round, but the
cut-out in the gasket **b** is. **Under no circumstances
must the opening in the gasket be cut to match the
shape of the manifold ports.** To avoid distortion of the
carburetter flange, the carburetter retaining nuts must be
evenly tightened to a torque of 11±.7 lb ft. If the seal

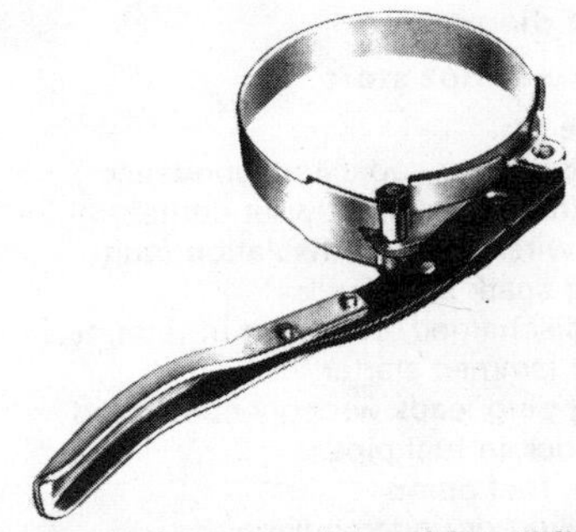

FIG 1:53 A typical commercial tool for oil filter removal

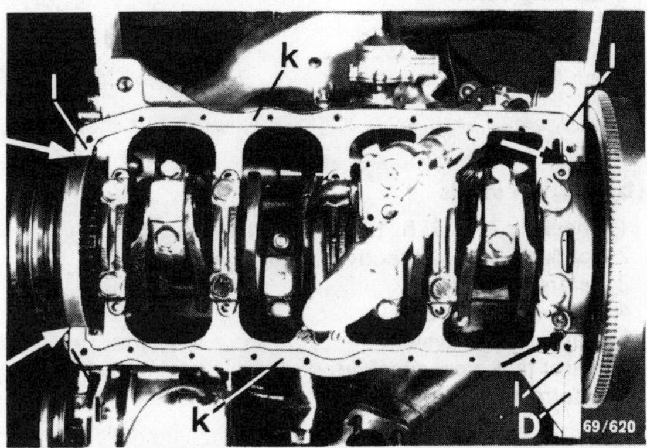

FIG 1:52 Fitting sump gaskets to the cylinder block

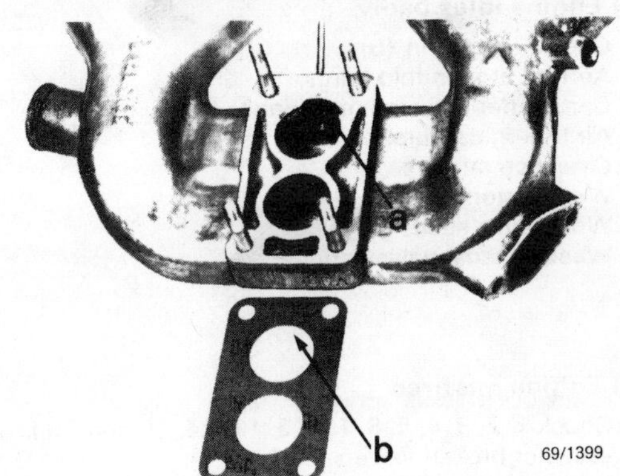

FIG 1:54 Modified inlet manifold and gasket, USA
versions

between manifold and carburetter is imperfect, as would
be indicated by the presence of fuel in the two depressions
in the manifold, a paper gasket, Part No. 059.129.799
should be inserted above and below the existing gasket.

Closed-circuit crankcase breathing is provided by
means of an oil separator in the rocker cover and a hose
located between the rocker cover and the air cleaner.
The exhaust gases and oil vapours pass through the hose
and are passed through the carburetter to be burnt in
the engine. A flap valve in the air cleaner ensures sufficient
intake vacuum for this operation and is described in
Chapter 2.

1:12 Fault diagnosis

(a) Engine will not start

1 Defective coil
2 Faulty distributor capacitor (condenser)
3 Dirty, pitted or incorrectly set contact points
4 Ignition wires loose or insulation faulty
5 Water on spark plug leads
6 Battery discharged, corrosion of terminals
7 Faulty or jammed starter
8 Sparking plug leads wrongly connected
9 Vapour lock in fuel pipes
10 Defective fuel pump
11 Overchoking or underchoking
12 Blocked fuel filter or carburetter jets
13 Leaking valves
14 Sticking valves
15 Valve timing incorrect
16 Ignition timing incorrect

(b) Engine stalls

1 Check 1, 2, 3, 4, 5, 10, 11, 12, 13 and 14 in (a)
2 Sparking plugs defective or gaps incorrect
3 Retarded ignition
4 Mixture too weak
5 Water in fuel system
6 Petrol tank vent blocked
7 Incorrect valve clearances

(c) Engine idles badly

1 Check 2 and 7 in (b)
2 Air leak at manifold joints
3 Carburetter adjustment wrong
4 Air leak in carburetter
5 Over-rich mixture
6 Worn piston rings
7 Worn valve stems or guides
8 Weak exhaust valve springs

(d) Engine misfires

1 Check 1, 2, 3, 4, 5, 8, 10, 12, 13, 14, 15 and 16 in (a)
2 Weak or broken valve springs

(e) Engine overheats (see Chapter 4)

(f) Compression low

1 Check 13 and 14 in (a)
2 Worn piston ring grooves
3 Scored or worn cylinder bores

(g) Engine lacks power

1 Check 3, 10, 11, 12, 13, 14, 15 and 16 in (a); 2, 3, 4 and 7 in (b); 6 and 7 in (c); and 2 in (d). Also check (e) and (f)
2 Leaking joint washers
3 Fouled spark plugs
4 Automatic advance not working

(h) Burnt valves or seats

1 Check 13 and 14 in (a); 7 in (b) and 2 in (d). Also check (e)
2 Excessive carbon round valve seats and heads

(j) Sticking valves

1 Check 2 in (d)
2 Bent valve stem
3 Scored valve stem or guide
4 Incorrect valve clearance

(k) Excessive cylinder wear

1 Check 11 in (a)
2 Lack of oil
3 Dirty oil
4 Piston rings gummed up or broken
5 Badly fitting piston rings
6 Connecting rod bent

(l) Excessive oil consumption

1 Check 6 and 7 in (c) and check (k)
2 Ring gaps too wide
3 Oil return holes in piston choked with carbon
4 Scored cylinders
5 Oil level too high
6 External oil leaks

(m) Crankshaft and connecting rod bearing failure

1 Check 2 in (k)
2 Restricted oilways
3 Worn journals or crankpins
4 Loose bearing caps
5 Extremely low oil pressure
6 Bent connecting rod

(n) Internal water leakage (see Chapter 4)

(o) Poor water circulation (see Chapter 4)

(p) Corrosion (see Chapter 4)

(q) High fuel consumption (see Chapter 2)

(r) Engine vibration

1 Loose alternator bolts
2 Engine mountings loose or ineffective
3 Cooling fan out of balance
4 Misfiring due to mixture, ignition or mechanical faults

CHAPTER 2

THE FUEL SYSTEM

2:1 Description
2:2 Fuel pump
2:3 35 PDSIT-5 single barrel carburetter
2:4 Adjusting 35 PDSIT-5 carburetter
2:5 32 TDID dual barrel carburetter
2:6 Adjusting 32 TDID carburetter

2:7 Modifications to 32 TDID carburetters
2:8 32/32 TDID USA export carburetter
2:9 Sealed fuel system, USA export models
2:10 Air cleaners
2:11 Solex carburetters type 32/35 TDID
2:12 Fault diagnosis

2:1 Description

The fuel tank is located at the rear of the car beneath the luggage compartment. The fuel pump, which is positioned on the side of the engine block, draws fuel from the tank and delivers it to the carburetter. An air cleaner containing a paper filter cartridge is mounted on the carburetter. Audi 100 and 100S engines are equipped with a Solex 35 PDSIT downdraught single barrel carburetter, the Audi 100LS being equipped with a Solex 32 downdraught dual barrel instrument. Cars for the USA export market are fitted with Solex 32/32 TDID downdraught dual barrel carburetters with idle air bypass bore and thermo starting valve, these instruments being designed to ensure minimum quantities of carbon monoxide in the exhaust gases to comply with regulations.

For 1971 certain models, including the 100GL, were fitted with Solex carburetters of type 32/35 TDID, while the Coupé S has twin carburetters of the same type. Details of settings and jet sizes for all carburetters are given in **Technical Data** in the **Appendix**.

2:2 Fuel pump

The mechanical fuel pump, operated by a pushrod from an eccentric on the camshaft, is shown in **FIG 2:1**. As can be seen in **FIG 2:2**, the pushrod moves a diaphragm which draws fuel into the pump body and discharges it through the outlet under pressure, this process being controlled by valves in the pump upper part.

Pump testing:

Before testing the pump ensure that the fuel tank vent is not blocked. If it is suspected that fuel is not reaching the carburetter, remove the feed pipe from the carburetter, hold the end of this pipe in a suitable small container and have an assistant turn the engine over several times with the starter. Watch for fuel squirting from the end of the pipe, which will indicate that the pump is working. If so, check that the carburetter needle valve is not stuck and preventing fuel reaching the float chamber.

Reduced flow can be caused by blocked fuel pipes or a clogged filter. Remove the pump cover and check the filter as described later. If an obstructed pipeline is suspected it may be cleared with compressed air. Disconnect the pipes at the carburetter and fuel pump. **Do not pass compressed air through the pump or the valves will be damaged.** If there is an obstruction between the pump and the tank, remove the tank filler cap before blowing the pipe through from the pump end.

If the pump delivers insufficient fuel, suspect an air leak between the pump and the fuel tank, dirt under the pump valves or faulty valve seatings. If the fault is traced to the pump itself, remove the pump for servicing as described in the next section.

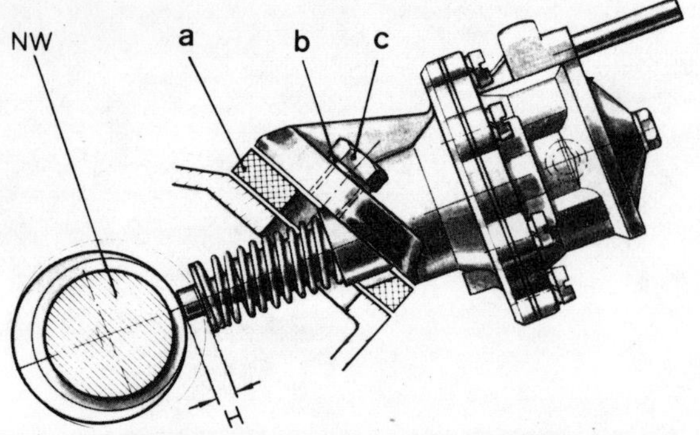

FIG 2:1   Fuel pump mounting details

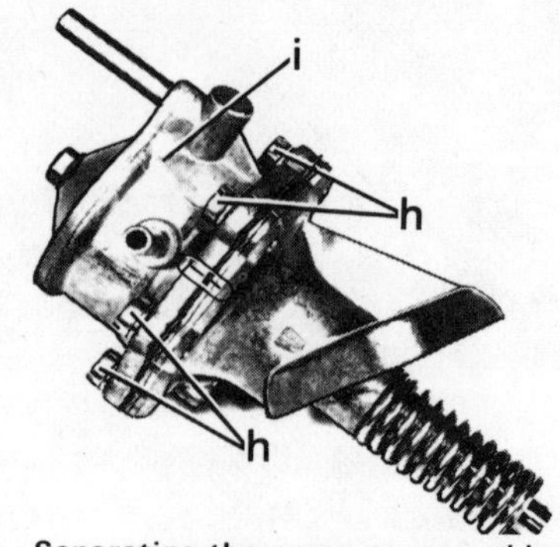

FIG 2:3   Separating the pump upper and lower halves

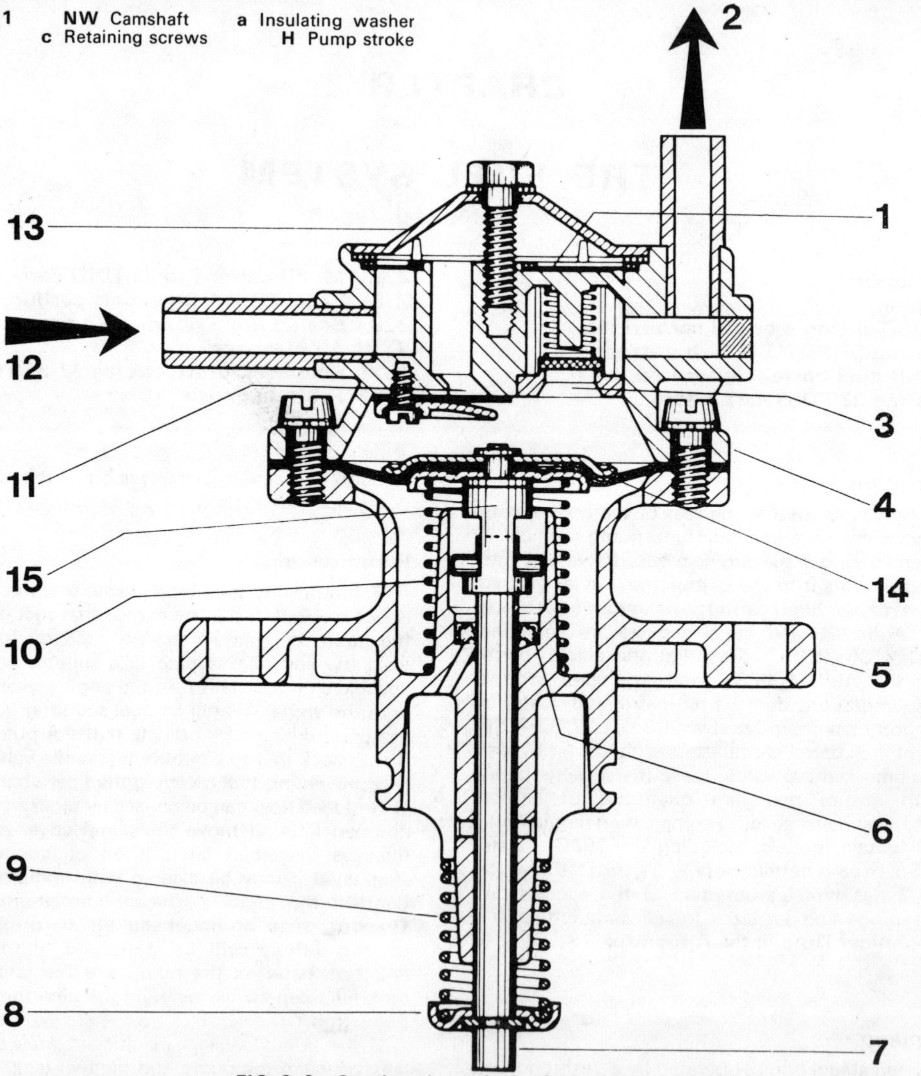

Key to Fig 2:1   **NW** Camshaft   **a** Insulating washer
b Washers   **c** Retaining screws   **H** Pump stroke

FIG 2:2   Section through the fuel pump

Key to Fig 2:2   1 Filter screen   2 Fuel outlet   3 Outlet valve   4 Pump upper part   5 Pump lower part   6 Oil scraper ring
7 Pushrod   8 Spring retainer   9 Spring, pushrod   10 Spring, diaphragm   11 Inlet valve   12 Fuel inlet   13 Cover
14 Diaphragm   15 Coupling

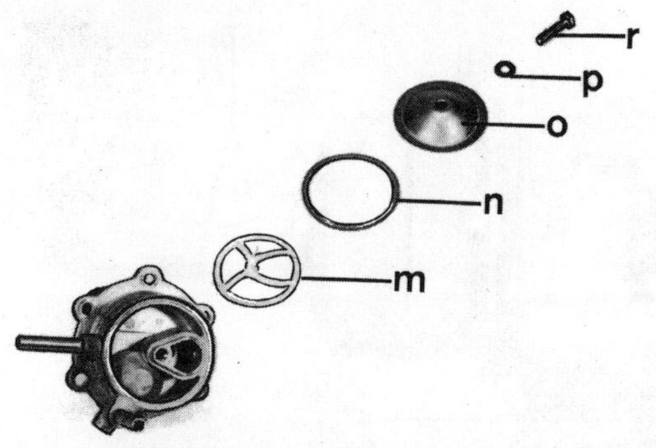

FIG 2:4   Pump filter and seals

Key to Fig 2:4   **m** Filter   **n** Seal   **o** Cover
p Seal   **r** Screw

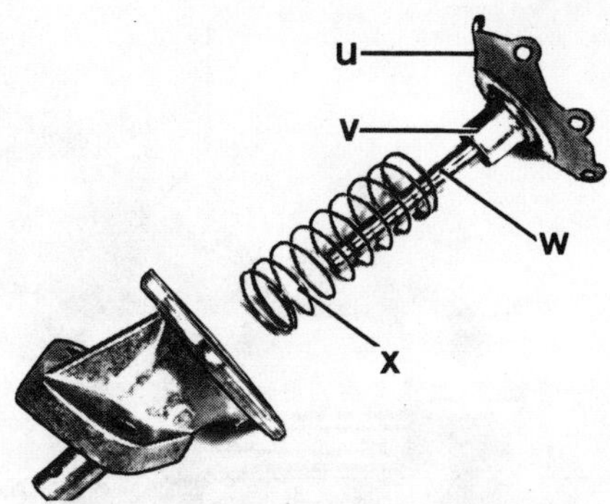

FIG 2:6   Pump diaphragm assembly

Key to Fig 2:6   **u** Diaphragm   **v** Coupling   **w** Pushrod
x Spring

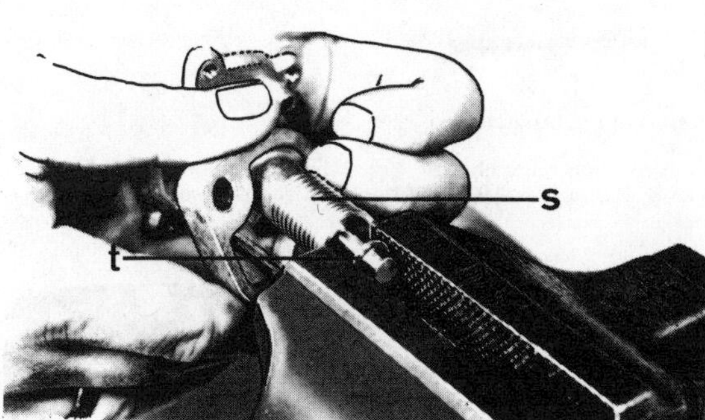

FIG 2:5   Removing the pump pushrod circlip

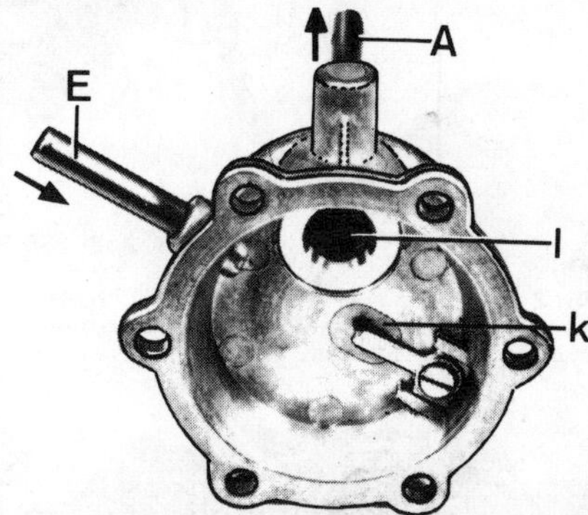

FIG 2:7   Fuel pump valves

Key to Fig 2:7   **A** Fuel outlet   **E** Fuel inlet   **1** Outlet valve
k inlet valve

Fuel pump removal:

Disconnect the fuel lines from the pump, plugging the pipe from the tank to prevent loss of fuel. Remove the two mounting screws shown at **c** in **FIG 2:1** and remove the pump from the engine block, collecting the insulating gasket.

Refitting:

This is the reverse of the removal instructions, using a new insulating gasket.

Dismantling:

Clean the outside of the fuel pump and mark the housing halves as shown in **FIG 2:3** to ensure correct reassembly. Remove the screws **h** and lift off the pump upper part **i**. Remove the cover screw from the upper part and carefully take out the cover, filter and seals as shown in **FIG 2:4**. Close the jaws of a vice until they clear the pushrod but not the spring as shown in **FIG 2:5,** then slide the pushrod between the jaws to compress the spring. With the spring compressed, remove the pushrod circlip, then remove the diaphragm, pushrod and spring shown in **FIG 2:6**.

Servicing:

Wash all parts in clean petrol and inspect them for wear, renewing any parts found defective. If fuel starvation has been traced to the pump, suspect a leaking diaphragm or valves. Renew the diaphragm if it is hardened, distorted or split. The pump inlet and outlet valves are shown in **FIG 2:7.** It must be possible to blow air in at the inlet **E** but not possible to suck air out, and possible to suck air out of the outlet **A** but not possible to blow air in. If the valves prove to be faulty when this test is made it will be necessary to renew the pump upper part. Clean the filter screen with petrol and a small brush. **Do not use cloth as particles of lint may remain on the filter and be drawn into the carburetter.** If the filter is damaged or will not clean up properly, fit a new filter. Inspect the filter and covers seals and renew them if not in good condition.

Reassembly:

This is the reverse of the dismantling instructions, indexing the alignment marks on the two parts that were made earlier. Start the pump upper part retaining screws in their threads then press in the pump pushrod a little, holding in this position while tightening the screws alternately and evenly. This will ensure that the diaphragm is not stressed or creased.

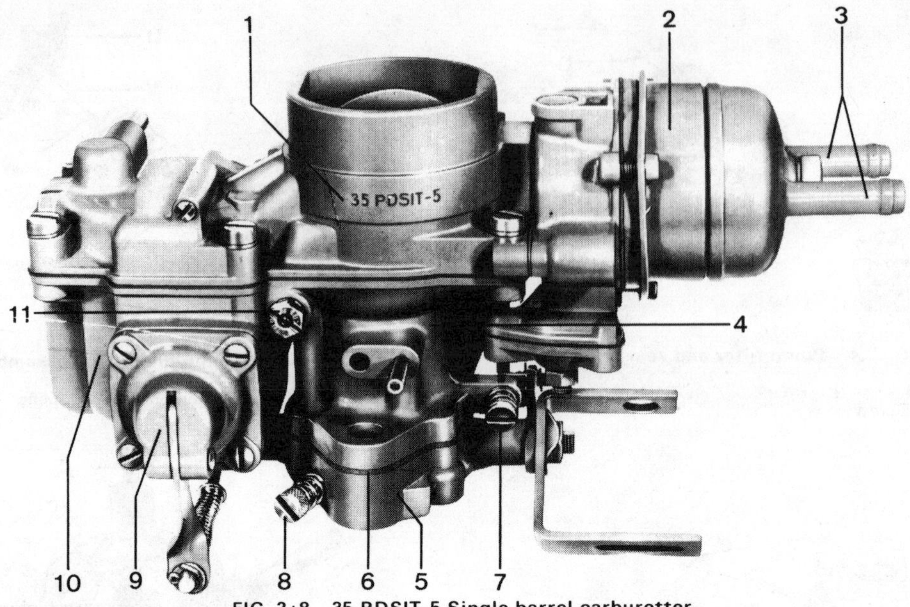

FIG 2:8   35 PDSIT-5 Single barrel carburetter

Key to Fig 2:8   1 Cover   2 Automatic choke   3 Water connections, automatic choke   4 Mixing chamber   5 Throttle
6 Insulator   7 Idle setscrew   8 Idle mixture regulating screw   9 Pump   10 Float housing, sometimes fitted with idle
cut-off valve   11 Idle jet

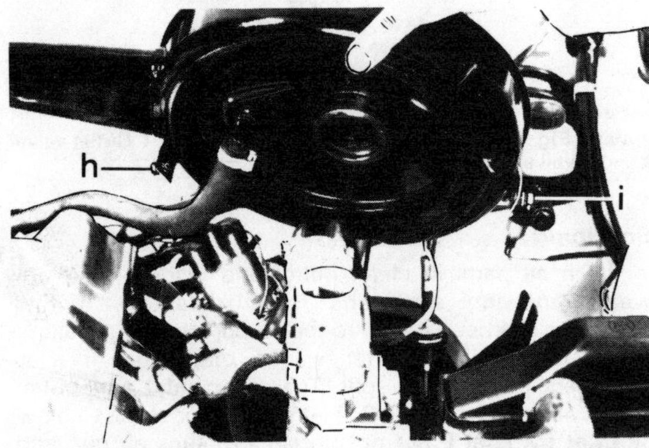

FIG 2:9   Removing the air cleaner

FIG 2:10   Disconnecting the accelerator linkage

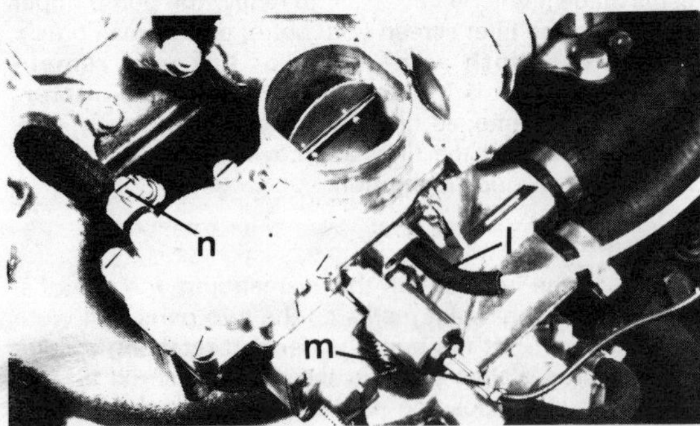

FIG 2:11   Disconnecting the vacuum hose, idle valve
lead and fuel hose

2:3 35 PDSIT-5 single barrel carburetter

This type of carburetter is shown in **FIG 2:8** and is
equipped with an automatic, engine temperature operated
choke 3 and an accelerator pump 9.

Removing and refitting:

Remove the air cleaner as shown in **FIG 2:9** after
loosening the nuts **h** and **i**. Loosen the accelerator linkage
clamp spring shown at **F** in **FIG 2:10** and disconnect
the linkage, noting the plastic washer. Loosen the hose
clips and disconnect the two water hoses from the
automatic choke, removing the radiator cap if the engine
is warm to prevent loss of coolant due to pressure. Refer
to **FIG 2:11** and disconnect vacuum hose **i** and lead **m**
at the idle cut-off valve. Loosen the hose clip **n** and

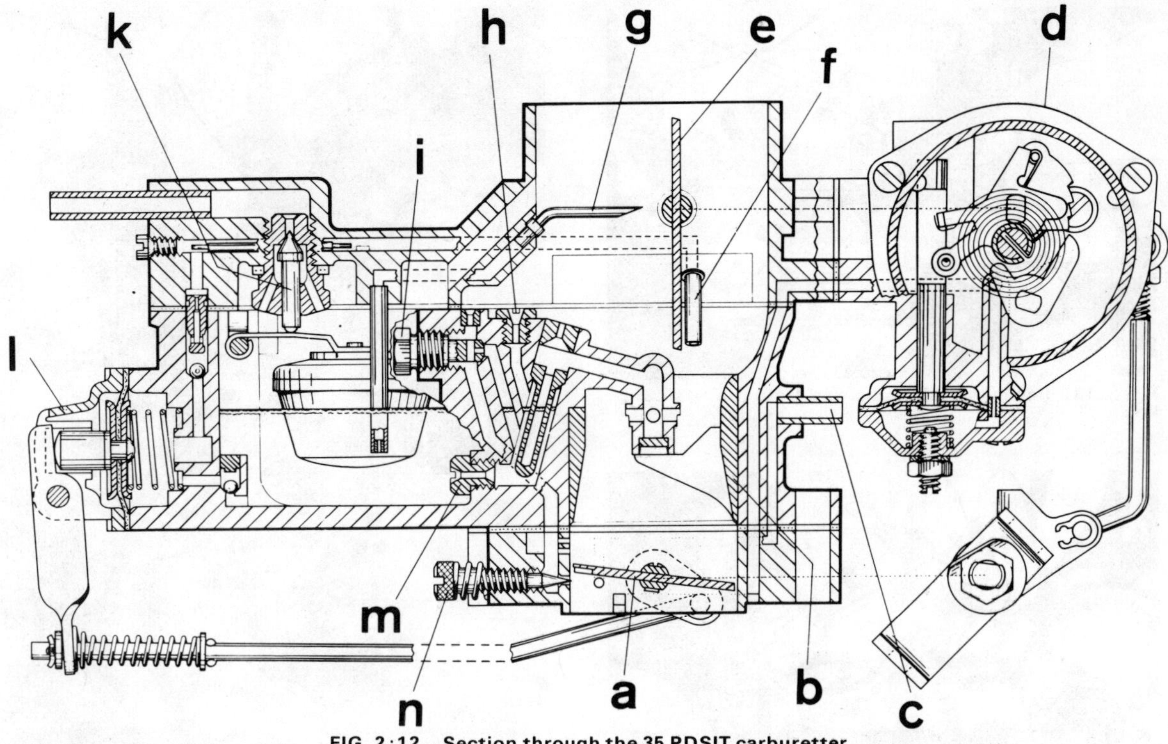

FIG 2:12   Section through the 35 PDSIT carburetter

Key to Fig 2:12   **a** Throttle   **b** Venturi   **c** Connecting tube, vacuumatic ignition timing   **d** Automatic choke   **e** Choke flap   **f** Injection tube   **g** Enrichment tube   **h** Air correction jet   **i** Idle jet   **k** Float needle valve   **l** Pump   **m** Main jet   **n** Idle mixture regulating screw

disconnect the fuel hose. Loosen both mounting nuts and remove the carburetter.

Refitting is a reversal of the removal procedure, using a new gasket between the carburetter and inlet manifold flange. On completion, check the throttle linkage for smooth operation.

Dismantling and servicing:

FIG 2:12 shows a section through the 35 PDSIT carburetter and illustrates the locations of the internal components. Undo the fixing screws and remove the carburetter top cover, then unscrew the needle valve assembly and collect its sealing washer. Take out the float pivot and remove the float. Remove the jets and emulsion tubes from inside the carburetter body, noting their locations for correct reassembly.

Clean and inspect all parts carefully. Clean out all sediment from the float chamber, jets and passages. Use compressed air, clean petrol and a small stiff brush. **Do not use cloth or a wire probe.** Check the needle valve assembly. If the needle or seat is damaged or if the unit will not seal correctly, it must be renewed. Inspect the float for leaks and check that its mounting flange is not bent. The float must be renewed if it is defective in any way.

Check the radial play of the throttle valve shaft in the throttle body. Too much play will allow the entry of air which will impair starting and slow-running. If the bearing surfaces are excessively worn the component should be renewed.

Reassembly:

Reassemble the carburetter in the reverse order of dismantling, using new gaskets and seal rings throughout. Fit the unit to the inlet manifold and carry out the adjustments described next.

2:4 Adjusting 35 PDSIT-5 carburetter

Checking fuel level:

With the car standing on level ground, run the engine at idle for about one minute to allow the float chamber to fill to its normal level. Remove the air cleaner as previously described and disconnect fuel hose from the carburetter. Take out the fixing screws that secure the carburetter top cover. Remove the clamp ring **e** shown in **FIG 2:13**, but do not loosen the nuts **f**. Lift off the carburetter top cover and gasket.

Using a suitable depth gauge, measure the distance between the flange surface and the surface of the fuel in the float chamber as shown in **FIG 2:14**. The distance should be .45 to .53 inch. Correct the fuel level if necessary by fitting fibre washers under the float needle valve assembly, refitting the cover and running the engine, then removing the cover again and checking the level as before until the correct thickness of washers has been determined. Adding washers will lower the level, removing washers will raise it.

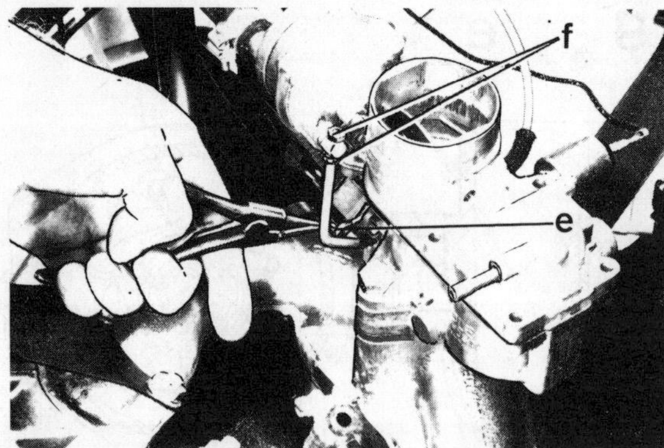

FIG 2:13   Removing the clamp ring from the operating link

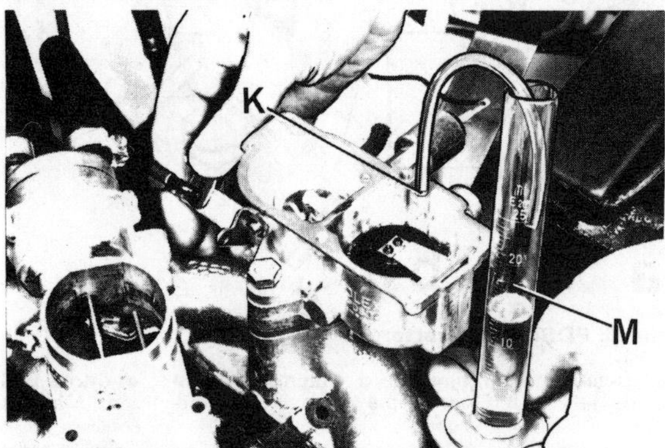

FIG 2:15   Checking the pump injection rate

FIG 2:16   Correcting pump injection rate

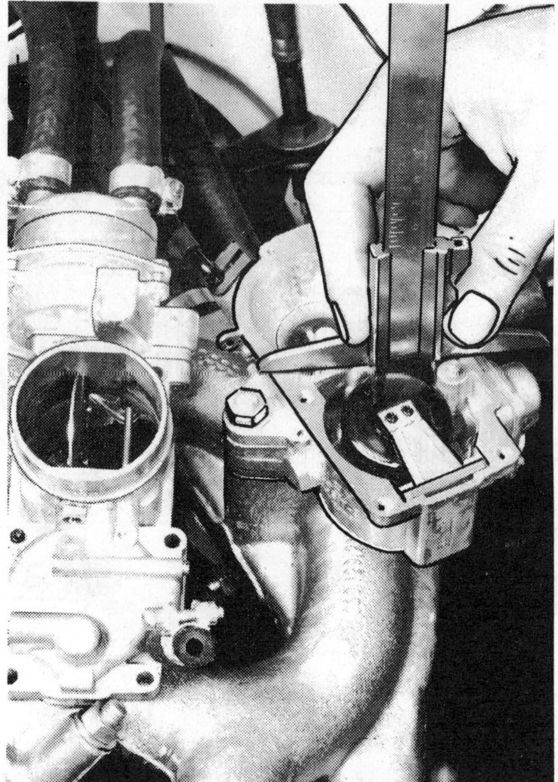

FIG 2:14   Checking the fuel level

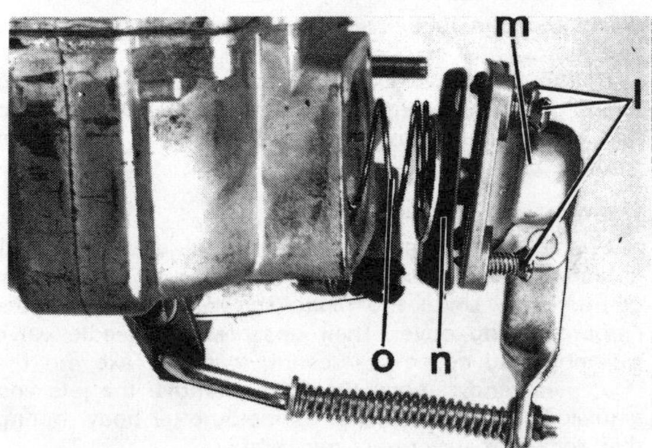

FIG 2:17   The accelerator pump assembly

Key to Fig 2:17   1 Screws   m Pump cover   n Diaphragm   o Spring

Checking pump injection rate:

Remove the carburetter top cover as described previously and loosen the idle adjusting screw completely. **Refer to FIG 2:15** and slide a length of thin plastic hose over connection **K.** Operate the throttle linkage as shown until the hose is full of fuel. Then place the end of the hose in a measuring cylinder. Move the throttle linkage from closed to fully open ten times in uninterrupted movements.

The injection rate will be the total amount of fuel in the measuring cylinder divided by ten. The injection rate should be $1.25 \pm .15$ cc per stroke.

To increase the pump injection rate, add additional washers between the cotterpin and the pump lever **k** shown in **FIG 2:16.** Note that no play must exist between the diaphragm and lever, that is, the injection cycle must begin as soon as the throttle lever is moved.

FIG 2:18   Checking the automatic choke position

To reduce the injection rate, remove washers from between the cotterpin and lever **k**, replace existing washers with thinner ones or move the cotterpin further towards the outside. After each adjustment check the injection rate until it is correct.

If the specified injection rate cannot be achieved, remove the cover and check the diaphragm **n** in **FIG 2:17** and renew it if worn, distorted or damaged then recheck the injection rate.

The stream of fuel that issues from the injection tube must be directed towards the opening throttle valve gap. If this is not so, carefully bend the injection tube as necessary.

Checking automatic choke:

Remove the carburetter as described in **Section 2:3**. Refer to **FIG 2:18** and mark the existing housing position. The standard setting is with notch 2 aligned with large tooth 1. Unscrew the mounting screws 4 and remove the housing complete with bi-metallic spring, noting the insulator **D**. Carefully clamp the carburetter in a vice in·such a manner that the throttle can be opened completely. Close the choke tight. Refer to **FIG 2:19** and press diaphragm rod **h** down to the stop with a screwdriver, at the same time holding choke follower **e** tight against the stop in closed position as shown in **FIG 2:20**. Check the gap between the choke and housing wall with a gauge **p** or a drill. The gap should be .0138± .004 inch. To adjust the choke gap, loosen nut **k** and turn the setscrew **i**. This changes the location of the lower stop for diaphragm rod **h**.

To set the throttle gap, close the choke tight and refer to **FIG 2:21**. Stop lever 1 is now positioned on the highest step of the stepped washer **m** and holds the throttle open by means of connecting rod **n**.

Check the gap between the throttle and housing wall with a gauge **o** or a drill. The gap should be .067± .004 inch. To adjust the throttle gap, adjust the nuts **p** on the connecting rod **n** shown in **FIG 2:22**.

FIG 2:19   Automatic choke mechanism

Key to Fig 2:19   **d** Eyelet, bi-metallic spring   **e** Follower   **f** Stepped washer   **g** Stop lever   **h** Diaphragm rod   **i** Setscrew, throttle gap   **k** Counter nut

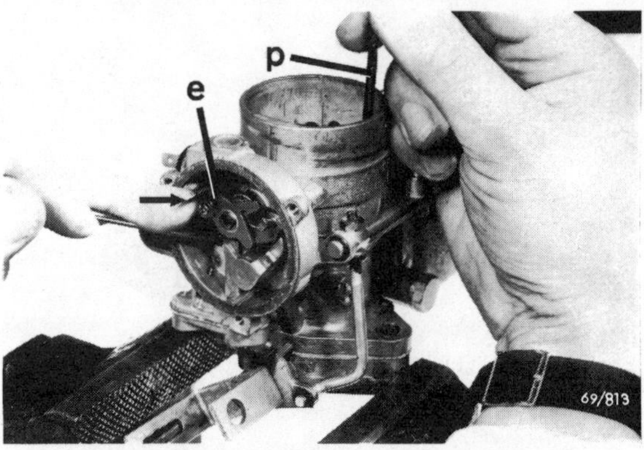

FIG 2:20   Checking the choke gap

FIG 2:21 Setting the choke mechanism to check the throttle gap

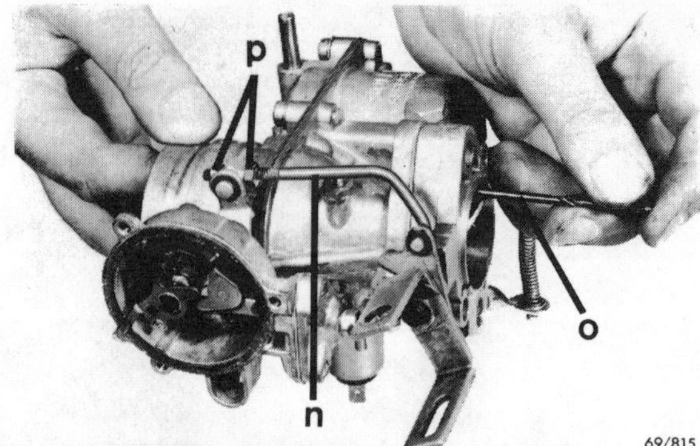

FIG 2:22 Checking the throttle gap

FIG 2:23 Idle speed screw E and mixture screw R

Idle speed adjustment:

Certain countries, such as West Germany, have laws requiring observation of the CO content of exhaust gases during carburetter idle adjustment procedure. If this is the case and approved exhaust analysing equipment is not available, the idle speed adjustments should be carried out by a service station with the necessary facilities.

The engine must be at operating temperature and the air cleaner fitted before idle speed adjustments are made to the carburetter. Adjustments will only be effective if the ignition timing, sparking plugs and contact breaker points are in order.

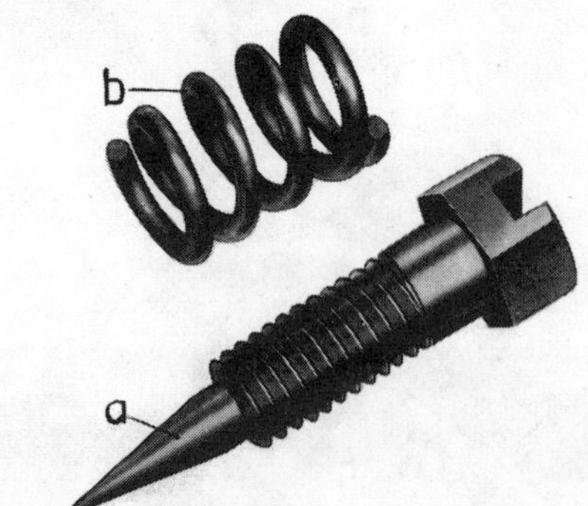

FIG 2:24 The idle mixture screw and spring

Refer to **FIG 2:23**. Start the engine and set it to idle at 950 rev/min by adjustments to screw **E**. Tighten the idle mixture screw **R** until the engine begins to run roughly, indicating a mixture which is slightly too weak. Now turn back the mixture screw approximately $\frac{1}{8}$ turn until the engine runs smoothly. Reset the idle to 950 rev/min if necessary by readjusting screw **E**. This is the point at which final CO measurement must be taken. If the CO content is above the legal minimum, tighten screw **R** a little until inside limits.

If the idle speed cannot be set satisfactorily, remove the idle mixture screw and spring as shown in **FIG 2:24**. Examine the tapered end of the screw and, if it is worn or damaged, fit a new screw and readjust the idle.

2:5 32 TDID dual barrel carburetter

This type of carburetter is shown in **FIG 2:25** and is equipped with an accelerator pump **i** and an engine temperature operated automatic choke. The automatic choke operates on the first barrel of the carburetter. Separate jets are fitted to each barrel, fed from a single common float chamber.

Removing and refitting:

Loosen the screws **a** and **b** shown in **FIG 2:26** and remove the air cleaner. Refer to **FIG 2:27** and loosen the throttle linkage clamp spring **f** and disconnect the linkage, paying attention to the plastic washer. Loosen the hose clips and disconnect the two hoses from the automatic

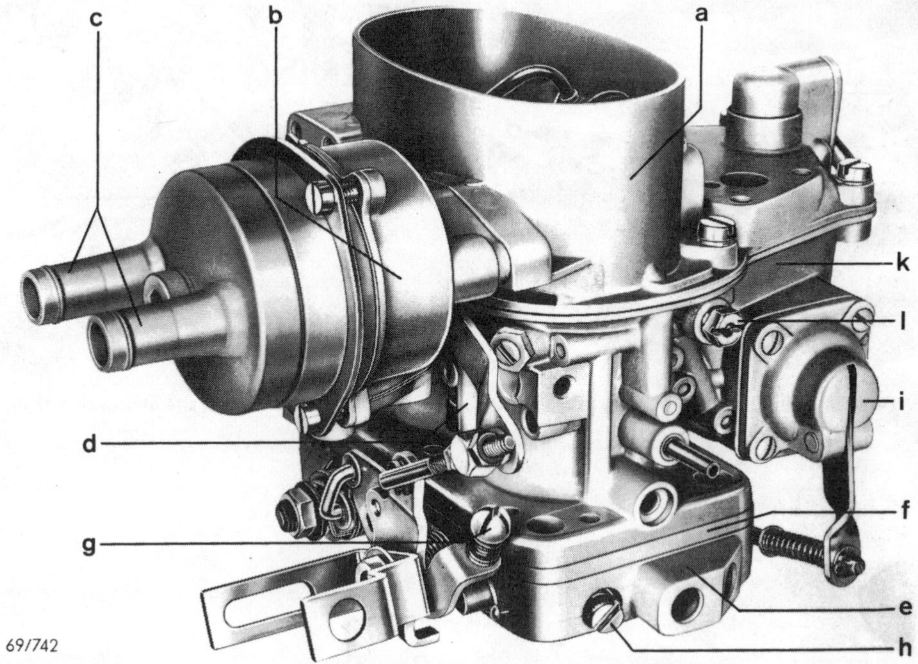

FIG 2:25 32 TDID dual barrel carburetter

Key to Fig 2:25   **a** Cover   **b** Automatic choke   **c** Water connections, automatic choke   **d** Mixing chamber I and II stage
e Throttle   **f** Insulator   **g** Idle setscrew   **h** Idle mixture regulating screw   **i** Delivery pump   **k** Float housing
l Idle jet (or idle cut-off valve)

choke, removing the radiator cap if the engine is warm to prevent loss of coolant due to pressure. Refer to **FIG 2:28** and disconnect vacuum hose **f** and the lead **g** at the idle cut-off valve. Loosen the clip **d** and disconnect the fuel hose. Loosen the four mounting nuts and remove the carburetter, preferably using a cranked ring spanner.

Refitting is a reversal of the removal instructions, using a new gasket between the carburetter and inlet manifold. On completion, check that both throttle linkages move easily.

Dismantling and servicing:

FIG 2:29 shows a section through the 32 TDID carburetter and illustrates the locations of the internal components. Undo the fixing screws and remove the carburetter top cover, then unscrew the needle valve assembly and collect its sealing washer. Take out the float pivot and remove the float. Remove the jets and emulsion tubes from the carburetter body, noting their locations for correct reassembly. **Do not mix the components of the first barrel with those of the second barrel.**

Clean and inspect all parts carefully. Clean out all sediment from the float chamber, jets and passages. Use compressed air, clean petrol and a small stiff brush. **Do not use cloth or a wire probe.** Check the needle valve assembly. If the needle or seat is damaged or if the unit will not seal properly, it must be renewed. Inspect the float for leaks and check that its mounting flange is not bent. The float must be renewed if it is defective in any way.

FIG 2:26   **Removing the air cleaner**

FIG 2:27   **Disconnecting the throttle linkage**

FIG 2:28   Disconnecting the vacuum hose, idle valve lead and fuel hose

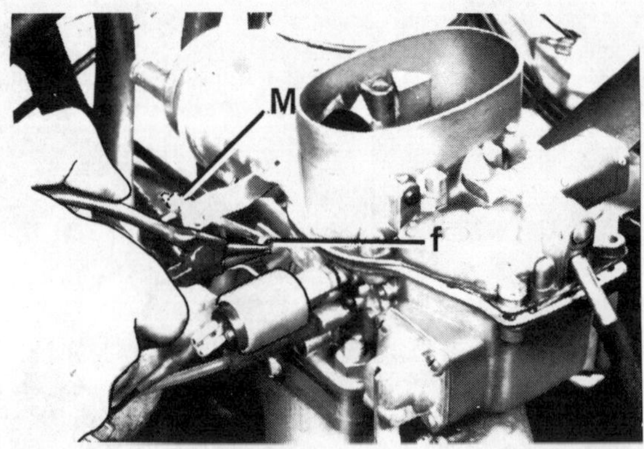

FIG 2:30   Removing the clamp ring from the operating link

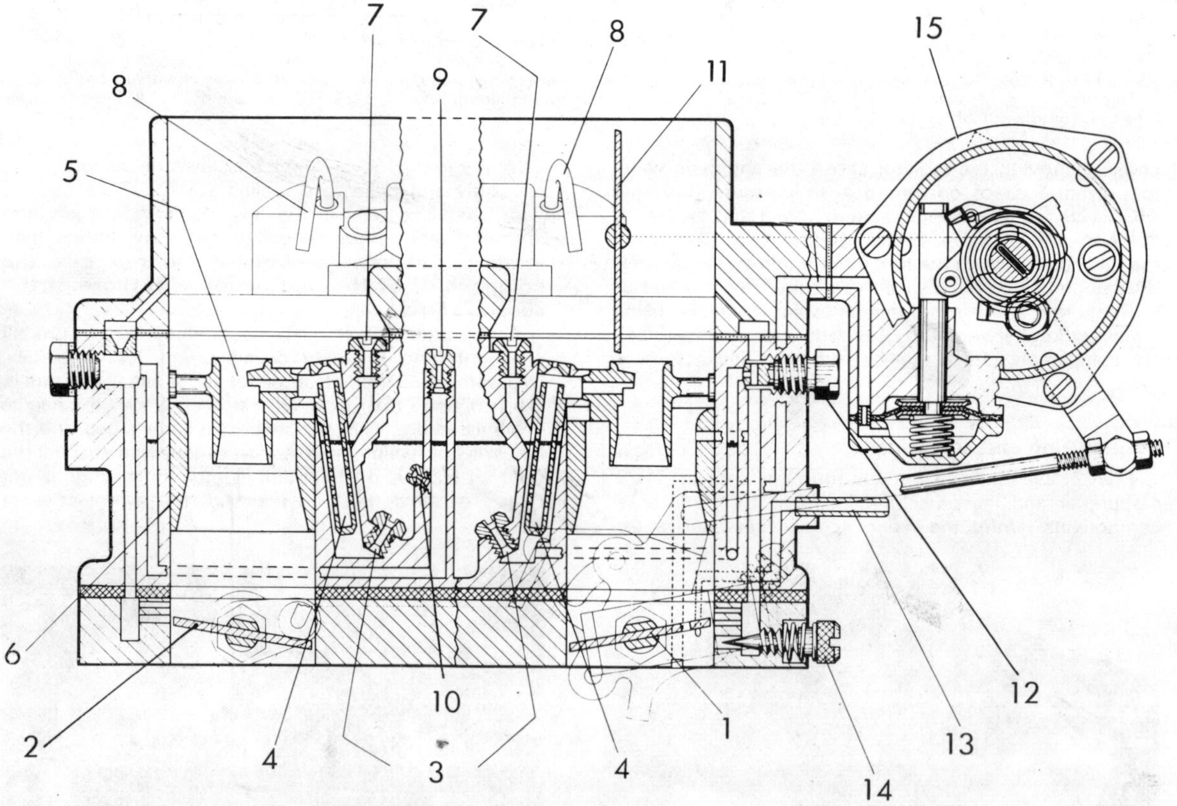

FIG 2:29   Section through the 32 TDID carburetter

Key to Fig 2:29   1 Throttle, I stage   2 Throttle, II stage   3 Main jet   4 Mixing tube   5 Outlet arm with atomizer   6 Venturi   7 Air correction jet   8 Enrichment tube   9 Breather jet   10 Transfer jet, II stage (idle reserve)   11 Choke   12 Idle jet   13 Connecting tube, vacuumatic ignition timing   14 Idle mixture regulating screw   15 Automatic choke

Check the radial play of the throttle shafts in the throttle body. Too much play will allow the entry of air which will impair starting and slow-running. If the bearing surfaces are excessively worn the component should be renewed.

Reassembly:

Reassemble the carburetter in the reverse order of dismantling, using new gaskets and seal rings throughout. Fit the unit to the inlet manifold and carry out the adjustments described in the next section.

2:6 Adjusting 32 TDID carburetter

Float location:

Remove the air cleaner and disconnect the hoses from the automatic choke as described previously. Take out the fixing screws that secure the carburetter top cover. Refer to **FIG 2:30** and remove the clamp ring **f** with angled, pointed pliers as shown. **Do not loosen the nuts M**. Lift off the carburetter cover.

Invert the carburetter cover and allow the float to rest against the needle valve assembly as shown in **FIG 2:31**. Fit the float gauge **g** (tool 20-100) and use it to check the float level as shown in **FIG 2:32**. The upper edge of the float bead must be within the slots of the gauge on both sides as indicated by the arrow. If not, the metal tab **h** on the float lever must be bent to obtain the correct setting.

FIG 2:31   Checking float height

Failing the special tool, the measurement can be carried out with a sliding rule. The measurement between the upper edge of the float flange and the cover flange surface should be .61 to .67 inch on both sides. Correct as described if the measurement is incorrect.

Checking pump injection rate:

With the carburetter installed, and all connections made, start the engine and allow it to run for a few moments to fill the float chamber with fuel. If the

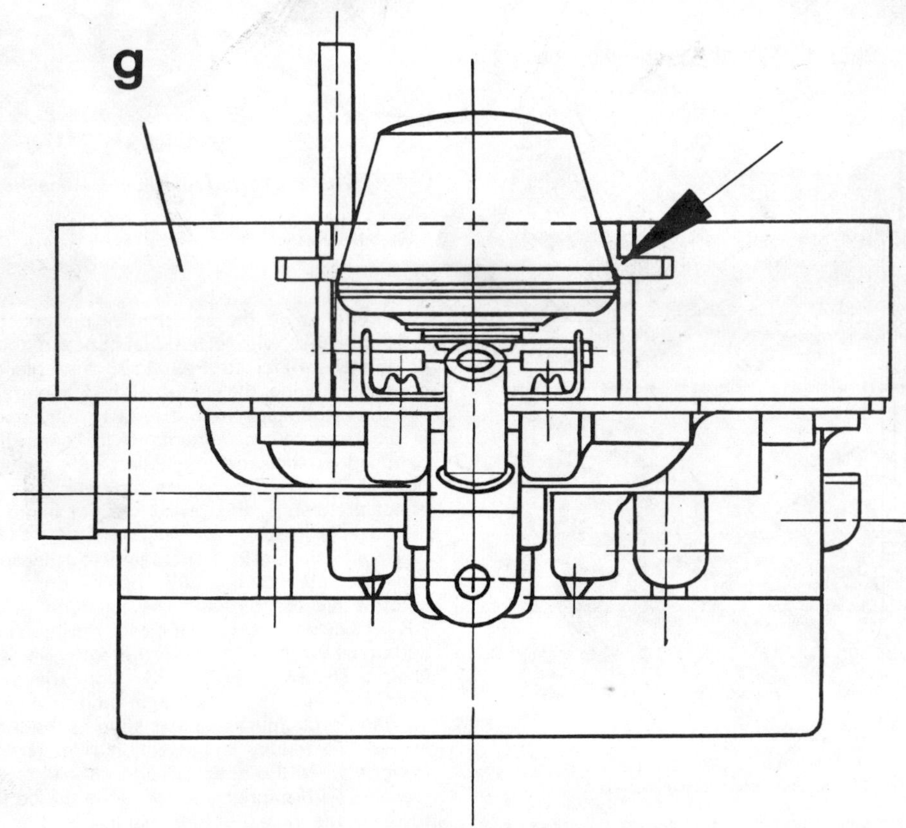

FIG 2:32   Installation of the checking gauge

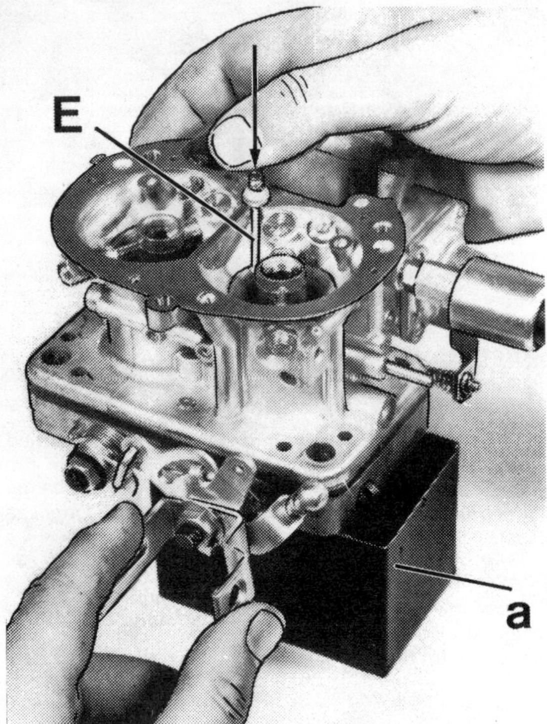

FIG 2:33   Checking the accelerator pump injection rate

FIG 2:34   Adjusting the accelerator pump injection rate

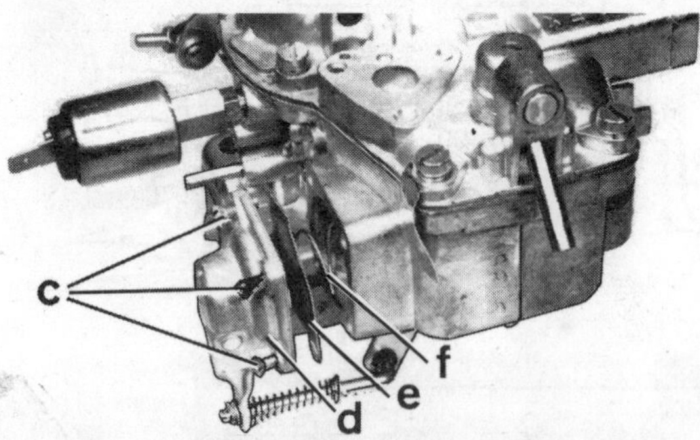

FIG 2:35   The accelerator pump assembly

Key to Fig 2:35   c Screws   d Pump cover   e Diaphragm
f Spring

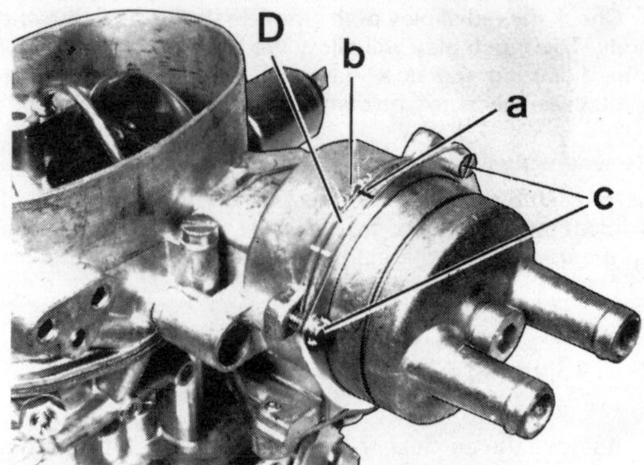

FIG 2:36   Checking the automatic choke position

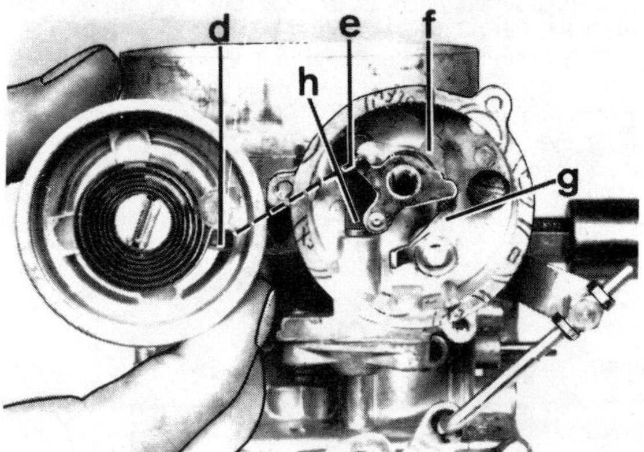

FIG 2:37   Automatic choke mechanism

Key to Fig 2:37   d Eyelet, bi-metallic spring   e Follower
f Stepped washer   g Stop lever   h Diaphragm rod

carburetter is off the car, remove the cover and fill the float chamber with clean fuel. Loosen the idle screw completely. Refer to .**FIG 2:33** and place a suitable container **a** under the venturi of the first barrel. Now move the throttle linkage from closed to fully open ten times in uninterrupted movements. If the carburetter cover is removed as shown the injection tube spring **e** must be pressed downwards to prevent leakage which would affect the results, this procedure not being necessary if the cover is fitted.

Transfer the fuel in the container to a measuring cylinder and check the total quantity. The injection rate will be this amount divided by ten. The injection rate should be $1.8 \pm .15$ cc per stroke. To increase the injection rate, place additional washers between the cotterpin and the pump lever **b** shown in **FIG 2:34**. Note that no play must exist between the diaphragm and lever, that is, the injection cycle must begin as soon as the throttle lever is moved. To reduce the injection rate, remove washers from between the cotterpin and lever **k**, replace existing washers with thinner ones or move the cotterpin further towards the outside. After each adjustment check the injection rate until it is correct.

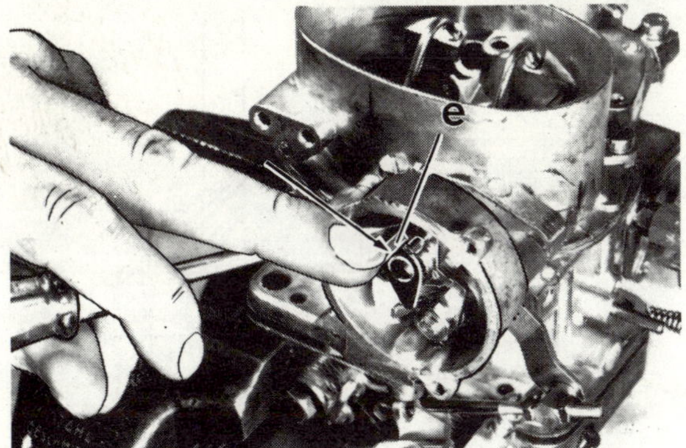

FIG 2:38 Setting the unit to check the choke gap

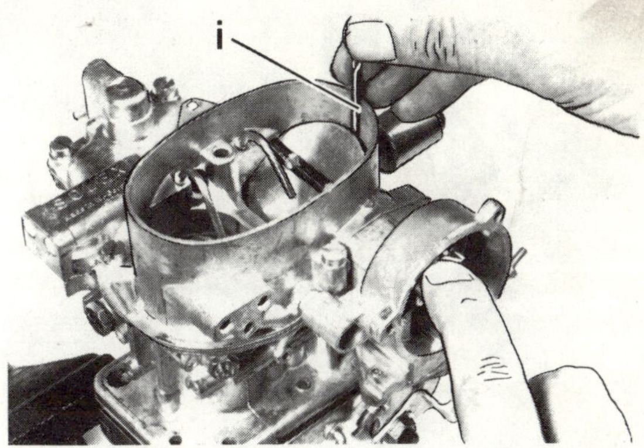

FIG 2:39 Checking the choke gap

If the specified injection rate cannot be achieved, remove the cover and check the diaphragm **e** in **FIG 2:35** and renew it if worn, distorted or damaged then recheck the injection rate.

The stream of fuel that issues from the injection tube must be directed towards the opening throttle gap. If this is not so, carefully bend the injection tube as necessary, this tube being shown at **E** in **FIG 2:33**. If fuel is injected from the tube in various directions and if the car has been accelerating roughly, the tube is probably partially blocked by dirt. In such a case it will be necessary to renew the injection tube.

Checking automatic choke:

Remove the carburetter as described in **Section 2:5**. Refer to **FIG 2:36** and mark the existing housing position. The standard setting is with notch **a** aligned with large tooth **b**. Unscrew the mounting screws **c** and remove the housing complete with bi-metallic spring, noting the insulator **D**. Carefully clamp the carburetter in a vice in such a manner that the throttle can be opened completely. Close the choke tight. Refer to **FIG 2:38** and press diaphragm rod **h** down to the stop with a screwdriver, at the same time holding choke follower **e** tight against the stop in closed position. Check the gap between the choke and the housing wall as shown in **FIG 2:39**, using a gauge **i** or a drill. The gap should be .09±.006 inch.

To adjust the choke gap, bend the pin **k** shown in **FIG 2:40** up or down with long-nosed pliers.

To set the throttle gap, close the choke tight and refer to **FIG 2:41**. Stop lever 1 is now positioned on the highest step of the stepped washer **m** and holds the throttle open by means of connecting rod **n**.

Check the gap between the throttle and the housing wall as shown in **FIG 2:42,** using a gauge **o** or a drill. The gap should be .063±.004 inch. To adjust the throttle gap, adjust the nuts **p** on the connecting rod **n**.

Idle speed adjustment:

Certain countries, such as West Germany, have laws requiring observation of the CO content of exhaust gases during carburetter idle adjustment procedure. If this is the case and approved exhaust analysing equipment is not available, the idle speed adjustments should be carried out by a service station with the necessary facilities.

The engine must be at operating temperature and the air cleaner fitted before idle speed adjustments are made to the carburetter. Adjustments will only be effective if the ignition timing, sparking plugs and contact breaker points are in order.

Refer to **FIG 2:43**. Start the engine and set it to idle at 950 rev/min by adjustments to screw **E**. Tighten the idle mixture screw **R** until the engine begins to run roughly,

FIG 2:40 Adjusting the choke gap

FIG 2:41 Setting the choke mechanism to check the throttle gap

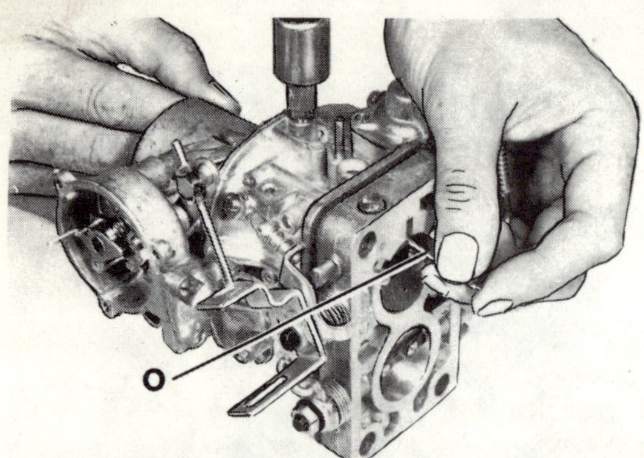

FIG 2:42 Checking the throttle gap

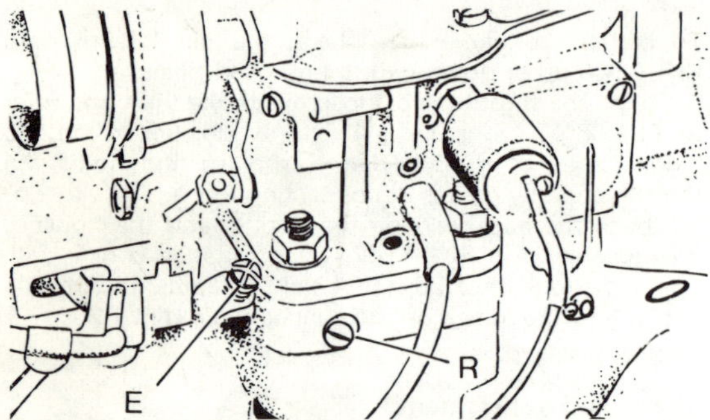

FIG 2:43 Idle speed screw **E** and mixture screw **R**

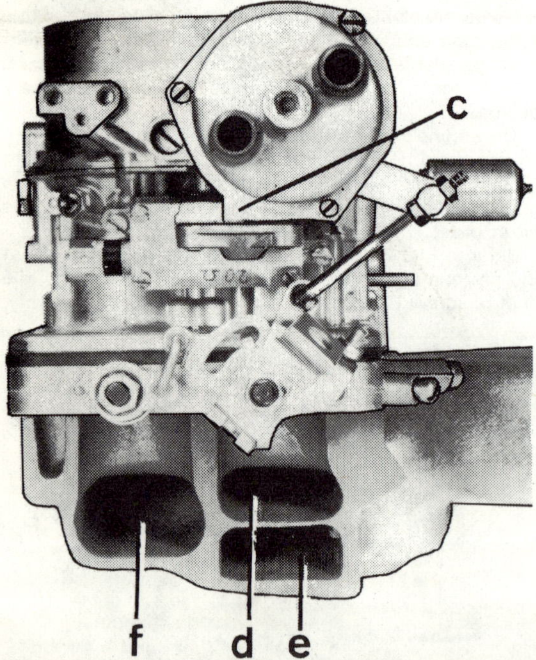

FIG 2:44 32/33 TDID USA export dual barrel carburetter, showing the mounting on the three-port inlet manifold

Key to Fig 2:44   **c** Carburetter   **d** Stage 1 gas port
e Stage 1 pre-heating port   **f** Stage 2 gas port

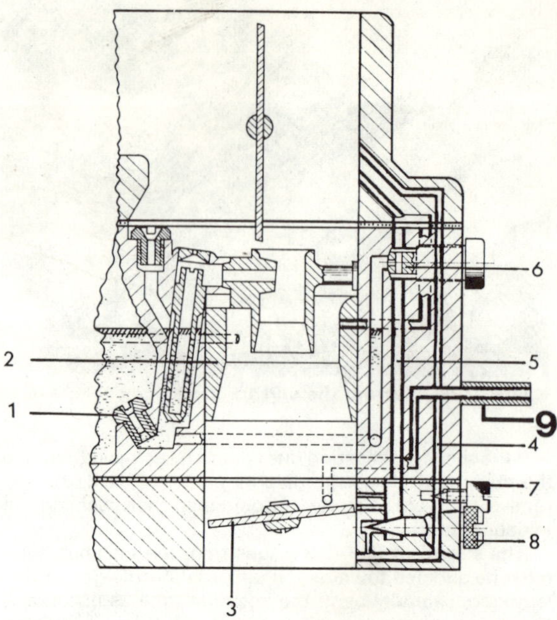

FIG 2:45 Cross section showing the idle bypass bore

Key to Fig 2:45   1 Main jet, stage I   2 Venturi, stage I
3 Throttle valve, stage I   4 Idle air bypass bore
5 Idle mixture bore   6 Idle fuel jet with electric cut-off valve
7 Idle air control screw   8 Idle mixture control screw
9 Vacuum connection

indicating a mixture which is slightly too weak. Now turn back the mixture screw approximately $\frac{1}{8}$ turn until the engine runs smoothly. Reset the idle to 950 rev/min if necessary by readjusting screw **E**. This is the point at which final CO measurement must be taken. If the CO content is above the legal minimum, tighten screw **R** a little until inside limits.

If the idle speed cannot be set satisfactorily, remove the idle mixture screw and spring as shown in **FIG 2:24**. Examine the tapered end of the screw and, if it is worn or damaged, fit a new screw and readjust the idle.

2:7 Modifications to 32 TDID carburetters

A more flexible transition between 2600 and 2800 rev/min can be attained on early models by means of the following modifications, models from Engine No. ZZ.016.349 being fitted with these modifications at the factory.

The main jet is changed from X.120 to X.125 with part number 059.129.405.C; the air correction jet changed from 150 to 160 with part number 059.129.435.C and the float level changed to give a measurement of .61 to .69 inch. This float level measurement is checked and adjusted to the figure quoted in the manner described in **Section 2:6**.

On models from Engine No. ZZ.002.331 onwards, g55 modified idle cut-off valve is fitted, this being part number 059.129.413. When exchanging the idle fuel jet against the idle cut-off valve make sure that the part is not overtightened. If it is too tight the part will be bent and the jet needle will no longer close or seal completely.

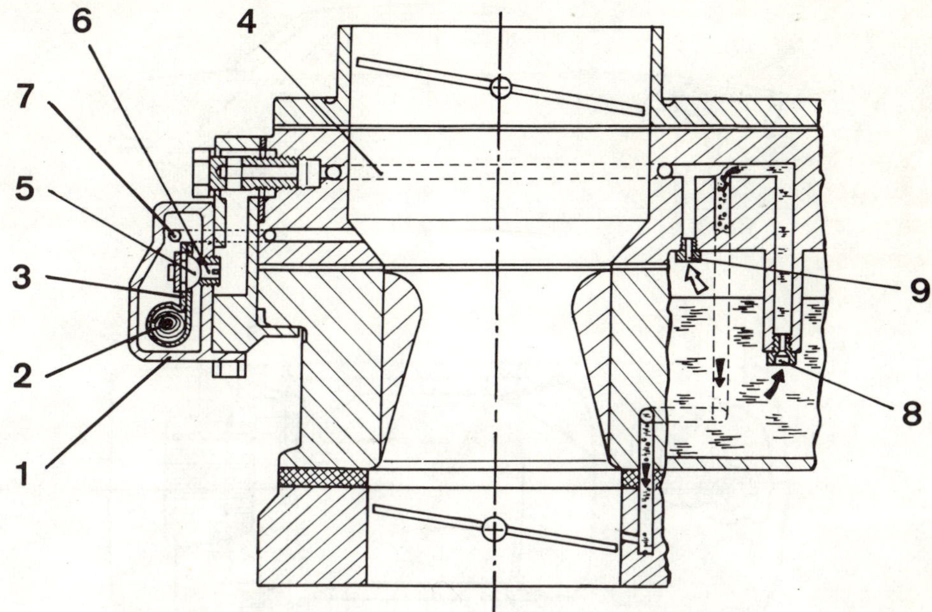

FIG 2:46   Cross section showing the thermo starting valve

Key to Fig 2:46 1 Thermo starting valve   2 Heating element
3 Bi-metallic spring   4 Pressure compensating bore
5 Valve cone   6 Valve seat (adjustable)   7 Breathing
bore (interior)   8 Compensating air jet   9 Fuel jet

2:8 32/32 TDID USA export carburetter

This carburetter is specially designed and adjusted to ensure very low CO content in the engine exhaust gases. **FIG 2:44** shows the 32/32 TDID carburetter, which is equipped with an idle air bypass bore and a thermo starting valve, illustrating the mounting arrangement on the three-port inlet manifold.

FIG 2:45 shows the arrangement of the idle air bypass bore. This has been developed in order to ensure constant vacumatic ignition timing. The pressure relief bore 9 for advanced timing at partial load is located above the throttle valve, so that the throttle valve controls the setting-in of advanced ignition timing. For this reason, the throttle valve adjustment is made at the factory, sealed with paint and must never be altered. The volume of air necessary for idling depends on engine dispersion. This volume is controlled by the idle air bypass bore 4 and is set by idle air screw 7.

The thermo starting valve 1 in **FIG 2:46** controls the mixture dispersion, in addition to the automatic choke and is a winter starting aid at extremely low temperatures. Fuel to enrich the mixture is taken from the float chamber. Valve 5 is closed when at a temperature of 23°F (—5°C). Additional fuel is received via jet 9 until the thermo starting valve opens. After valve 5 has opened, the vacuum necessary to transfer the fuel via pressure compensating bore 4 is discontinued and fuel delivery ceases. The flow of additional fuel is governed by the thermo starting valve as follows:

Under cold operating conditions, temperatures below 23°F, type bi-metallic spring 3 closes valve 5. When starting up the engine the right amount of vacuum can operate up to and within the float chamber and draws in fuel. Switching on the ignition simultaneously brings heating element 2 into operation. As its own temperature increases (to above 23°F) the bi-metallic spring expands and opens the valve. This breaks the vacuum in the additional enrichment tube and no more fuel is supplied.

Removal:

The 32/32 TDID USA export carburetter is removed and refitted in the manner described for 32 TDID carburetters in **Section 2:5.** Note, however, the instructions concerning the carburetter to inlet manifold gasket given in **Chapter 1, Section 1:11.**

Dismantling and servicing:

The basic design of this carburetter is similar to that of the 32 TDID model and the instructions for dismantling and cleaning given earlier will apply. However, due to the need for special tools and gauges when assembling to ensure low CO levels, it is recommended that the carburetter be dismantled and serviced only by an Audi agent.

Similarly, correct adjustment of the carburetter requires the use of infra-red absorption analyser to check CO content of the exhaust gas, an electric tachometer for accurate measurement of engine rev/min and a stroboscopic lamp to check the ignition timing. For these reasons the carburetter tuning should be entrusted to an Audi agent in order that legal requirements for CO emissions can be achieved.

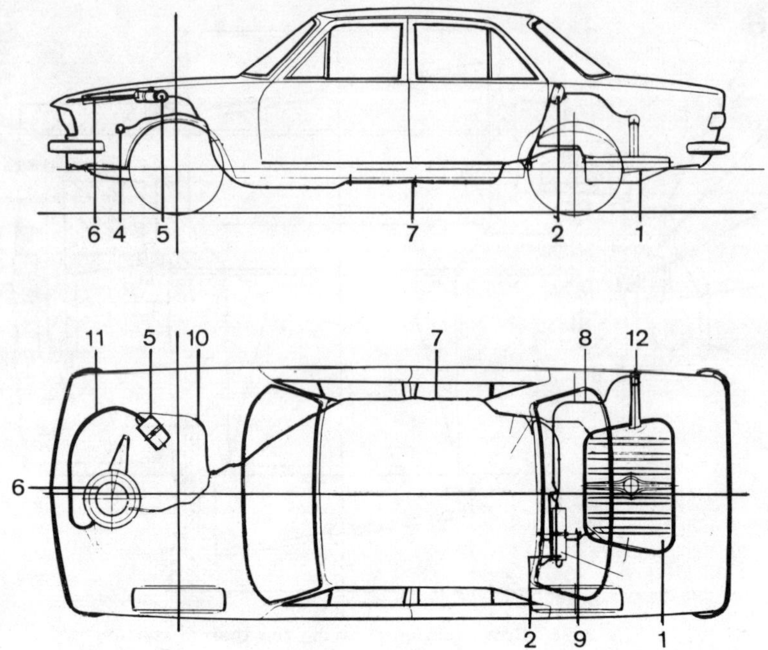

FIG 2:47   Sealed fuel system, USA export models

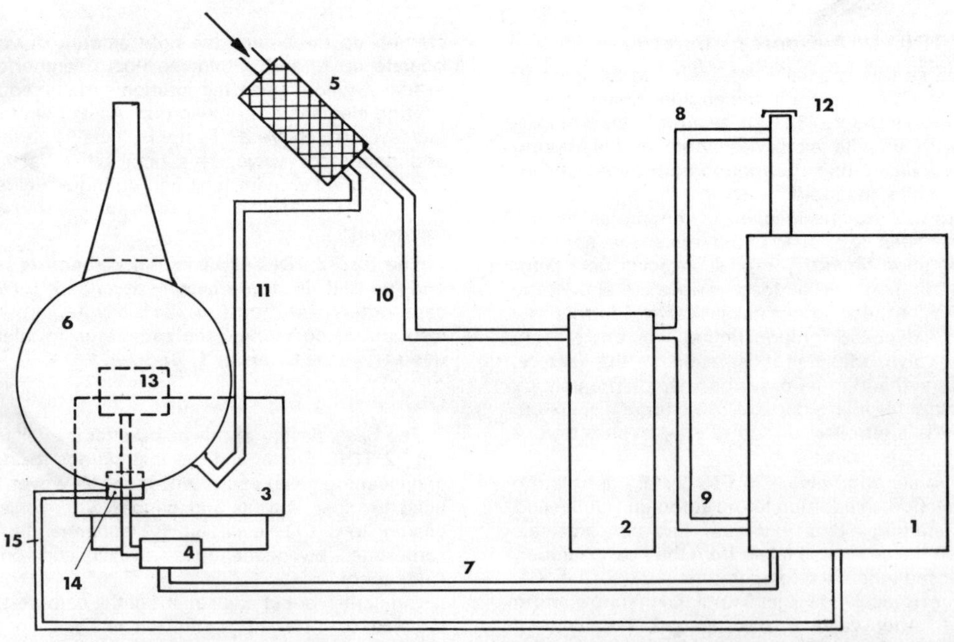

FIG 2:48   Diagram showing components and connections in the sealed fuel system

Key to Figs 2:47 and 2:48   1 Fuel tank   2 Expansion container   3 Engine   4 Fuel pump   5 Activated carbon container   6 Air cleaner   7 Fuel line from tank to fuel pump   8 Breather line from filler neck to expansion container   9 Connecting line from tank to expansion container   10 Breather line to activated carbon container   11 Connecting line from activated carbon container to filter   12 Cap, fuel tank   13 Line from carburetter to intake manifold   14 Fuel return valve   15 Fuel return pipe

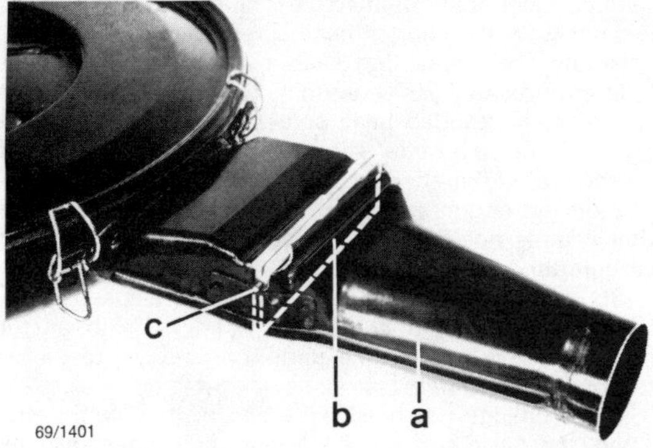

FIG 2:49 Air cleaner flap, USA export models

FIG 2:50 Twin carburetter installation. Adjustment

Key to Fig 2:50 **a** Idle mixture control screws **b** Idle speed control screws **c** Synchronizers **d** Tachometer **e** Intermediate linkage

FIG 2:51 Synchronizing twin carburetters

Key to Fig 2:51 **d** Tachometer **f** Knurled head screw **g** Locknut **h** Carburetter connecting shaft

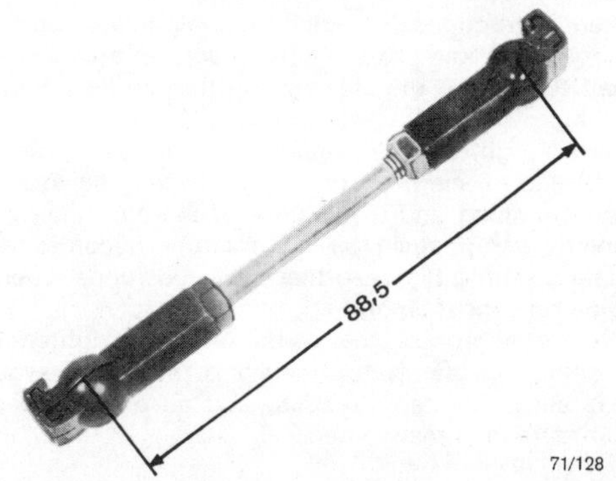

FIG 2:52 Rear carburetter link—from centre of ball to ball=3.48 inch (88.5 mm)

2:9 Sealed fuel system, USA export models

This fuel system, illustrated in **FIGS 2:47** and **2:48** is used to prevent air contamination due to evaporation losses from the system. The fuel tank filler cap 12 has no breathing device in order that fumes will not escape from the tank. Surplus fuel due to rising temperatures flows into expansion container 2 via line 9. The expansion container is located at the highest point in the luggage compartment.

Fuel fumes from tank 1 and filler neck 12 pass through lines 8, 9 and 10 into the activated carbon container 5 where they are absorbed. The activated carbon container is located in the engine compartment, connected to the air cleaner assembly by means of line 11 and continually regenerated by fumes drawn in from the engine 3.

From 1972 a vacuum-controlled fuel return valve is included in the fuel line between the pump and the carburetter, with a fuel return pipe to the fuel tank. These are shown as items 14 and 15 in **FIG 2:48**.

The return valve is operated by means of a vacuum obtained from the vacuum line between carburetter and distributor and is opened at periods of idle or low vacuum in the intake manifold to permit the return of surplus fuel to the tank. As the engine speed increases, and there is higher vacuum in the line, the return valve closes and the total fuel delivery flows into the carburetter.

Maintenance is limited to periodic checks on the condition of the pipes and hoses, and on the tightness of all clips and hose connections. Make sure that no fuel can pass into the activated carbon container 5.

2:10 Air cleaners

All air cleaners are fitted with paper filter cartridges which must be serviced as described in the owners handbook. Access to the filter cartridge is by removal of the air cleaner top cover.

The air cleaner fitted to USA export models is shown in **FIG 2:49**. Flap **b** is fitted in the inlet **a** in order to ensure sufficient vacuum in the air cleaner at all times. This flap blocks the air intake completely or partially at idle and low engine speeds, to guarantee suction of gases from the engine crankcase and rocker cover. The flap must operate easily to ensure perfect functioning. Check the operation occasionally. To do so, turn the flap by hand at the shaft end **c**. If any stiffness is apparent, clean the bearing surfaces, wash with petrol and apply a light coat of oil.

2:11 Solex carburetters type 32/35 TDID

Apart from jet sizes etc. these carburetters are very similar to the type already described, but it may be of assistance to give some details of the twin installation on Coupé S models.

Removal:

Loosen the three mounting screws for the air cleaner, pull the oil vent hose out of the cylinder head cover and disconnect the preheating hose from the exhaust manifold. Pull the air cleaner upwards and remove.

Disconnect the vacuum hose for the ignition control from the rear carburetter and the idle cutoff valve lead from both carburetters.

Disconnect the intermediate linkage and the operating link from the rear carburetter.

Loosen the clips for the water hoses to the automatic choke from both carburetters, pull off the hoses and tie them up to a higher level to prevent water running out.

Disconnect the fuel supply pipes from both carburetters. Remove the flange mounting nuts (a special ring spanner may be needed for this), and the mounting nuts on the connecting shaft console of the rear carburetter, for which a fork wrench is required.

Lift off first the front and then the rear carburetter and cover the intakes immediately.

The installation of these carburetters will be a reversal of the removal procedure.

Adjusting and synchronizing:

These instructions are given assuming that the carburetters are clean and correctly assembled and that all engine services are properly adjusted and functioning correctly. The engine should be at normal working temperature.

Refer to **FIG 2:50** after removing the air cleaner as described earlier.

Disconnect the intermediate linkage **e** from the front carburetter and fit the synchronizers **c** according to the makers instructions. Connect a reliable tachometer **d**.

Loosen the idle mixture control screws **a** by one-and-a-half turns from the starting position while the engine is idling.

Slowly tighten up the mixture control screw until the weakening of the mixture causes the engine to lose its smooth running and then turn it back until the engine is running evenly again as the mixture becomes richer. Obtain a setting between these two positions where the engine runs most smoothly.

Now synchronise the carburetters by tightening or loosening the idle control screw **b** until both synchronizers show the same reading and an engine speed of 1100 rev/min is maintained.

Reconnect the intermediate linkage and loosen the locknut **g** for the knurled head screw (see **FIG 2:51**).

Rotate the connecting shaft by hand as shown and hold an indicated 2000 rev/min. Adjust the intermediate rod with the knurled head screw until the synchronizer on the front carburetter shows the same reading as that on the rear carburetter.

Stop the engine and refit the air cleaner, making sure that it does not foul the idle cut off valve on the front carburetter.

Start the engine again and note that the speed should be 950 ± 50 rev/min. If necessary, adjust both mixture control screws by the same amount probably $\frac{1}{4}$ to $\frac{1}{2}$ a turn to obtain this speed.

If the linkage has been disturbed or new carburetters fitted, the basic setting of the rear carburetter link must be checked as shown in **FIG 2:52**.

2:12 Fault diagnosis

(a) Leakage or insufficient fuel delivered

1 Air vent to tank restricted
2 Fuel pipes blocked
3 Air leaks at pipe connections
4 Pump filter blocked
5 Pump gaskets faulty
6 Pump diaphragm defective
7 Pump valve sticking or seating badly
8 Fuel vapourizing in pipelines due to heat

(b) Excessive fuel consumption

1 Carburetter requires adjustment
2 Fuel leakage
3 Sticking mixture control
4 Dirty air cleaner
5 Excessive engine temperature
6 Brakes binding
7 Tyres under-inflated
8 Idling speed too high
9 Car overloaded

(c) Idling speed too high

1 Rich fuel mixture
2 Carburetter control sticking
3 Incorrect slow-running adjustment
4 Worn throttle valves

(d) Noisy fuel pump

1 Loose mountings
2 Air leaks at suction side or at diaphragm
3 Obstruction in fuel pipe
4 Clogged pump filter

(e) No fuel delivery

1 Float needle stuck
2 Tank vent blocked
3 Pipeline obstructed
4 Pump diaphragm stiff or damaged
5 Pump inlet valve stuck open
6 Bad air leak on suction side of pump

CHAPTER 3

THE IGNITION SYSTEM

3:1 Description
3:2 Routine maintenance
3:3 Ignition faults
3:4 Removing and dismantling distributor

3:5 Timing the ignition
3:6 Sparking plugs
3:7 Fault diagnosis

3:1 Description

The distributor is of Bosch manufacture and is mounted on the rear of the engine block. The distributor shaft rotates clockwise and is driven via the oil pump shaft from a gear on the engine camshaft.

The distributor incorporates automatic timing control by means of a centrifugal mechanism and a vacuum controlled unit. As engine speed increases, the centrifugal action of rotating weights pivoting against the tension of small springs moves the contact breaker cam relative to the distributor drive shaft and progressively advances the ignition. The vacuum unit is connected by small bore pipe to a fitting on the carburetter. At high degrees of vacuum the unit advances the ignition, but under load, at reduced vacuum, the unit progressively retards the ignition.

The distributor fitted to USA export models is equipped with a dual-acting vacuum control unit which controls the advance and retard to very fine limits according to engine load. This is necessary to ensure low percentages of noxious gases being emitted from the exhaust system.

The ignition coil is of Bosch manufacture. It is a high-output type and has a series resistance incorporated. When the starter is switched on, the series resistance is disconnected and battery voltage fed to the coil, but when the starter is switched off the series resistor functions to reduce current to the coil.

3:2 Routine maintenance

Remove the air cleaner and refer to **FIG 3:1**. Pull off the two spring clips **b** and remove the distributor cap **a**. Pull off the rotor and remove the dust cap. Apply a small drop of oil to the pivot point of the moving contact point and lightly grease the distributor shaft cam at the point shown by the arrow in **FIG 3:2**. Avoid allowing grease or oil to contaminate the contact breaker points, lubricating sparingly for this reason.

Adjusting the contact breaker points:

Turn the engine until one of the cams has opened the points to the fullest extent, then check the gap between the points with a feeler gauge. The correct gap is .016 inch. To adjust the gap, loosen the screw **p** in **FIG 3:2** and insert a screwdriver into the groove **o** and use bosses **n** as supports. Turn the screwdriver to adjust the gap to correct specifications and tighten the screw **p**. Recheck the gap.

Cleaning the contact points:

Use a fine carborundum stone or contact point file to polish the points if they are dirty or pitted, taking care to keep the faces flat and square. On completion, wipe away

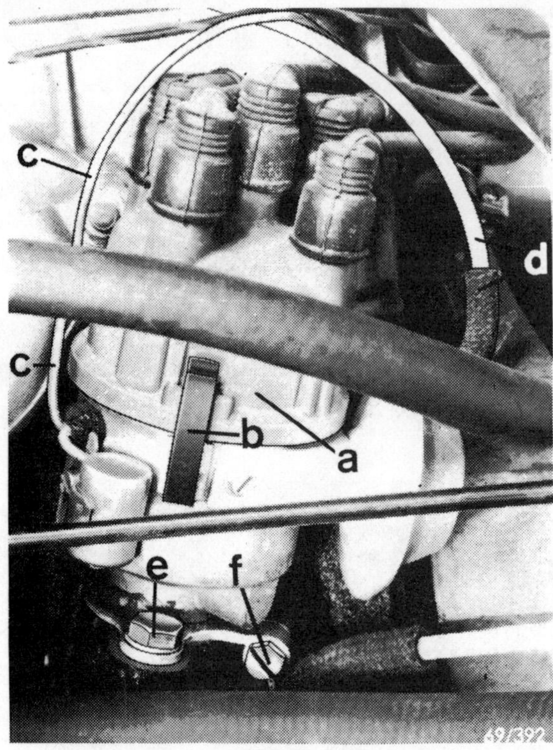

FIG 3:1 Distributor installation

Key to Fig 3:1 **a** Distributor cap **b** Spring clips
c Primary wire **d** Vacuum line **e** Mounting screw
f Clamp screw

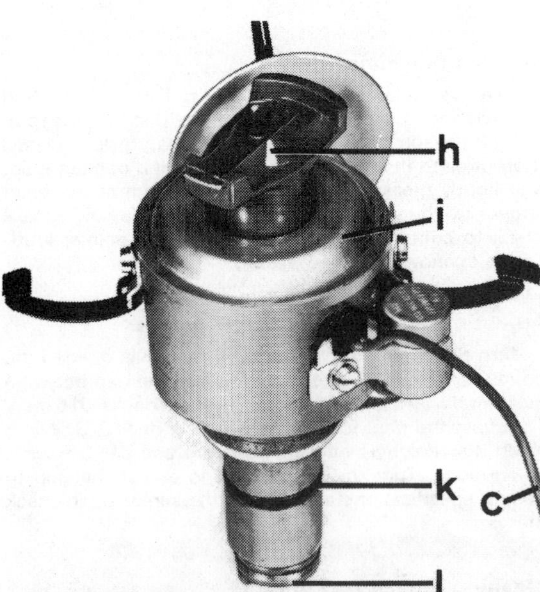

FIG 3:3 Removing the rotor and dust cover

Key to Fig 3:3 **c** Primary wire **h** Rotor **i** Dust cover
k Rubber seal **l** Drive dog

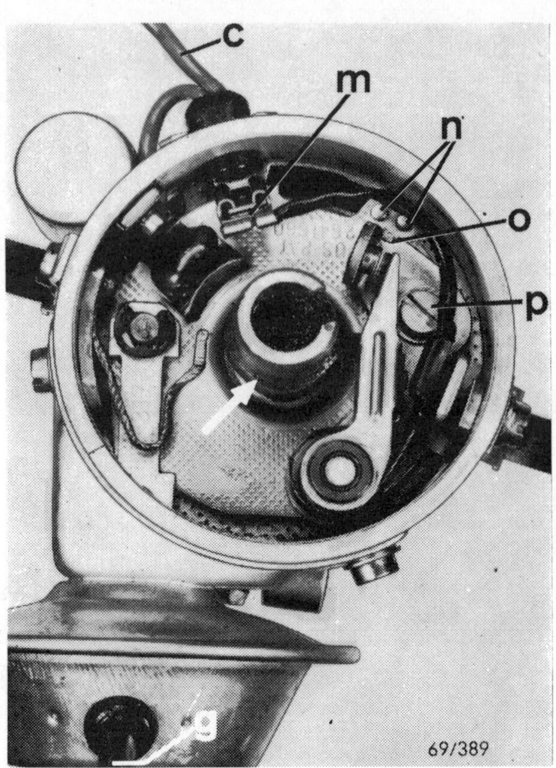

FIG 3:2 The contact breaker assembly

Key to Fig 3:2 **c** Primary wire **g** Plastic vacuum connection
m Flat plug connection **n** Bosses **o** Groove **p** Screw

all dust with a cloth moistened in petrol. The contact
points may be dismantled to assist cleaning by removing
screw **p** and plug **m** and pulling off the contact breaker
assembly.

3:3 Ignition faults

If the engine runs unevenly, set it to idle at about
1000 rev/min and, taking care not to touch any metal part
of the sparking plug leads, remove and replace each lead
from its plug in turn. Doing this to a plug which is firing
properly will accentuate the uneven running but will
make no difference if the plug is not firing.

Having located the faulty cylinder, stop the engine and
remove the plug lead. Pull back the insulation so that the
metal end of the lead is exposed. Start the engine and
hold the lead carefully to avoid shocks so that the metal
end is about $\frac{1}{8}$ inch away from the cylinder head. A strong,
regular spark confirms that the fault lies with the sparking
plug which should be cleaned as described in **Section
3:6** or renewed if defective.

If the spark is weak and irregular, check the condition
of the lead and, if it is perished or cracked, renew it and
repeat the test. If no improvement results, check that the
inside of the distributor cap is clean and dry and that
there is no sign of 'tracking', which can be seen as a thin
black line between the electrodes or to some metal part
in contact with the cap. 'Tracking' can only be rectified
by fitting a new cap. Check that the spring contact in the
cap is clean and that it makes good contact with the rotor.

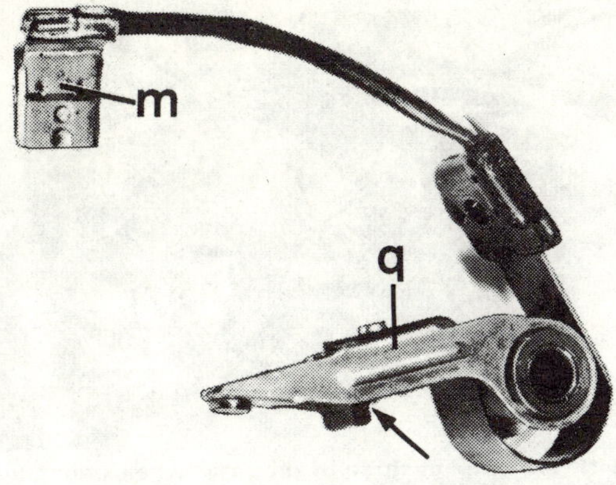

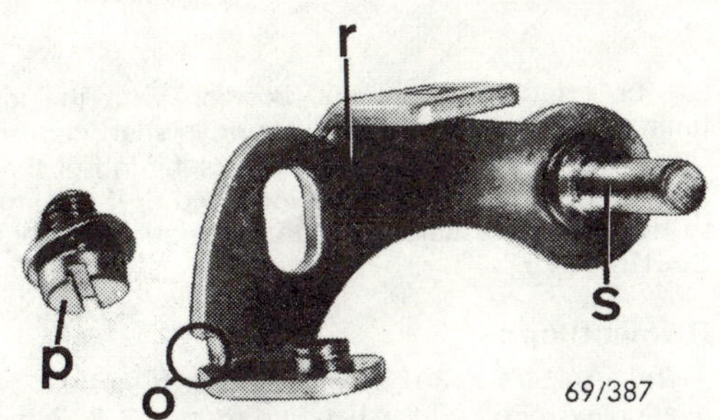

FIG 3:4 The contact breaker points dismantled

Key to Fig 3:4   **m** Flat plug connection   **o** Groove
p Screw   **q** Moving contact   **r** Fixed contact   **s** Pivot pin

Testing the low-tension circuit:

Check that the contact breaker points are clean and correctly set, then proceed as follows:

Disconnect the thin wire from the coil that connects to the distributor. Connect a 12-volt test lamp between these terminals, turn on the ignition and turn the engine slowly. If, when the contacts close the lamp lights and goes out when they open the circuit is in order. If the lamp fails to light, there is a fault in the low-tension circuit. Remove the test lamp and reconnect the wire to the coil and distributor.

If the fault lies in the low-tension circuit, use the test lamp to carry out the following tests with the ignition switched on.

Remove the wire from the ignition switch side of the coil and connect the lamp between the end of this wire and earth. If the lamp fails to light, it indicates a fault in the wiring or connections between the battery and the coil, or in the ignition switch. Reconnect the wire if the lamp lights.

Disconnect the wire from the coil that connects to the distributor. Connect the lamp between the coil terminal and earth. If the lamp fails to light it indicates a fault in the primary winding and a new coil must be fitted. Reconnect the wire if the lamp lights and disconnect its other end from the distributor. If the test lamp does not light when connected between the end of this wire and earth, it indicates a fault in the section of wire.

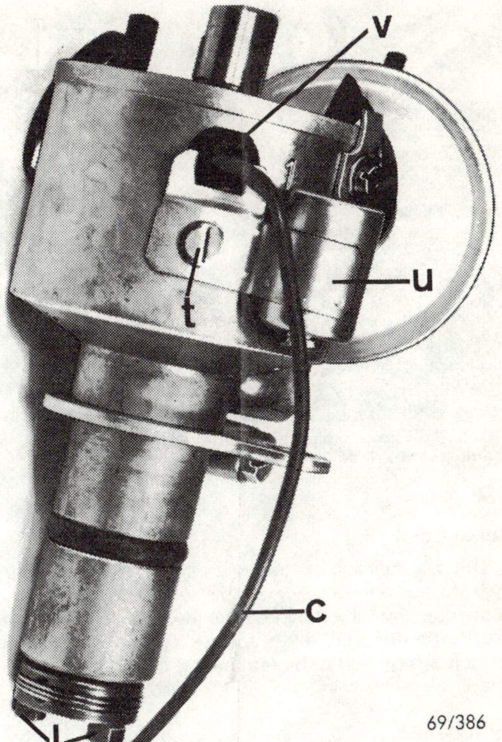

FIG 3:5 Capacitor mounting

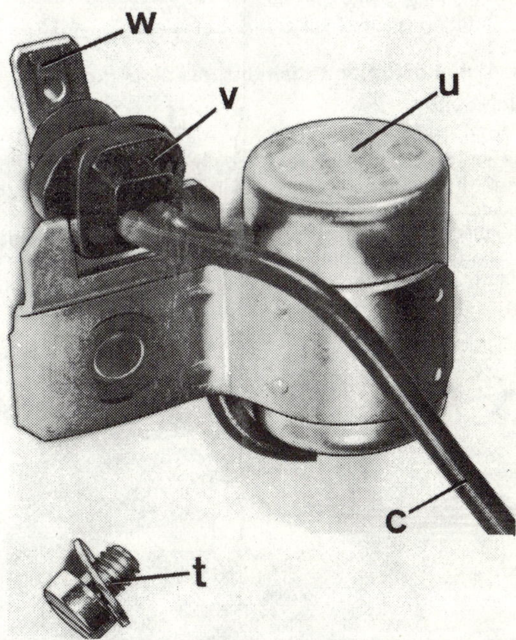

FIG 3:6 Capacitor, plastic mounting and connection

Key to Figs 3:5 and 3:6   **c** Primary wire   **l** Drive dog
t Screw   **u** Capacitor   **v** Plastic mounting   **w** Flat plug terminal

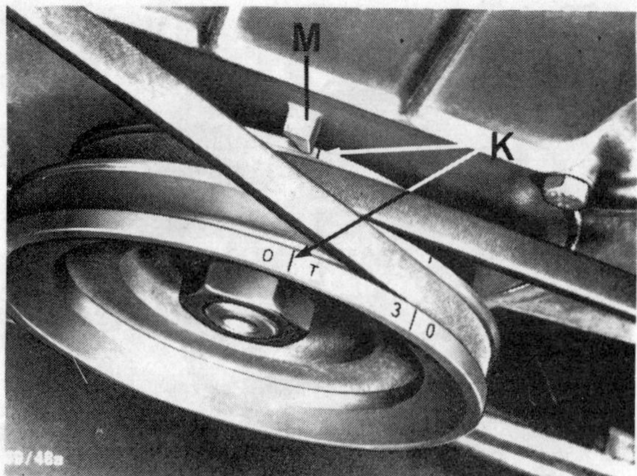

FIG 3:7 The crankshaft pulley timing mark **K** and crankcase mark **M**

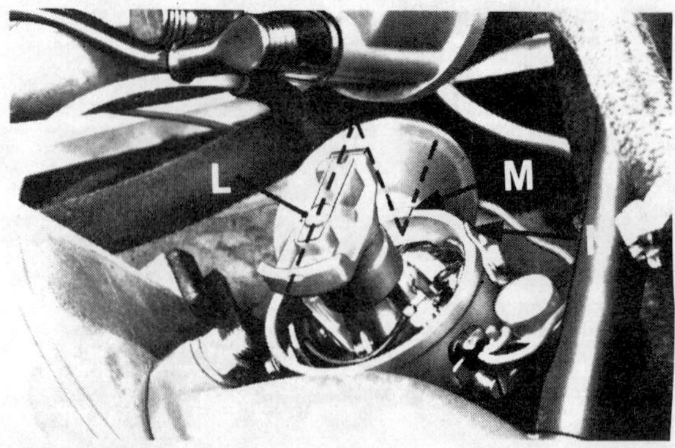

FIG 3:8 The position of the rotor when timing marks are correctly aligned

Key to Fig 3:8   **L** Rotor   **M** Mark on housing
N Primary terminal

Capacitor:

The best method of testing a capacitor (condenser) is by substitution. Disconnect the original capacitor and connect a new one between the low-tension terminal on the distributor and earth for test purposes. If a new capacitor is proved to be required, it can then be properly fitted.

Removal:

Pull off the connector on the wire leading to the capacitor from the contact breaker assembly, take out the retaining screw and remove the capacitor.

Refitting is a reversal of this procedure.

3:4 Removing and dismantling distributor

Removal:

Refer to **FIG 3:1**. Remove the air cleaner and the distributor cap **a**. Disconnect the green lead **c** at the coil. Pull off the vacuum line **d**, taking care not to break the plastic tube connector. Take out screw **e** and pull out the distributor, using a screwdriver to assist this operation if the distributor rubber seal sticks. Do not loosen the clamp screw **f**. If this screw is untouched, the distributor

FIG 3:9 Checking vacuum retard, USA export models

can be fitted in its original position with the ignition timing unaltered. The distributor drive shaft can only be fitted correctly, due to off-centre machining of the drive parts. If the clamp screw **f** is loosened or if the timing is to be reset, instructions for this operation are given in **Section 3:5**.

Dismantling:

Refer to **FIG 3:3**. Pull off the rotor **h** and remove the dust cover **i**. Pull off the flat plug **m** in **FIG 3:2** and take out the screw **p**. The contact point set can then be removed and the components separated as shown in **FIG 3:4**.

FIG 3:5 shows the capacitor mounting. Remove the retaining screw **t** and detach capacitor **u** together with the plastic fitting **v** and connection **w**, as shown in **FIG 3:6**.

Servicing:

Clean and inspect all parts, renewing any found worn or damaged. If there is excessive play in the shaft bearings or if the shaft is bent or the housing damaged, an exchange unit should be obtained and fitted. Do not dismantle the centrifugal advance mechanism unless absolutely necessary.

Reassembly and refitting:

Reassembly is a reversal of the dismantling procedure. Grease the moving parts of the centrifugal advance mechanism and apply a thin film of grease to the distributor drive shaft cam. Refit the contact points if they are in good condition, if not they should be renewed. Apply a small drop of oil to the pivot pin shown at **s** in **FIG 3:4**.

Align the distributor body in the engine block and turn the rotor to rotate the drive shaft. When the drive pegs on the shaft align correctly with the slot in the oil pump shaft the distributor will seat in the block under hand pressure. Tighten the mounting screw **e** in **FIG 3:1**, then reconnect the low-tension wire and vacuum line and refit the distributor cap. If the clamp screw **f** has not been loosened, the ignition timing should not have been affected. If the timing has been lost it must be reset as described in the next section.

3:5 Timing the ignition

In order to turn the engine to align the timing marks, make sure that the car is standing on level ground so that it will not tend to move under its own weight when the handbrake is released. Remove the air cleaner and the rocker cover. Engage top gear and release the handbrake, then push the car to turn the engine until the mark **K** on the crankshaft pulley shown in **FIG 3:7** aligns with the point **M** on the crankcase with No. 1 piston at TDC. This position for No. 1 cylinder is when both valves are closed. The distributor rotor should now be pointing to the mark on the distributor housing as shown in **FIG 3:8**. Make sure that the timing marks are aligned as described, then apply the handbrake and move the gearlever to neutral.

Connect a 12-volt test lamp between the terminal **N** in **FIG 3:8** and earth, then switch on the ignition. Now loosen the distributor clamp screw shown at **a** in **FIG 3:9** and turn the distributor body right (clockwise) until the lamp goes out. Turn the distributor slowly to the left (anticlockwise) until the lamp just lights, which indicates that the points are just beginning to open. In this position, tighten the clamp screw **a**. The ignition timing will now be correctly set for static advance. Precise setting should now be carried out with the engine running, using a stroboscopic timing lamp. If such equipment is not available, the work should be carried out by a service station. This only takes a few minutes and the method is as follows:

Stroboscopic timing:

To assist identification when the engine is running, the timing mark **K** can be coloured with white paint. Connect the stroboscopic lamp to the ignition circuit of No. 1 cylinder in accordance with the manufacturers instructions. Connect a suitable tachometer to measure engine rev/min. Loosen the distributor clamp screw so that the distributor can just be turned by hand and disconnect the vacuum hose from its connection.

With the engine running at 3000 rev/min, aim the timing lamp at the timing marks and turn the distributor as necessary until the marks appear in alignment, then tighten the clamp screw.

Checking centrifugal advance:

If the engine speed is slowly increased from idle to about 4500 rev/min with the vacuum hose connected, the ignition timing must advance progressively as seen when the lamp is aimed at the timing marks.

Checking vacuum advance:

Let the engine run at 3000 rev/min and aim the lamp at the timing marks. If the vacuum hose is now connected, the ignition should advance noticeably.

USA export models:

Check the ignition timing as described for standard models, but with the engine at 2500 rev/min. Check the action of the centrifugal advance as described for standard models at the engine speeds stated, noting that there are two vacuum hoses to be removed and replaced.

Check the vacuum control as follows for correct advance and retard characteristics. First connect the

70/89

FIG 3:10 Checking vacuum advance, USA export models

FIG 3:11   Setting the sparking plug electrode gap

retard vacuum hose which runs from the intake manifold to the metal tube on the side of the distributor. At idle speed and with the lamp aimed at the pulley the 9 deg. ATDC mark must appear aligned with the crankcase mark **M**, as shown in **FIG 3:9**. Now connect the advance vacuum hose which runs from the carburetter vacuum tube to the plastic tube on the distributor vacuum box. With the engine running at 2500 rev/min and with the lamp aimed at the pulley the mark must appear away from the mark **M** in an anticlockwise direction, as shown in **FIG 3:10**. This should represent a maximum advanced ignition setting of 40 deg. before TDC for manual transmission models, 31 deg. before TDC for automatic transmission models.

3:6 Sparking plugs

Inspect, clean and adjust sparking plugs regularly. New sparking plugs of the correct grade should be fitted at about 10,000 mile intervals.

When removing sparking plugs, ensure that their recesses are clean and dry so that nothing can fall into the cylinders. Plug gaskets can be re-used provided they are not less than half their original thickness. Have sparking plugs cleaned on an abrasive-blasting machine and tested under pressure with the electrode gaps correctly set at .020 to .024 inch as shown in **FIG 3:11**. The electrodes should be filed until they are bright and parallel. The gaps must be set by adjusting the earth electrode. **Do not try to bend the centre electrode.**

Before refitting the plugs, clean the threads with a wire brush. Do not use a brass wire brush for this job as small particles of brass may enter the plug body and cause internal shorts. Clean the threads in the cylinder head with a tap if the plugs cannot be screwed in by hand. Failing a tap, use an old sparking plug with cross-cuts down the threads. Plugs should be tightened to a torque of 22 lb ft

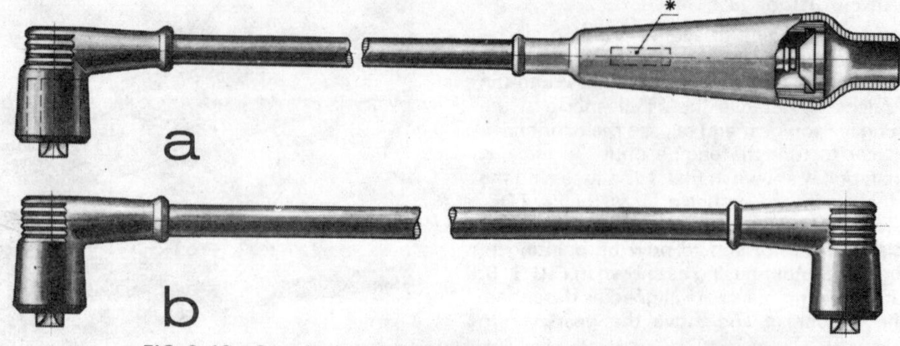

FIG 3:12   Standard ignition cable **a** and coil/distributor lead **b**

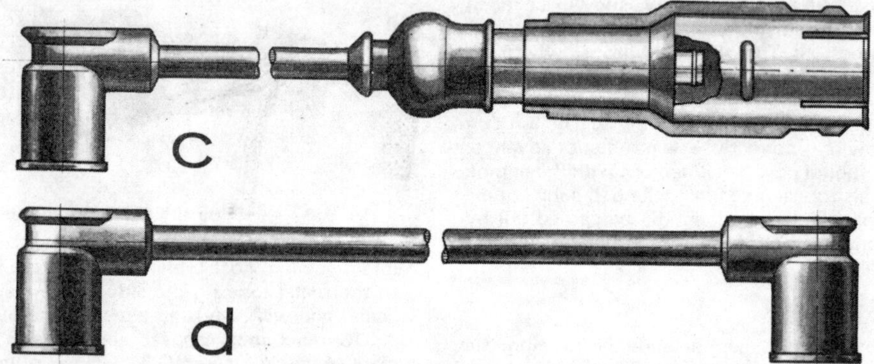

FIG 3:13   Special ignition cable **c** and coil/distributor lead **d**, suppressed for USW (VHF)

but, in the absence of a torque wrench, tighten with a normal box spanner through half a turn. Avoid over-tightening the plugs due to the possibility of stripping the threads in the light-alloy cylinder head.

Inspection of the deposits on the elctrodes can be helpful when tuning. Normally, from mixed periods of high- and low-speed driving, the deposit should be powdery and range in colour from brown to greyish-tan. There will also be slight wear of the electrodes. Long periods of constant speed driving or low-speed city driving will give white or yellowish deposits. Dry, black, fluffy deposits are due to incomplete combustion and indicate running with a rich mixture, excessive idling and, possibly, defective ignition. Overheated plugs have a white, blistered look about the centre electrode and the side electrode may be badly eroded. This may be caused by poor cooling, incorrect ignition or sustained high speeds with heavy loads.

Black, wet deposits result from oil in the combustion chamber from worn pistons, rings, valve stems or guides. Sparking plugs which run hotter may alleviate the problem but the cure is an engine overhaul.

Sparking plug leads:

Renew high-tension leads if they are defective in any way. Inspect for broken, swollen or deteriorated insulation which can be the cause of 'tracking', especially in wet weather conditions. Ignition cables are supplied in one piece, it not being possible to renew connectors or suppressors separately. When renewing a sparking plug lead, make sure that the correct length is obtained as each of the four leads is a different length. **FIG 3:12** shows the construction of standard suppressed leads, **FIG 3:13** the leads which are available specially suppressed for USW (VHF).

3:7 Fault diagnosis

(a) Engine will not fire

1 Battery discharged
2 Distributor contact points dirty, pitted or maladjusted
3 Distributor cap dirty, cracked or 'tracking'
4 Contact in distributor cap not touching rotor
5 Faulty cable or connection in low-tension circuit
6 Cracked or damaged rotor
7 Faulty coil
8 Broken contact breaker spring
9 Contact points stuck open

(b) Engine misfires

1 Check 2, 3, 5 and 7 in (a)
2 Weak contact breaker spring
3 High-tension plug and coil leads cracked or perished
4 Sparking plug(s) loose
5 Sparking plug insulation cracked
6 Sparking plug gap incorrectly set
7 Ignition timing too far advanced

CHAPTER 4

THE COOLING SYSTEM

4:1 Description
4:2 Maintenance
4:3 Removing the radiator
4:4 Adjusting fan belt
4:5 Removing and refitting fan

4:6 The thermostat
4:7 The water pump
4:8 Frost precuations
4:9 Fault diagnosis

4:1 Description

All models covered by this Manual have the same type of pressurized, thermostatically controlled cooling system. Water circulation is assisted by a centrifugal pump which is mounted at the front of the cylinder block and the cooling fan, which draws air through the radiator, is mounted on a support to one side of the engine. The fan is driven by a belt, except in the case of certain USA export models fitted with an electrically driven cooling fan.

The pump takes coolant from the bottom of the radiator and delivers it to the cylinder block from which it rises to the cylinder head. The warmed coolant then circulates through the inlet manifold passage, automatic choke unit and car heater. At normal temperatures the thermostat is open and the coolant returns to the top of the radiator. At lower temperature, the thermostat closes and coolant bypasses the radiator and returns to the pump inlet to provide a rapid warm-up.

4:2 Maintenance

The cooling system should periodically be drained, flushed to remove sediment and refilled. If antifreeze is in use, the coolant may be collected and returned to the system after flushing but should be discarded after two winters. Check the tightness of all clips on all hoses including those on the heater pipes.

Draining:

Drain the system when the engine is cool. Place the centre heater lever in the 'warm' position. Remove the radiator cap and open the breather screw shown at **c** in **FIG 4:1**. Unscrew the drain plug at the bottom of the radiator shown at **a** in **FIG 4:2** and allow the coolant to drain from the system, using a clean container to collect it if it is to be re-used. Always use a socket wrench to loosen or tighten the drain plug.

Flushing:

Use a water hose to flush the system, allowing the water to enter the radiator filler and to run out through the drain plug until it is clean. If the radiator is blocked, remove it as described in **Section 4:3**. Invert the radiator and reverse flush it by running clean water in through the drain plug hole and out of the filler neck.

Filling:

Refit the radiator drain plug, using a new seal if necessary. Set the heater lever to 'warm' and make sure that the breather screw is opened. Check all the hose connections to ensure that leaks will not develop in the system. Fill the cooling system until it runs from the breather screw. Now start the engine and allow it to run

FIG 4:1 The cooling system breather screw

FIG 4:2 The radiator drain plug

at idle for a short while to bleed air from the system, then tighten the breather screw. Top up the system until the level is at the filler mark in the radiator as shown by the arrow in **FIG 4:3,** then fit and tighten the radiator cap.

4:3 Removing the radiator
Removal:

Allow the engine to cool, then remove the radiator cap. Drain the cooling system as described in **Section 4:2.** Refer to **FIG 4:4** and loosen the clip **a** and pull off the top hose. Remove the screw **c** and turn the strut **b** forwards. Loosen the hose clip **a** in **FIG 4:5** and pull off the bottom hose. Unscrew the nut **b** from the rear rubber bearing, noting the plain and spring washers. Refer to **FIG 4:6** and loosen the nut **a** on the rubber bearing **b** at the right side of the radiator. Lift out the radiator complete with cowl. If necessary the cowl can be removed after taking out the six screws which secure it.

Refitting:

Refitting is a reversal of the removal procedure. If the cowl was detached from the radiator, make sure that the upper and lower sealing strips are correctly positioned, retaining them with rubber cement. Make sure that the large washer **c** in **FIG 4:6** is positioned outside the mounting tabs **d** as shown. On completion, make sure that the rubber fan cover shown at **c** in **FIG 4:5** rests flat against the cowl around its complete circumference.

4:4 Adjusting fan belt

A tight fan belt will cause rapid wear of the fan bearings, a loose belt will slip and wear excessively with the consequent possibility of engine overheating. The tension is correct when the belt can be flexed manually by approximately $\frac{1}{2}$ inch midway between the two pulleys. Adjustment is made at the fan air guide ring mounting screws shown at **a** in **FIG 4:7.** Slacken the screws, then move the guide ring as necessary before retightening the screws.

The belt which drives the alternator and water pump is adjusted for tension in the normal manner, by slackening the alternator pivot and adjustment bolts, swinging the alternator in or out to adjust the tension then retightening the bolts.

4:5 Removing and refitting fan

Loosen both screws shown at **a** in **FIG 4:7** and loosen and remove the fan belt. Undo the three screws **b** and pull off the fan and support in the direction of the arrow. The fan can now be removed from its mounting.

When refitting the fan **a** always use a new lock plate **b** to secure the fixing screws as shown in **FIG 4:8.** Refit in the reverse order of removal, first pressing pad **c** (see **FIG 4:7**) on the stop **d** then sliding on the support **e** from the side. If the fan support is under tension when tightening the screws, loosen both screws **a** shown in **FIG 4:9** which mount the stop **b.** Afterwards, check the engine and transmission unit alignment as described in **Chapter 1, Section 1:2.**

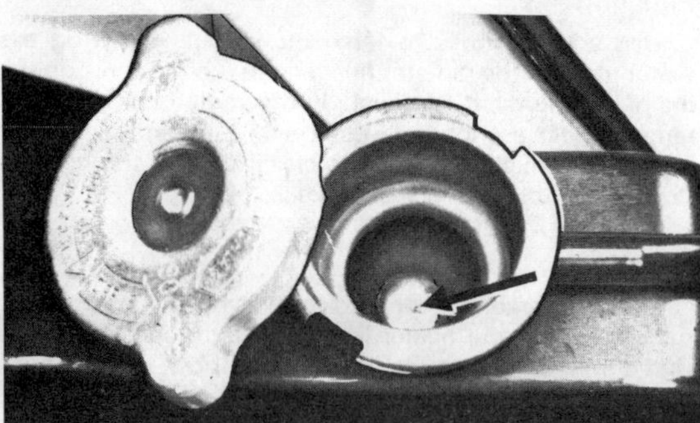
FIG 4:3 Correct coolant level in the radiator

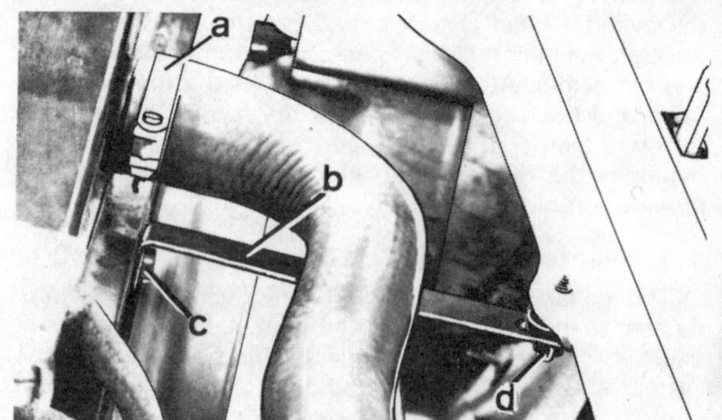
FIG 4:4 Removing the top hose

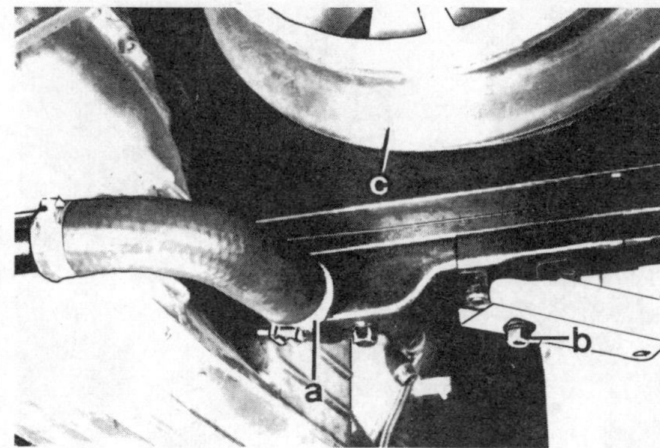

FIG 4:5   Removing the bottom hose

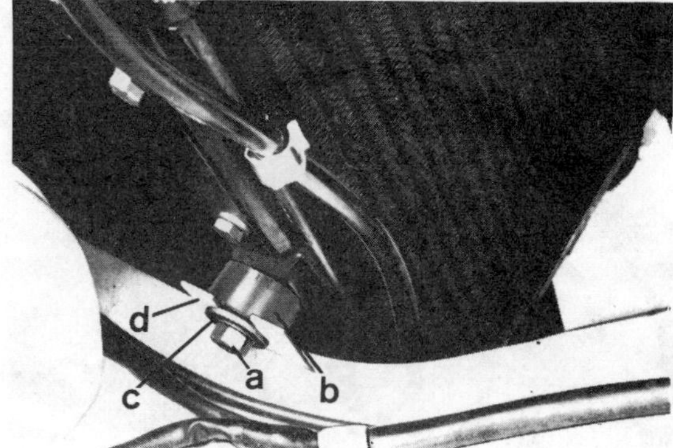

FIG 4:6   Radiator rubber mounting location

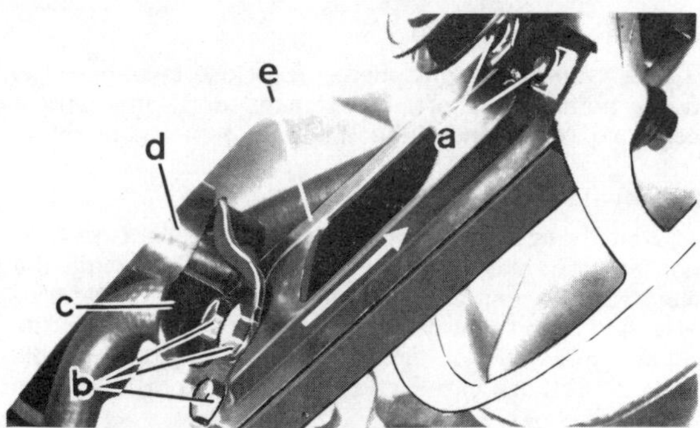

FIG 4:7   Fan mounting details

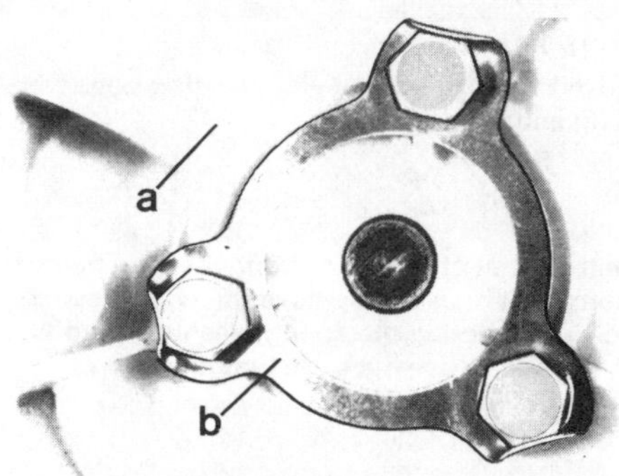

FIG 4:8   The fan fixing screw lock plate

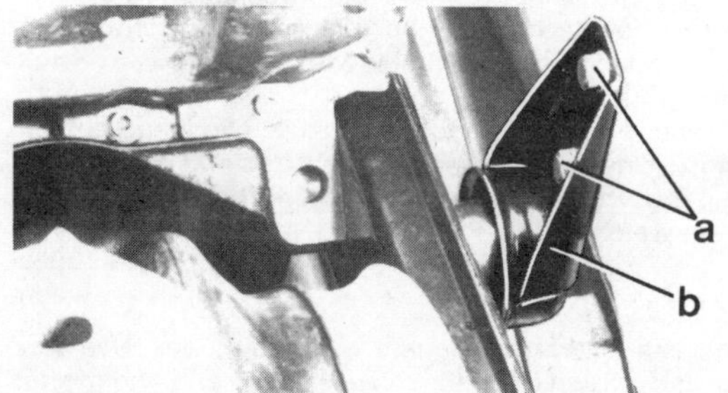

FIG 4:9   Releasing tension on the fan support if necessary

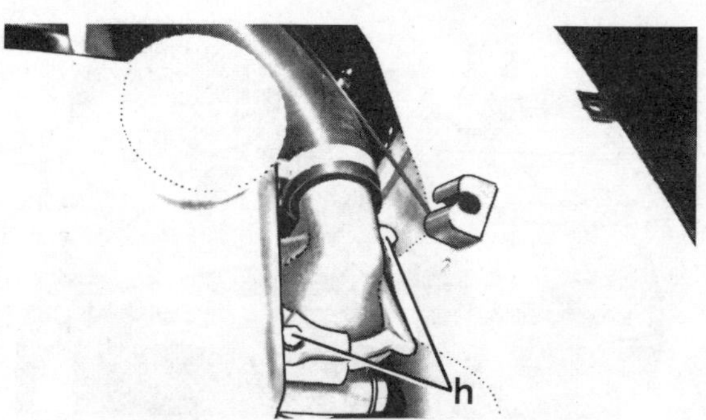

FIG 4:10   Removing the thermostat

FIG 4:11   Installing the thermostat

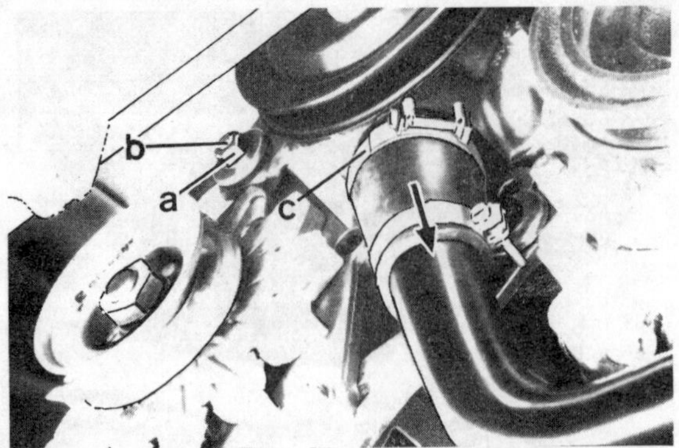

FIG 4:12 Removing the bottom hose and the mounting bolt

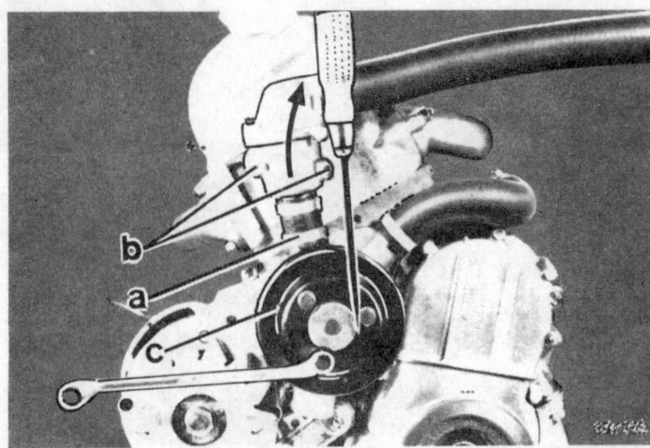

FIG 4:13 Removing the thermostat housing complete

4:6 The thermostat

The thermostat is located in an elbow fitting between the water pump and the top hose.

Removal:

Drain a small amount of coolant to bring the level below that of the thermostat housing. Remove the two screws **h** shown in **FIG 4:10**, noting the spring washers, then lift off the cover and seal and remove the thermostat.

Testing:

Clean the thermostat and immerse it in a container of cold water together with a zero to 100°C thermometer. Heat the water, keeping it stirred and observe the operation of the valve. As the temperature rises the valve should begin to open at approximately 83°C and be fully open at approximately 93°C. If the thermostat does not operate correctly it must be renewed.

Refitting:

Refit the thermostat in the housing with the bar facing forward as shown in **FIG 4:11**. Check the thermostat sealing ring and renew it if not in good condition. Refit the housing cover with a new gasket and tighten the fixing screws.

4:7 The water pump

Due to intricate adjustments and close tolerances the water pump must not be dismantled. If the unit is defective, it is intended that a replacement unit be fitted.

Removal:

Drain the cooling system as described in **Section 4:2**. Loosen the alternator mounting screws, swing the alternator inwards and remove the drive belt. Refer to **FIG 4:12** and unscrew the nut **a** then remove the screw **b** from the mounting plate by pushing it rearwards. Loosen the hose clip **c** and pull the bottom hose from the pump.

Remove the complete thermostat by loosening the lower clip **a** in **FIG 4:13**, unscrewing both screws **b** and lifting the unit aside. Remove the three screws from the pulley **c**, counterholding the pulley with a screwdriver as shown. Lever off the pulley with two screwdrivers as shown in **FIG 4:14**.

Refer to **FIG 4:15**. Loosen the hose clip **a** and pull off the hose. Unscrew the fixing screws **b**, **c** and **d** collecting the spring washers, then remove the mounting plate **e** and the water pump.

Refitting:

This is a reversal of the removal instructions. Use new seals and gaskets for the water pump and thermostat units. On completion, tension the alternator and water pump drive belt as described previously.

FIG 4:14 Levering off the water pump pulley

FIG 4:15 Removing the water pump

4:8 Frost precautions

If antifreeze is to be used the system should first be drained and flushed as described in **Section 4:2**. Ethylene-glycol type antifreeze must be added to the cooling system in the correct proportion recommended by the manufacturer, to give protection from freezing in the lowest temperatures in which the car is to be operated. After the second winter, drain and flush the system and refill with fresh solution. When topping up the radiator when antifreeze is in use, use a mixture of antifreeze and water in the correct proportions, as neat water will weaken the solution, perhaps below a safe level.

4:9 Fault diagnosis

(a) Internal water leakage

1 Cracked cylinder wall
2 Loose cylinder head nuts
3 Cracked cylinder head
4 Faulty head gasket

(b) Poor circulation

1 Radiator matrix blocked
2 Engine water passages restricted
3 Low water level
4 Slack fan belt
5 Defective thermostat
6 Perished or collapsed radiator hoses

(c) Corrosion

1 Impurities in the water
2 Infrequent draining and flushing

(d) Overheating

1 Check (b)
2 Sludge in crankcase
3 Faulty ignition timing
4 Low oil level in sump
5 Tight engine
6 Choked exhaust system
7 Binding brakes
8 Slipping clutch
9 Incorrect valve timing
10 Retarded ignition
11 Mixture too weak

CHAPTER 5

THE CLUTCH

5:1 Description
5:2 Checking and adjusting pedal travel
5:3 Removing and dismantling clutch

5:4 Assembling and refitting clutch
5:5 Fault diagnosis

5:1 Description

The clutch is a single dry-plate unit operating on the rear face of the flywheel. Operational pressure is obtained from a radially slotted diaphragm spring fitted in the clutch pressure plate. When the clutch is fully engaged, the driven plate which is splined to the gearbox primary shaft is nipped between the pressure plate and the flywheel, causing it to rotate with the flywheel and transmit torque to the gearbox. The clutch is disengaged when the pressure plate is withdrawn from the driven plate by means of a cable control operated from the clutch pedal, which transmits pedal pressure through a linkage to the clutch release bearing. The driven plate then ceases to transmit torque. The clutch assembly is enclosed in a bellhousing which is integral with the gearbox. Access to the clutch assembly can only be gained by removing the engine and transmission unit from the car, then detaching the transmission from the engine. For this reason, it would be wise to check the condition of the clutch if the engine and transmission are removed for any reason. Remedial work carried out at this stage, if necessary, may prevent the need to remove the unit solely for work on the clutch at a later time.

5:2 Checking and adjusting pedal travel

Usually, the reason for the clutch releasing too late can be traced to a lack of pedal travel. This can lead to difficulty in engaging gears and premature wear on the gearbox synchronizing components.

Refer to **FIG 5:1** and check the clutch pedal free play as shown. This should be between .6 and .8 inch. If above or below the limits stated, loosen the adjusting nut **d** in **FIG 5:2** then adjust the nut **c** to bring the pedal free play within specifications and retighten nut **d**.

With the clutch pedal free play correctly adjusted, check the condition of the linings on the clutch driven plate. To do this, place a wooden block one inch in thickness below the clutch pedal as shown in **FIG 5:3**. Start the engine, press the pedal down against the block, then select reverse gear while the engine is idling. If it is difficult or impossible to select reverse under these conditions, recheck the pedal free play measurement and, if it is correct, the difficulty in engaging reverse will indicate **X** badly worn driven plate linings. Although it may still be possible to release the clutch sufficiently with the test block removed, the driven plate should be reconditioned as soon as possible to avoid possible clutch slip and wear or damage to the pressure plate assembly and flywheel.

Removing clutch cable:

Remove the knee protector pad in order to gain the necessary access by taking out the screws **a** shown in **FIG 5:4** and pulling the pad away in the direction of the

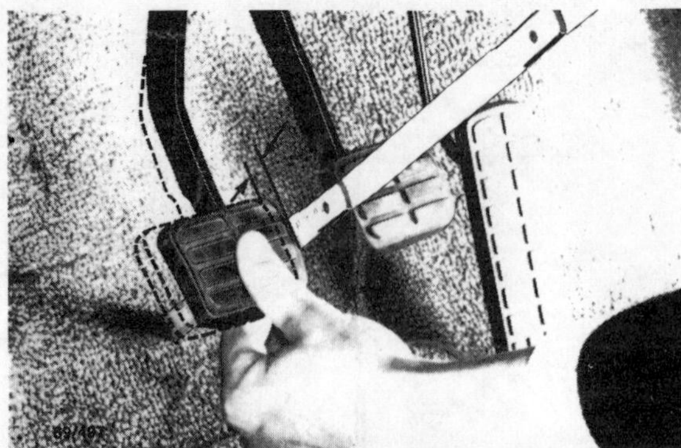

FIG 5:1   Checking the clutch pedal free play

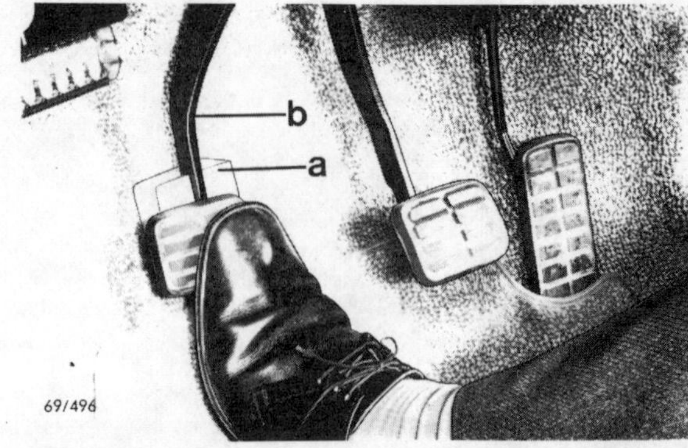

FIG 5:3 Checking the clutch driven plate lining condition

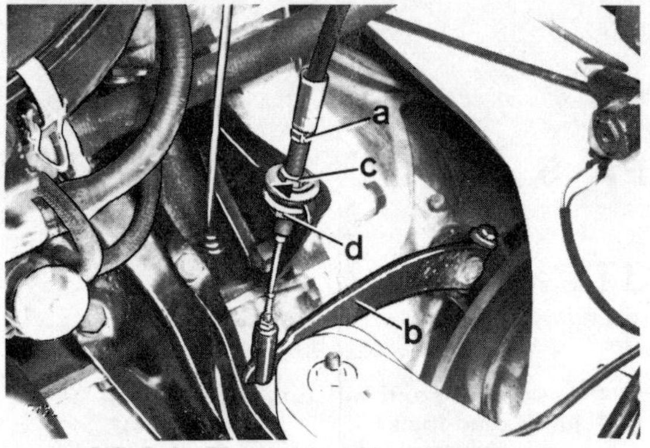

FIG 5:2   The clutch cable adjusting nuts

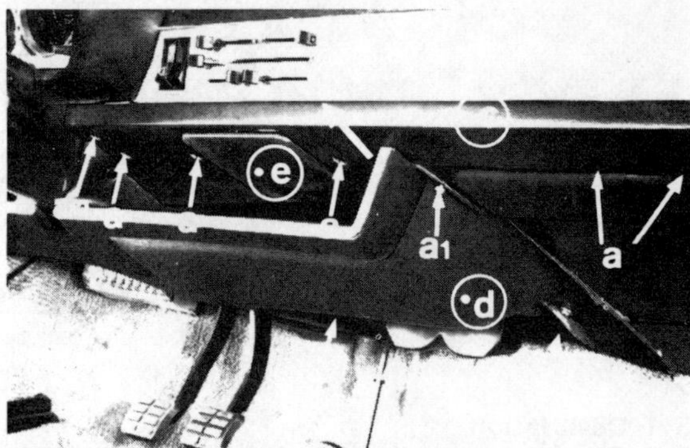

FIG 5:4   Removing the knee protector pad for access to the clutch cable

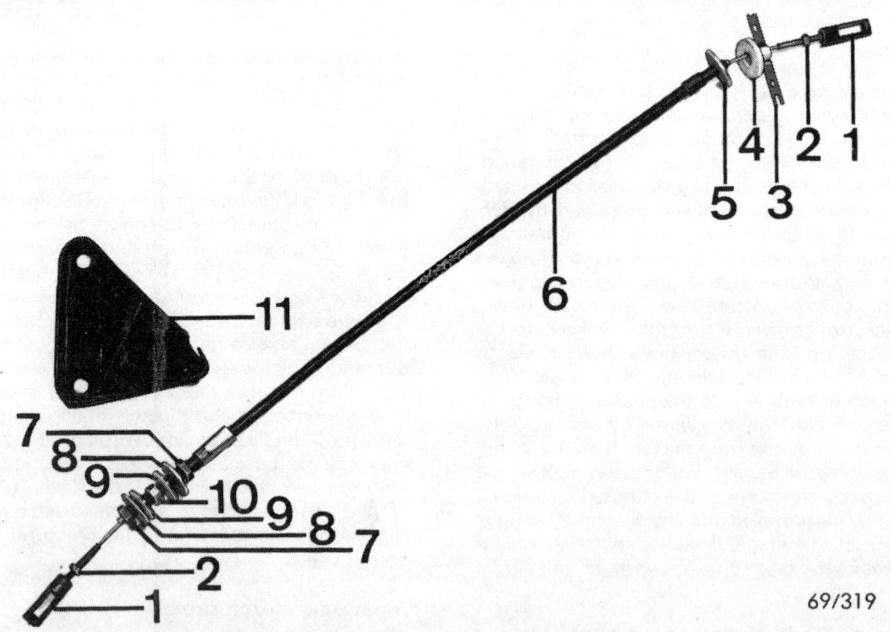

FIG 5:5   The clutch cable and connections

Key to Fig 5:5   1 Threaded eyelet   2 Nut   3 Bulkhead   4 Bushing   5 Washer   6 Cable   7 Nut   8 Washer
9 Rubber washer   10 Bushing   11 Mounting

arrow. Refer to **FIG 5:5**. Loosen the adjusting nuts 7 and lift the cable from the mounting 11. Disconnect the threaded eyelets 1 at the clutch pedal hook and at the clutch lever. Remove the eyelet 1 and nut 2 at the pedal end and pull out the cable from the engine compartment side, paying attention to the bushing 4 and washer 5.

Refitting:

Renew any parts found worn or damaged, then refit the cable in the reverse order of removal. The clutch lever **a** in **FIG 5:6** should be checked for correct positioning. The distance **x** from the clutch lever hook to the edge of the mounting should be 6.3 inches. To adjust the position of the lever, remove the clamp bolt and reposition the lever correctly on its splined shaft. Tighten the clamp bolt to 10.1 lb ft. On completion, adjust the clutch cable as described previously.

5:3 Removing and dismantling clutch

Remove the engine and transmission assembly from the car then separate the transmission from the engine, as described in **Chapter 1, Section 1:2**.

Refer to **FIG 5:7**. Mark the position of the pressure plate on the flywheel with paint as shown by the arrow. This is necessary to ensure correct refitting as the clutch and flywheel are balanced together. Loosen and remove the retaining screws **a** evenly and alternately, then remove the pressure plate and slide off the driven plate. Take care not to get oil or grease on the driven face linings if it is to be refitted. **FIG 5:8** shows the pressure and driven plates.

Servicing:

The clutch cover, spring and pressure plate assembly is an integral unit and must not be dismantled. If any part is defective the assembly must be renewed.

Inspect the surfaces of the flywheel where the driven plate makes contact. Small cracks or scratches are unimportant, but if there are signs of heavy scoring the flywheel should be resurfaced. Check the pressure plate for scoring or damage and check that the working surface is flat and true, using a metal straightedge. Check the diaphragm spring for cracks or other damage.

The clutch release bearing can be removed from the shaft by levering out the spring clips **a** shown in **FIG 5:9**. The release bearing should be renewed if there is any sign of roughness when it is pressed and turned by hand. Do not clean the release bearing with solvents as this would wash away the internal lubricant, merely wipe it with clean cloth to remove surface dirt.

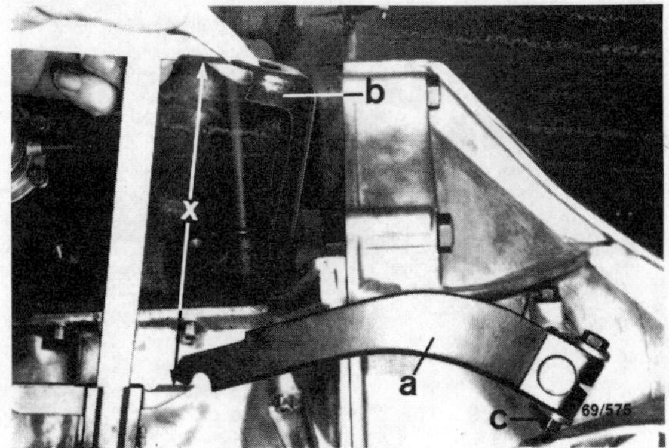

FIG 5:6   Checking the clutch lever position

FIG 5:7   Removing or fitting the clutch assembly

Key to Fig 5:7 a Retaining screws **b** Pressure plate assembly **c** Special tool to align the driven plate during installation

Check the driven plate for loose rivets and broken or very loose torsional springs. The friction linings should be well proud of the rivets and have a light colour, with a polished glaze through which the grain of the material is clearly visible. A dark, glazed deposit indicates oil on the facings and, as this condition cannot be rectified, a new or relined plate will be required. Any sign of oil on the clutch will call for examination of the crankshaft main bearing oil seal as described in **Chapter 1, Section 1:6**.

It is not recommended that owners attempt to reline the clutch driven plate themselves, as special equipment

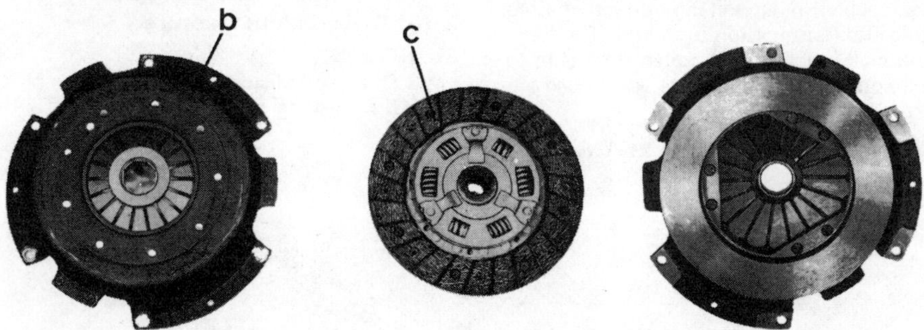

FIG 5:8   **The clutch driven plate c and both sides of the pressure plate assembly**

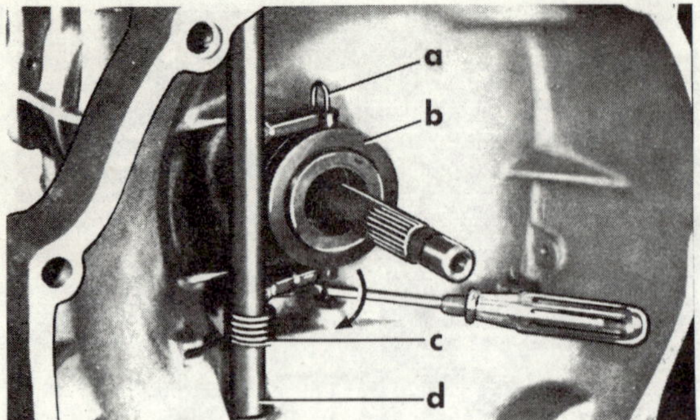

FIG 5:9   The clutch release bearing

Key to Fig 5:9   **a** Spring clip   **b** Release bearing
c Return spring   **d** Shaft

is needed to ensure correct attachment of the lining material. For this reason, the driven plate should be relined at a service station or an exchange unit obtained and fitted. Check the driven plate for a smooth sliding fit on the splined shaft, removing any burrs from the shaft or hub. Check the plate for distortion which can cause faulty operation. Driven disc runout should not exceed .019 inch at the outer circumference, runout beyond this figure dictating renewal of the component.

5:4 Assembling and refitting clutch

The use of special tool Ku-2 aligning arbour is necessary when refitting the clutch assembly, in order to ensure that the driven plate will be concentric with the gearbox primary shaft when the transmission is refitted to the engine.

Slide the driven plate over the aligning tool, then enter the tool into the crankshaft needle bearing. Install the pressure plate assembly in accordance with the alignment marks made when dismantling and enter the retaining screws in their threads. Tighten the retaining screws alternately and evenly to a final torque of 25 to 27 lb ft. The aligning tool may now be withdrawn. **FIG 5:7 illustrates the use of the aligning tool, which is shown at d.** Refit the release bearing and grease the release shaft arms.

Carefully slide the transmission into position, making sure that no strain or side load is imposed on the clutch disc when the splined shaft is entered, as this would distort the driven plate seriously. Tighten the fixings between the engine and transmission, then check that the clutch release mechanism is working correctly before refitting the engine and transmission to the car. On completion, check the clutch action and adjust the cable to give the correct pedal free travel as described in **Section 5:2.**

5:5 Fault diagnosis

(a) Drag or spin

1 Oil or grease on driven plate linings
2 Misalignment between engine and splined shaft
3 Driven plate hub binding on splines
4 Distorted driven plate
5 Warped or damaged pressure plate or clutch cover
6 Broken driven plate linings
7 Dirt or foreign matter in clutch
8 Incorrect clutch pedal free travel

(b) Fierceness or snatch

1 Check 1, 2 and 3 in (a)
2 Worn driven plate linings

(c) Slip

1 Check 1, 2 and 8 in (a)
2 Check 2 in (b)
3 Weak diaphragm spring
4 Seized clutch cable

(d) Judder

1 Check 1 and 2 in (a)
2 Pressure plate not parallel with flywheel face
3 Contact area of driven plate linings not evenly distributed
4 Bent or worn splined shaft
5 Badly worn splines in driven plate hub
6 Buckled driven plate
7 Faulty engine or transmission mountings

(e) Rattle

1 Check 3 in (c)
2 Check 4 and 5 in (d)
3 Broken springs in driven plate
4 Worn release mechanism
5 Excessive backlash in transmission
6 Wear in transmission bearings
7 Release bearing loose on shaft

(f) Tick or knock

1 Check 4 and 5 in (d)
2 Release plate out of line
3 Loose flywheel

(g) Driven plate fracture

1 Check 2 in (a)
2 Drag and distortion due to hanging transmission in driven plate hub

CHAPTER 6

MANUAL TRANSMISSION

6:1 Description
6:2 Removing and refitting transmission
6:3 Dismantling and reassembling transmission

6:4 Selector lever adjustment
6:5 Fault diagnosis

6:1 Description

The transmission is specially designed for front-wheel drive and is constructed as an integral unit incorporating the gearbox, differential assembly and inner stub axles. **FIGS 6:1** and **6:2** show the transmission components and layout.

The gearbox is a two-shaft unit with Porsche system synchromesh assemblies, all gear wheels having helically cut teeth and being matched for silent operation. Third and fourth gears are pressed onto the mainshaft; first, second and reverse gears being integral with the main-shaft. If first, second or reverse gears are damaged then the mainshaft assembly must be renewed. If third or fourth gears are damaged then they must be pressed off, this being a specialist operation requiring the use of press equipment capable of supplying a load of 10 to 12 tons.

In order to dismantle and service the transmission, the use of several special tools is necessary. These tools are numbered and their applications described in the text.

6:2 Removing and refitting transmission

The engine and transmission assembly must be removed as a unit, then the transmission separated from the engine. The instructions for this procedure will be found in **Chapter 1, Section 1:2.**

6:3 Dismantling and reassembling transmission

1 The transmission should be fitted to an assembly stand or suitably supported on a bench so that it can be dismantled without damage. Drain the oil from the transmission.
2 Refer to **FIG 6:3** and remove the reversing light switch **b** and the screw **a**. This screw must be coated with sealing compound when refitted. Remove the clutch release bearing as described in **Chapter 5** and, if necessary, remove the clutch release shaft. **FIG 6:4** shows the correct fitting of the eccentric bushing at the clutch release shaft. Remove the speedometer bushing **h**.

Gear selector rod:

3 Refer to **FIG 6:5.** Remove the two screws 2 and the screw 7 and drive the selector rod and cover out from the opposite side. Should it be necessary to renew the shaft seal, lever out the old seal with a screwdriver and drive in a new seal, keeping it square. The seal lip faces toward the inside of the transmission.
4 The selector rod can be dismantled by removing the plug 7 and withdrawing the internal parts as shown in **FIG 6:6.** When the rod assembly is refitted use a suitable sealing compound on the flange surfaces and screws.

Key to Figs 6:1 and 6:2 1 Drive pinion 2 Roller bearing 3 Spacer 4 Sliding gear, 4th speed 5th speed gear 6 Needle bearing inner race 7 Operating sleeve 8 Guide sleeve 9 Sliding gear, 3rd speed 10 Two-part needle bearing 11 Thrust washer 12 Sliding gear, 2nd speed 13 Guide sleeve 14 Sliding gear, 1st speed 15 Needle bearing 16 Needle bearing inner race 17 Reverse gear 18 Shim, selected thickness 19 Shim, selected thickness 20 .15 mm shim 21 Four point bearing 22 Lock plate 23 Nut 24 Shim 25 Reverse gear assembly 26 Snap ring 27 Grooved ballbearing 28 Circlip 29 Support disc 30 End cover 31 Shim, selected thickness 32 Gasket, selected thickness 33 Transmission cover 34 Transmission case 35 Needle bearing 36 Screw 37 Mainshaft 38 Breather valve 39 Oil slinger 40 Shaft seal 41 Bushing 50 Stub axle, left 51 Flange 52 Drain hose 53 Cord seal 54 Shaft seal 55 Grooved ballbearings 56 Washer 57 Circlip 58 Washer 59 Spring 60 Shim, selected thickness 61 Thrust washer 62 Taper roller bearing 63 Screw 64 Differential housing 65 Crownwheel 66 Differential bevel gear 67 Shaft 68 Tubular key 69 Differential pinion 70 Magnetic plug 71 O-ring 72 Gasket 73 Stub axle, right 74 Nut and washer 75 Circlip 76 Differential flange 77 Nut and washer 78 Pressure pin 79 Seal 80 Reversing light switch

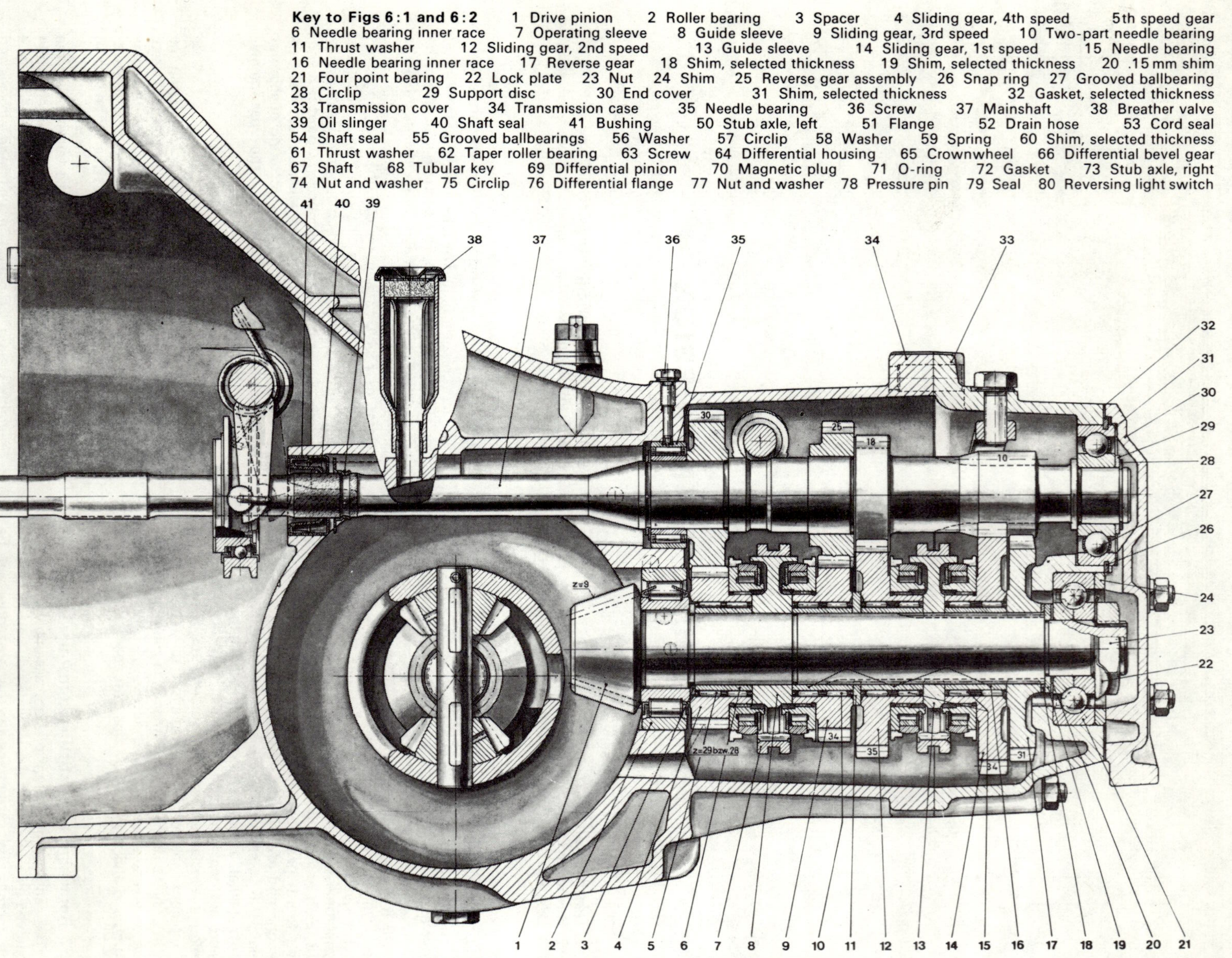

FIG 6:1 Section through the manual transmission assembly

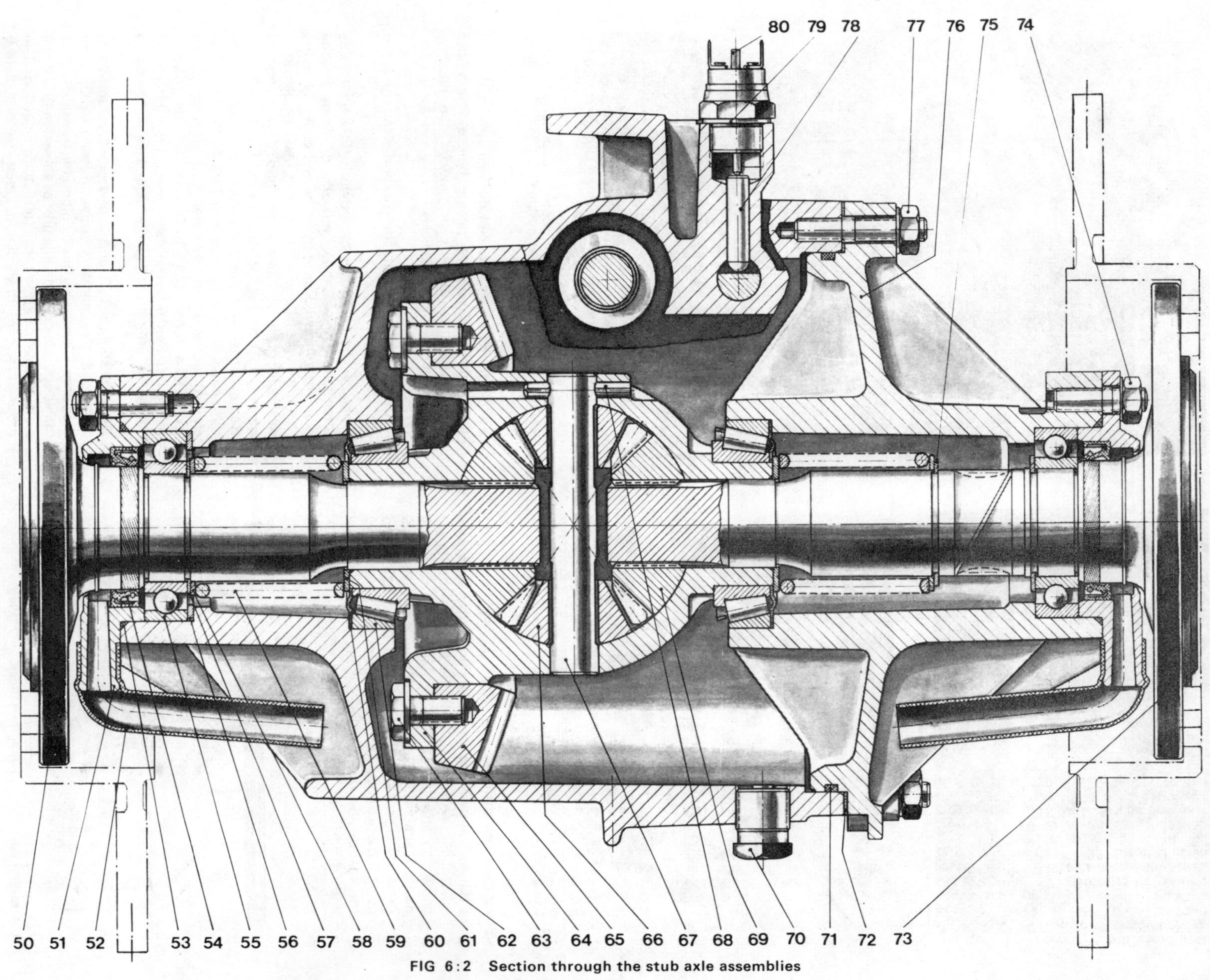

FIG 6:2 Section through the stub axle assemblies

FIG 6:3 The breather **c** and reversing light switch **b**

FIG 6:5 Removing the selector rod

Key to Fig 6:5   1 Selector rod cover   2 Screws
3 Washer   4 Shaft seal   5 Selector rod   6 Washer
7 Screw

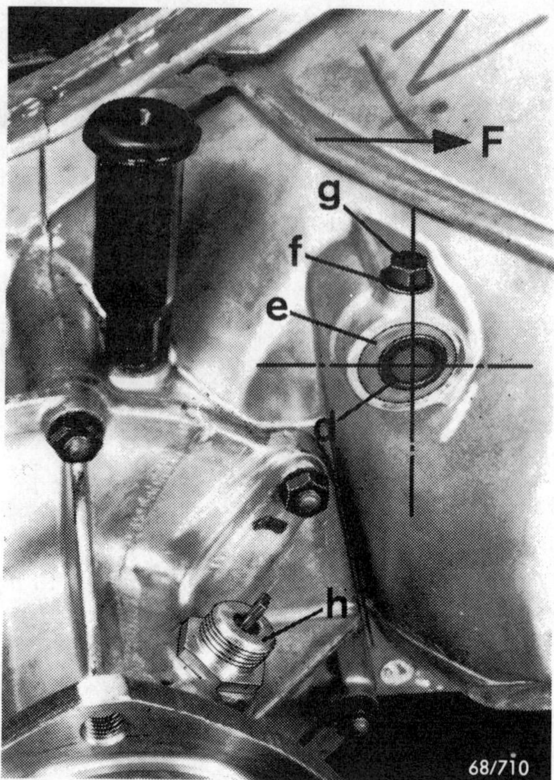

FIG 6:4 Clutch release shaft bushing and speedometer bushing

Key to Fig 6:4   **d** Shaft   **e** Eccentric bushing   **f** Washer
g Screw   **h** Speedometer bushing

Stub axle assemblies:

5 **FIG 6:7** shows the components of the stub axle assemblies. Working through the holes in the flange shown by arrows in **FIG 6:8,** remove the four nuts on each side. Using tool G-6 shown at **a** in **FIG 6:9** press out the stub axles. Remove the circlips and pull off the bearings with a suitable puller. If necessary the seal can be renewed by driving out the old seal with a drift and pressing a new seal into position.

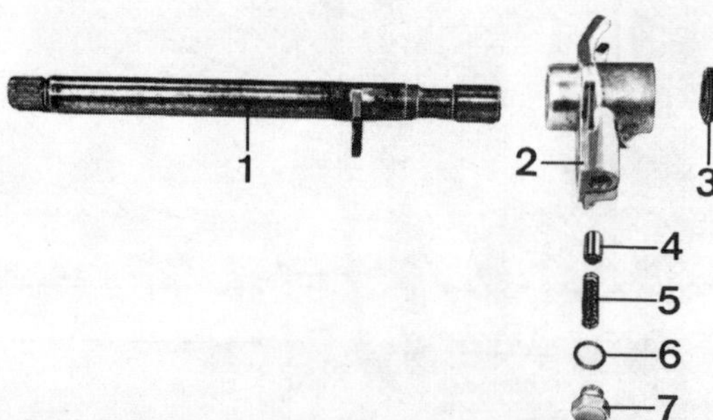

FIG 6:6 Selector rod components

Key to Fig 6:6   1 Selector rod   2 Cover   3 Shaft seal
4 Arresting pin   5 Spring   6 Seal   7 Plug

Fill the round cavity between the seal inner and outer lips with multi-purpose grease before fitting and make sure that the lips are toward the bearing. Always renew the cord seal 4.

End cover, differential flange and transmission cover:

6 Unscrew the end cover as shown in **FIG 6:10**. Pay attention to the number and size of shims for the mainshaft grooved bearing in the end cover. Measure the thickness of the cover gasket, as this gasket is available in three thicknesses and a new correct gasket must be used when refitting the cover.

7 Remove the nine nuts and washers mounting the differential flange as shown in **FIG 6:11**. Place the special tool G-11 in the differential housing. Screw tool G-8 **a** in tool G-15 **b.** Bolt the adjusting flange to the differential flange then lever off the differential flange by turning the spindle clockwise as shown in **FIG 6:12**.

8 Remove springs 1, 2 and 3 and pin 4 as shown in **FIG 6:13**. Pay attention to the arresting pin beneath the springs, removing this by tilting the transmission as necessary. Using a suitable drift as shown in **FIG 6:14** slide in reverse gear rod 1 and third gear rod 3 in order to lock the drive pinion. Open the lock plate **b**

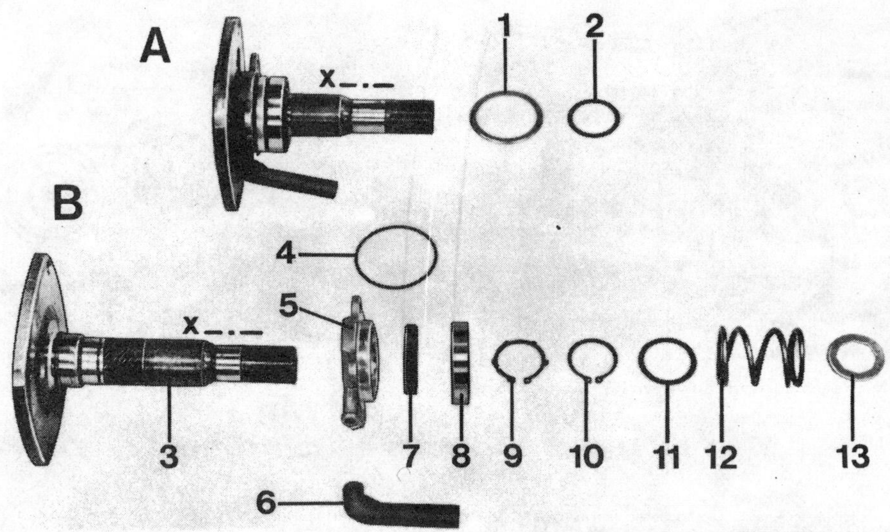

FIG 6:7   Stub axle components

Key to Fig 6:7   **A** Left stub axle   **B** Right stub axle   1 Washer   2 Washer   3 Axle with speedometer drive   4 Cord seal
5 Flange   6 Drain hose   7 Shaft seal   8 Grooved ballbearing   9/10 Circlips   11 Washer   12 Spring   13 Thrust washer

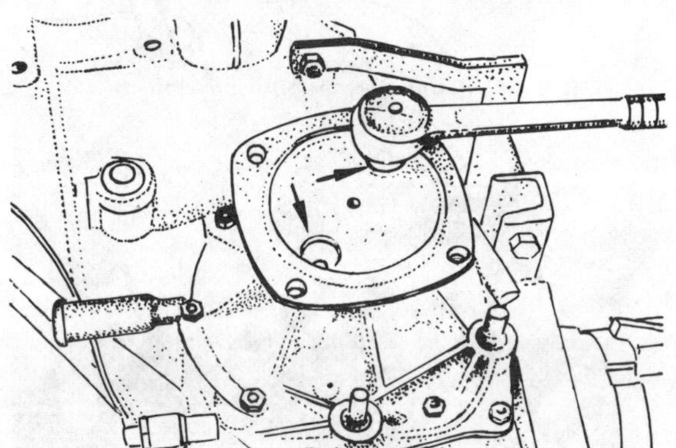

FIG 6:8   The stub axle retaining nuts

FIG 6:9   Removing the stub axles

FIG 6:10   Removing the end cover

FIG 6:11   The differential flange retaining nuts

FIG 6:12   Removing the differential flange

Key to Fig 6:12   a Removing spindle   **b** Adjusting flange
c Plate (not visible)

FIG 6:13   Removing springs and locating pin

Key to Fig 6:13   1 Spring, reverse 30.0 mm long   **2** Spring,
1st/2nd gears 34.7 mm long   **3** Spring, 3rd/4th gears
34.7 mm long   **4** Locating pin, roller bearing outer race
a/b Standards   **c** Special tool G-11

FIG 6:14   Locking the drive pinion by selecting reverse
and 3rd gears

Key to Fig 6:14   1 Selector rod, reverse   **2** Selector rod,
1st/2nd gears   **3** Selector rod, 3rd/4th gears   **a** Nut
b Lock plate

FIG 6:15   The transmission cover retaining nuts

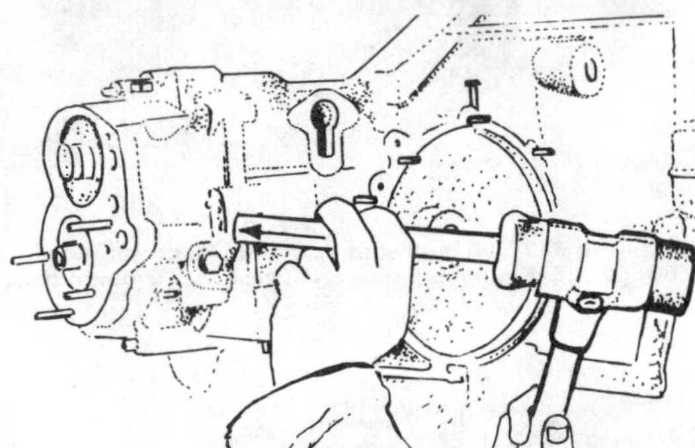

FIG 6:16   Removing the transmission cover

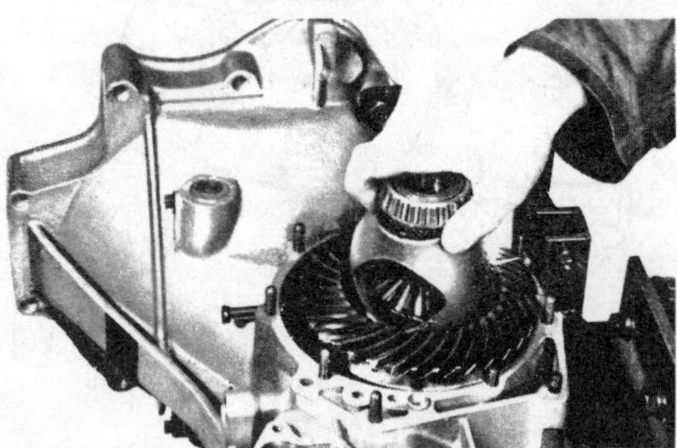

FIG 6:17   Lifting out the differential assembly

FIG 6:18   Removing the circlip and washer from the
mainshaft

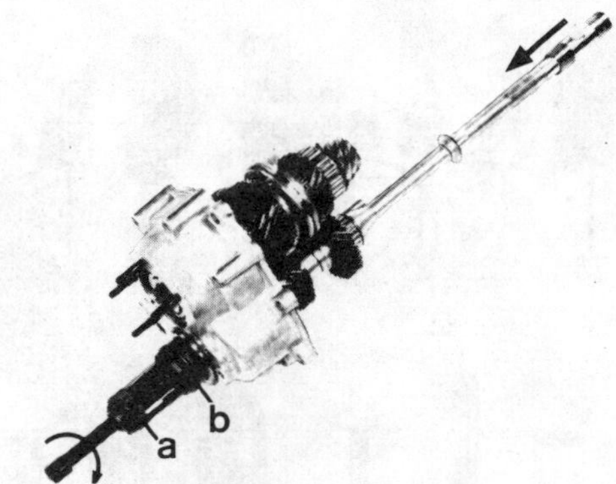

FIG 6:19   Removing the mainshaft and bearing

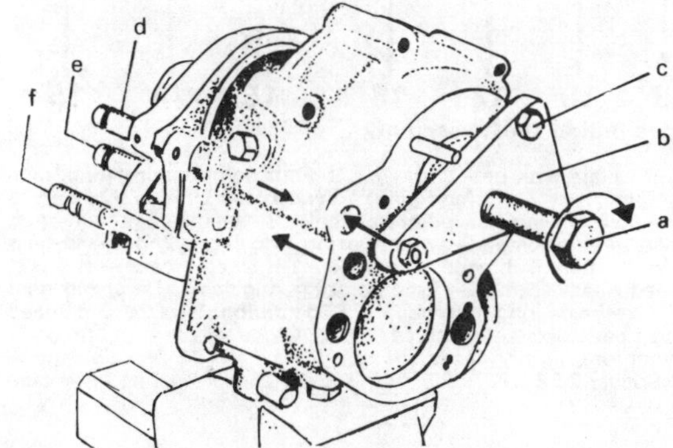

FIG 6:21   Removing the drive pinion shaft assembly

Key to Fig 6:21   **a/b** Special tool G-16   **c** Nut
d Selector rod, 3rd/4th gears   **e** Selector rod, 1st/2nd gears
f Selector rod, reverse

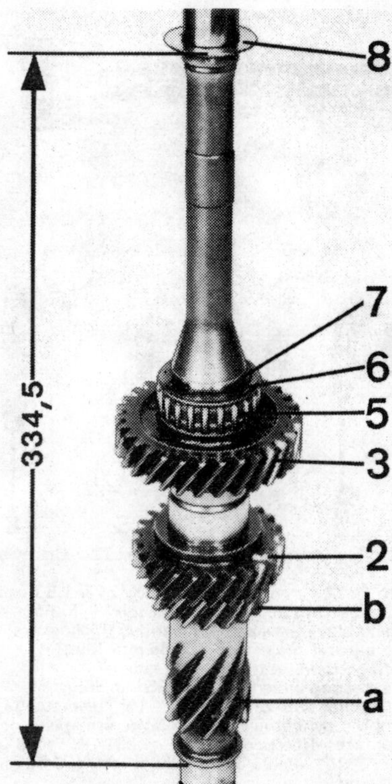

FIG 6:20   Mainshaft assembly

Key to Fig 6:20   **a** Gear, reverse and 1st speed   **b** Gear,
2nd speed   1 Mainshaft   2 Gear, 3rd speed   3 Gear,
4th speed   4 Needle bearing   5 Needle cage   6 Shim
7 Circlip   8 Oil slinger

and remove nut **a.** Unscrew the nine nuts and washers
from the transmission cover shown in **FIG 6:15** and
use a suitable drift to drive the dowel pin out of the
case. Use a drift or suitable lever to remove the cover,
working against the cast reinforcements on the cover
as shown in **FIG 6:16.**

9 Lift the differential assembly out of the transmission
case as shown in **FIG 6:17** and lay to one side.
Details of differential servicing procedures are given
in **Chapter 8.**

The mainshaft assembly:

10 Refer to **FIG 6:18** and remove the circlip **c** and the
washer **d.** Place the grooved ballbearing extractor **a**
in the bearing as shown in **FIG 6:19,** then press the
clamp ring **b** downwards. Carefully turn the spindle
in a clockwise direction, applying plastic-hammer
blows against the end of the mainshaft at the same
time in order to drive the shaft and bearing from the
cover. **FIG 6:20** shows the mainshaft components.
Examine the components for wear or damage and, if
renewal of any part is necessary, refer the work to a
service station having the necessary hydraulic press
equipment.

Drive pinion shaft:

11 Refer to **FIG 6:21.** Clamp the transmission in a vice
having padded jaws. Fit the pressure plate **b** (tool
G-16) with screw **a** loosened completely. Slide the
reverse selector rod **f** to neutral position, sliding the
rod in approximately ½ inch from the end cover mating
surface to do this.

12 Place the first and second selector rod **e** in second by
sliding in the direction of the arrow, then place the
third and fourth selector rod in neutral. Tighten the
screw **a** to remove the pinion shaft assembly, being
careful of the selector rods. Remove the selector rods
and their arresting pins, noting their positions for
correct refitting.

13 **FIG 6:22** shows the components of the drive pinion
shaft assembly. Use a puller as shown in **FIG 6:23**
to remove parts 5, 6, 7, 8 and 11 and lay them aside.
Remove one part needle cage 9 from the pinion shaft
and operating sleeve 12 from the guide sleeve 13.

14 Use a puller to remove parts 10, 13 and 16 as shown
in **FIG 6:24.** Remove one part needle cage 14.

15 Remove parts 15, 17, 20, 21, 22 and 23 in two stages
as shown in **FIGS 6:25** and **6:26,** using tool G-14
for the first stage. After removal, two each two-part
needle cages 18 and 24 and spacer 19 will be cleared.

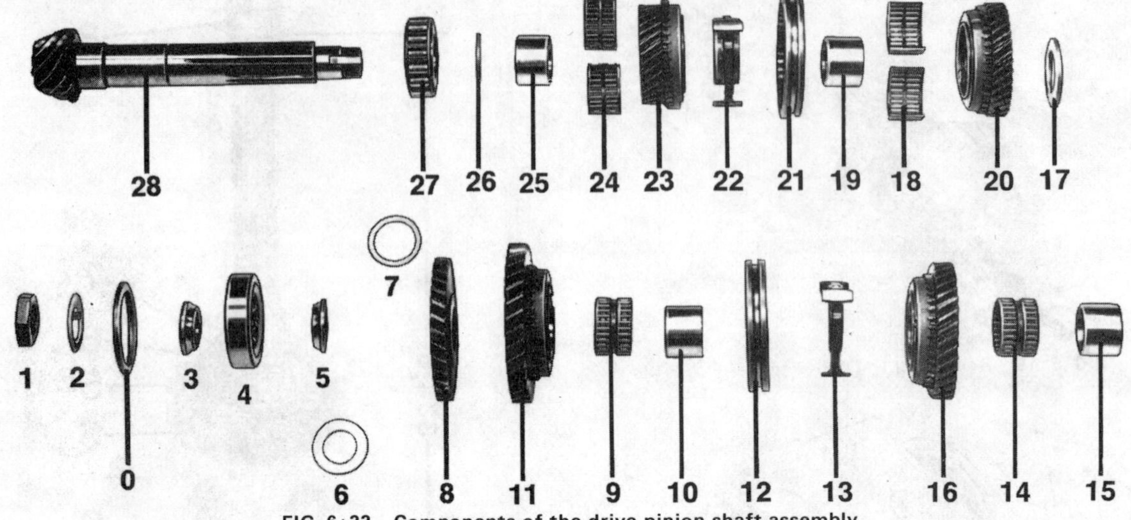

FIG 6:22   Components of the drive pinion shaft assembly

Key to Fig 6:22   0 Shim   1 M24 x 1.5 hexagon nut   2 Lock plate with projection   3 Four point bearing inner race
4 Four point bearing outer race and cage   5 Four point bearing inner race   6 Shim (end play)—available in various thicknesses
7 Shim (gear play)—available in various thicknesses   8 Reverse gear—collar facing four point bearing   9 Needle cage—one part
10 Needle bearing inner race (25.35 mm long)   11 1st speed gear assembly—synchronizing ring faces 2nd speed gear
12 Operating sleeve with short threads   13 Guide sleeve with internal threads   14 Needle cage—one part
15 Needle bearing inner race (27.35 mm long)   16 2nd speed gear assembly—synchronizing ring faces 1st speed gear
17 Thrust washer with projection   18 Needle cage—two part   19 Needle bearing inner race (27.35 mm long)   20 3rd speed
gear assembly—synchronizing ring faces 4th speed gear   21 Operating sleeve with short threads   22 Guide sleeve—shrunk on—
wider collar faces 4th speed gear   23 4th speed gear assembly—synchronizing ring faces 3rd speed gear   24 Needle cage—
two part   25 Needle bearing inner race (25.35 mm long)   26 Spacer 32.2 x 41 x 2.5 mm   27 Roller bearing inner race
28 Drive pinion

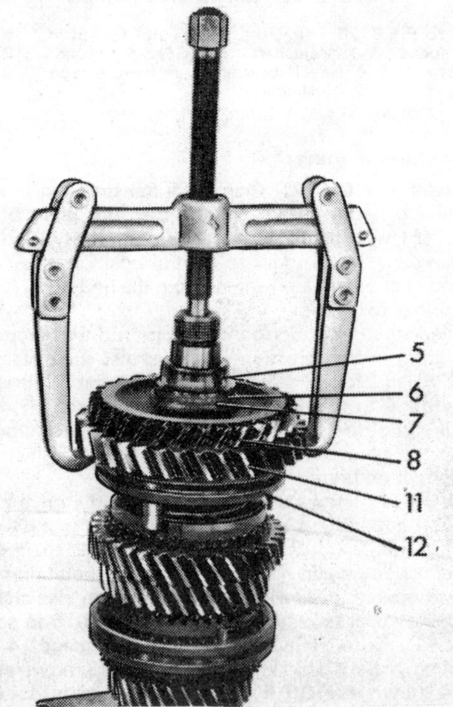

FIG 6:23   Dismantled the drive pinion shaft assembly, first stage

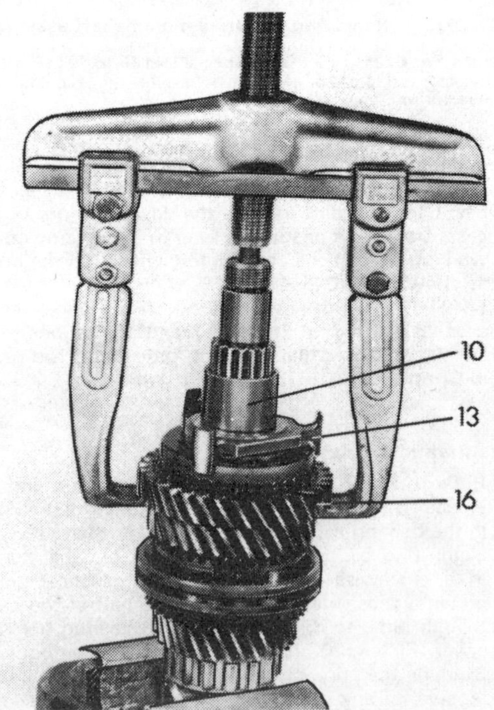

FIG 6:24   Dismantling the drive pinion shaft assembly, second stage

66

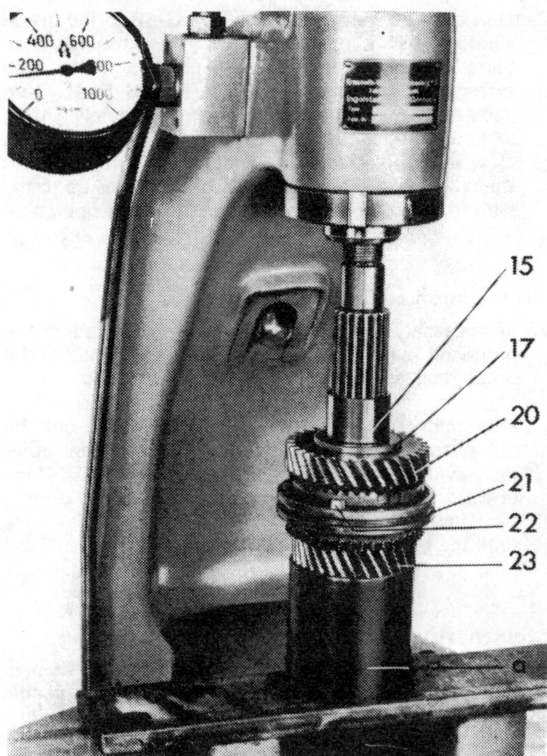

FIG 6:25   Dismantling the drive pinion shaft assembly, third stage

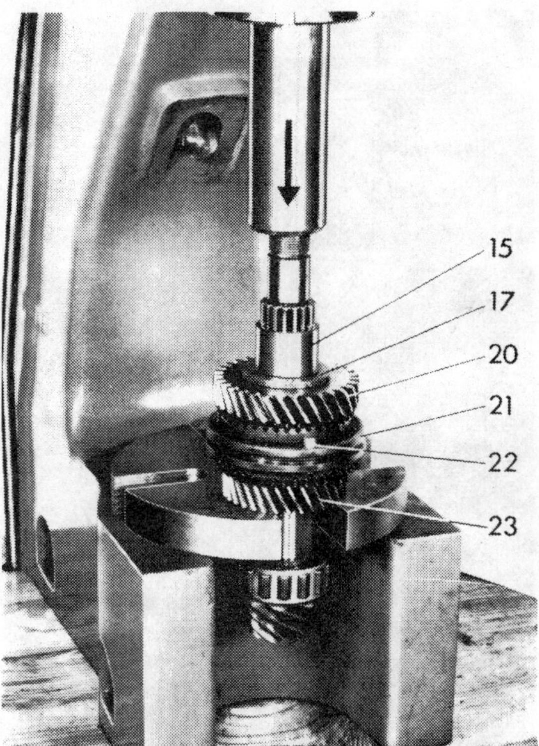

FIG 6:26   Dismantling the drive pinion shaft assembly, fourth stage

16 Suspend tool G-27 **b** as shown in **FIG 6:27** in a press. Place tool G-12 **a** in position and remove parts 25, 26 and 27.

17 Check all parts for wear or damage, renewing any that are found unserviceable. The synchromesh assemblies are dismantled and serviced as follows.

Synchromesh assemblies:

17 First gear synchromesh differs from that for second, third and fourth gears in that only one lock is installed and its key has a projection engaging in a milled opening. First gear web has two milled openings shown by arrows in **FIG 6:28** compared to the other gears which have only one opening. Remove the circlip from first gear and remove the synchronizing parts. Check the removed parts for wear and renew as necessary. Always use new circlips. When circlips are removed they are deformed and would cause faulty synchromesh operation if refitted. Refit the parts to first gear as shown in **FIG 6:28**. Make sure that the key projection is positioned in the wider milled opening so that the projection just faces towards the milled side. Fit the criclip with special pliers as shown in **FIG 6:29.** Slide the side of the ring without a projection in the gear groove and hold in this position. Lift the other end of the ring, which has a projection, a little and spread it. Press the ring downwards in the direction of the arrow with the thumb and release, allowing the circlip to snap into the groove.

18 This instruction concerns synchromesh assemblies for all gears except first gear. Remove the circlip to release the parts and check them for wear, renewing worn parts as necessary. Always use new circlips. Refit the parts after servicing in accordance with **FIG 6:28** and refit the circlip in the manner described for first gear in instruction 17.

Reverse gear assembly:

19 Refer to **FIG 6:30.** Remove screw **b** and washer. Pull out the selector rod **a** in the direction of the arrow. Remove lever **g** together with the selector fork. Carefully remove stop plungers **k** and **k1**. Should it be necessary to remove the gear, press out shaft **d.** If the four-point bearing **e** is to be renewed, carefully press out the old bearing. Heat the transmission cover in an oil bath to about 80°C then press in a new bearing up to the stop on the case collar, preferably using tool VG-20 for this operation.

Renewing bearing races, seals and studs:

Tapered roller bearing, crownwheel end:

20 If the backlash at the crownwheel and pinion assembly is to be reset at the reassembly stage, due to the fitting of new parts or to correct noisy operation, the tapered roller bearing outer race at the crownwheel end must be removed and refitted without shims, using tools G-15 and G-18.

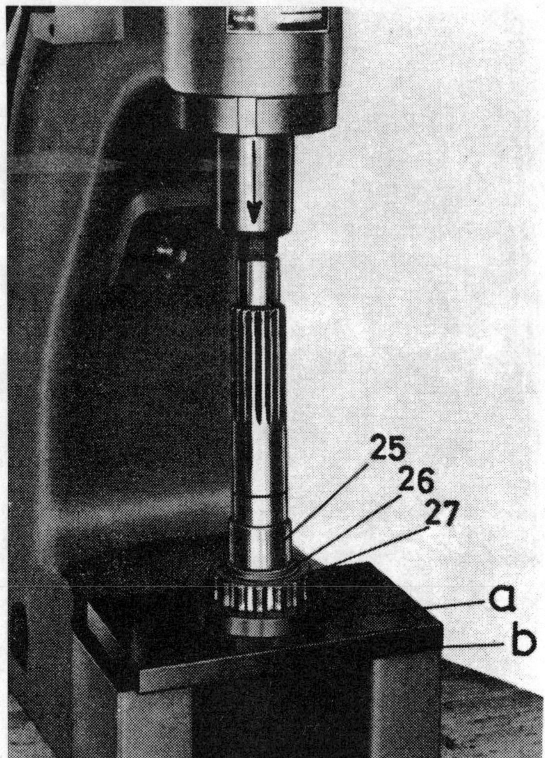

FIG 6:27   Dismantling the drive pinion shaft assembly, fifith stage

Key to Figs 6:23, 6:24, 6:25, 6:26 and 6:27 All numbers as **Fig 6:22**   **a** Special tool G-12   **b** Special tool G-27

21 Turn both pressure pieces on tool G-18 to the inside a little and slide into the cavities in the stub axle hub. Slide the special tool into the position of the stub axle grooved bearing, as shown in **FIG 6:31**. Turn back the screw **b** on tool G-15 approximately $\frac{2}{3}$ turn, then bolt the tool into position as shown in **FIG 6:32**. Now tighten the screw to remove the outer race and shims. Drive in the outer race without shims up to the stop, preferably using tool VG-20 for this operation.

Drive pinion roller bearing outer race:

22 If necessary the outer race can be removed in the following manner. Note that a groove is milled in the outer race as shown in **FIG 6:33** in which pin **b** engages. It is essential to remove this pin before attempting to remove the outer race. Drive out the outer race with tool G-25, then refit the new outer race with the same tool. The groove must face upwards to engage the pin and the wide end **d** must face towards the clutch housing. Drive in the race until the pin engages in the groove.

Mainshaft needle bearing outer race:

23 If not already carried out, remove the stud at **a** in **FIG 6:3**. This stud locates the mainshaft needle bearing outer race in position. Using a long soft-metal drift of approximately 18 mm diameter, drive out the race together with the seal and bushing, working from the inside of the case.
24 Place the stepped-down end of tool G-10 in the bearing outer race and cool both parts in a freezer if possible, as this will shrink them and assist alignment.

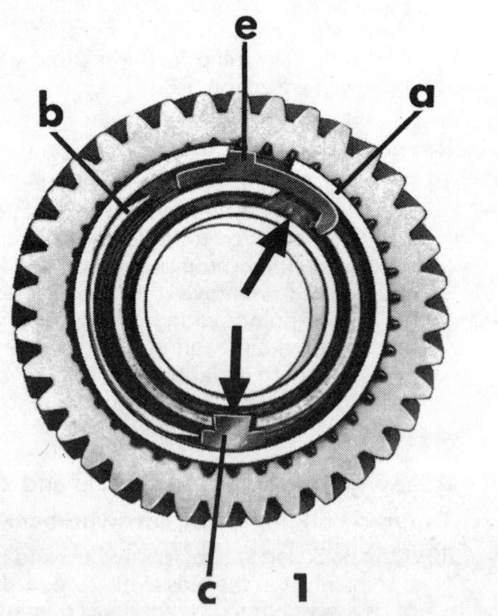
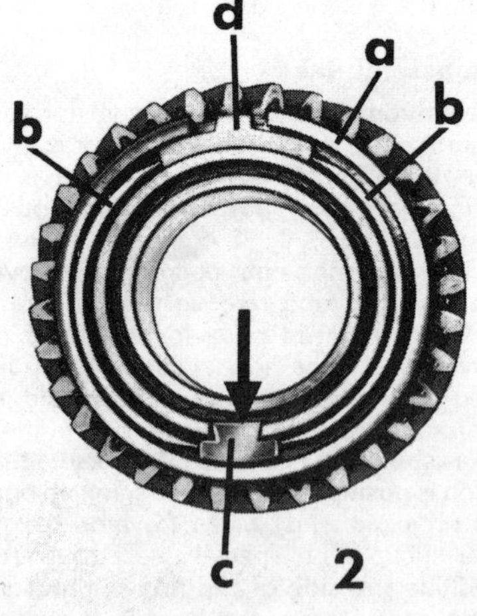

FIG 6:28   The synchromesh assemblies

Key to Fig 6:28   **1** Gear, 1st speed   **2** Gears, 2nd, 3rd and 4th speed   **a** Synchromesh ring   **b** Lock   **c** Stop   **d** Key, 2nd, 3rd and 4th speed   **e** Key, 1st speed

FIG 6:29   Installing the synchromesh circlip

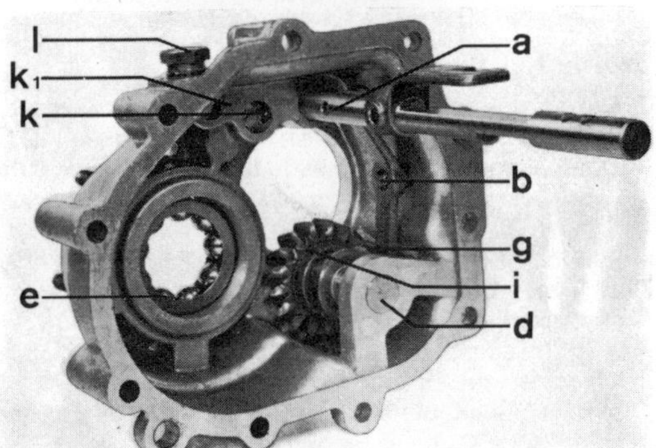

FIG 6:30   Removing reverse gear assembly

Key to Fig 6:30　　　**a** Selector rod, reverse　　**b** Screw
c Washer　　　**d** Reverse shaft　　　**e** Four point bearing
f Stud　　**g** Reverse lever with selector fork　　**i** Reverse gear
with bushing　　**k** Stop plunger, reverse and 1st/2nd speeds
k1 Stop plunger, 1st, 2nd, 3rd and 4th speeds　　**l** Filler plug

The outer race has a locating hole in its outer side in which the stud end of the locating stud must fit exactly. Place race and tool in position with the holes lined up, then drive into place with tool G-20, making sure that the alignment is precise. Refit the stud and tighten, using a suitable sealer on the threads. Note that if the stud does not correctly engage the outer race, the race will tilt in operation and cause excessive bearing wear and gearbox noise.

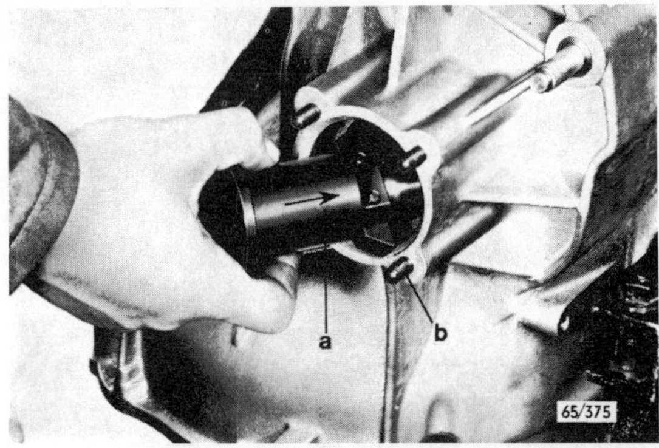

FIG 6:31   Inserting tool G-18 into the stub axle cavity

FIG 6:32   Using tool G-15 to remove the outer race

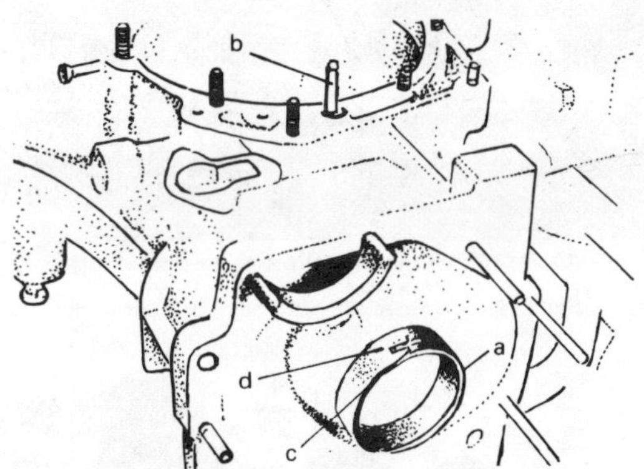

FIG 6:33   The drive pinion roller bearing outer race

Key to Fig 6:33　　　**a** Outer race　　**b** Pin　　**c** Narrow end
d Wide end

Mainshaft seal:

25 **FIG 6:34** shows the mainshaft oil seal and bushing, which should always be renewed when servicing the transmission. Place the stepped-down end of tool G-10 on the seal and drive it out with tool G-23 as shown in **FIG 6:35**. Use tool G-23 to drive in the new bushing until it is approximately 5 mm below the upper surface. Use tool G-21 to drive in the new seal until it is flush with the upper surface of the bore.

FIG 6:34   Mainshaft oil seal **a** and bushing **b**

FIG 6:35   Removing the seal and bushing

Key to Fig 6:35   **c** Special tool G-10   **d** Special tool G-23

FIG 6:36   Removing or refitting a left brake caliper mounting stud

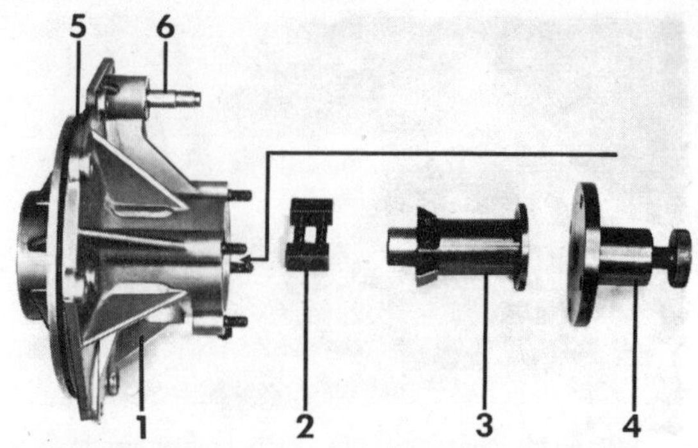

FIG 6:37   The differential flange and special tools for bearing removal

Key to Fig 6:37   1 Differential flange   2 Intermediate piece of tool G-17   3 Special tool G-18   4 Special tool G-15   5 O-ring   6 Stud, right brake caliper

Left brake caliper studs:

26 Should it be necessary to renew the left front brake caliper studs, the old studs should be removed with an extractor tool, or by locking two nuts together on the stud as shown in **FIG 6:36** and removing the stud with a spanner. Before refitting studs, treat the threads on stud and in the case with Loctite-Aktivator then apply Loctite binder AAV. Tighten the studs to a torque of 29 to 36 lb ft and allow 48 hours for the loctite to dry.

Differential flange needle bearing:

27 The differential flange (stub axle bore) has two cavities. Refer to **FIG 6:37.** Press the intermediate piece 2 together somewhat and slide it into the cavities. Press both pressure pieces of tool G-18 towards the inside somewhat and also place the removing bolt in position. Turn back the screw on tool G-15 shown at 4, then bolt the tool to the flange. Now tighten the the screw to press out the bearing outer race together with the shims. If it is necessary to renew stud 6, refer to instruction 26 for the necessary procedure.

28 Extract the needle bearing from the differential flange using tool G-1, as shown in **FIG 6:38.** Pull out spreader 1 then turn back nut 2 completely. Fit washer 3 in position and press extractor 4 into the needle bearing 5. Slide in spreader 1 and extract the bearing by turning the nut 2 clockwise.

29 The new bearing must be pressed into position to a depth of 2.22±.008 inch as measured from the upper surface **c** as shown in **FIG 6:39.** By using tool G-102 shown at **a**, the bearing **b** will be correctly positioned when the tool rests against the surface **c**.

30 The needle bearing can be removed from the speedometer bushing with tool G-2. This tool is operated in the same manner as tool G-1, the method being as stated in instruction 28.

31 Use a 20 mm diameter aluminium drift to drive a new needle bearing, with the lettering facing upwards, into the speedometer bushing until it is flush.

Checking drive pinion end play:

The crownwheel and drive pinion assembly are paired by the manufacturer to show the best wear patterns and noise levels when rotated together. For these reasons the crownwheel and drive pinion must always be renewed together if wear or damage is noted at either component. The pairing code numbers and backlash settings are marked on the parts as shown in **FIG 6:40**. End play is the distance measured from the face of the drive pinion to the centre axis of the crownwheel. A distance of 51.7 mm has been determined as a reference dimension for end play. The amount of end play in excess of the reference dimension is stamped on the pinion face in hundredths of a millimetre as shown at **b1**.

For example, if 15 is stamped on the pinion then the end play is 51.7 plus .15 which equals 51.85 mm. The correct shim thickness must be determined as follows in order to carry out proper adjustments to ensure smooth running and long life. Shims for adjustment purposes are available in .15 mm thickness, and in twelve .1 mm steps from 3.2 to 4.3 mm thickness.

32 If the parts have been removed from the pinion shaft, refit them. Press the parts onto the shaft in the order shown in **FIG 6:22**, heating the roller bearing inner race 27 to 100°C and the guide sleeve 22 to 150°C to facilitate fitting of these parts.

33 With the parts pressed onto the shaft, place the drive pinion on a surface plate as shown in **FIG 6:41** and use a dial gauge to check the difference in height between the splined shaft **a** and reverse gear **b**. The difference in height must be compensated for by fitting a shim which will leave a play of approximately .1 mm. For example, if the difference in height as measured is .6 mm, then a shim of .5 mm will be needed to leave a play of .1 mm. Shims are available in nine .1 mm steps from .2 to 1.0 mm thickness.

34 Place the axial play shim as determined in position at **a** in **FIG 6:42** and the 3.2 mm shim **b** for the end

FIG 6:38   Removing the needle bearing

Key to Fig 6:38   1 Spreader   **2** Nut   **3** Washer
4 Extractor   **5** Needle bearing   **6** Stud

FIG 6:39   Pressing in the needle bearing

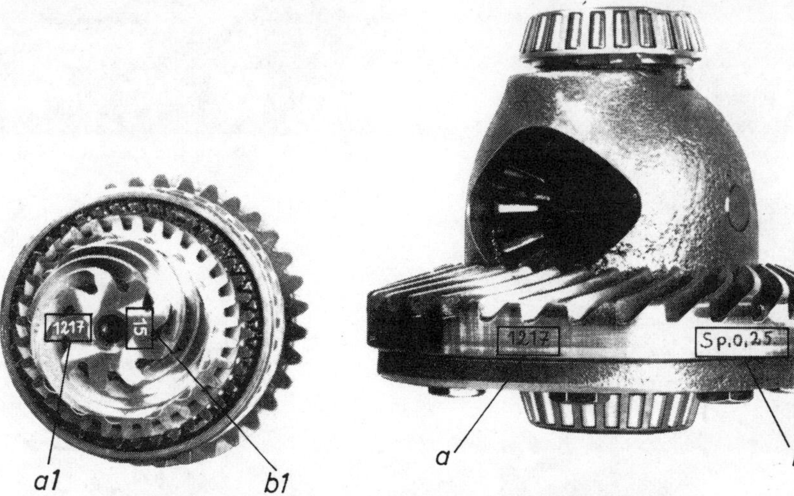

FIG 6:40   The crownwheel and drive pinion markings

Key to Fig 6:40   a Pair code on crownwheel   **b** Backlash figure   **a1** Pair code on pinion   **b1** End play figure

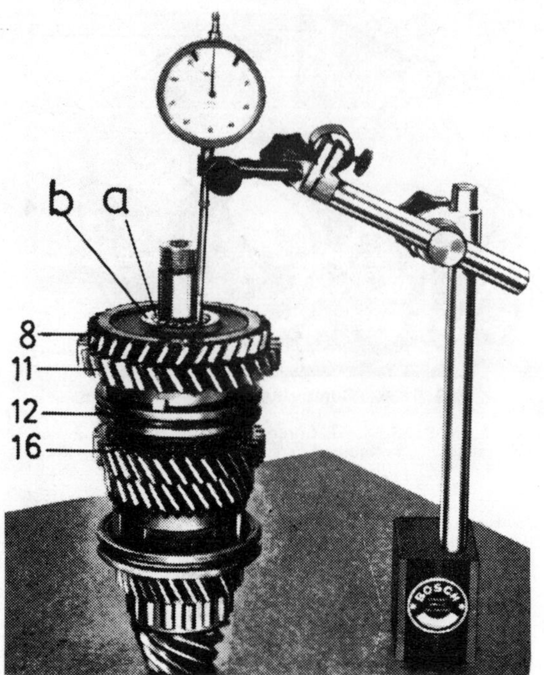

FIG 6:41 Checking the height difference between splined shaft **a** and reverse gear **b**

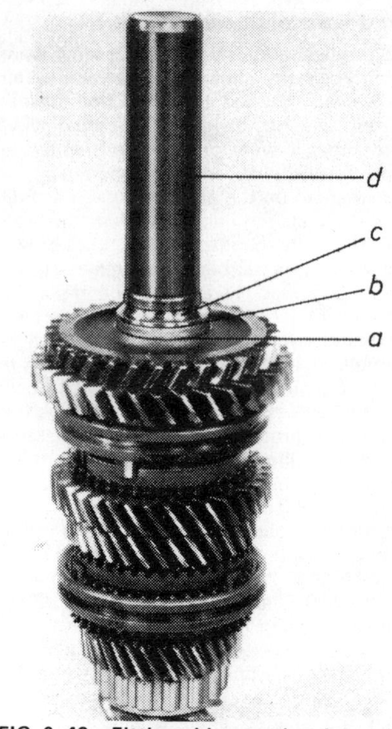

FIG 6:42 Fitting shims to the pinion shaft

FIG 6:43 Fitting the transmission cover to the pinion shaft

FIG 6:44 Fitting the special tool G-16 to the cover

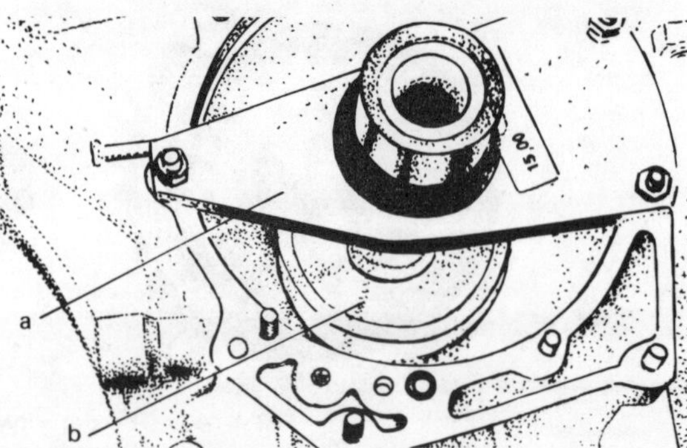

FIG 6:45 Installing tools G-42 at **a** and G-41 at **b**

FIG 6:46 Measuring the distance between the pinion and the special tool

FIG 6:47 Mounting the gauge G-44 in position

Key to Fig 6:47 **a** Gauge shaft **b** Socket head screw
c Dial gauge caliper (mounted later)

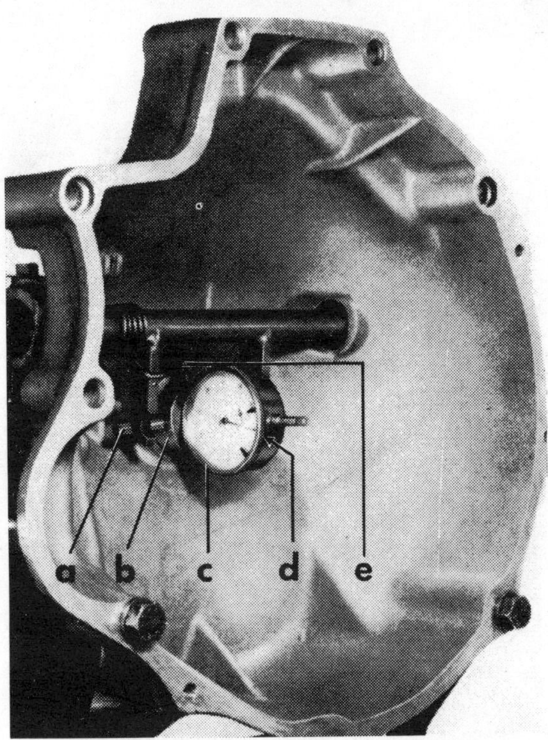

FIG 6:48 Fitting the dial to the transmission

Key to Fig 6:48 **a** Dial gauge holder retaining pin
b Dial gauge holder, tool G-48 **c** Dial gauge and caliper,
tools G-43 and G-45 **d** Gauge ring **e** Setscrew

play in position. Heat the angular bearing inner race **c** to about 100°C and drive into position with tool B-23 as shown. Clamp the pinion shaft assembly in a vice having thick aluminium jaws as shown in **FIG 6:43,** clamping above 4th gear. Press the 3rd and 4th speed synchromesh operating sleeve **a** in the direction of the arrow until it is positioned in the 4th speed gear body. Heat the transmission cover and the second four-point bearing inner race to about 100°C in an oil bath, then fit these parts in position and tighten the nut at the shaft end to a torque of 72 to 79 lb ft.

35 Place the cover and drive pinion assembly in the transmission case and fasten crosswise with at least four nuts. Fit special tool G-16 as shown in **FIG 6:44** and tighten evenly. Refer to **FIG 6:45** and place tool G-41 in the seat for the tapered roller bearing outer race, then slide tool G-42 over tool G-41 and fasten with nuts. The radius of the tool shaft collar is 51.5 mm.

36 Refer to **FIG 6:46** and use a feeler gauge **c** to measure the distance between the pinion face and the tool at **b**. Do this as accurately as possible. The shim thickness required is then calculated as shown by the following example, assuming a feeler gauge measurement of .60 mm.

Example: Radius of tool shaft collar	..	51.5 mm
Standard shim used ..	..	3.2 mm
Feeler gauge measurement	..	.6 mm
Total		55.3 mm

The reference figure of 51.7 mm must be added to the figure stamped on the pinion face and the result deducted from the total figure just calculated.

Example: Reference dimension	..	51.7 mm
Dimension stamped on pinion		.15 mm
Total		51.85 mm

The difference between the two figures is then 3.45 mm which is the thickness of shims that must be fitted in place of the 3.2 mm shim fitted for measuring purposes, this being one 3.3 mm shim and one .15 mm shim fitted together.

37 Remove the pressure plate. Clamp the pinion shaft unit in a vice as before at the 4th gear position and move the synchromesh into the 4th gear. Unscrew the nut and reinstall the pressure plate and press out the drive pinion assembly as shown in **FIG 6:21** and described in instructions 11 and 12. Use a puller to remove parts 5, 6, 7, 8 and 11 as shown in **FIG 6:23** and described in instruction 13. Slide on parts 11, 8 and 7 and press into position, then slide on the shims as determined in instruction 36. Install the four point bearing inner race in accordance with instruction 34. The correct setting will now be established.

Adjusting backlash:

38 The backlash figure for the crownwheel is marked as shown at **b** in **FIG 6:40**. If not already carried out, fit the taper roller bearing outer race in position without shims and drive it into position as described in

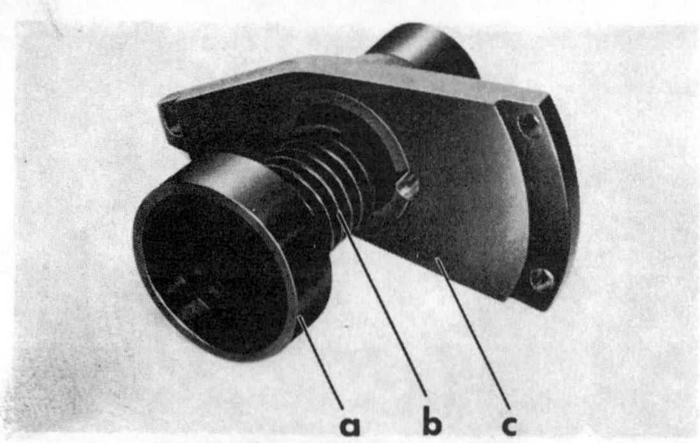

FIG 6:49   Special tool G-42

Key to Fig 6:49   **a** Centre   **b** Spring   **c** Gauge flange

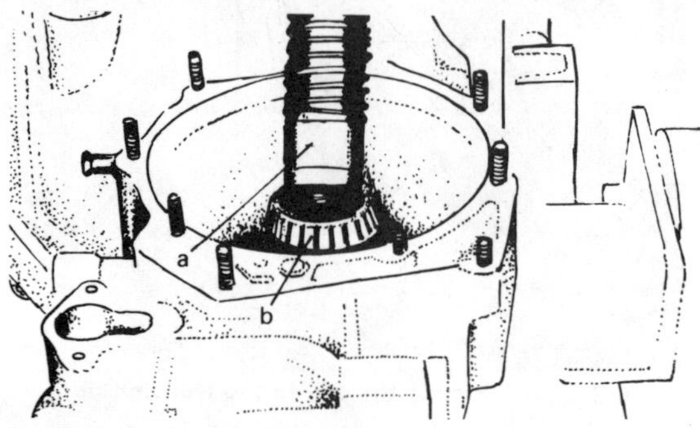

FIG 6:50   Fitting the taper roller bearing assembly

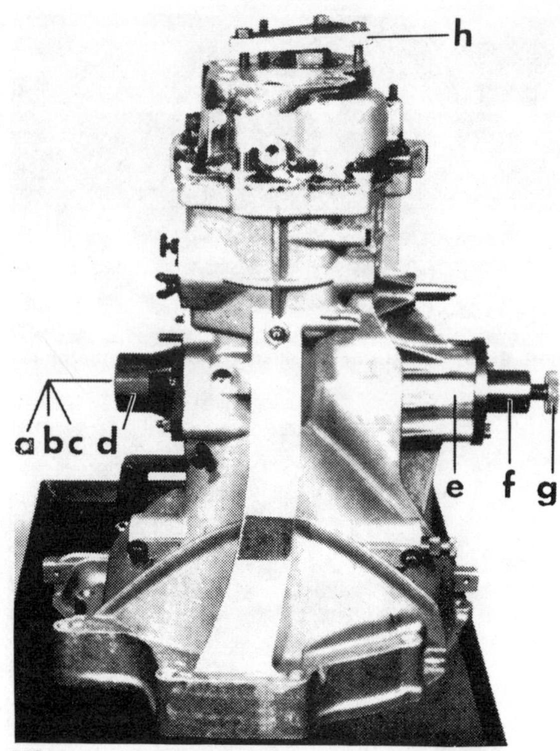

FIG 6:51   The special tools fitted for the adjustment of backlash

Key to Fig 6:51   **a** Taper roller bearing outer race   **b** Centre   **c** Spring   **d** Gauge flange   **e** Tool G-18   **f** Adjusting flange   **g** Screw   **h** Tool G-16

FIG 6:52   Seating the roller bearing races

instructions 20 and 21. Install the differential housing. Place the gauge shaft of tool G-44 in the differential housing in such a manner that its gauge surface is in vertical alignment with the centre axis of the crownwheel, as shown in **FIG 6:48**. Lock the gauge shaft in position with the socket head screw.

39 Place the axial play and the end play shims previously determined into position, and fit the pinion shaft parts and the transmission cover as described in instruction 34. Place the transmission cover complete with drive pinion assembly in the transmission case and tighten crosswise with at least four nuts.

40 Turn the crownwheel by rotating the pinion shaft nut until gauge shaft **a** in **FIG 6:47** is at right angles to dial gauge caliper **c**. Install the dial gauge and holder as shown in **FIG 6:48**. Fit the special tool G-16 as shown in **FIG 6:44** and tighten evenly.

41 Fit the parts of tool G-42 together as shown in **FIG 6:49**. Place the taper roller bearing outer race **a** in the centre and position both on the bearing cage **b**, as shown in **FIG 6:50**. Screw the gauge flange **c** of tool G-42 to the transmission case. Slide the special tools G-18 and G-15 into the transmission at the crownwheel end as described in instruction 21 and shown in **FIG 6:31**.

42 **FIG 6:51** shows the arrangement of special tools required for adjustment of backlash, items **b**, **c** and **d**

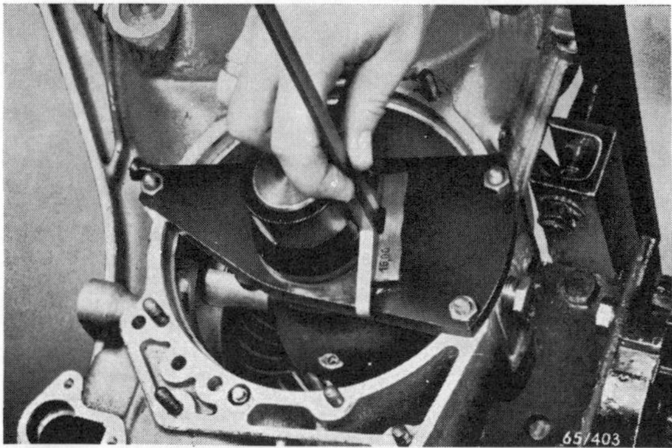
FIG 6:53 Measuring the distance between the tool surface to the outer race

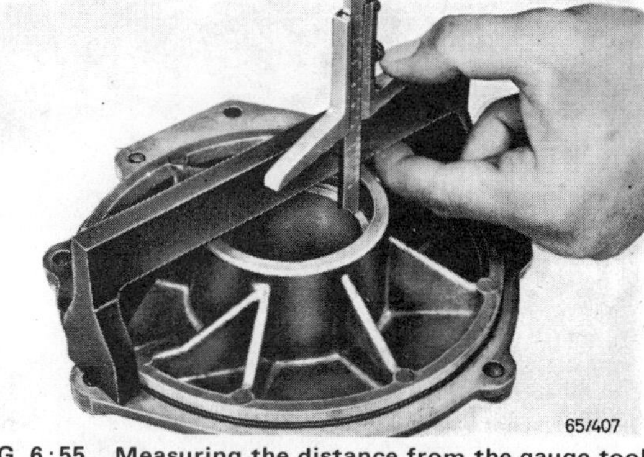
FIG 6:55 Measuring the distance from the gauge tool to the bearing surface

FIG 6:54 Measuring the distance from the gauge tool to the differential flange

being tool G-42, item **e** tool G-18, items **f, g** special tool G-15 and item **h** tool G-16. The screw **g** is to be loosened fully to remove any pressure from part **e**. In order to correctly seat the taper roller bearing outer races, apply several blows with a soft-faced hammer to the bottom side of the differential housing as shown in **FIG 6:52**.

43 Working through the opening in the gauge flange, measure the distance from the measuring surface to the upper edge of the taper roller bearing outer race, the depth gauge caliper resting on the outer race as shown in **FIG 6:53**. Note the measurement for use in later calculations. (For the purposes of the example given later, a measurement of 38.7 mm is assumed.)

44 Refer to **FIG 6:48** and install the dial gauge holder **b** so that its retaining pins **a** are positioned below the arms of the clutch release shaft. Fit the gauge and caliper and slide the gauge in its holder so that approximately 2 mm preload is present when the caliper rests against the gauge shaft (see **FIG 6:47**). Clamp the dial gauge in position and set the gauge ring at 0.

45 Turn the differential to the right and left and take a reading from the dial gauge. Carefully tighten the screw **g** in **FIG 6:51** until the reading is reduced to agree with the backlash figure stamped on the crown-wheel (.25 mm in the example given).

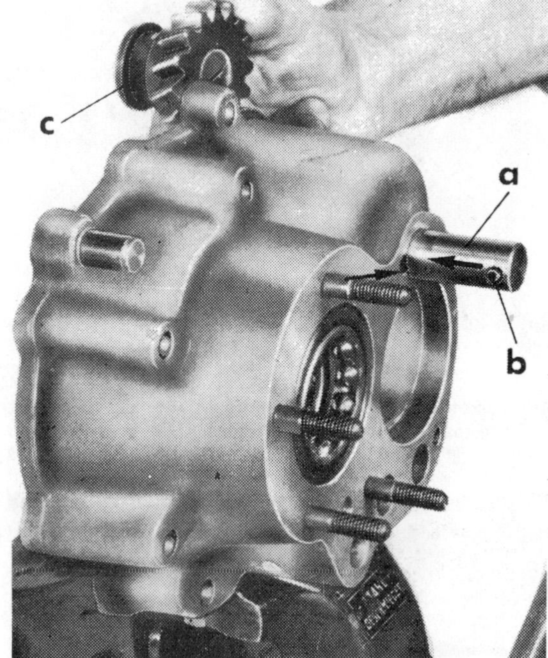
FIG 6:56 Fitting reverse gear and shaft

FIG 6:57 Fitting the stop plungers **a** and **b**, showing the 3rd/4th speed selector rod bore, **1**, the 1st/2nd bore **2** and the reverse bore **3**

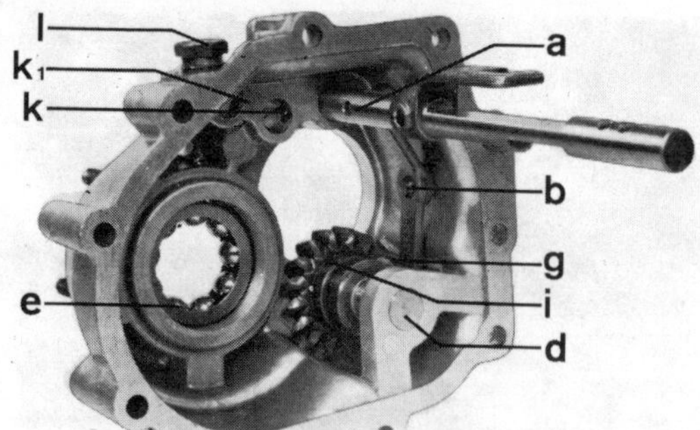

FIG 6:58   Installing reverse selector rod

Key to Fig 6:58   **a** Reverse selector rod   **b** Screw
g Lever   **i** Reverse gear and bushing   **k** Stop plunger, reverse and 1st/2nd speeds

FIG 6:60   Fitting 1st/2nd selector rod **a** and 3rd/4th selector rod **b**

FIG 6:59   Checking the four point bearing protrusion

46 Working through the opening in the gauge flange, measure the depth to the taper roller bearing outer race as described in instruction 43 and note this figure. (For the example given a measurement of 37.4 is assumed.) The thickness of shims required under the taper roller bearing outer race on the crown-wheel end can now be determined in the manner shown in the following example.

Example: 1st measurement according to
instruction 43   ..   ..   38.7 mm
2nd measurement according to
instruction 46   ..   ..   37.4 mm
Difference   11.3 mm
Add .1 mm for bearing preload   0.1 mm
Shim thickness required   ..   1.4 mm

Shims for adjusting the backlash are available in the following thicknesses: 1.5, 1.0, .8, .5, .25, .2 and .15 mm. Select the minimum number of shims to make up the thickness required.

47 The shim for the differential flange must now be determined. Place a new differential flange gasket in position and make sure that the flange surface is clean. Place gauge G-40 on the flange as shown in **FIG 6:54** and measure the distance from the gauge to the flange with a depth gauge. (For the purposes of the example given, a measurement of 70.0 mm is assumed.)

48 Now measure the distance between the gauge tool and the taper roller bearing surface as shown in

FIG 6:55. (For the example given a measurement of 47.0 mm is assumed.)

49 The shim thickness for the differential flange can now be determined in the manner shown in the following example.

Example: 1st measurement according to
instruction 47   ..   ..   70.0 mm
2nd measurement according to
instruction 48   ..   ..   47.0 mm
Difference (1)   23.0 mm

Measurement taken as shown
in **FIG 6:53**, e.g. ..   ..   38.6 mm
Thickness of flange as stamped,
e.g.   ..   ..   ..   15.0 mm
Difference (2)   23.6 mm

Dimension (2)   23.6 mm
Dimension (1)   23.0 mm
Difference   0.60 mm
Add .1 mm for bearing preload   0.10 mm
Differential flange shim thick-
ness required   ..   ..   0.70 mm

50 Unscrew the pressure plate. Unscrew and remove the transmission cover and drive pinion. Unscrew the gauge flange and remove the taper roller bearing outer race from the centre. Remove the differential assembly from the transmission case. Continue tightening the knurled head screw of the gauge flange to press out

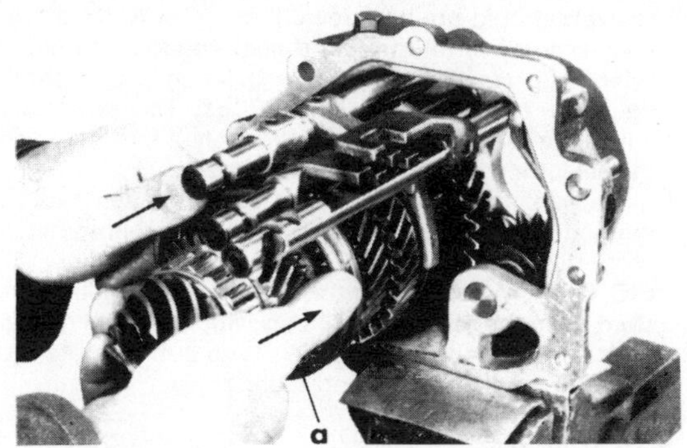

FIG 6:61 Fitting the drive pinion assembly and selector rod

FIG 6:64 Setting the selector rods in neutral

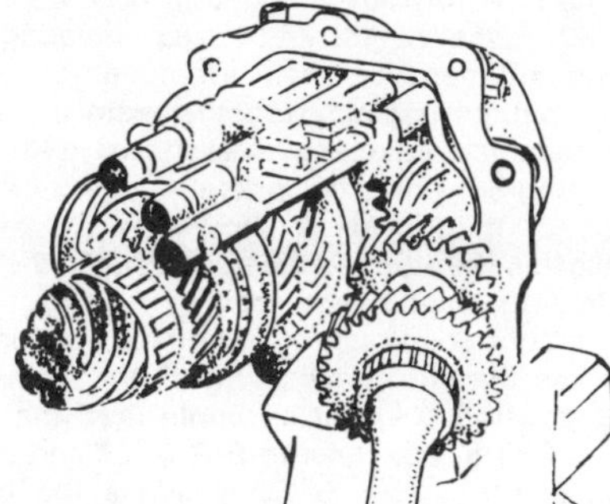

FIG 6:62 Installing the mainshaft

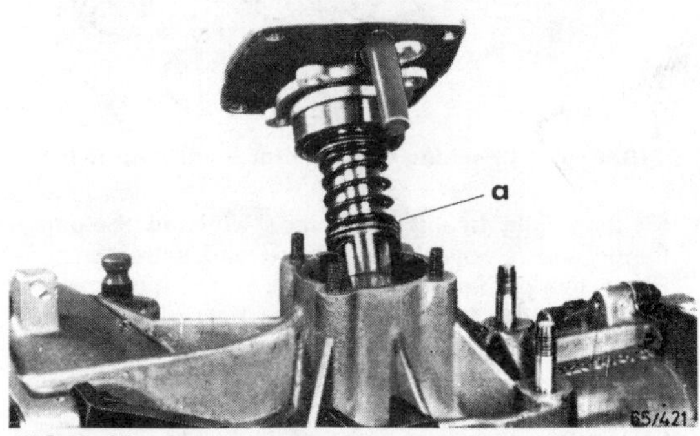

FIG 6:65 Retaining the thrust washer with grease

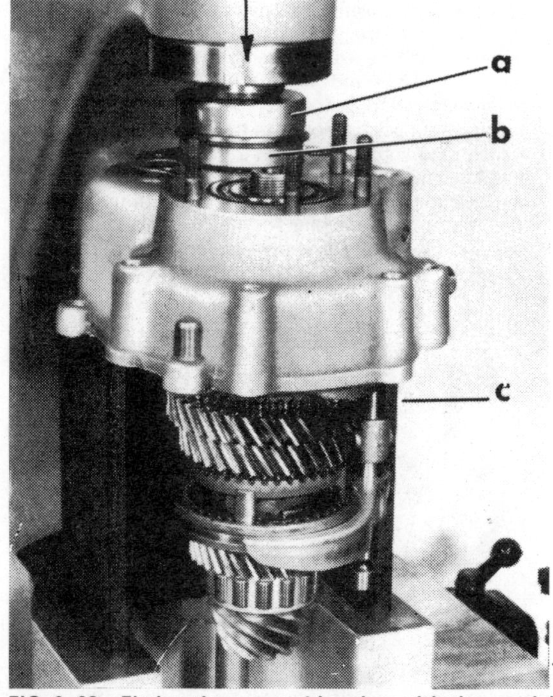

FIG 6:63 Fitting the grooved bearing with the special tools

FIG 6:66 Checking the selector lever position

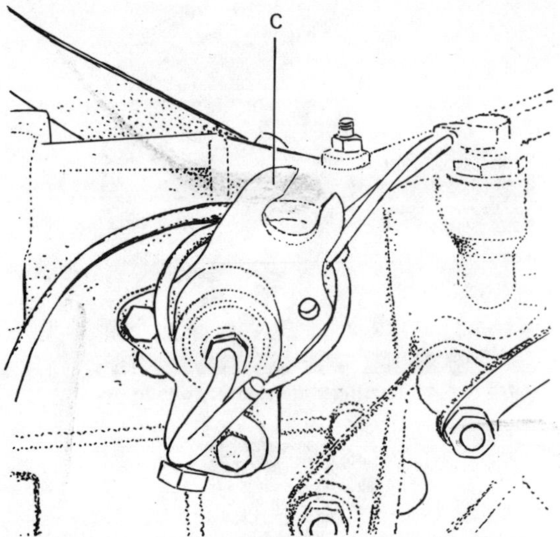

FIG 6:67 Checking the selector lever alignment

the taper roller bearing outer race. Unscrew the gauge flange and remove the adjusting and extracting pin. Place the predetermined shims in the transmission case and drive in the taper roller bearing outer race, using tool G-20. Mount the pinion and cover assembly as shown in **FIG 6:43** and remove the pinion shaft nut. Refit the pressure plate and press out the drive pinion assembly as shown in **FIG 6:21**.

Reassembling transmission assemblies:

51 Refer to **FIG 6:56** and install the reverse gear **c** so that it faces the end cover. Turn shaft **a** until tubular key **b** aligns with the cavity shown arrowed. Slide in the shaft completely. Slide in the 17mm long stop plunger **a** and the 11.7mm long stop plunger **b**, both shown in **FIG 6:57**.

52 Refer to **FIG 6:58** and install the selector rod **a** together with selector fork and lever **g** and clamp in position as follows. Tighten screw **b** in the transmission cover until, firstly, the lever rests against the selector rod and, secondly, against the selector fork in the groove of the reverse gear. When doing so,

screw **b** should not be screwed into lever **g**. Now turn back screw **b** until the first thread engages, whereby lever **g** is pressed against screw **b**. Afterwards, tighten the screw to a torque of 22 to 28 lb ft. This procedure ensures a clearance of approximately 1 mm between the selector fork and the reverse gear.

53 Make sure that the four-point bearing outer race is pressed fully home, then check the amount that it protrudes from the case with a dial gauge as shown in **FIG 6:59**. When taking this measurement, place the shim 0 shown in **FIG 6:22** in position. A new gasket must be selected by measuring with a micrometer, to conform with the following table:

.10 to .15 mm	.2 mm
.16 to .18 mm	.25 mm
.19 to .22 mm	.3 mm
.23 to .28 mm	.4 mm

54 Install the selector rods **a** and **b** in accordance with **FIG 6:60**. Place the 1st/2nd speed operating sleeve in second and the reverse selector rod in neutral. Slide the drive pinion assembly together with the selector rod into the transmission cover as shown in **FIG 6:61**. When doing so, press the operating sleeve **a** in the direction of third gear as shown by the arrow in order to allow the stop plunger to engage in the groove in the 3rd/4th speed selector rod.

55 Install the four point bearing inner race and lock plate and tighten the nut by hand. Install the mainshaft in the transmission cover at an angle from the side as shown in **FIG 6:62**. Refer to **FIG 6:63** and suspend the mainshaft in tool G-19 **c**. Place the grooved bearing **b** on the mainshaft and using tool G-4 **a**, carefully press it on a small amount. Align the transmission cover and continue installing the bearing until it is correctly positioned against the snap ring in the bore and on the mainshaft. Place the differential assembly in the transmission case. Align the drive pinion selector rod and operating sleeve so that reverse and third gear are in mesh.

56 Apply a thin coat of sealer to the flange surfaces of the transmission case and cover. Carefully install the transmission cover and shafts in the case, taking care not to damage the mainshaft oil seal in the clutch housing. Drive in both dowel pins for the cover and tighten the cover nuts. Tighten the drive pinion nut to a torque of 73 to 79 lb ft. Working through the selector rod and

FIG 6:68 Checking the gearchange lever on the transmission

FIG 6:69 Checking the distance between the lever and the case

differential flange openings, set all the selector rods in the neutral position as shown in **FIG 6:64**.

57 Place the shims as determined by instruction 49 in the differential flange, installing the thicker shim first, then drive in the taper roller bearing outer race with tool G-20. Use a new O-ring seal and differential flange gasket, coating the O-ring with grease or oil when fitting. Check to make sure that the selector rod stop plungers are positioned in bores 1, 2 and 3 and install the springs, as shown in **FIG 6:13**. Fit the pin 4, making sure that the groove in the pin is visible.

58 Install the differential flange in the transmission case and tighten the nuts alternately and evenly to 18 to 23 lb ft. Apply a light coat of grease to the thrust washer **a** shown in **FIG 6:65** so that it sticks to the circlip. Install the left and right stub axles, being careful with the drain hose. Tighten the four stub axle nuts crosswise to 18 to 23 lb ft.

59 Fit the shims as removed, a new correct thickness gasket and the end cover, referring to instruction 6. Coat the screws **a** and **b** in **FIG 6:10** with sealer when installing them. Refit the gear selector rod and cover, the clutch release bearing, reversing light switch and seal and the speedometer bushing, referring to instructions 2, 3 and 4. Make sure that the transmission drain plug is tight, then fill the transmission with two litres of hypoid oil in accordance with the instructions in the Owners Manual and fit the filler plug.

6:4 Selector lever adjustment

Refer to **FIGS 6:66, 6:67, 6:68** and **6:69**. The selector lever **b** is to be adjusted so that dimension **d** is within the range 48 to 50 mm and it must be aligned with the holder **c**. Lock in the correct position with nut **a**.

Place the selector rod in neutral and slide on the gear-change lever **e**. The dimension **f** as measured from the centre of the screw must be 84 mm, this giving the correct angle of 23 deg. as shown.

Place the selector rod in second gear. In this position the distance between the lever and the transmission case should be 3 mm as shown at **g**. This distance can be set correctly by altering the position of the lever on the rod.

6:5 Fault diagnosis

(a) Jumping out of gear

1 Excessively worn selector shafts
2 Worn synchromesh assemblies
3 Loose or worn selector fork

(b) Noisy transmission

1 Insufficient oil
2 Mainshaft or bearings worn or damaged
3 Worn pinion shaft bearings
4 Worn gear or synchromesh teeth
5 Incorrect differential or drive pinion adjustment

(c) Difficulty in engaging gear

1 Incorrect clutch adjustment
2 Worn synchromesh assemblies
3 Worn selector shafts or forks

(d) Oil leaks

1 Damaged joint washers or gaskets
2 Worn or damaged oil seals
3 Faulty joint faces on covers

CHAPTER 7

AUTOMATIC TRANSMISSION

7:1 Description
7:2 Maintenance
7:3 Power flow (mechanical)

7:4 Fault diagnosis
7:5 Removing and refitting automatic
transmission

7:1 Description

The Audi 100 automatic transmission is an hydraulically operated threespeed unit combined with a hydrodynamic torque converter. All speeds change automatically within a preselected driving range. Up and down changes take place at the appropriate road speed and in accordance with the engine speed and loading. The clutch pedal is omitted and the planetary gears in the unit allow gearchanging without interrupting the power flow.

The various components of the automatic transmission are housed in a complex, cast aluminium casing. The main parts of the transmission are the oil pump, gearchange components, planetary gears, valve body, differential (final drive) and the torque converter assembly. **FIG 7:1** shows a cutaway view of the transmission and **FIG 7:2** a section view.

The action of the torque converter shown in **FIG 7:3** is as follows. The torque converter housing, parts 1 and 3 are welded together to form a single unit. When the engine is running, the torque converter is continually supplied with automatic transmission fluid by the pump. The impeller, driven by the engine, transmits torque by means of the fluid to the turbine which drives the automatic gearbox. The stator redirects the flow of fluid as it leaves the turbine so that it re-enters the impeller at the most effective angle.

When the engine is idling, the converter impeller is being driven slowly and the energy of the transmission fluid leaving it is therefore low, so little torque is imparted to the turbine. For this reason, with the engine idling and drive engaged the car will have little or no tendency to 'creep'. As the throttle is opened impeller speed increases and the process of torque multiplication begins. As the turbine picks up speed and the slip between it and the impeller becomes less, the torque multiplication reduces progressively until, when their speeds become substantially equal, the unit acts as a fluid coupling. When the turbine speed is higher than that of the impeller, as when the car is decelerating, the torque converter works in reverse. In this situation, the turbine drives the impeller and thus the engine, so that the braking effort of the engine is then fully effective. When decelerating the torque converter only functions as a fluid coupling.

7:2 Maintenance

Every 6000 miles the fluid level in the automatic transmission and the oil level in the differential housing must be checked and, if necessary, topped up to the correct level. The filler tube and dipstick for the automatic transmission are shown at 7 in **FIG 7:1**, those for the differential being shown at 4.

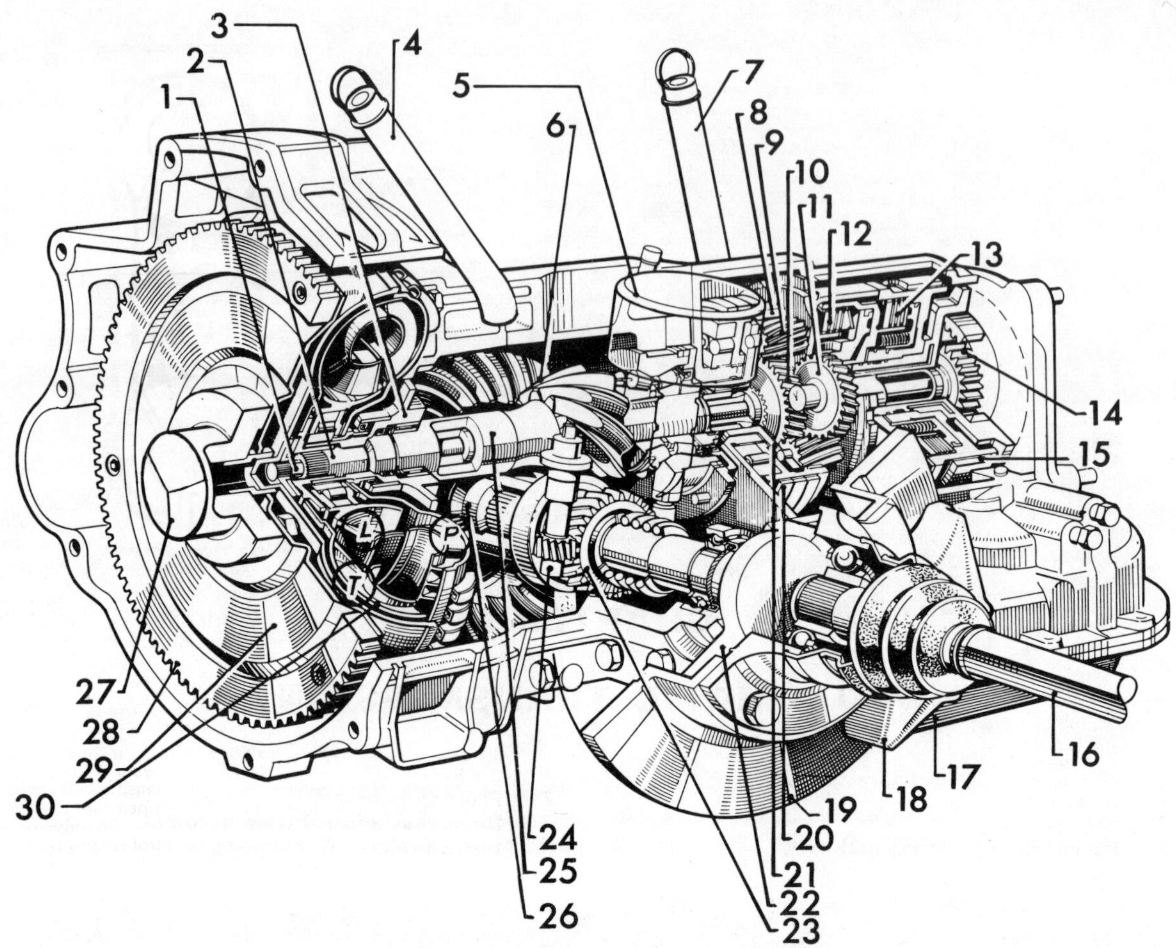

FIG 7:1 Cutaway view of the automatic transmission

Key to Fig 7:1 1 Pump shaft 2 Turbine shaft 3 Stator support 4 Oil filler tube, differential 5 Governor 6 Drive pinion 7 Oil filler tube, planetary gear 8 Annulus 9 Small planetary gear 10 Large sun gear 11 Large planetary pinion 12 Forward clutch 13 Direct and reverse clutch 14 Oil pump 15 2nd gear brake band 16 Drive shaft 17 Oil pan 18 Brake caliper 19 Brake disc 20 1st gear and reverse brake band 21 Planetary gear carrier 22 Stub axle 23 Impeller, governor and speedometer drive 24 Speedometer pinion shaft 25 Drive pinion shaft 26 Differential 27 Crankshaft, engine 28 Gear ring 29 Drive plate 30 Torque converter **P** Impeller **L** Stator **T** Turbine

The fluid in the automatic transmission and the oil in the differential unit must be changed every 18,000 miles, or every 12,000 miles if the car is operated under extreme conditions such as hauling trailers, excessive city driving, operating in mountainous country or at extremely high temperatures.

Transmission fluid:

Checking:

When checking the fluid level always hold the ring handle of the dipstick vertically as shown in **FIG 7:4**, otherwise the dipstick will be twisted in the filler tube. The specified fluid level is most important to ensure correct operation of the automatic transmission, so check it carefully. The level must be between the upper and lower marks on the dipstick at normal temperatures. If the transmission is very hot or very cold, the level will be somewhat above or below the marks. **Always check the level when the fluid is lukewarm, with the engine idling in neutral.** The difference between the upper and lower marks on the dipstick is approximately .1 gallon (.4 litre).

If the level is not correct as stated, add fluid or drain off some fluid as the case may be. The approved fluid for the automatic transmission is that designated Dexron B, as marketed by the major oil companies. **Do not use anything but the recommended fluid.** It is safe to mix different brands of Dexron B fluid if necessary.

Changing:

Remove the transmission fluid drain plug shown at **a** in **FIG 7:5** and allow the fluid to drain into a suitable container, then take out the screws **x** and detach the transmission oil pan. Thoroughly clean the inside of the oil

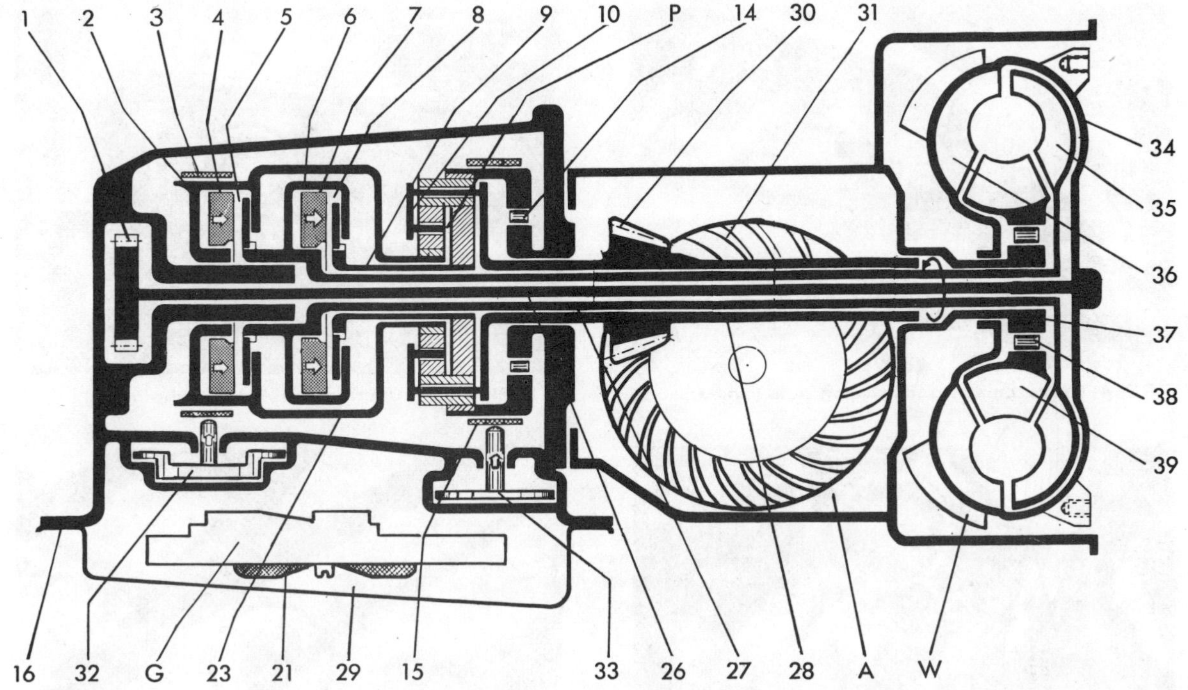

FIG 7:2 Sectional view of the automatic transmission

Key to Fig 7:2 1 Oil pump 2 Clutch drum 3 2nd gear brake band 4 Piston, direct and reverse clutch 5 Direct and reverse clutch 6 Forward clutch drum with ball valve 7 Piston, forward clutch 8 Forward clutch 9 Forward clutch hub 10 Planetary gear carrier 14 1st gear one-way clutch 15 1st gear and reverse brake band 16 Transmission case 21 Oil strainer 23 Drive shell 26 Oil pump shaft 27 Turbine shaft 28 Drive pinion shaft 29 Oil pan (automatic transmission fluid) 30 Drive pinion 31 Crownwheel 34 Torque converter housing 35 Turbine 36 Impeller 37 Stator support 38 One-way clutch 39 Stator **P** Planetary gears **G** Transmission control—valve body **A** Differential—final drive **W** Torque converter

FIG 7:3 The torque converter assembly

70/300

FIG 7:4 The automatic transmission fluid level dipstick

FIG 7:5   The transmission fluid drain plug

FIG 7:6   The differential unit oil level dipstick

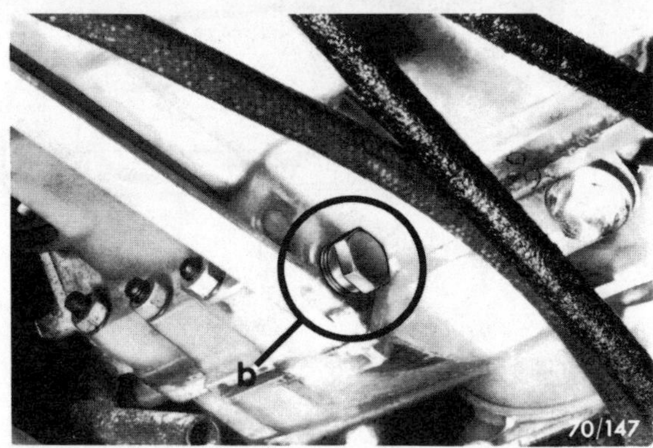

FIG 7:7   The differential unit oil drain plug

FIG 7:8   The planetary gear assembly

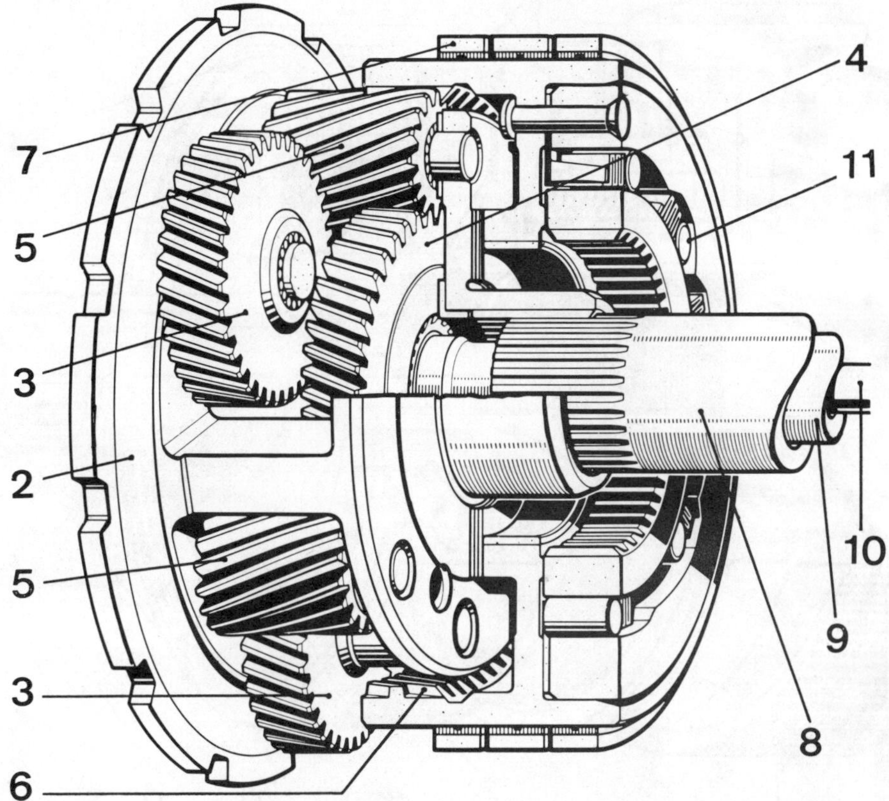

FIG 7:9 Section through the planetary gear assembly

Key to Figs 7:8 and 7:9 1 Small sun gear—30 teeth 2 Planetary gear carrier 3 Large planetary pinions—35 teeth 4 Large sun gear—51 teeth 5 Small planetary pinions—16 teeth 6 Annulus gear—84 teeth 7 1st gear and reverse brake band 8 Drive pinion 9 Turbine shaft 10 Drive shaft, oil pump 11 Roller-type one-way clutch, annulus gear

pan with a lint-free cloth and refit it to the transmission, using a new gasket. Tighten the pan mounting screws to a torque of 7.25 lb ft, working crosswise to ensure even tension.

Use a clean funnel and add .55 Imp. gallons of new fluid to the transmission through the filler tube shown in **FIG 7:4.** Start the engine, depress the brake pedal and move the selector lever through all positions before returning it to the N (neutral) position. Check the fluid level with the selector in N and correct the level as necessary, as described previously. Finally, recheck the tightness of the pan mounting screws as the gasket is likely to settle after the transmission has warmed up. Always check the level with the engine idling in neutral.

Differential unit oil:

Checking:

Check the oil level in the differential unit with the dipstick shown in **FIG 7:6.** The level should be at the mark on the dipstick. If not, top up to the correct level with SAE.90 hypoid transmission oil.

Changing:

When the transmission is warm after a drive, remove the drain plug shown at **b** in **FIG 7:7** and drain the oil into a suitable container. Use a clean funnel and fill the differential unit with the correct grade of oil to the level marked on the dipstick.

7:3 Power flow (mechanical)

The layout of the various components of the automatic transmission is shown in **FIG 7:2.** The torque converter described in **Section 7:1** transmits engine power to the planetary gear assembly and thence to the final drive pinion shaft. The pinion turns the differential assembly in the normal manner, the differential transmitting power to the drive shafts which turn the road wheels.

FIGS 7:8 and **7:9** show the planetary gear assembly. One small sun gear 1 and one large sun gear 4 are located one behind the other. Three small planetary pinions 5 are in mesh with the large sun gear 4 and three large planetary pinions 3 are in mesh with the small sun gear 1. The six planetary pinions are mounted together on one planetary gear carrier 2, in such a manner that one

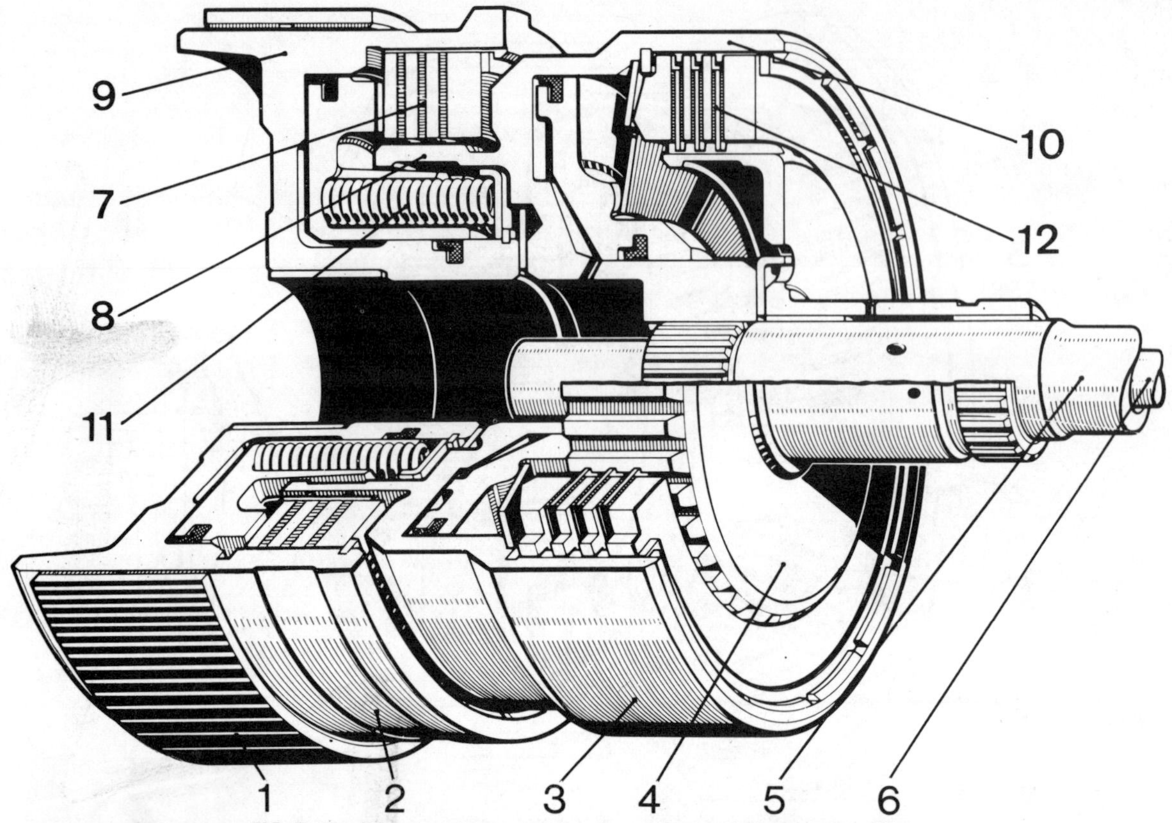

FIG 7:10 **Direct and reverse clutch and forward clutch assemblies**

Key to Fig 7:10   1 2nd gear brake band   2 Direct and reverse clutch   3 Forward clutch   4 Clutch hub   5 Turbine shaft
6 Drive shaft, oil pump   7 Internal and external splined discs   8 Hub, forward clutch drum   9 Direct and reverse clutch drum
10 Forward clutch drum   11 Springs (eighteen)   12 Forward clutch discs

small and one large planetary pinion mesh in pairs. The internal teeth of the annulus gear 6 are in mesh with the three small planetary pinions 5.

Depending on the gear ratio selected, either the large or the small sun gear is driven or, in the case of direct (top) gear, both sun gears are driven at the same time. A roller-type one-way clutch 11 is installed in the annulus gear 6 in order to prevent that gear from rotating in the opposite direction to the engine while allowing free rotation in the direction of engine rotation. The planetary gear carrier 2 provides the driving force through its splined connection to the drive pinion 8.

The various gear ratios are obtained by holding, releasing or driving different parts of the planetary gear assembly. These operations are carried out by two disc clutches, two brake bands and the one-way clutch. The disc clutches and the bands are controlled hydraulically by the valve body unit, which operates according to fluid pressure supplied by the pump, this fluid pressure being dependant on engine speed, road speed and engine load. The gear selector and kick-down mechanisms operate through the valve body to give overriding manual control over the automatic gearbox functions.

FIG 7:10 shows the components of the disc clutch assemblies. Both disc clutches 2 and 3 transmit torque from the turbine shaft 5 to the large sun gear 4, these being shown in **FIGS 7:8** and **7:9**, the small sun gear or, in top gear, to both sun gears at the same time. The internal splined discs of the clutches are coated with a friction material, the external splined discs being of plain steel. The clutches are operated by ring shaped pistons, which are moved axially by fluid pressure to press the splined discs together. The clutches are released when the fluid pressure is removed, springs returning the splined discs to the free position.

The direct and reverse clutch is installed in the drum 9. The external splined discs 7 engage in the hub 8 of the forward clutch drum 10. The internal splined discs are driven from the turbine shaft 5 via hub 8. Piston pressure is applied directly to the discs and release is by means of the springs 11. The direct and reverse clutch is in operation with the selector lever at **D** or **R** and connects clutch drum 9 to the small sun gear via the driving shell.

The forward clutch is installed in clutch drum 10 which is splined to the turbine shaft 5. The external splined discs 12 of the forward clutch 3 engage in the splines of clutch drum 10. The return spring is a spring disc which also acts as a lever for the piston force. The piston force is increased two and a half times and transmitted to the clutch discs 12. The forward clutch 3 is in operation in all

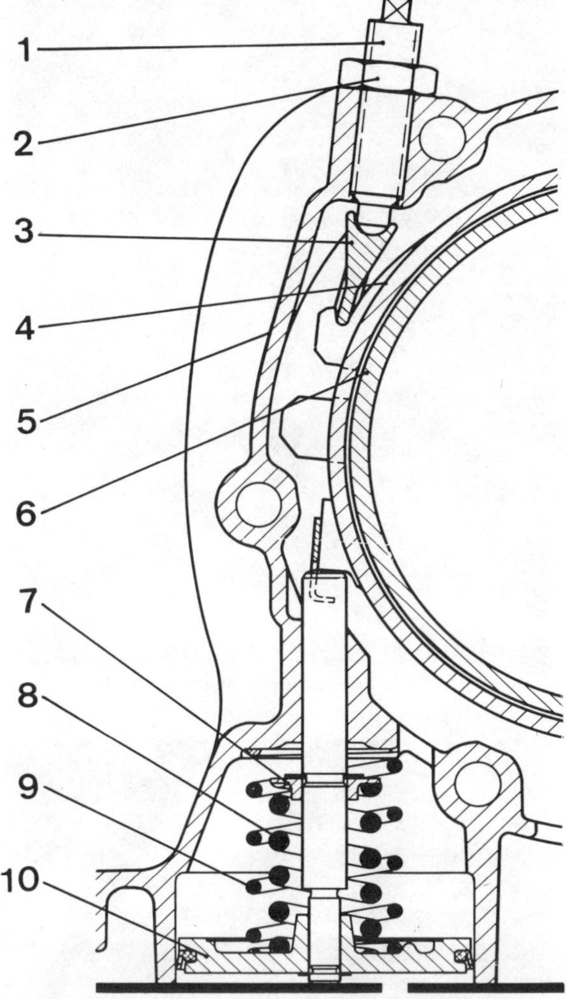

FIG 7:11   First gear and reverse brake band

Key to Fig 7:11   1 Setscrew   2 Counter nut   3 Support
4 Brake band   5 Transmission case   6 Ring gear and
one-way clutch   7 Spring disc   8 Spring, strong
9 Return spring   10 Piston

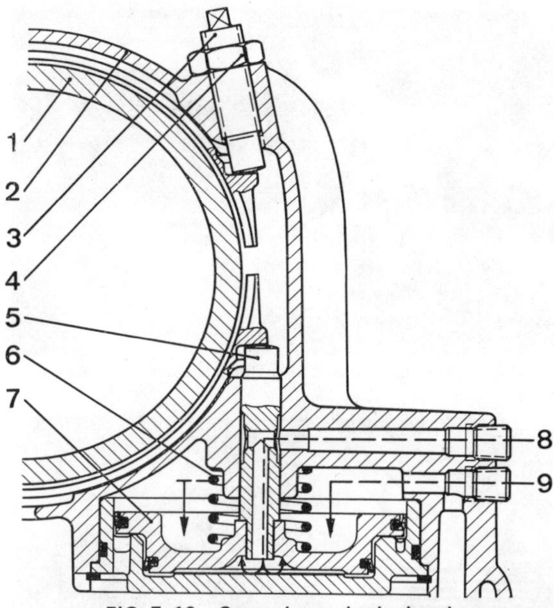

FIG 7:12   Second gear brake band

Key to Fig 7:12   1 Clutch drum   2 Brake band   3 Setscrew
4 Counter nut   5 Piston rod   6 Return spring   7 Piston
8 Oil bore (to small piston surface)   9 Oil bore (to large
piston surface)

FIG 7:13   Bolting the engine holder to the stop

FIG 7:14   Disconnecting the brake lines

forward gears. The turbine shaft 5 drives the clutch
drum 10 and its external splined discs 12. The driving
torque is transmitted to the large sun gear via the internal
splined discs 12 and the clutch hub 4.

Various ratios are obtained by holding or releasing
annulus gear 6 (see **FIG 7:8**) or clutch drum 9 (see
FIG 7:10). The first gear and reverse brake band shown
in **FIG 7:11** holds the annulus gear when the selector
lever is in 1 or R. With the selector lever in R the direct
and reverse clutch is engaged and the small sun gear is
driven. With the selector lever in 1 the direct and reverse
clutch is released, the forward clutch is engaged, the
large sun gear is driven and the ring gear is held.

The brake band 4 is coiled twice around the ring gear
and has a bonded lining. Piston 10 is inserted into the
transmission case from below and is held in position

FIG 7:15   Disconnecting the accelerator linkage

FIG 7:16   Removing the oil filter and starter motor

FIG 7:17   Disconnecting the drive shafts

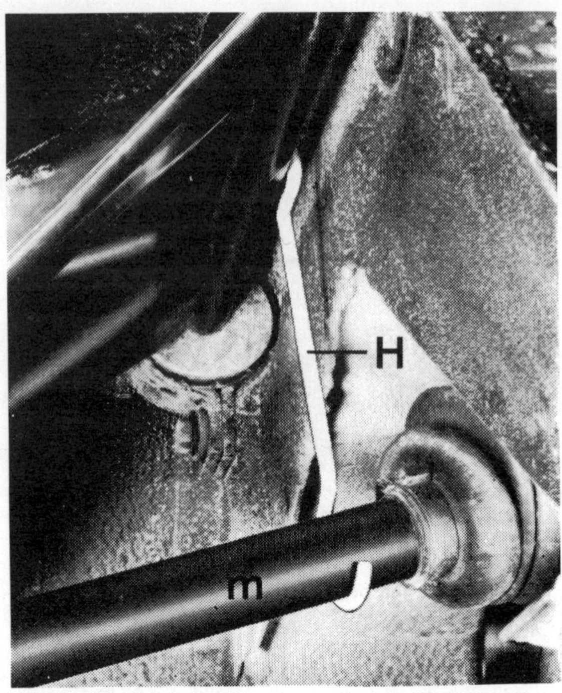

FIG 7:18   Supporting the drive shafts

FIG 7:19   Disconnecting the anti-roll bar

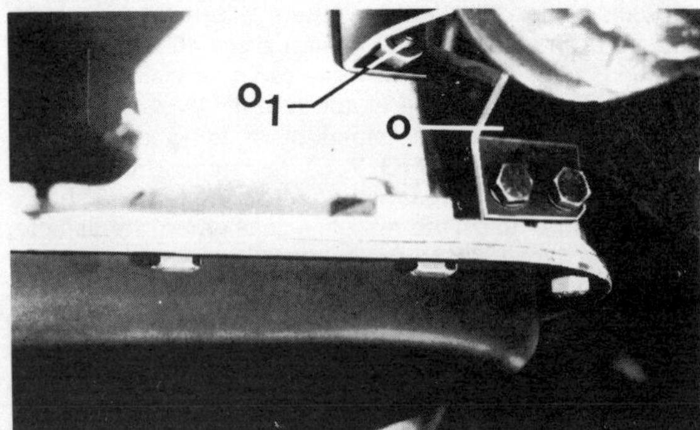

FIG 7:20   Disconnecting the selector cable

by the weaker return spring 9. To apply the brake band, fluid pressure is supplied to the lower surface of the piston. A stronger spring 8 and a spring disc 7 transmit the piston force at a steadily increasing rate to the piston rod and brake band 4, in order to hold ring gear 6 and engage first gear or reverse gear smoothly.

The second gear brake band is shown in **FIG 7:12**. This band, in second gear, holds the clutch drum 1 and also the small sun gear via the driving shell in the case of non-engaged direct and reverse clutch 2 (see **FIG 7:10**). The power flows via the large sun gear and drive pinion. In third and first gears the second gear brake band is released, the direct and reverse clutch as well as the forward clutch being engaged. The large and small sun gears are driven by the clutch drum.

A single coil brake band with a bonded friction lining 2 is wrapped around the clutch drum 1. A two-stage piston 7 is inserted in the transmission case from below. With the selector lever at 1, piston 7 is released through pressure of return spring 6. With the selector lever at 2 fluid pressure is supplied against the small piston surface, via bore 8 and a bore in the piston, to press the piston upward. With the selector lever at **D**, fluid pressure remains on the small piston surface. Fluid pressure is also supplied to the large piston surface via bore 9 and presses the piston downward smoothly due to the larger piston surface and spring tension, to release the brake band. The brake band is pressed together smoothly by a pressure regulating valve and an accumulator.

7:4 Fault diagnosis

This section contains a list of faults which may occur in the automatic transmission and a list of possible causes, followed by a list of appropriate remedial procedures. Any adjustments that may be required or the renewal of components where listed should be entrusted to a fully equipped service station, due to the need for specialized knowledge, test equipment and special tools to carry out this work. The automatic transmission assembly must not be dismantled, even by a service station. In the event of an internal component failure, the transmission must be removed and a factory reconditioned unit obtained and fitted.

Fault	Possible cause
No power transmission in any selector position	1, 2, 3, 4
No power transmission in any forward range	5
Car does not move until accelerator pressed several times	1, 6
Car jerks on acceleration	1, 6
Erratic gearchanges	1, 6
Noises in reverse gear	1, 6
No power transmission when coasting in 1st gear and in reverse when accelerating, selector in 1 or R	7
Changes into 3rd gear only	9
Insufficient power transmission in reverse, slip noticed	10
No upchange from 1st gear	11, 12
Power transmission only at high engine speeds, jerky changes	1
Erratic power transmission	1, 6
No power transmission in 1st with selector in D	13
No power transmission in 2nd with selector at 2 and D	14
Delayed engagement, engine races	15, 16, 17, 18
Gearchanges occur when speed is too low	16, 19, 20
Gearchanges occur when speed is too high	16, 19, 21
No change to 3rd with selector in D	19, 22
Harsh engagement when selector moved from N into a gear	21, 23
Car 'creeps' excessively at idle speed	23
No 'kick-down'	24, 25, 26
Poor initial acceleration, low top speed despite full engine power	1, 27, 28
Poor acceleration and a screeching noise when moving off	13, 29
Scraping, grinding noise from torque converter	30
Fluid consumption without external leakage	31, 32
Fluid very dirty or discoloured and smells burnt	33
Fluid leaking from housing breather	34
Parking lock not working	6, 35
Heavy fluid loss, fluid splashed over transmission and car body floor	36
Final drive noisy (crownwheel and pinion)	37

Possible causes key:	Repair procedure
1 Low fluid level	1
2 Drive plate broken	2
3 Pump or drive defective	3
4 Shafts or planetary gear set broken	3
5 Forward clutch defective	3
6 Selector lever cable incorrectly adjusted	4
7 1st and reverse brake bands or pistons defective	3
8 Direct and reverse clutches burnt or piston seals defective	3
9 Governor dirty	3
10 Fluid pressure too low due to incorrect selector cable adjustment	4
11 Governor drive defective	3
12 Governor valve sticking	3
13 1st gear one-way clutch defective	3
14 2nd gear brake band or piston defective	3
15 Fluid level too high or too low	1
16 Fluid pressure incorrect due to incorrect vacuum unit adjustment	5
17 Friction linings burnt or worn	3
18 Fluid pressure incorrect due to internal leakage	3
19 Governor or valve body defective	3
20 Fluid pressure incorrect due to leakage in transmission	3
21 Vacuum unit or hose leaking or hose disconnected	6
22 Direct and reverse clutch defective	3
23 Engine idle speed too high	7
24 Incorrect throttle linkage and kick-down switch adjustment	8
25 Electrical fault in switch or cables	9
26 Valve body dirty	3
27 Torque converter defective	10
28 Bands or clutches slipping	3
29 Torque converter or one-way clutch slipping	10
30 Thrust washer in torque converter worn	10
31 Vacuum unit leaking	6
32 Oil seals on pinion or governor defective	11
33 Friction linings burnt, clutch plates or brake bands	3
34 Fluid flowing into final drive housing, oil seal damaged	11
35 Operating linkage broken	3
36 Weld seam on torque converter leaking	10
37 Gear set incorrectly adjusted, pinion bearings or gears worn	3

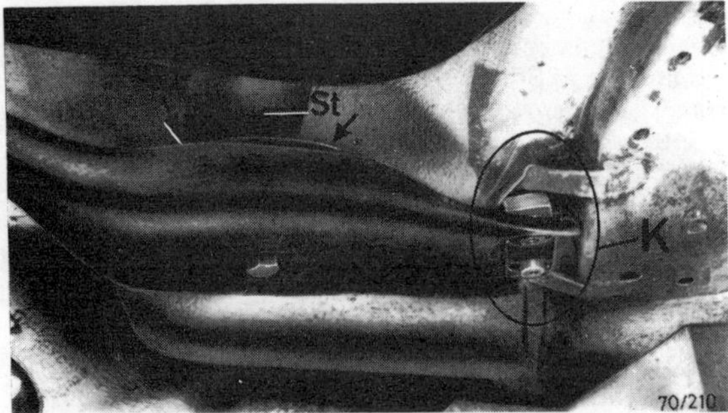

FIG 7:21 Disconnecting the crossmember and engine mountings

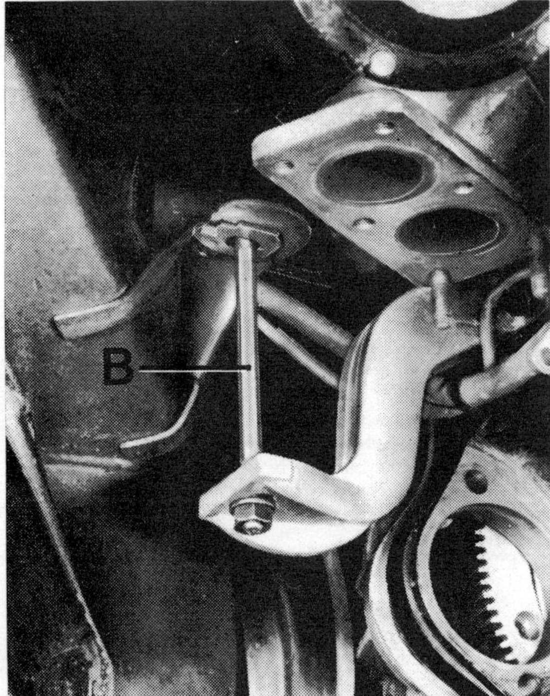

FIG 7:23 Fitting M10 x 200 bolts in place of the engine mountings

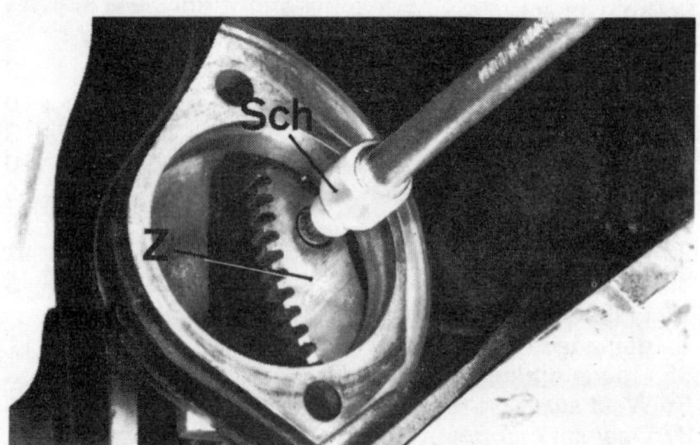

FIG 7:24 Loosening the torque converter

FIG 7:22 Disconnecting the left and right engine mountings

FIG 7:25 The engine and transmission connections

FIG 7:26   Fitting the torque converter holding tool

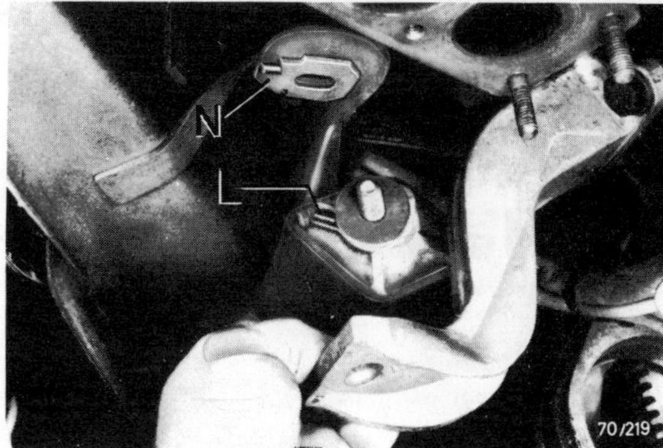

FIG 7:27   Correct assembly of the engine mountings

Repair procedure key:

1 Check fluid level and correct if necessary. Eliminate any oil leaks found
2 Renew broken drive plate
3 Fit an exchange transmission assembly complete
4 Adjust cable
5 Adjust vacuum unit
6 Renew vacuum unit or hose, or reconnect hose
7 Adjust the engine idle speed to specifications
8 Readjust the throttle linkage and kick-down switch
9 Check cables and switches, repairing if necessary
10 Renew the torque converter assembly
11 Renew defective oil seals

7:5 Removing and refitting automatic transmission

The automatic transmission assembly can be disconnected and removed from the car without the need to remove the engine unit. Proceed as follows:

Removal:

1 Remove the front grill and apron from the bodywork. Engine holder **a** must be bolted to stop **c** with an M8 x 100 screw and nut, fitted through stop pad **b** as shown in **FIG 7:13**. This prevents the engine from slipping off after the mountings have been loosened.
2 Loosen the brake pipes **e** from the hoses **f** as shown in **FIG 7:14**, securely plugging the brake hoses to prevent fluid loss. When the pipes are refitted, make certain that the right hose **f1** is connected to pipe **e1** as shown. Disconnect the accelerator pedal connecting rod **g** at shaft **h** as shown in **FIG 7:15**. Press bearing bush **i** out of the bracket **i1** in the direction of the arrow.
3 Refer to **FIG 7:16**. Disconnect the front exhaust pipe at the exhaust manifold and primary silencer. Remove the oil filter **k**. Disconnect the battery, then disconnect and remove the starter motor 1.
4 Disconnect both drive shafts **m** as shown in **FIG 7:17**, then support them with hooks **h** as shown in **FIG 7:18**. Disconnect the anti-roll bar **n** at both lower wishbones as shown in **FIG 7:19**.

5 Unscrew the selector cable holder **o** from the transmission. Disconnect the cable from the selector lever at the transmission. Remove the holder from the transmission by pulling it over bolt **o1** as shown in **FIG 7:20**. Disconnect the crossmember **p** and the engine mounting at body **K** and support **St** as shown in **FIG 7:21**. Place a lift or jack fitted with a support fixture beneath the transmission to support it.
6 Remove the guard and unscrew the left and right engine mountings **r** shown in **FIG 7:22**. When doing so, be sure not to alter the position of the left mounting, which is fixed by means of counter nuts. Insert M10 x 200 bolts on both sides in place of the engine mountings, as shown in **FIG 7:23**. Now lower the engine and transmission assembly until it rests on the bolts **B**. Disconnect the vacuum hose either at the vacuum unit or at the T-connector.
7 Loosen the torque converter by working through the bore for the starter gear ring **Z** shown in **FIG 7:24**. Loosen the three screws with a special wrench as shown, or with a suitable socket wrench. Loosen the engine and transmission connections **s** as shown in **FIG 7:25**.
8 Disconnect the transmission from the engine by pulling rearwards off the bolts while supporting on a jack, then lowering and removing from beneath the car. Immediately the transmission has been removed, install special tool 30-105 torque converter holder in position, as shown by the solid arrows in **FIG 7:26**, to hold the torque converter in position. The holder is removed for transmission refitting by moving in the direction of the broken arrows.

Refitting:

Refitting the transmission is a reversal of the removal procedure, noting the following points:

Lift the transmission and bolt it to the engine. Lift both engine and transmission. Install the selector lever holder. When installing the left and right engine mountings, make sure that projection **N** engages in the groove of the mounting **L** as shown in **FIG 7:27**. On completion, the engine and transmission assembly alignment must be checked as described in **Chapter 1, Section 1:2**, and the brakes bled as described in **Chapter 11**.

CHAPTER 8

THE DIFFERENTIAL ASSEMBLY

8:1 Description
8:2 Removing and refitting differential

8:3 Dismantling and reassembling differential
8:4 Fault diagnosis

8:1 Description

The crownwheel and pinion are a matched pair, being tested together as a unit for correct meshing and the optimum setting for minimum noise is measured. The key measurements for the crownwheel and pinion assembly are the distance from the end face of the pinion to the centre of the crownwheel and the backlash between the teeth. These measurements and the mating number are stamped onto both parts and, when the crownwheel and pinion shaft assembly are installed, these measurements must be accurately adjusted, using shims and special measuring tools. The instructions for crownwheel and pinion measurement and adjustment are given in **Chapter 6, Section 6:3,** as these settings must be established during transmission reassembly.

8:2 Removing and refitting differential

This section deals only with the differential assembly fitted to manual transmission units. The assembly cannot be removed from automatic transmission units, it being intended that the transmission be replaced with a service exchange unit in the event of a defective final drive unit.

The engine and transmission assembly must be removed as a unit, then the transmission separated from the engine. The instructions for this procedure will be found in **Chapter 1, Section 1:2.**

Refer to **Chapter 6, Section 6:3** and carry out instructions 1 to 9 to remove the differential assembly from the transmission case. Due to the amount of transmission dismantling necessary to remove the differential, it would be wise to carry out all servicing operations detailed in **Section 6:3** while checking the final drive components.

Refit the differential assembly as described in **Chapter 6, Section 6:3** and carry out the measurement and adjustments as described in that section.

8:3 Dismantling and reassembling differential

In order to dismantle and service the differential assembly, the use of two special tools, V-11 and G-25 is required, also the use of a commercial bearing puller. These tools are detailed and their application described in the text.

1 Use a puller as shown in **FIGS 8:1** and **8:2** to remove the taper roller bearing inner races from each side of the differential assembly. The differential assembly has cast pockets to allow the legs of a puller to fit under the bearings. Place tool V-11 in the differential housing.

2 Refer to **FIG 8:3** and drive out the tubular key **a** with a 5 mm diameter punch as shown at **b.**

FIG 8:1   Removing the first taper roller bearing from the differential assembly

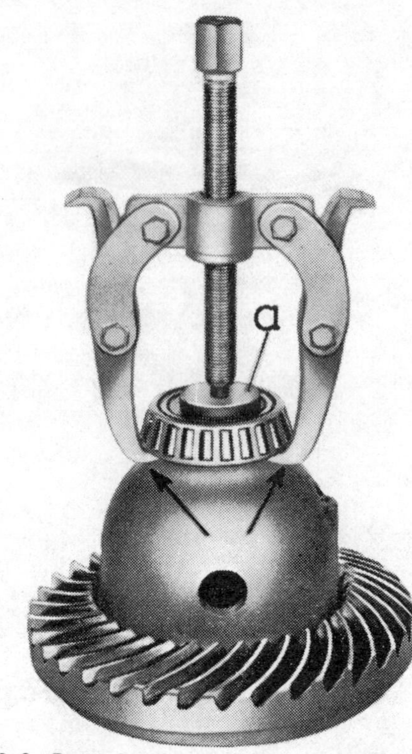

FIG 8:2   Removing the second taper roller bearing from the differential assembly

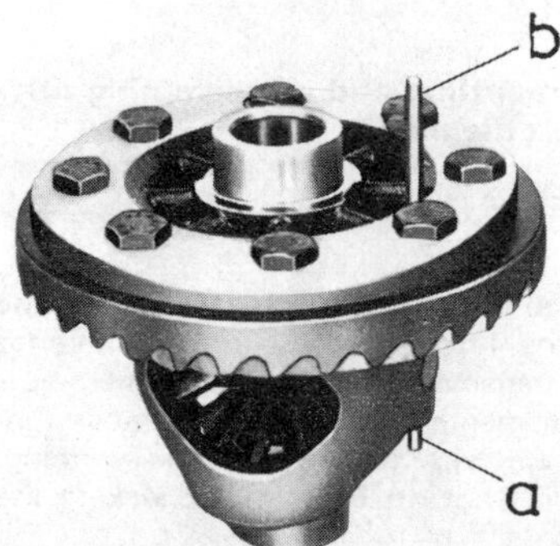

FIG 8:3   Driving out the tubular key **a** with a punch **b**

FIG 8:4   Driving out the differential pinion shaft

FIG 8:5   Removing the eight crownwheel mounting screws

3 Drive out the differential pinion shaft with a hammer and drift as shown in **FIG 8:4**. Roll the differential pinions over the bevel gears in the direction of the opening in the housing and remove them. Remove the bevel gears from the housing.

4 If necessary, remove the crownwheel from the housing as follows. Slacken the mounting screws shown in **FIG 8:5** evenly and alternately and remove them. Remove the crownwheel from the differential housing by placing on a hard wooden block and pressing out as shown in **FIG 8:6**.

5 Clean all parts in petrol or paraffin and dry them. Examine the bearings for wear and looseness and the gears and crownwheel for worn or chipped teeth.

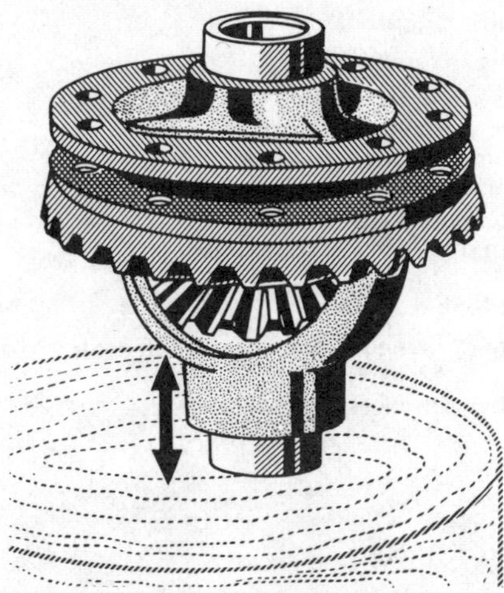

FIG 8:6 Pressing off the crownwheel

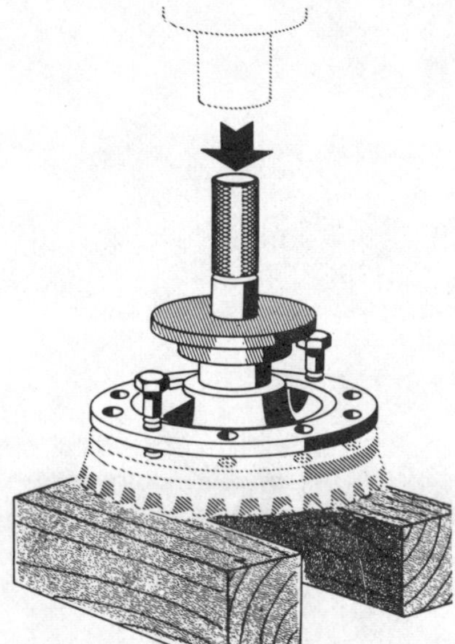

FIG 8:7 Refitting the crownwheel

FIG 8:8 Installing one differential pinion and one bevel gear into the housing

FIG 8:9 Installing the second differential pinion and bevel gear

FIG 8:10 Fitting the taper roller bearing inner races to the housing

Renew all parts found defective, noting that, if the crownwheel is to be renewed a matched crownwheel and drive pinion must be fitted. Refer to **Chapter 6** for pinion shaft details.

6 Thoroughly clean the mating surfaces of the crownwheel and differential housing. Heat the crownwheel to approximately 80°C in an oil bath, then install it as shown in **FIG 8:7** using special tool G-25. Use two mounting screws to guide the crownwheel into position as shown. Tighten the eight screws evenly to a torque of 50.6 lb ft.

7 Install the differential pinions and bevel gears in the following manner. First place one differential pinion and one bevel gear in the housing as shown in **FIG 8:8**.

Then slide in the second bevel gear through the opening and hold it in place by installing the second differential pinion as shown in **FIG 8:9**.

8 Swing the differential pinions together with the bevel gears in an axial direction 90 deg. around the bevel gears in order that the shaft can be installed. Drive in the differential pinion shaft. When fitting the shaft, pay attention to the tubular key bore. Drive in a new tubular key.

9 Heat the taper roller bearing inner races in an oil bath to approximately 100°C and press them into position as shown in **FIG 8:10**, using special tool G-25. The differential assembly is now ready for reinstallation in the transmission case.

8:4 Fault diagnosis

(a) Noisy transmission

1 Insufficient oil
2 Incorrect pinion adjustment
3 Incorrect crownwheel backlash
4 Incorrect side bearing adjustment
5 Side bearings worn
6 Worn differential components

(b) Oil leaks

1 Worn or damaged bearing or shaft seals
2 Worn or broken gaskets
3 Faulty joint faces on covers or case

CHAPTER 9

DRIVE SHAFTS AND SUSPENSION

9:1 Description
9:2 Front springs and dampers
9:3 Drive shafts and wheel hubs
9:4 Renewing drive shaft rubber boots
9:5 Removing and refitting upper wishbone assembly
9:6 Anti-roll bar and lower wishbone assembly

9:7 Checking and adjusting front wheel bearings
9:8 Suspension geometry
9:9 Removing and refitting rear axle assembly
9:10 Suspension arms and torsion bars
9:11 Rear stub axle and hub assemblies
9:12 Checking and adjusting rear wheel bearings
9:13 Fault diagnosis

9:1 Description

The front wheel drive shafts are equipped with Rzeppa synchronized universal joints. Suspension movement is accommodated by the inner joints, steering movement by the outer joints. Each front wheel is mounted on a steering swivel and supported on upper and lower wishbones. Suspension is by means of coil springs controlled by telescopic hydraulic dampers. A rubber mounted anti-roll bar is connected between the lower wishbone assemblies to improve the stability of the car when turning.

The rear suspension consists of a tubular steel axle assembly, controlled by two suspension arms and a panhard rod. Two torsion bar springs are fully enclosed in the cross tube, spring action being controlled by telescopic hydraulic dampers. The slotted rear axle tube is relatively flexible and functions as a stabilizer, assisted by the anti-roll bar which is welded to the tube. It should be noted that the car must never be jacked up at or supported by the slotted rear axle tube or the tube will be deformed. Jacking should be carried out at the cross tube.

9:2 Front springs and dampers

Removal:

Jack up the front of the car and support it with the suspension hanging free. Refer to **FIG 9:2** and unscrew the spring leg and damper **a** from the upper wishbone **b**. Remove the spring leg upper end **a** by unscrewing the three nuts **d** shown in **FIG 9:3**. **Do not loosen the nuts s at the upper damper mounting.** Refer to **FIG 9:4**. Pull the spring leg downwards, swing to the outside as arrow 1 and turn it through 90 deg. as arrow 2. If necessary, press the steering knuckle downwards slightly. Pull out the spring leg as arrow 3.

Dismantling:

Put the complete spring leg assembly into the special compressor tool V-100 as shown in **FIG 9:5**. Tighten the tool slightly to ease the load on the damper upper mounting nuts, then remove the nuts. Pull out the damper, carefully release the spring, then remove the components. **FIG 9:6** shows the spring and damper components. If both front coil spring assemblies are dismantled at the

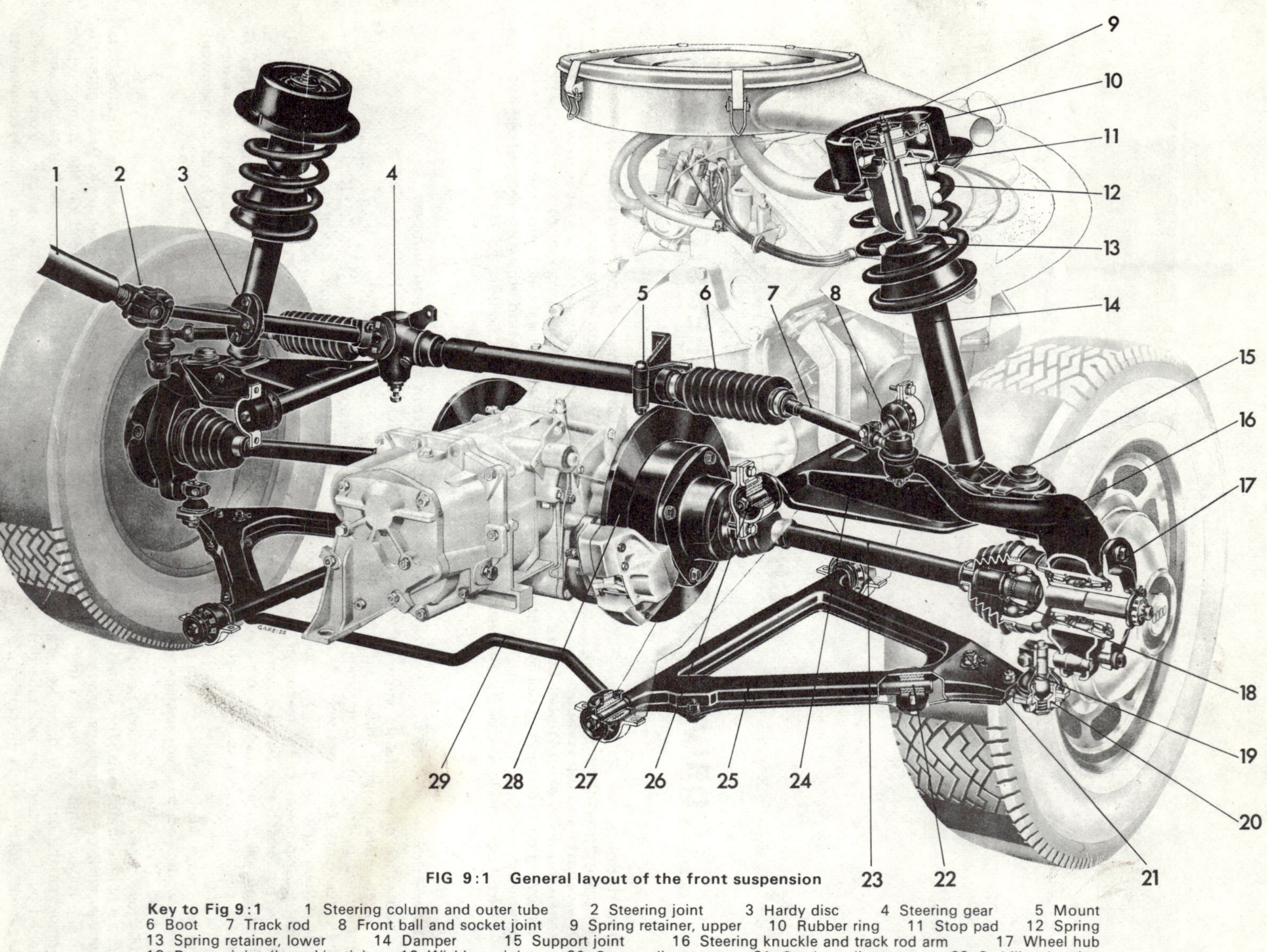

FIG 9:1 General layout of the front suspension

Key to Fig 9:1   1 Steering column and outer tube   2 Steering joint   3 Hardy disc   4 Steering gear   5 Mount
6 Boot   7 Track rod   8 Front ball and socket joint   9 Spring retainer, upper   10 Rubber ring   11 Stop pad   12 Spring
13 Spring retainer, lower   14 Damper   15 Support joint   16 Steering knuckle and track rod arm   17 Wheel hub
18 Rzeppa joint (homokinetic)   19 Wishbone joint   20 Caster adjustment   21 Camber adjustment   22 Stabilizer bearing
23 Drive shaft   24 Wishbone, upper   25 Wishbone, lower   26 Wishbone bearing, upper   27 Wishbone bearing, lower
28 Brake disc   29 Anti-roll bar

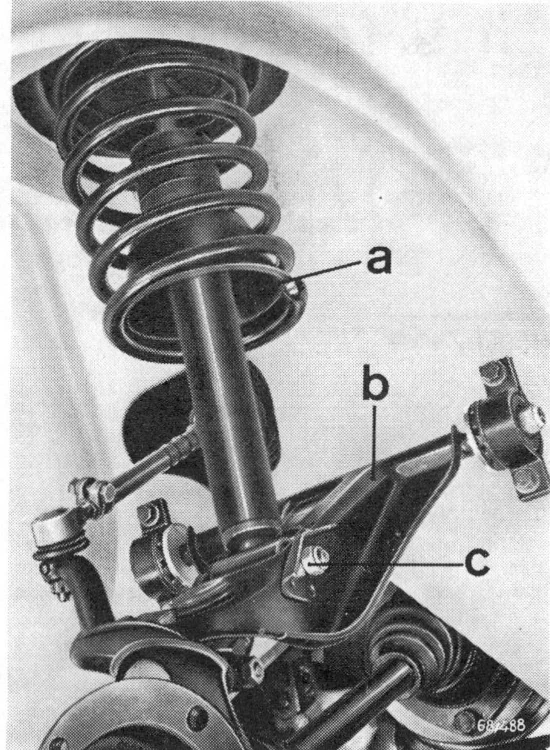
FIG 9:2 Disconnecting the spring leg from the upper wishbone

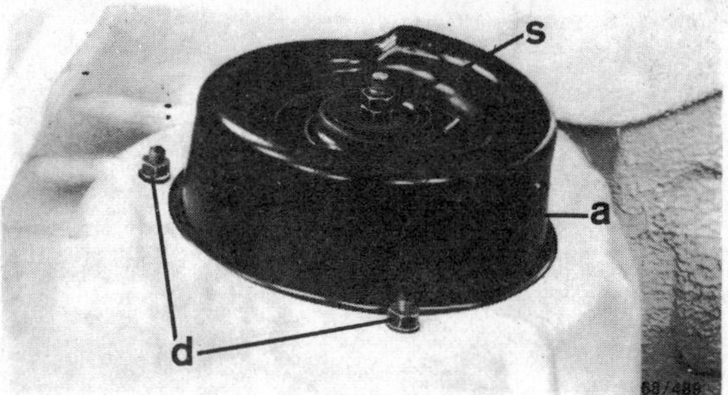
FIG 9:3 Disconnecting the upper spring mountings

FIG 9:4 Removing the spring and damper assembly

same time, keep the parts for the left and right side units separate for correct refitting. If springs or spring rings are to be renewed, make sure that correctly matching parts are obtained from the suppliers.

Reassembly:

The ring **h** must be placed in the retainer **d** so that the lug **N** is fitted in the notch **A**, as shown in **FIG 9:7**. When fitting the spring, make sure that the front end of the spring is engaged in the notch in the rubber ring **h**. Before compressing the spring, place stop pad **g** into the spring.

Compress the spring in the special tool, then slide in the damper and add parts **g, f, e, c** and **b**. Note that the side play between the spring and spring retainer must be at least 2 mm all round, in the fitted position. Turn the spring the other way round if necessary. Noisy operation may result if the spring is touching the retainer.

Before tightening the damper upper retaining nuts, make sure that the bore for the lower damper fixing screw is parallel to the flat on the spring retainer. Tighten the upper damper retaining nuts and lock them together. Release the compressor and remove the spring leg assembly.

Refitting:

Refitting the spring leg assembly to the car is a reversal of the removal instructions, making sure that the flat on the spring retainer is facing to the centre of the car.

9:3 Drive shafts and wheel hubs

Removal:

Refer to **FIG 9:8** and remove the drive shaft **a** from the brake disc **c**, taking care of the insulating washer **d** between the shaft and the brake disc. Unscrew the mounting screws **f** in **FIG 9:9** and take out the setscrew. Remove the cotterpin and unscrew the castle nut **g**. Extract the track rod ball joint **h** from the steering knuckle arm **e** as shown in **FIG 9:10,** using a universal joint extractor **i**. Remove the drive shaft and hub assembly, complete with steering knuckle, from the car.

FIG 9:5 Compressing the spring in the special tool

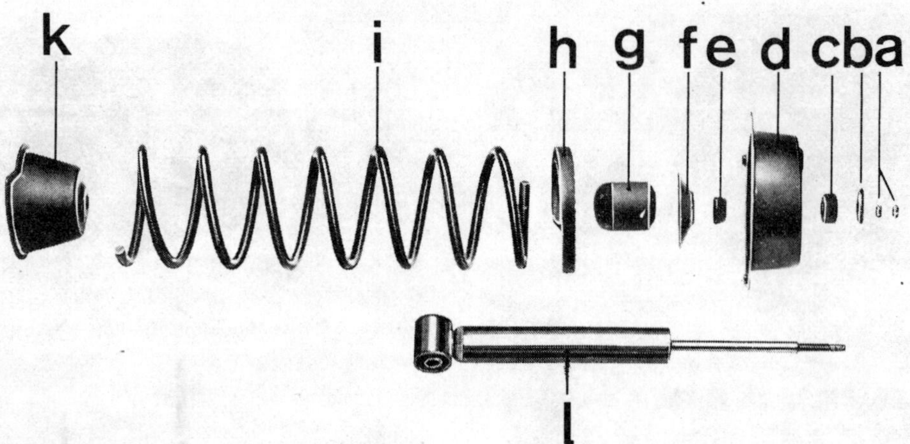

FIG 9:6 Spring and damper components

Dismantling:

Clamp the steering knuckle in a vice as shown in **FIG 9:11**. Pull out the cotterpin **f** and remove the castle locking cap **g**. Remove the nut and pull off spacer **h**. Fasten the intermediate flange tool V-23 to the hub and fasten the extractor tool V-26 to the flange with the wheel screws. Clamp the drive shaft and extractor assembly in a vice as shown in **FIG 9:12** and press the drive shaft from the steering knuckle.

Clamp the steering knuckle **g** in a vice as shown in **FIG 9:13** and use special screws **x** (tool V-17) and washers **y** to press out the wheel hub **a**. Take off the spacer, Nilos ring and the ballbearing inner ring. Place the steering knuckle on a piece of suitable tubing for support, then drive out the ballbearing outer ring with a drift. Remove the retaining rings and press out the second outer ballbearing ring.

Slightly press out the second ballbearing inner ring, Nilos ring and spacer bushing as shown in **FIG 9:13**. Extract the spacer bushing and ballbearing inner ring, placing the pressure piece **b** into the hub and using a puller as shown in **FIG 9:14**. **FIG 9:15** shows the components of the steering knuckle and wheel hub. Examine all parts and renew any found worn or damaged. Always fit a new spacer bushing **e**. Clean off all old grease before reassembly.

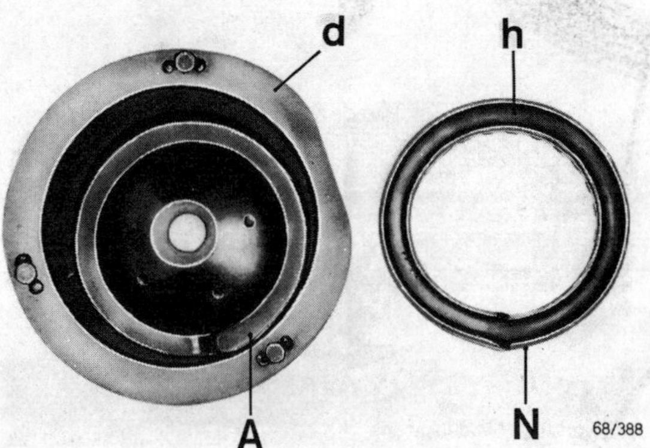

FIG 9:7 Spring retainer details

Reassembly:

Fit the retaining rings **i** and **l**. Press in the outer rings, preferably with driver tool VG-20. Fill the space between the two outer rings with approximately 50 g. of Calypsol 5974.LS.5999 grease.

Place the spacer **a** and Nilos ring **b** onto the wheel hub. Press on the ballbearing inner ring **d** and fit the new spacer bushing **e**. Place the hub **a** into the pre-assembled steering knuckle and press in the second ballbearing inner ring **f**. Using the special outer drive shaft installer tool, press the drive shaft into the steering knuckle in the following manner. Screw the threaded insert **a** in **FIG 9:16** onto the drive shaft. Apply thick grease to spacer **n** (flat side towards the ballbearing) and to the Nilos ring **m** and stick these parts to the drive shaft. Push the drive shaft into the fitted wheel hub. Put on the tool spindle **b** and bushing **c** and screw on the nut **d**. Fit the drive shaft as shown in **FIG 9:17**, making sure that the spacer does not move out of its proper position.

Refit the drive shaft and steering knuckle in the reverse order of removal. Check the wheel bearing adjustment as described in **Section 9:7** and the front wheel tracking as described in **Chapter 10**.

9:4 Renewing drive shaft rubber boots

FIGS 9:18 and **9:19** show the components of the drive shafts. Only a 96.5 mm diameter band clip or a Noppen clip can be used to mount the outer rubber boot **c**. Under no circumstances must any other type of clip be used, as the clamp screw on the clip will contact the wishbone joint during suspension movement and be damaged.

1 Remove the drive shaft assembly as previously described and thoroughly clean the outside of the assembly. Remove both clamps or clips and slide the rubber boot off the Rzeppa joint. Clean the joint with methylated spirits and dry with compressed air.

2 Clamp the drive shaft in a vice as shown in **FIG 9:21**. Spread open the snap ring **b** with special pliers **a** and at the same time deliver a powerful blow to the polygon shaft with a plastic or rubber hammer. The pretensioned disc springs press the housing upwards somewhat.

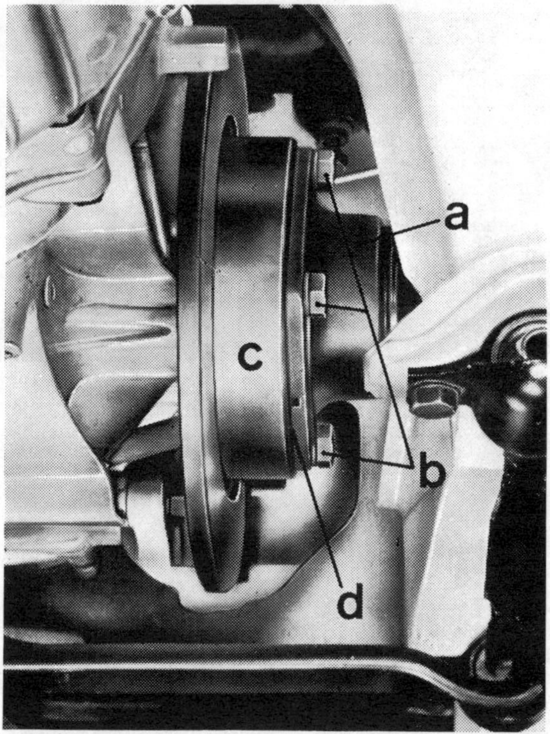

FIG 9:8   Removing the drive shaft from the brake disc

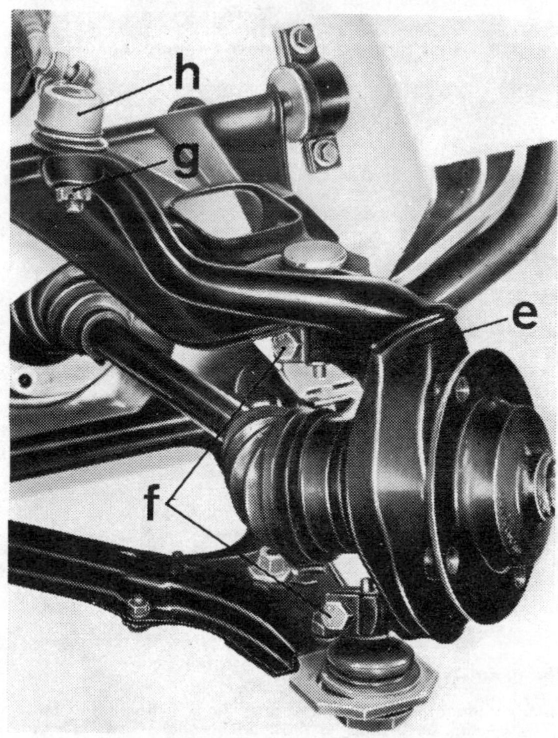

FIG 9:9   Disconnecting the steering knuckle

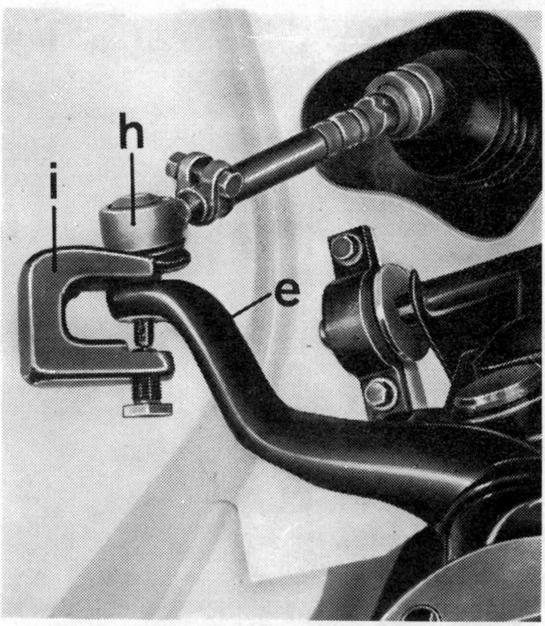

FIG 9:10   Pressing out the track rod end ball joint

FIG 9:11   Removing the castle nut and spacer

FIG 9:12   Pressing the drive shaft from the steering knuckle

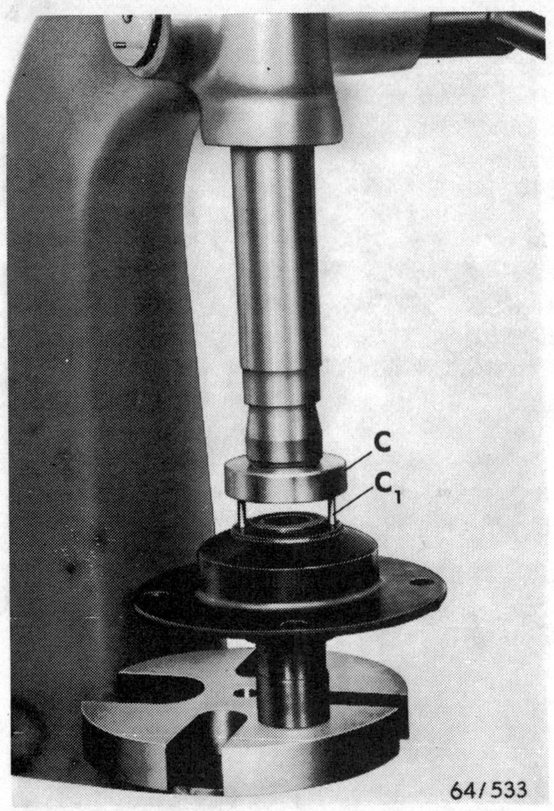

FIG 9:13 Pressing the inner ring with the pressure plate **c** and pins **c1**

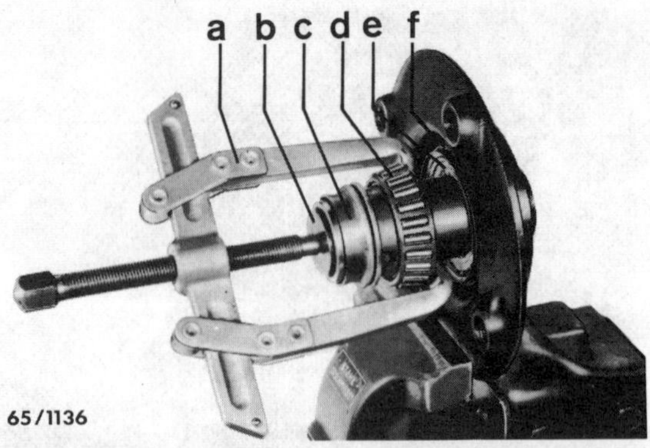

FIG 9:14 Extracting the spacer ring and bearing from the wheel hub

Key to Fig 9:14   a Extractor tool   b Pressure piece
c Spacer bushing   d Ballbearing inner ring   e Nilos ring
f Spacer

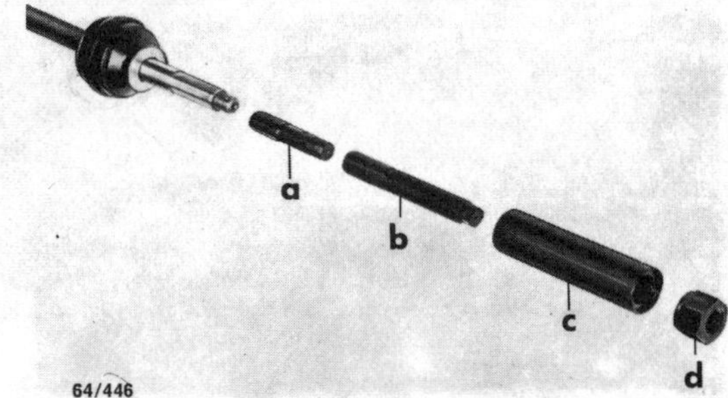

FIG 9:16 The drive shaft installer tool

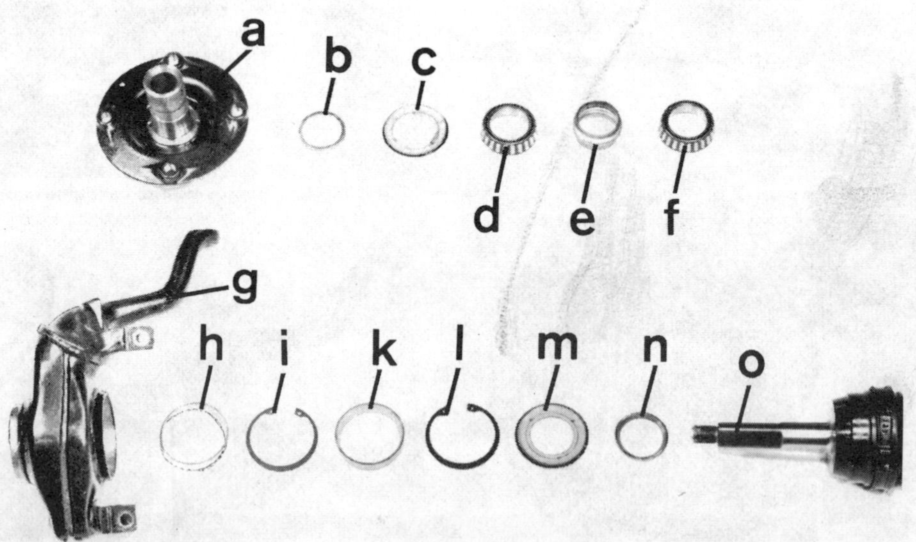

FIG 9:15 Components of the steering knuckle and wheel hub

Key to Fig 9:15   a Wheel hub   b Spacer   c Nilos ring   d Bearing inner ring   e Spacer bushing   f Bearing inner ring
g Steering knuckle   h Bearing outer ring   i Retaining ring   k Bearing outer ring   l Retaining ring   m Nilos ring
n Spacer   o Drive shaft

FIG 9:17 Pressing the drive shaft into the steering knuckle

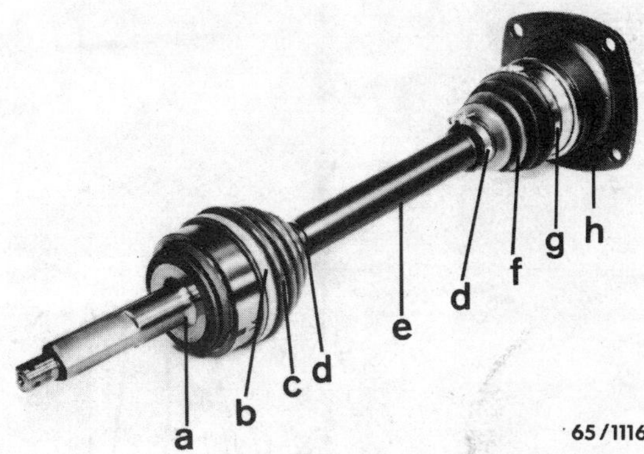

FIG 9:18 The drive shaft assembly. For key see FIG 9:20

Drive the housing off the shaft as shown in **FIG 9:22** and pull the rubber boot from the shaft. Loosen the clamp or clip and remove the inner rubber boot.

3 Place new rubber boots in position. Refer to **FIG 9:23**. Place two disc springs **b** on the inner drive shaft with their domed side facing outwards, then slide on pressure ring **c** with its slanting side facing outwards. Place a new snap ring **a** in **FIG 9:24** in the groove in the housing. Both ends fit in the machined groove as shown by the arrow **b**. Carefully slide the Rzeppa joint onto the inner drive shaft so that the snap ring starts into place. Without holding the snap ring, drive in the Rzeppa joint as shown in **FIG 9:21** until the snap ring snaps into place in the inner drive shaft groove. Fill each joint with 60 cc of Molykote grease BR2.

4 Slide the rubber boot on the Rzeppa joint and retain with the correct type of band or clip. Make sure that the end of the clip **b** faces the direction of shaft rotation as shown in **FIG 9:25**. Tighten the clamp by hand as tightly as possible, then secure by pressing the nose **c** together with pincers. Mount the boot so that the small collar is over the shaft collar and that the folds are equally spaced. Fit the clamp **d**. The inner boot is then fitted in similar manner.

9:5 Removing and refitting upper wishbone assembly

Removal:

Disconnect the lower spring leg mounting at the upper wishbone as described in **Section 9:2**. Disconnect the wishbone from the steering knuckle. Take out the four screws **b** in **FIG 9:26** and remove the upper wishbone **a**.

Dismantling:

Refer to **FIG 9:27**. Unscrew the nuts **f**, take off bearing **e** and washers **d**. Remove retaining ring **c**. Press out the support joint **b**, using a suitable tubular support under the wishbone when doing so. Examine all parts and renew any found worn or damaged.

Reassembly:

This is a reversal of the dismantling procedure, again using a tubular support when pressing in the support joint **b**.

Refitting:

Before fitting the upper wishbone, the lower wishbone assembly must be removed as described in the next section, in order that the special adjusting tool may be

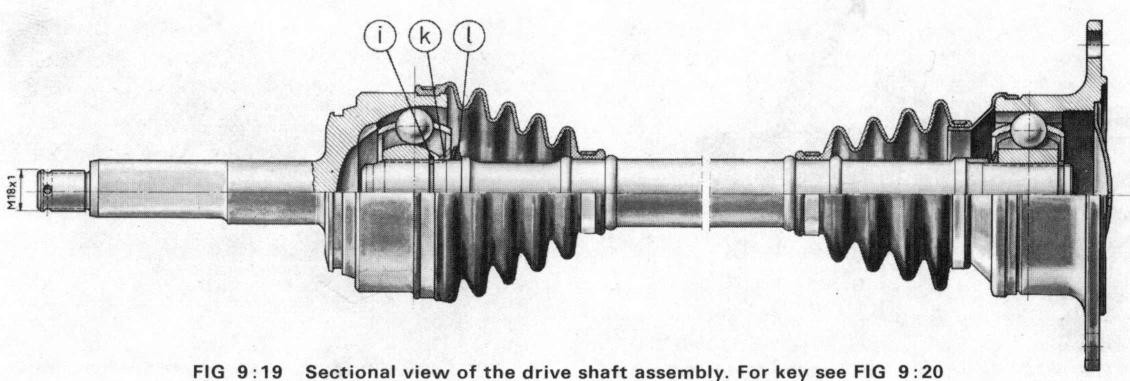

FIG 9:19 Sectional view of the drive shaft assembly. For key see FIG 9:20

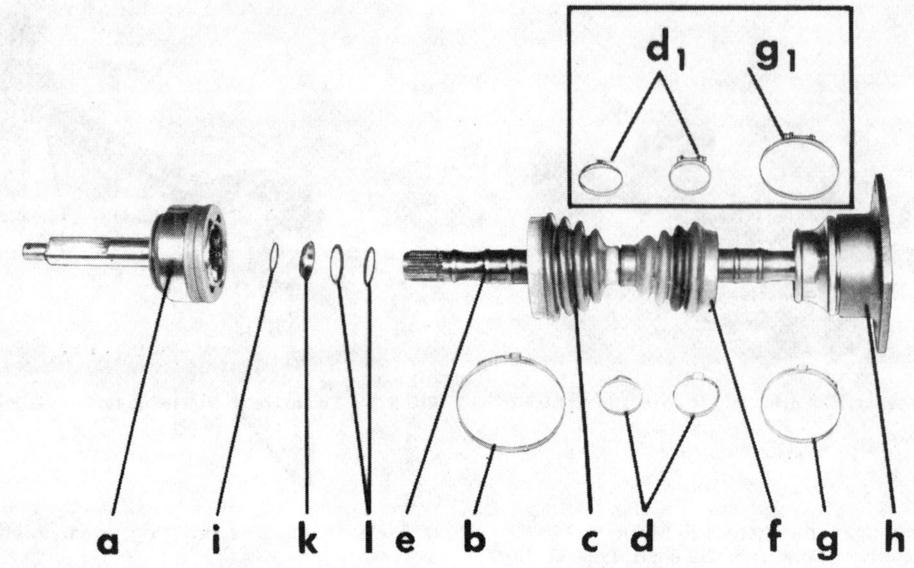

FIG 9:20   Components of the drive shaft

Key to Figs 9:18, 9:19 and 9:20   **a** Outer drive shaft with Rzeppa joint   **b** Clamp   **c** Outer rubber boot   **d** Clamp
e Inner drive shaft   **f** Inner rubber boot   **g** Clamp   **h** Rzeppa joint   **i** Snap ring   **k** Pressure ring   **l** Disc springs

Removing the snap ring

FIG 9:22   Driving off the housing

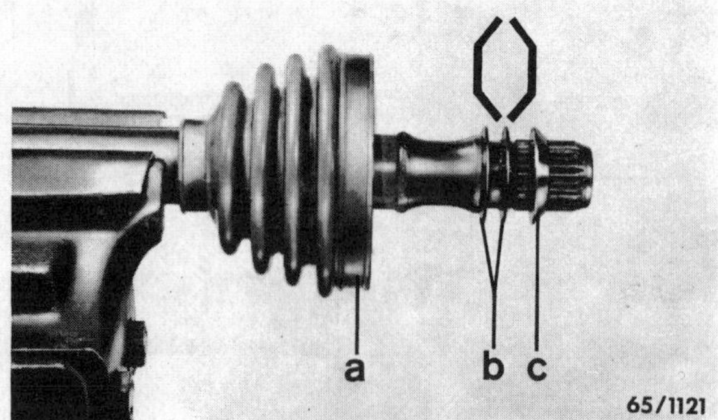

FIG 9:23   Fitting disc springs and pressure ring

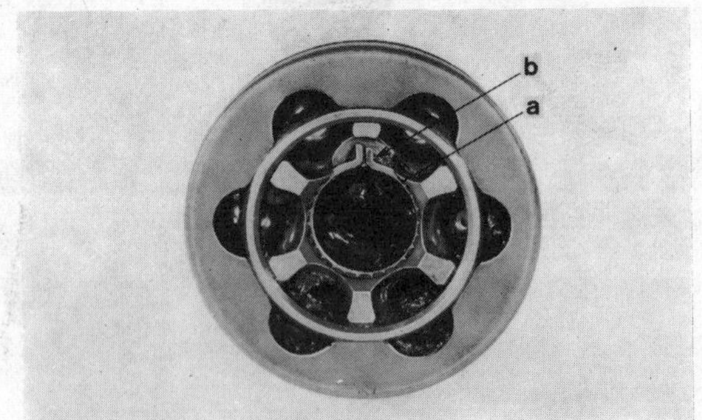

FIG 9:24   Fitting the snap ring to the housing

104

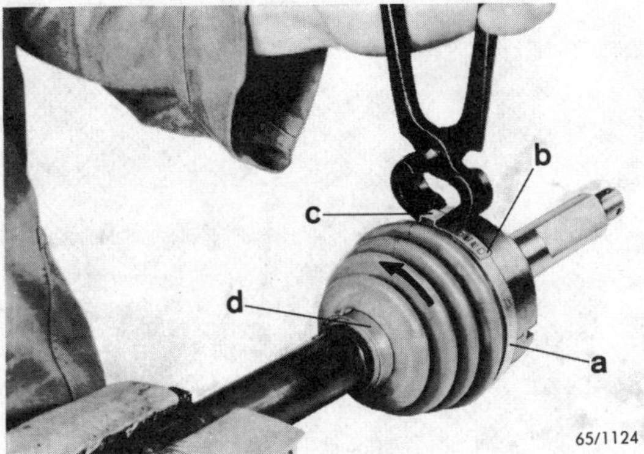

FIG 9:25   Fitting the clamp to the rubber boot

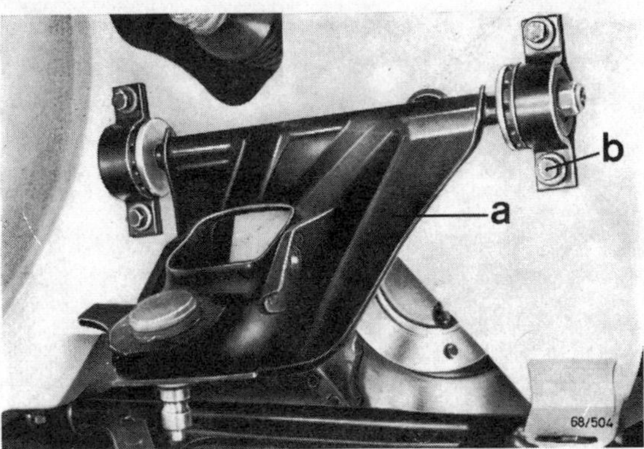

FIG 9:26   Removing the upper wishbone

used to correctly align the upper wishbone. The special tool is V-101 for the left side of the car, V-102 for the right side of the car. The longer arm of the tool must always be situated towards the front of the car when the tool is in use.

Mount the special tool in the lower wishbone mountings as shown in **FIG 9:28**. Turn the arms of the tool upwards and bring the upper wishbone into position and install the mounting screws. Angle the wishbone to a position where the untensioned spring leg can be connected, then tighten the wishbone mountings fully to a torque of 16 lb ft. Refit the remaining components in the reverse order of removal.

9:6 Anti-roll bar and lower wishbone assembly

Removal:

Jack up the car clear of the suspension and safely support it. Remove the front road wheels. Refer to **FIG 9:29** and detach the anti-roll bar **a** by removing the screws **b** on both sides of the car. Detach the lower wishbone at the points **e** in **FIG 9:30** and at the steering swivel, then remove the unit from the car.

Dismantling:

Refer the **FIG 9:31**. Unscrew the nuts at points **b** and **c** and remove the bearings and washers. Remove the retaining ring **h**, unscrew the nut **g**, take off disc springs **f** and pull the wishbone joint **d** out of the joint plate **e**. Remove the screws **i** and pull out the joint plate. Examine all parts and renew any found worn or damaged.

Reassembly:

Put the wishbone joint **d** into the joint plate **e**. Fit the disc springs **f**, tighten the nut **g** and fit the retaining ring **h**. Finish reassembly in the reverse order of removal.

Renewing anti-roll bar bearings:

If the anti-roll bar rubber bearing blocks are defective, remove the old blocks and fit new parts according to the dimensions shown in **FIG 9:32**.

Refitting:

This is the reverse of the removal instructions. The rear bearing **f** of the lower wishbone shown in **FIG 9:33** should be situated exactly between the points **g** on the bearing bracket **h**. The mounting brackets must be finally

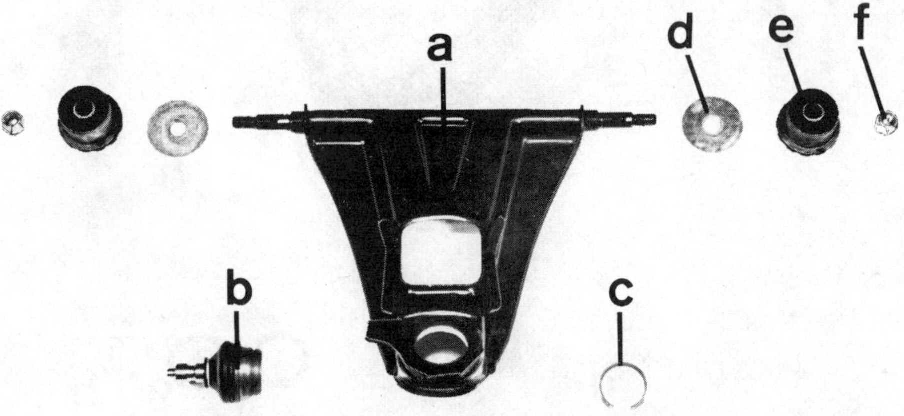

FIG 9:27   Components of the upper wishbone assembly

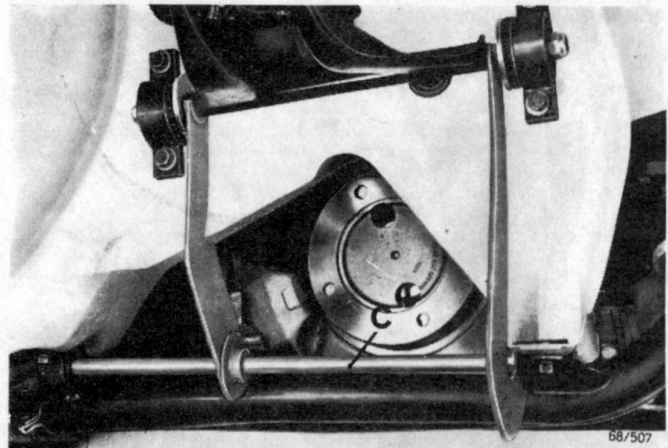

FIG 9:28 Fitting the special tool for upper wishbone alignment

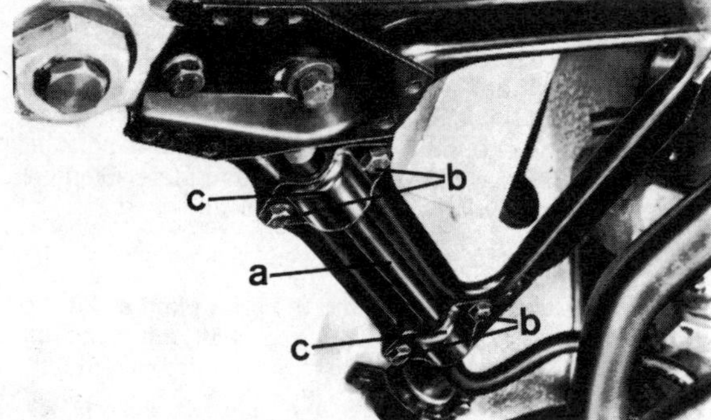

FIG 9:29 Detaching the anti-roll bar

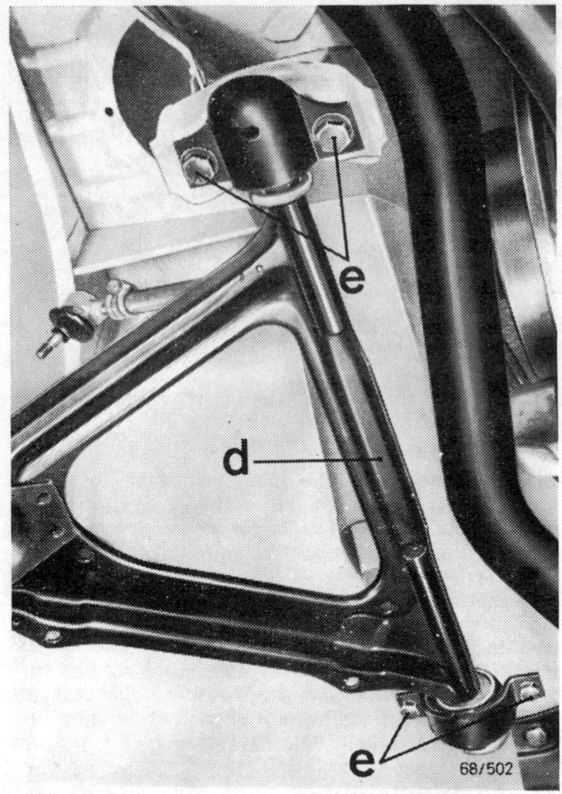

FIG 9:30 Detaching the lower wishbone

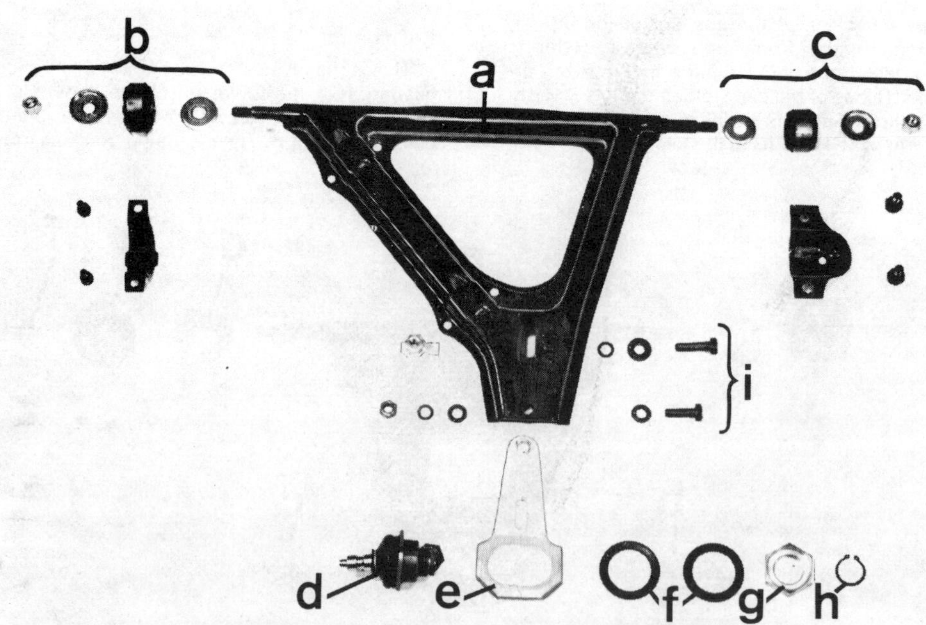

FIG 9:31 Components of the lower wishbone assembly

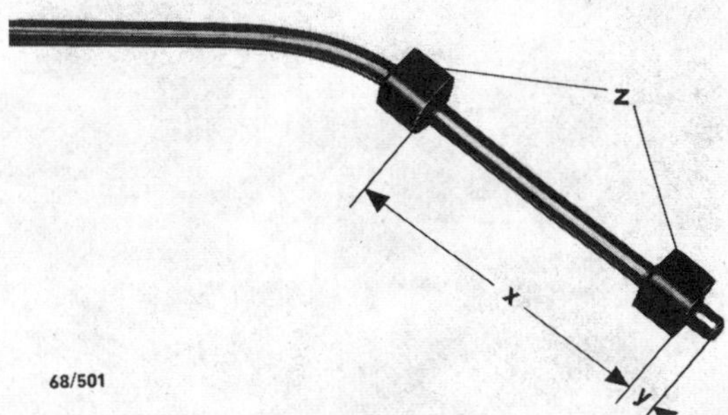

FIG 9:32   Anti-roll bar rubber bearing positions

Key to Fig 9:32   **x** 207 mm (8.15 inches)   **y** 12.5 mm (.492 inch)   **z** Rubber bearings

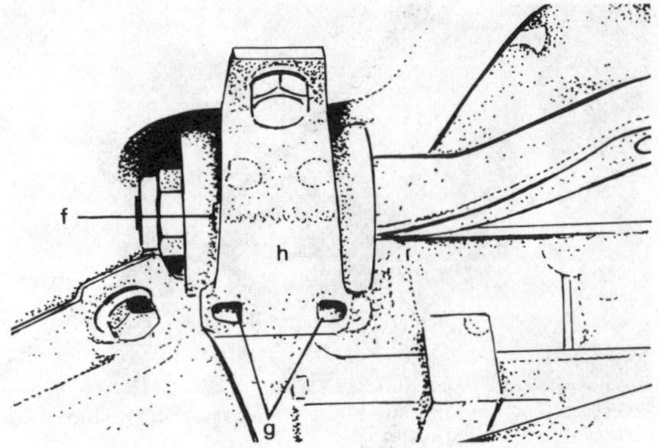

FIG 9:33   Refitting the lower wishbone assembly

tightened when the steering knuckle is fitted and the components are in their original positions. Tighten the mounting screws to 16 lb ft at the rear, and 31 lb ft at the front. Check the castor and camber angles as described in **Section 9:8** and the tracking as described in **Chapter 10**.

9:7 Checking and adjusting front wheel bearings

Front wheel bearing play must be .04 to .07 mm (.0016 to .0027 inch). The play must first be checked, then adjusted in one of two ways, according to the measurement taken.

Checking:

Jack up the front of the car and remove the road wheels. Refer to **FIG 9:34**. Position the special tools V-104 (retaining screw **a**), G-43 (gauge **b**) and V-1 (wheel hub lever **c**) on the hub. When doing so, the gauge should be pretensioned to approximately 1 mm and should rest against the steering knuckle **d**. By moving the lever **c** in the direction of the arrow, it is possible to check the wheel bearing play on the dial gauge. If the play is too large or too small, the bearing must be adjusted in the appropriate following manner.

FIG 9:34   Mounting the special tools to check front wheel bearing play

FIG 9:35   Special tools mounted to adjust the front wheel bearing

FIG 9:36   Checking the clearance between the hub and nut with a feeler gauge

FIG 9:38   Steering geometry adjustment points

FIG 9:39   Disconnecting the dampers from the rear axle assembly

FIG 9:37   Loosening the wheel bearing with the special tools

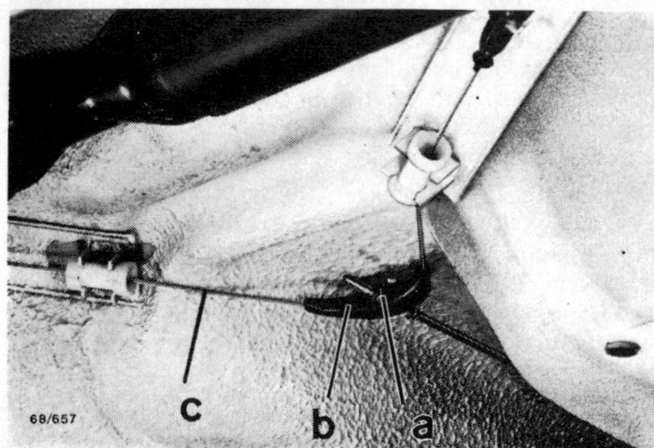

FIG 9:40   Disconnecting the handbrake cable

Adjustment, play too large:

Remove the cotterpin shown at **e** FIG 9:34, remove the castle nut **f** and unscrew the nut **f**2. Position special tools V-2, V-3, V-5 and V-8, fixtures for pulling in the outer drive shaft, as shown in FIG 9:35 then mount the dial gauge as before. Tighten the nut **g** until the bearing play is as specified, checking in the manner previously described. When checking it is always necessary to loosen the nut **g** and pull out the bushing **h** somewhat.

After the correct setting has been achieved, remove the special tools, tighten the nut **f**2 and replace the castle nut **f** in such a manner that the cotterpin can be fitted and locked.

Adjustment, play too small:

Pull out the cotterpin and remove the castle nut. Unscrew the nut **f** and remove the shim. Unscrew the nut shown at **a** in FIG 9:36 until a gap of 1 mm maximum exists between the nut and the hub. Place tool V-12 **b** in position. Position the special tool V-26 extractor shown at **k** in FIG 9:37 and the special tool intermediate flange **l**. By tightening the tool nut as shown the shaft will be brought back to the nut which was previously loosened for this purpose. By this means sufficient bearing play is assured. Remove the special tools and carry out the adjustments as detailed for a bearing play which is too large, given previously.

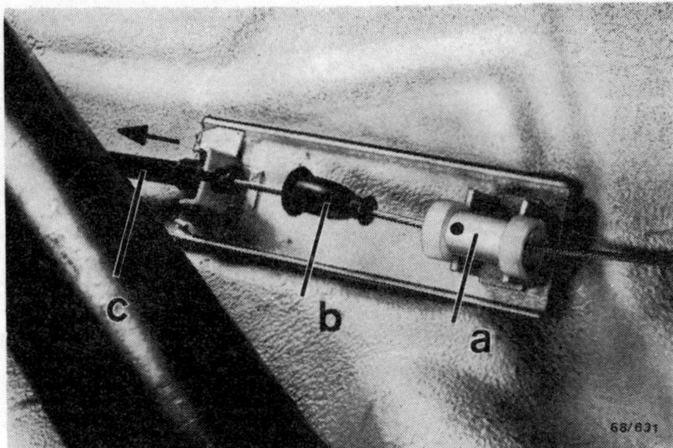

FIG 9:41   Removing the handbrake cable

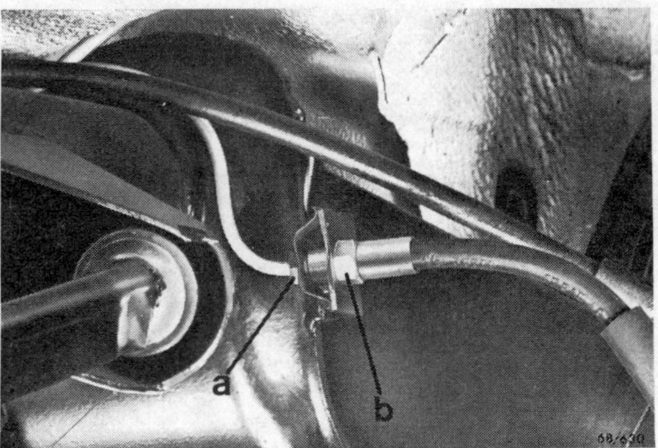

FIG 9:42   Disconnecting the brake line

9:8 Suspension geometry

As special equipment is necessary to carry out the operations accurately, the car should be taken to a service station or wheel and tyre specialist for castor and camber angles to be checked and adjusted.

Castor is adjusted by turning the eccentric nut **a** in **FIG 9:38** after loosening the nut **b** and screw **c**. An equal figure should be obtained on each wheel, then the nuts **b** and screws **c** tightened. Camber is adjusted by turning the eccentric nut **e** after loosening the nut **d**. Retighten the nut when the adjustment is correct.

Castor and camber angles are given in **Technical Data** in the **Appendix**.

9:9 Removing and refitting rear axle assembly

The rear axle assembly can be removed from the car as a complete unit and refitted in the same manner. It is essential, however, to use special tool H-100 when refitting the unit, to ensure correct alignment with the car body.

Removal:

Remove the rear silencer and disconnect both dampers from the rear axle assembly as shown in **FIG 9:39**. Jack up the car and support it safely on floor stands placed beneath the body clear of the rear axle unit. Remove the rear wheels. Remove the nut **a** and metal grommet **b** shown in **FIG 9:40** to slacken the handbrake cable **c**. Refer to **FIG 9:41**. Push out the protective

FIG 9:43   Removing the axle assembly mounting screws

plastic sleeve **a** on the right and left sides. Push out the rubber boot **b**. Pull out the handbrake cable **c** in the direction of the arrow, then pull the cable downwards through the slot in the holding bracket.

Disconnect the brake line **a** in **FIG 9:42** from the brake hose **b** on the right side of the rear axle. Seal the brake line to prevent fluid loss with a dust cap taken from the brake bleeding connection and seal the hose with a suitable plug. Support the cross-tube and rear axle assembly, then remove the mounting screws shown at **a** and **b** in **FIG 9:43** from both sides of the car. Lower the rear axle assembly and remove it from beneath the car. **FIG 9:44** shows the complete rear axle assembly.

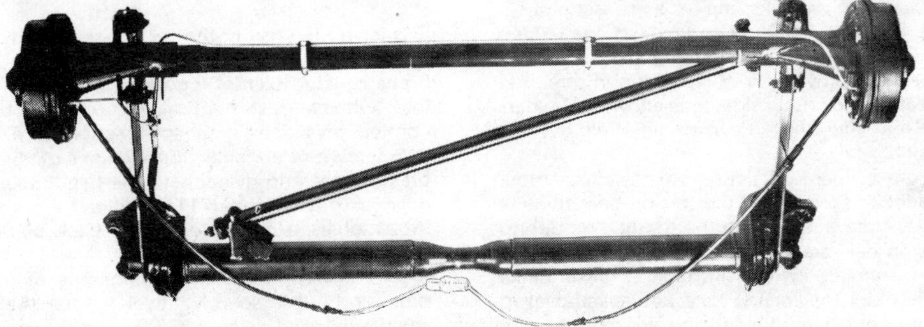

FIG 9:44   The rear axle assembly complete

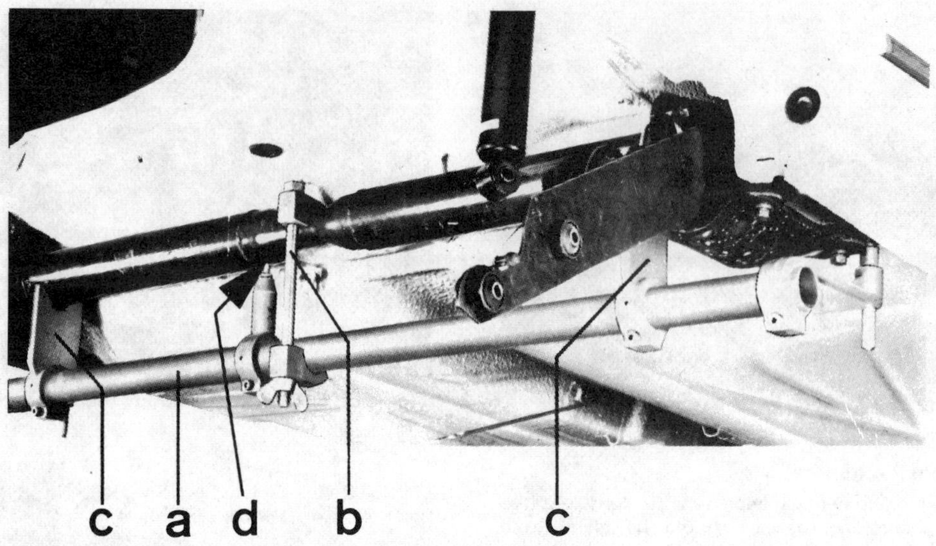

FIG 9:45 The use of the special gauge for refitting. Rear axle tube omitted for clarity

Refitting:

Attach the cross-tube with the screws **a** and **b** shown in **FIG 9:43**. Do not tighten these screws as the unit must remain moveable. Attach the centring gauge H-100 **a** with clamp **b** onto the cross-tube, as shown in **FIG 9:45**. The prisms **c** are resting on the cross-tube and the centring bolt **d** has to be inserted into the measuring hole provided in the cross-tube. **The bolt d must not be forced into the hole nor must it be distorted.**

Move the cross-tube laterally in order to be able to insert the bolts **e** on the right and left sides into the holes **f** provided in the car body, as shown in **FIG 9:46**. **Do not use force when fitting these bolts.** Tighten the cross-tube mounting screws and check to make sure that the bolts **e** can still be inserted in the holes **f** without using force. Remove the centring gauge. Refit the remaining components in the reverse order of removal.

On completion, bleed the brakes and adjust the handbrake cable as described in **Chapter 11.**

9:10 Suspension arms and torsion bars

Removal:

Remove the rear axle assembly as described in **Section 9:9.** Refer to **FIG 9:47** and extract one torsion bar from the suspension arm, using a puller as shown. The torsion bars are provided with 40 teeth on the inner side and 44 teeth on the outer side, thus allowing the bars to be pulled out after they are released. Pull out the extracted torsion bar.

Unscrew both suspension arms from the cross-tube, collecting the lockwashers. Pull the torsion bar which is still in the cross-tube out through the toothed mounting tube. The torsion bars are marked for right and left sides with an R or L stamped on the end face. If these marks are not visible, mark the torsion bars before removal in order to ensure correct refitting to the appropriate side of the car.

If the rubber mounting shown at **a** in **FIG 9:48** is to be renewed, use special tool H-103 to press the mounting in and out as shown. Apply soapy water to the rubber mounting as a lubricant to assist fitting. Note that the rubber mountings which are pressed into the flange of the suspension arms cannot be renewed.

Refitting:

Attach the suspension arms to the cross-tube, leaving the mounting screws loose. When tightening the fixings, including the .73 inch clearance make sure that the measurement **x** in **FIG 9:49** is 8.46 ±.14 inch on both sides. To ensure this, adjust special tool H-101 according to the measurement and screw it on to the cross-tube as shown.

When fitting the torsion bars, slide special tool H-102 grip sleeve approximately half an inch onto the 44 tooth side of the bar and tighten it. Keep turning the torsion bar by one tooth at a time until it will slide in smoothly, this being when the inner and outer teeth are correctly engaged. **FIG 9:50** shows this operation.

9:11 Rear stub axle and hub assemblies

Removal:

Jack up the rear of the car and remove the road wheel. Detach the brake lines from the wheel cylinder on the brake backing plate. Plug the brake line to prevent fluid loss with a dust cap taken from the brake bleeder connection and seal the connection bore at the wheel cylinder with a suitable plug. Remove the brake drum and brake shoes and disconnect the handbrake cable, all as described in **Chapter 11.** Unscrew the six screws and lockwashers **a** and take off the back plate **b** and stub axle **c** as shown in **FIG 9:51.**

FIG 9:52 shows the components of the rear brake drum and hub assembly. Lever out the shaft seal with a screwdriver and discard it. Take out the inner ring of the taper roller bearing. Remove the outer ring of the inner

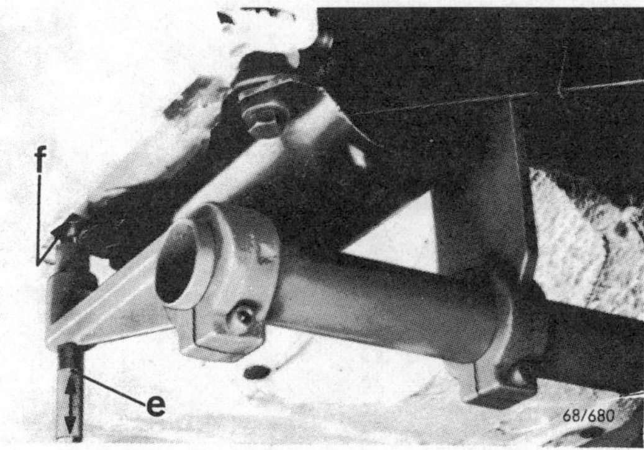

FIG 9:46 Aligning the cross-tube

FIG 9:47 Removing a torsion bar

FIG 9:48 Pressing out the rubber mounting

FIG 9:49 Setting the suspension arms at the correct angle

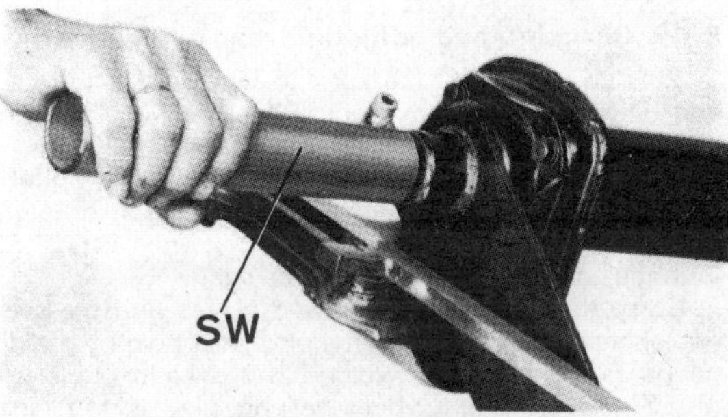

FIG 9:50 Refitting a torsion bar

taper roller bearing, using a suitable drift. For this purpose, three grooves are machined in the brake drum. Remove the circlip and remove the outer bearing rings in similar manner. Examine all parts after cleaning, renewing any found worn or damaged.

Refitting:

This is a reversal of the removal procedure. Make sure that the bearing rings are pressed fully home. Apply Calypsol grease to the roller bearings when refitting. Place a new shaft seal in position with the open side facing toward the bearings and drive it into position, keeping it square. Fill the space between the two roller bearings with approximately 30 g. of Calypsol grease.

FIG 9:51 Removing the brake backplate and the stub axle

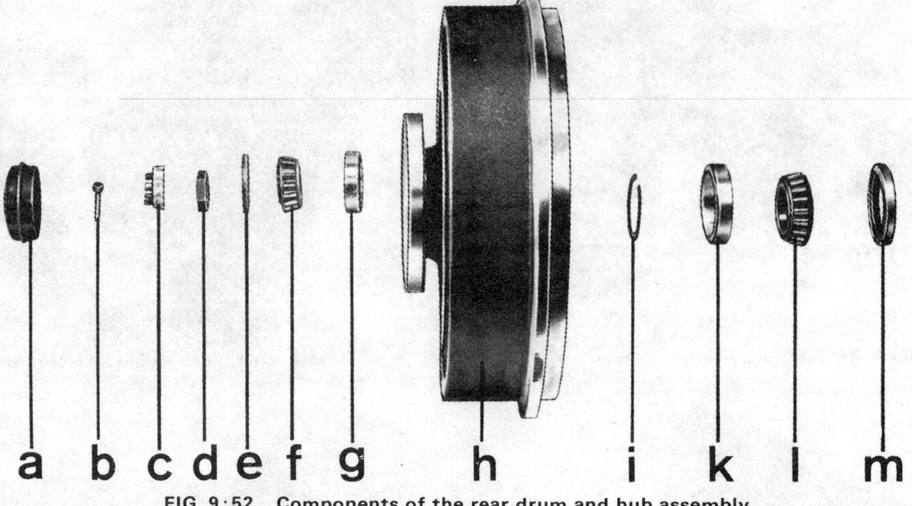

FIG 9:52   Components of the rear drum and hub assembly

Key to Fig 9:52   **a** Cap   **b** Cotterpin   **c** Castle nut   **d** Nut   **e** Washer   **f** Bearing inner ring   **g** Bearing outer ring
h Brake drum   **i** Circlip   **k** Bearing outer ring   **l** Bearing inner ring   **m** Shaft seal

On completion, adjust the wheel bearing play as described in **Section 9:12**, bleed the brakes and adjust the handbrake cable as described in **Chapter 11**. Fill the bearing cap with approximately 10 g of grease before refitting.

9:12 Checking and adjusting rear wheel bearings

Jack up the rear of the car and remove the hub caps and wheel trims. Remove one wheel bolt and lever off the grease cap. It is not necessary to remove the cotterpin and castle nut when checking the play. Fit a suitably threaded dial gauge clamp to the wheel bolt hole and mount a dial gauge in the holder as shown in **FIG 9:53**, with the gauge pin on the stub axle shaft.

Grasp the tyre at two opposed places and press the wheel in and out, checking the play as shown by the dial gauge. Play must be between .02 to .04 mm (.00078 to .00157 inch). If the wheel bearing play is too large, remove the cotterpin and castle nut must be removed. Carefully tighten the hexagon nut until the play is correct, then secure the nut with the castle nut and a new cotterpin.

FIG 9:53   Checking rear wheel bearing play

9:13 Fault diagnosis

(a) Wheel wobble

1 Worn hub bearings
2 Broken or weak front spring
3 Uneven tyre wear
4 Worn suspension components
5 Loose wheel fixings
6 Incorrect tracking
7 Worn suspension joints

(b) 'Bottoming' of suspension

1 Check 2 in (a)
2 Worn stop pads
3 Dampers not working

(c) Heavy steering

1 Defective wheel swivels
2 Wrong suspension geometry

(d) Excessive tyre wear

1 Check 4 and 6 in (a) and 2 in (c)

(e) Rattles

1 Check 2 in (a) and 1 in (c)
2 Worn suspension joints or bushes
3 Damper attachments loose
4 Front spring contacting spring retainer

(f) Excessive rolling

1 Check 2 in (a) and 3 in (b)

CHAPTER 10

THE STEERING SYSTEM

10:1 Description
10:2 The steering wheel
10:3 The steering column

10:4 The steering gear
10:5 Tracking
10:6 Fault diagnosis

10:1 Description

Rack and pinion steering gear is employed on all Audi 100 models. The pinion shaft is turned by the lower end of the steering column and moves the toothed rack to the left or right, transmitting the steering motion to the front wheels by means of the track rods and the steering arms on the wheel swivels. The design of the steering gear is such, that the steering operates progressively, that is, when the steering is near the straight-ahead position the ratio is 21.6:1 and is progressively reduced to 14.4:1 as the turning circle is tightened. The steering therefore becomes more direct with increasing lock applied.

For safety reasons a divided steering column, located at a certain angle, has been fitted. Additionally, a steering joint and a Hardy disc have been provided so that, in the event of a frontal collision, the column cannot move towards the inside of the car but will break away in a certain direction.

A rack and pinion assembly with or without a damper unit may be fitted and, in either case, the assembly cannot be dismantled and serviced in the event of failure. The unit is set up at the factory and, if defective, a new unit must be obtained and fitted.

10:2 The steering wheel

Removal:

Lever off the steering wheel pad in the direction of the arrow as shown in **FIG 10:1**. Unscrew and remove the steering wheel as shown in **FIG 10:2**.

Dismantling and reassembly:

Refer to **FIGS 10:3** and **10:4**. Remove the screw 6 and washer 7. Remove the horn bar 2, paying attention to the three each springs 5, washer 4 and contact rings 3. The insulating bushes 8 must be pressed in hole 12 of the horn bar from below, as shown in **FIG 10:4**.

If a new contact brush is to be fitted, make sure that the projection **N** of the brush engages in the cut-out **A** as shown in **FIG 10:5**. The horn bar upper section shown at 14 in **FIG 10:6** is pressed onto the horn bar 2 after the steering wheel has been refitted. Renew the plastic studs 15 if necessary, these being simply screwed into place.

Refitting:

This is the reverse of the removal procedure, tightening the steering wheel fixing to a torque of 36 lb ft.

FIG 10:1   Removing the steering wheel pad

FIG 10:2   Removing the steering wheel

FIG 10:5   Installing the contact brush in the holder

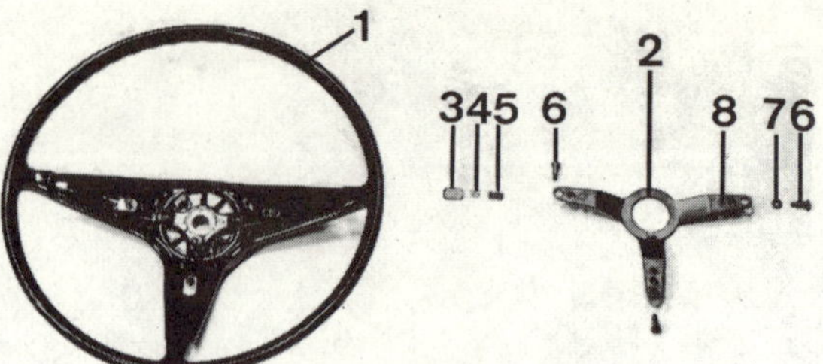
FIG 10:3   Steering wheel components

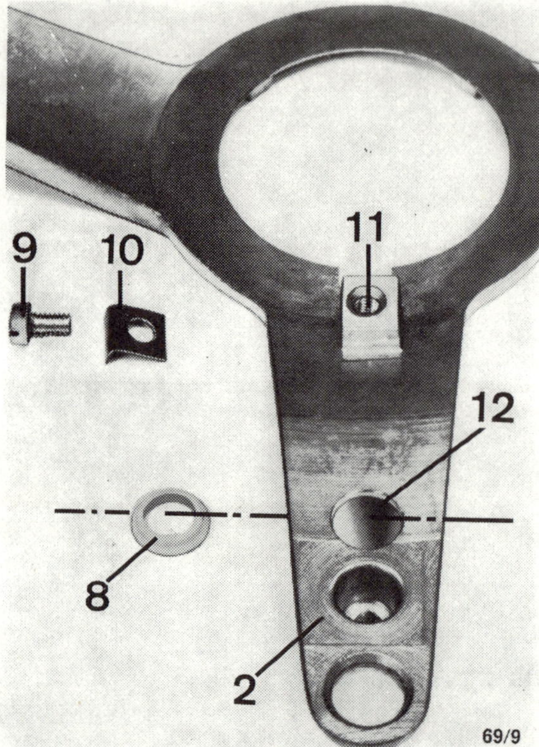
FIG 10:4   Steering wheel components

Key to Figs 10:3 and 10:4   1 Steering wheel   2 Horn bar
3 Contact ring   4 Toothed washer   5 Spring   6 Screw
7 Washer   8 Insulating bushing   9 Screw   10 Horn
cable clamp   11 Thread for 9   12 Hole for 8

10:3 The steering column

Removal:

Remove the steering wheel as described in **Section 10:2.** Remove the instrument panel trim **a** shown in **FIG 10:7.** Refer to **FIG 10:8** and unscrew and remove the slip ring **d** at point **e** and the casing **f** at point **g.** Pull the earth lead **h** off the slip ring. Remove the washers **i** shown in **FIG 10:9.** When refitting, the thicker washer must be fitted first with the cut-out facing downwards. Unscrew the gearlever **k** and press to one side. Unscrew tube **l** from the instrument panel at point **m,** upper.

Refer to **FIG 10:10.** Remove the combination switch **n** from tube **l,** pull off the white lead from the terminal **p**

of the combination switch. Separate the ignition lock connecting cable at the connections, noting the colours of the leads for correct refitting. Loosen clip 9 from the steering column and tube 6 and pinion **r** as shown in **FIG 10:11.** Pull out the screw. Loosen the lower tube mounting at point **m** in **FIG 10:11,** then pull out the steering column and tube assembly in the direction of the arrow.

Dismantling:

Refer to **FIG 10:13.** Remove the tube 6 from Hardy disc 5. When the tube is refitted the clip **S** must be upwards and the stop for the indicator self-cancelling

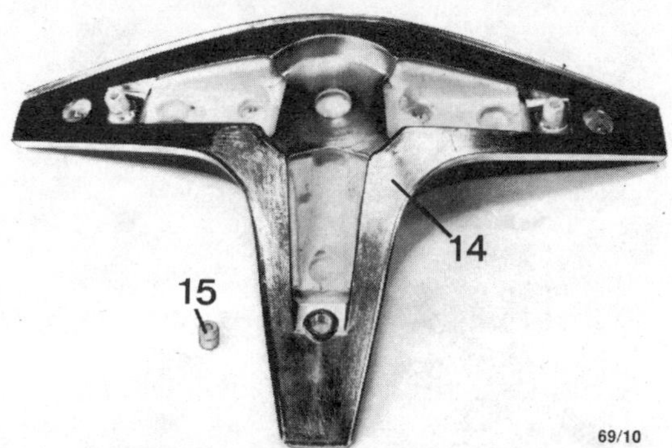

FIG 10:6   The horn bar and plastic studs

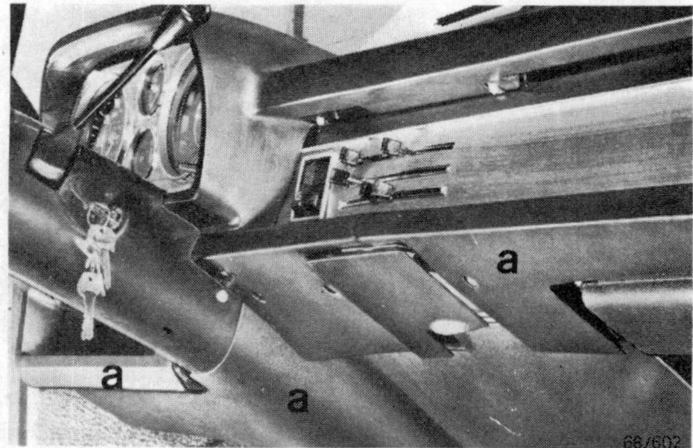

FIG 10:7   Removing the instrument panel trim

device **B** forwards. Pull the steering column 2 out of tube 1 somewhat, or press the tube downwards. Remove the snap ring 7 shown in **FIG 10:14** and pull off the support ring 8.

After loosening the connection, pull off the steering joint 3 and remove the spring, support ring and washer, these components being shown in **FIG 10:15**. When refitting the steering joint, refer to the note on steering column modifications at the end of this section, as modified screws 9 should be fitted. Remove the steering

column bearing 12 from the tube by pulling out the steering column 2. When refitting, first place the column in the tube then drive the bearing into position with a suitable length of metal tube. If necessary, the Hardy disc can be removed from the steering joint and dismantled. Drive the upper steering column bearing 12 out of the tube with a suitable drift.

Clean and inspect all parts, renewing any found worn or damaged. Grease the steering column bearings during reassembly.

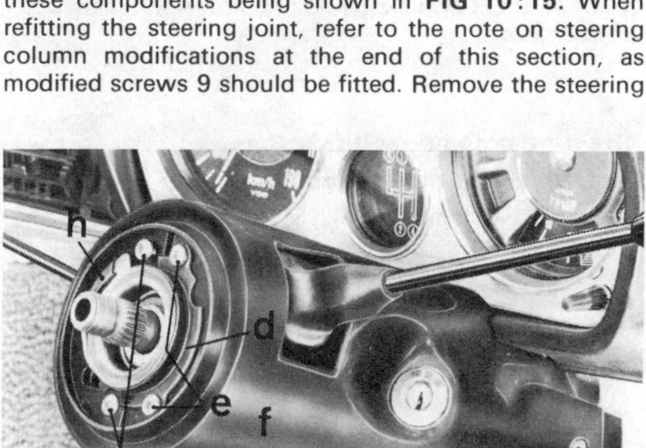

FIG 10:8   Removing the steering column casing

FIG 10:9   Upper steering column components

FIG 10:10   Removing the combination switch

FIG 10:11   Loosening the clip from the steering column

FIG 10:12   Removing the steering column assembly

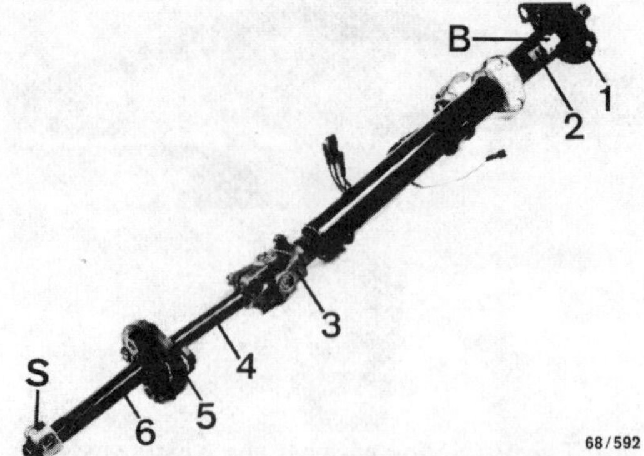

FIG 10:13   The steering column assembly

Key to Fig 10:13   1 Tube   2 Steering column
3 Steering joint   4 Intermediate shaft   5 Hardy disc
6 Tube   **B** Indicator self cancelling device   **S** Clip

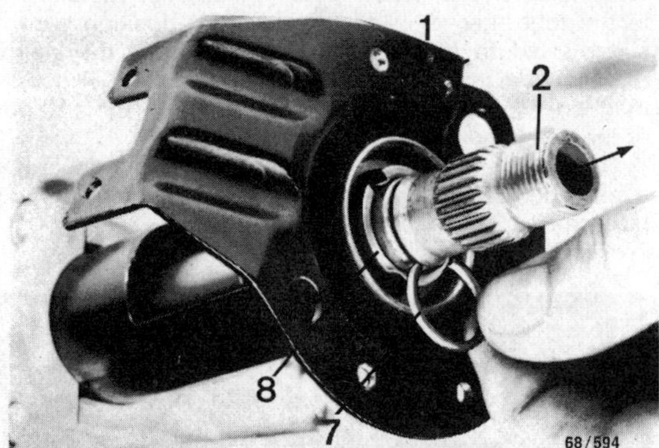

FIG 10:14   Removing the support ring

Reassembly and refitting:

This is a reversal of the dismantling and removal instructions, paying attention to the notes concerning reassembly.

Steering column modifications:
Steering joint mountings:

From chassis number 80/81.9.025.684 modified nuts and screws 9 in **FIG 10:15** are fitted. These are part number 10.340.4 screws and 8G nuts. Use only these screws and nuts when servicing any steering column assembly, including early types.

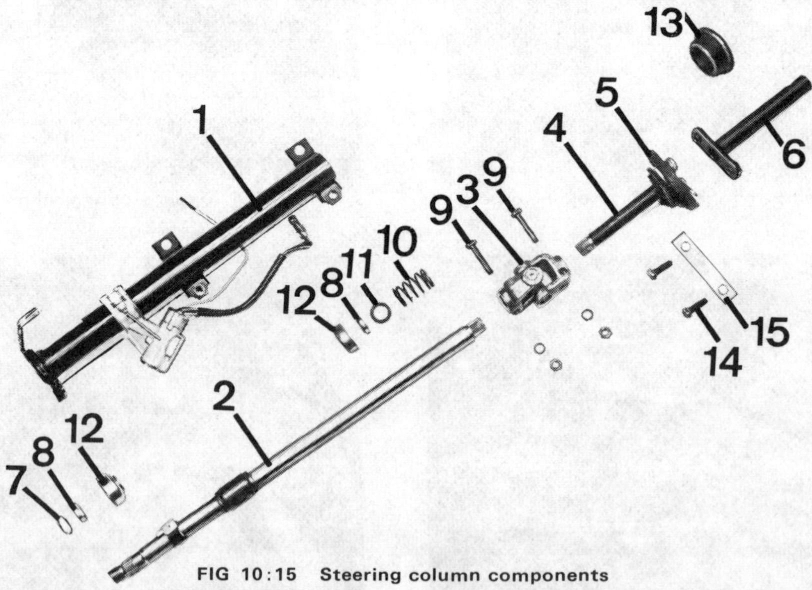

FIG 10:15   Steering column components

Key to Fig 10:15   1 Tube   2 Steering column   3 Steering joint   4 Intermediate shaft   5 Hardy disc   6 Tube
7 Snap ring   8 Support ring   9 Screw   10 Spring   11 Washer   12 Steering column bearing   13 Cap   14 Screw
15 Lock plate

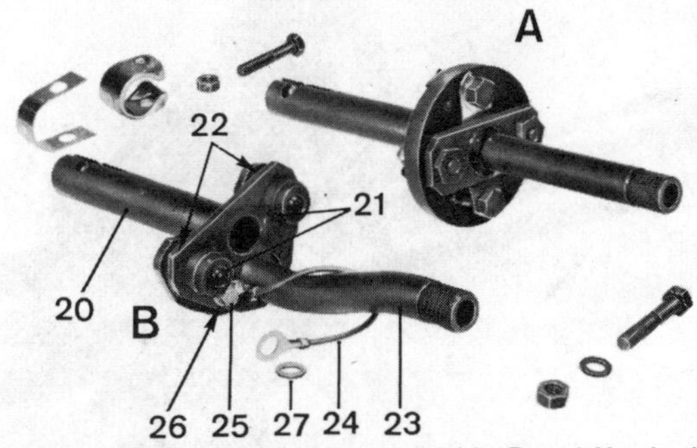

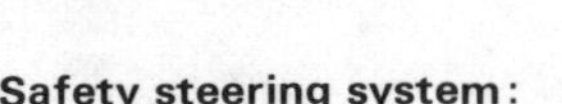

FIG 10:16   Safety steering assembly **B** and Hardy disc assembly **A**

Key to Fig 10:16   **A** Hardy disc assembly   **B** Safety steering system   20 Tube   21 Bushing   22 Sleeve   23 Intermediate shaft   24 Earth wire   25 Self-tapping screw   26/27 Washers

FIG 10:17   Installing bushings and sleeves in the safety system plate

Safety steering system:

From chassis number 80/81.01.026.044 LHD and 80/81.01.028.447 RHD a safety steering system is installed in series production. The Hardy disc is replaced by a joint and plug-in type safety element. Steering column removal and dismantling instructions are the same for both units. **FIG 10:16** shows the safety steering system **B** compared with the Hardy disc system **A**. If required, the safety steering system can be installed on cars with earlier systems, in the following manner.

Installation:

Remove the Hardy disc as described previously and detach the intermediate shaft from the disc. Refer to **FIG 10:17**. Press bushings 21 in the appropriate bores in

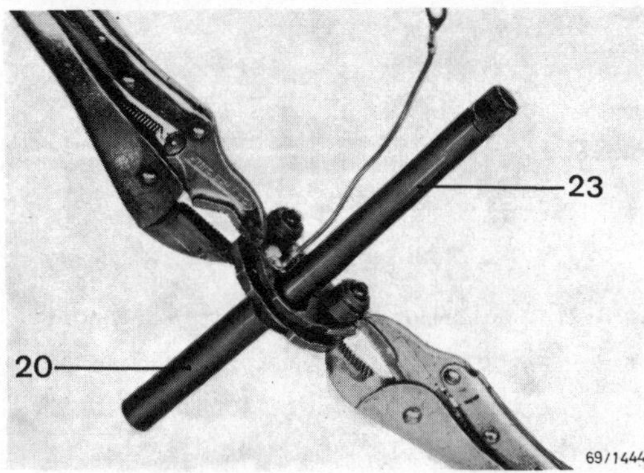

FIG 10:18   Clamping the tube and shaft together

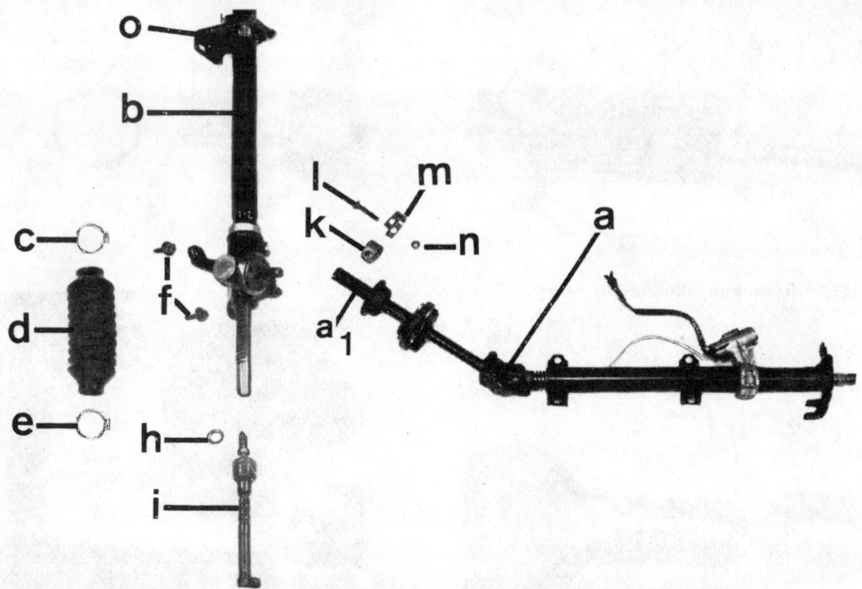

FIG 10:19   Components of the rack and pinion steering gear

Key to Fig 10:19   **a** Steering column   **a1** Tube   **b** Steering gear, LHD shown   **c** Hose clip   **d** Boot   **e** Hose clip   **f** Screw, washer and spring washer   **h** Lock plate   **i** Track rod   **k** Clip   **l** Screw   **m** Lock plate   **n** Nut   **o** Mount

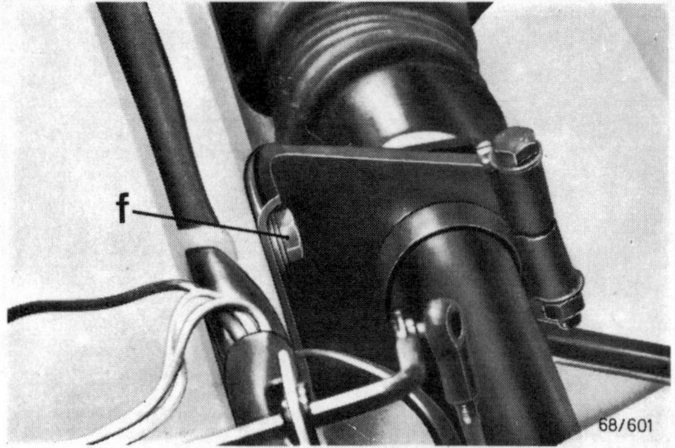

FIG 10:20   The mounting connection

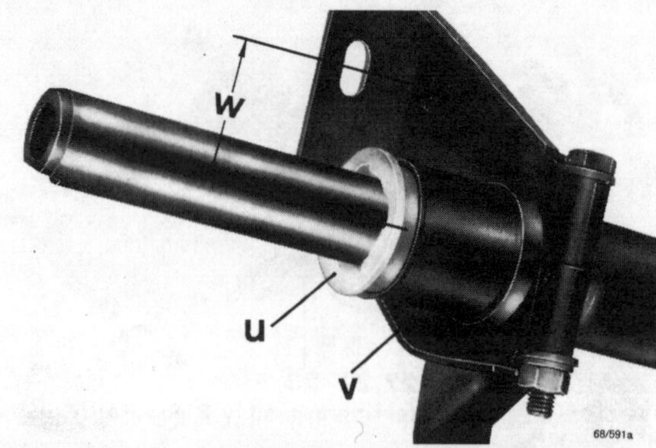

FIG 10:24   The stop ring fitted to models without steering dampers

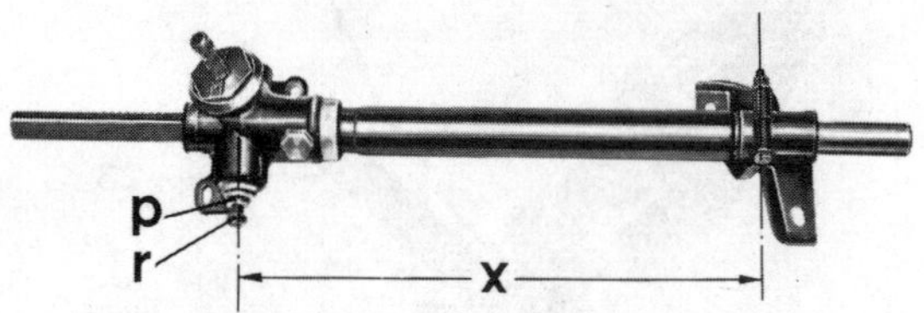

FIG 10:21   Installation of the steering gear mount

Key to Fig 10:21   x 412 mm (16.22 inches)

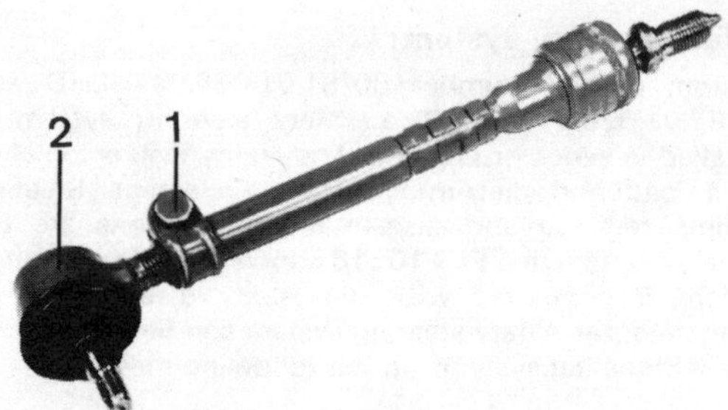

FIG 10:25   Removing a track rod ball joint

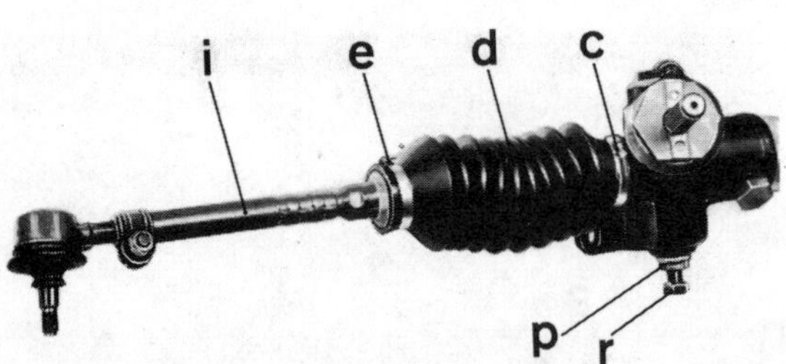

FIG 10:22   Removing the rubber boot

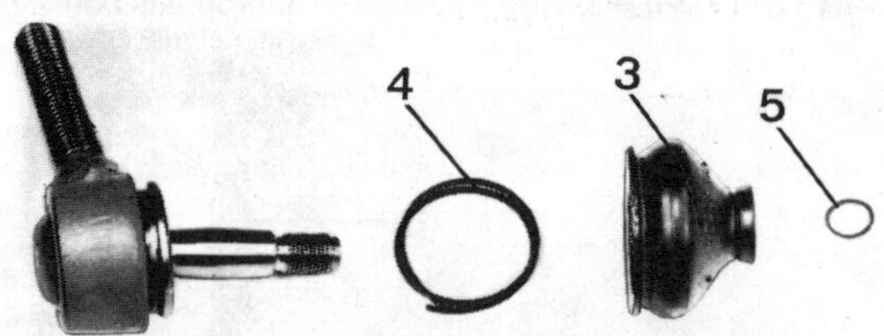

FIG 10:26   Ball joint components

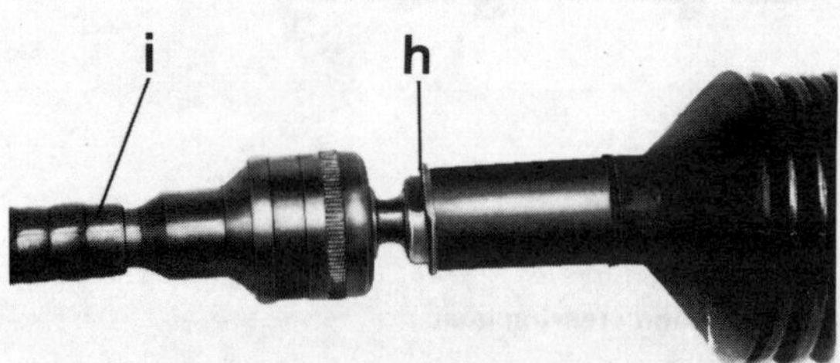

FIG 10:23   Removing the track rods

FIG 10:27   Fitting the steering gear alignment gauge

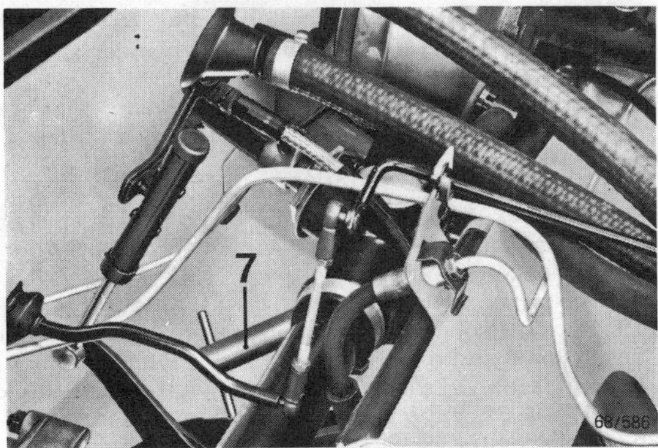

FIG 10:28   Fitting the centring fixture

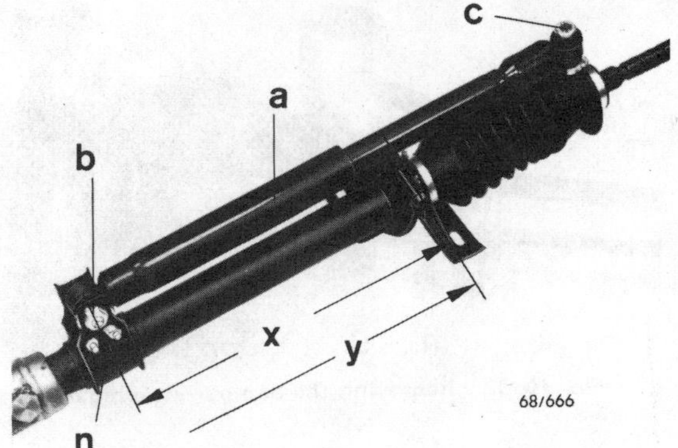

FIG 10:30   The steering gear with damper

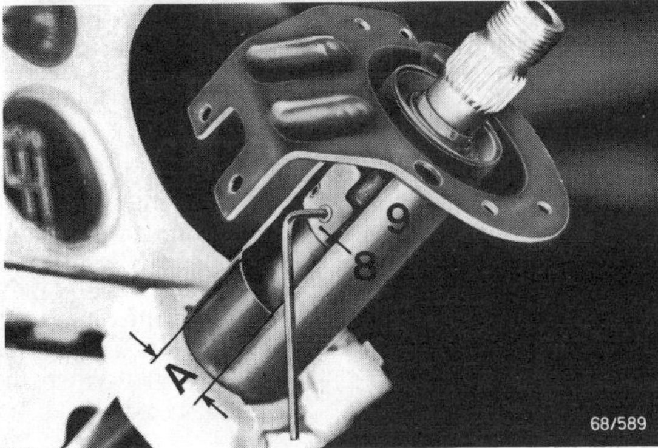

FIG 10:29   Aligning the indicator self-cancelling device

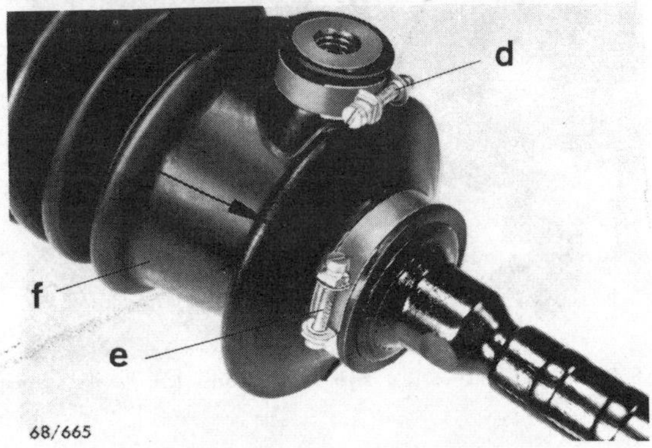

FIG 10:31   Removing the rubber boot

the plate of tube 20 and slide sleeves 22 in the bushings. Press and clamp the tube 20 and intermediate shaft 23 together. The tube and shaft must be pressed together up to the stop so that no play exists, as shown in **FIG 10:18**.

Install the tube and shaft assembly in the steering joint and secure the earth lead to the screw 9. Further installation instructions are as previously described. After the safety system has been installed to earlier cars, it will be necessary to bend the side of the mount in the car a fraction, in order that it will clear the assembly.

10:4 The steering gear

Instructions for removing the rack and pinion steering gear are given in this section, but it should be noted that no repair work can be carried out on the assembly and, if it is found to be worn or damaged, an exchange steering gear unit must be obtained and fitted. Additional points covering steering gear assemblies fitted with dampers are given at the end of this section. **FIG 10:19** shows the components of the steering gear.

Removal:

Loosen the steering column and tube **a** from the bulkhead and connection **k-n** of the pinion and pull the tube from the pinion. Remove the track rod end joints from the steering swivels as shown in **FIG 9:10** in **Chapter 9**.

Loosen the connection (see **FIG 10:20**) from the mount and steering gear. First slide the steering gear towards the right, then pull it out upwards through the engine compartment.

Dismantling:

If mount **o** is to be replaced, install in accordance with the dimensions shown in **FIG 10:21**. The mount is not symmetrical, the larger distance **w** in **FIG 10:24** must face upwards. Always renew parts **k** and **m** when servicing the steering gear. If the tube **a1** has been damaged by the pinion, this also must be renewed.

Open and remove the hose clips **c** and **e** shown in **FIG 10:22** and pull off boot **d**. The settings of screw **r** and nut **p** should not be altered, except in cases where the steering clearance is too great. In such cases the following operation should be carried out: Loosen nut **p** and tighten the screw **r** until it is possible to slide the track rod over the full amount of its travel easily. Under no circumstances must the torque required to turn the pinion exceed 10.42 lb in. Tighten the nut **p** when setting is correct and seal with paint.

Bend open the lock plate **h** shown in **FIG 10:23** and unscrew the track rod **i**. On the right side a stop ring **u** is slid into tube **v** on models without steering dampers only. If this ring is defective in any way, it can be renewed. Loosen the clamp 1 in **FIG 10:25** and unscrew the outer

FIG 10:32 Removing the damper attachment

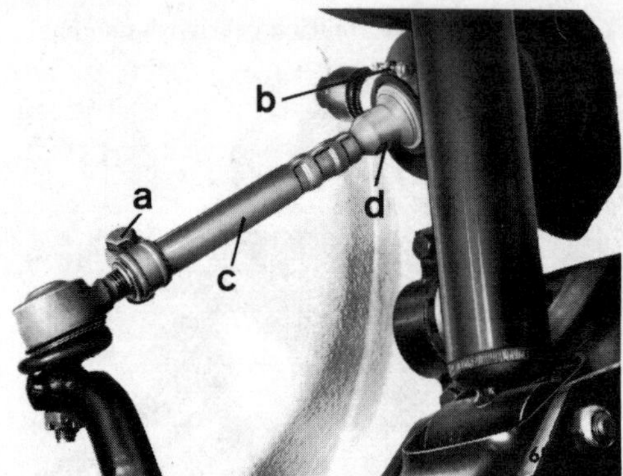

FIG 10:33 Adjusting the track rods for front wheel alignment

ball joint. The ball joint boots shown in **FIG 10:26** can be renewed separately if they are damaged, after removing the clamping rings 4 and 5. When fitting, fill the boot with Molykote BR2 grease and carefully install new clamping rings.

Reassembly:

Reassembly of the steering gear is carried out in the reverse order of dismantling.

Refitting:

Place the steering gear assembly in the car and tighten the mounting screws a little. Slide back both outer boots and install tool L-100/101 steering alignment gauge 6 as shown in **FIG 10:27**. Remove the screw and place the oval edge of the gauge on the upper wishbone. The gauge must be vertical, so smooth off the underseal on the wheel arch if necessary. Tighten the wingnut slightly. The track rod must rest on the left and right arms of the gauge. Tighten the steering gear, swing out the arms and remove the gauge. Tighten the outer rubber boots.

Set the track rod in approximately the central position and install special tool L-1 centring fixture as shown in **FIG 10:28**. Continue turning until the pin of the special tool snaps into position. This is the straight-ahead position for the steering wheel, which can then be installed.

The stop 8 for the indicator self cancelling device must be in the centre of cut-out **A** when the wheel is in the straight-ahead position, as shown in **FIG 10:29**. Both socket head screw must be loosened in order to carry out corrections.

On completion, the front wheel alignment must be checked and adjusted as described in **Section 10:5**.

Steering gear with damper:

Removing, servicing and refitting this type of steering gear is as described previously, noting the following points concerning dismantling.

Loosen the connections shown at **b** and **c** in **FIG 10:30** and remove the steering damper **a**. Unscrew the hose clips **d** and **e** in **FIG 10:31** and pull off the boot **f** in the direction of the arrow. Bend open the lock plate **g** in **FIG 10:32** and unscrew the track rod. Unscrew the nut **h**, slide out stud **i** and remove the attachment **k**.

When refitting, first place the boot over the track rod and attachment. The attachment **k** must be slid onto the track rod in such a manner that the threaded hole for stud **i** is exactly aligned with the groove in the shaft. When installing clip **n** the dimension **x** in **FIG 10:30** must be achieved.

10:5 Tracking

The front wheels must be aligned parallel to .079 inch toe-out. This operation should be carried out by a service station or wheel and tyre specialist having access to the special equipment required. The means of adjustment is shown in **FIG 10:33**. The clamps **a** and hose clips **b** on each side of the car must be loosened, then the track rods **c** turned equally by means of the flats **d**. The clamps and hose clips must be securely retightened when the setting is correct.

10:6 Fault diagnosis

(a) Wheel wobble

1 Unbalanced wheels and tyres
2 Slack steering connections
3 Incorrect steering geometry
4 Excessive play in steering gear
5 Faulty suspension
6 Worn hub bearings

(b) Wander

1 Check 2, 3 and 4 in (a)
2 Uneven tyre pressures
3 Uneven tyre wear
4 Ineffective dampers

(c) Heavy steering

1 Check 3 in (a)
2 Very low tyre pressures
3 Wheels out of track
4 Rack and pinion assembly faulty
5 Inner steering column bent
6 Steering column bearings tight

(d) Lost motion

1 Loose steering wheel
2 Worn rack and pinion teeth
3 Worn ball joints
4 Worn steering swivel joints
5 Slack pinion bearings

CHAPTER 11

THE BRAKING SYSTEM

11:1 Description
11:2 Maintenance
11:3 Disc brakes
11:4 Drum brakes
11:5 The master cylinder

11:6 Bleeding the system
11:7 Vacuum servo unit
11:8 The handbrake
11:9 Fault diagnosis

11:1 Description

The Audi 100 is equipped with a dual-circuit brake system, using disc front brakes and drum rear. A similar system is fitted to 100S, 100LS and 100GL models, boosted by a vacuum servo unit. The brakes on all four wheels are hydraulically operated by the brake pedal, the handbrake operating the rear brakes only through a mechanical linkage.

Drum brakes are each fitted with one leading and one trailing shoe. Drum brake systems require that a small fluid pressure acts at all times to hold the wheel cylinder seals against the cylinder walls, preventing the entry of air or the loss of fluid. To achieve this, the rear brake circuit is equipped with a static pressure valve at the master cylinder.

Disc brakes have a fixed caliper with two self-adjusting friction pads between which the disc rotates. The friction pads are applied by two pistons operated by hydraulic pressure from the master cylinder, both pistons operating simultaneously to exert equal pressure on the pads. Disc brakes require that all pressure is released to disengage the pistons, no pressure valve being incorporated in the circuit.

The master cylinder supplies fluid pressure simultaneously to both front and rear brake circuits when the pedal is depressed, the master cylinder pushrod being directly connected to the pedal. The vacuum servo unit, where fitted, is mounted on the master cylinder body and operates to increase the effort applied to the brake fluid, using power supplied by a diaphragm actuated by engine vacuum.

11:2 Maintenance

Regularly check the level of the fluid in the master cylinder supply tank shown in **FIG 11:1** and replenish if necessary up to the 'MAX' mark on the side of the tank. Wipe dirt from around the cap before removing it and check that the vent hole in the cap is unobstructed. If frequent topping up is required the system should be checked for leaks, but it should be noted that, with disc brake systems, the fluid level will drop gradually over a period of time, due to the movement of caliper pistons compensating for friction pad wear. The recommended fluid is that complying to the specification SAE.70.R3, such as ATE Blue Original Brake Fluid or Lockheed Brake Fluid. **Never use anything but the recommended fluid.**

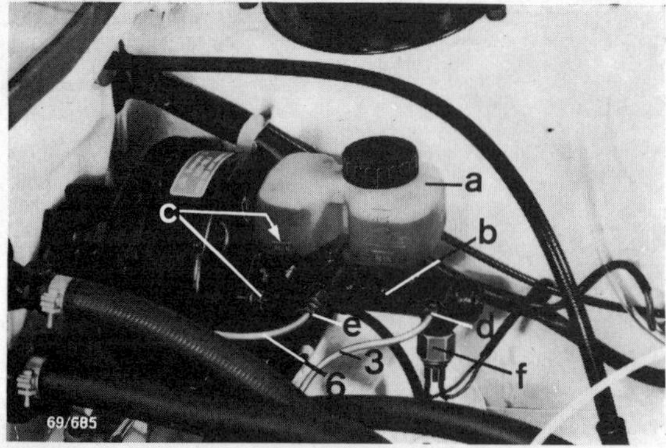
FIG 11:1 The brake master cylinder and fluid supply tank

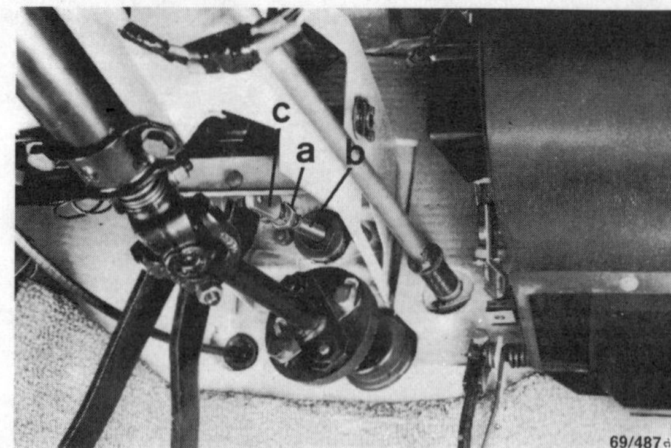
FIG 11:3 Checking the master cylinder pushrod free play

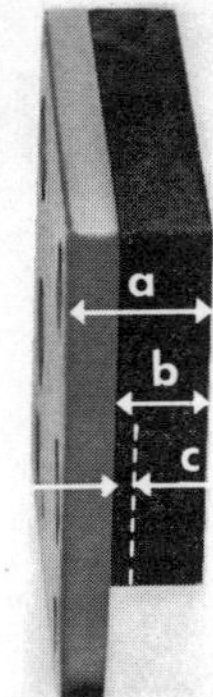
FIG 11:2 Checking the disc brake friction pads
Key to Fig 11:2 a Thickness of disc pad with backplate 15 mm (.59 inch) b Thickness of disc pad—new 10 mm (.394 inch) c Thickness of disc pad—aluminium 2 mm (.078 inch)

FIG 11:4 Adjusting the rear brake shoes

Checking brake pads and linings:

New disc brake friction pads have a thickness of 10 mm, the total thickness of pad and backplate being 15 mm. If any friction pad has worn down to 2 mm or if any pad is cracked or oily, all four friction pads must be renewed. **Do not renew pads singly or on one side only as uneven braking will result.** The friction pad is shown in **FIG 11:2**.

To check the condition of the rear brake shoe linings, jack up the rear of the car and remove the road wheels. A visual check can then be made through the holes in the brake drums. If the linings are worn down to the rivets, exchange brake shoes must be fitted.

Adjusting brakes:

Adjust the rear brake shoes when pedal travel becomes excessive. Remove the instrument panel trim to gain access to the master cylinder pushrod as shown in **FIG 11:3**. The play between the pushrod and the brake pedal should be 1 mm. The play must be corrected to this figure if necessary, by loosening nut **a** and turning the pushrod **b** in the swivel joint **c**. Tighten the nut **a** when the play is correct.

Check the level of fluid in the master cylinder supply tank and top up if necessary. Chock the front wheels, raise the rear of the car and release the handbrake. Two adjusters are provided at each rear brake, one for each shoe, these being shown in **FIG 11:4**. Use a 17 mm wrench to tighten an adjuster **A** in the direction of arrow **a** until the wheel becomes stiff to turn. Now loosen the adjuster slightly in the direction of arrow **b** until the wheel just turns freely. Repeat the adjustment on the second adjuster **A**. In the same manner, adjust the brakes on the opposite wheel, then pump the brake pedal several times and check the wheels for smooth rotation, slackening the adjusters a fraction if necessary. Top up the fluid in the supply tank and test the brakes.

Handbrake cable adjustment will normally be corrected by the drum adjustment just described. However, if the cables have been disconnected for servicing or have been stretched after a long period of use, the cable should be adjusted as follows:

Adjust the rear brake shoes as described previously. With the rear of the car raised, tighten the adjusting nut shown in **FIG 11:5** until the rear wheels start to bind when the handbrake lever is pulled on to the first or second notch. As the lever is pulled to the third or fourth notch, the wheels should be locked. When the handbrake is set as stated, pull the lever on and off several times, then check the wheels for free rotation with the brakes off.

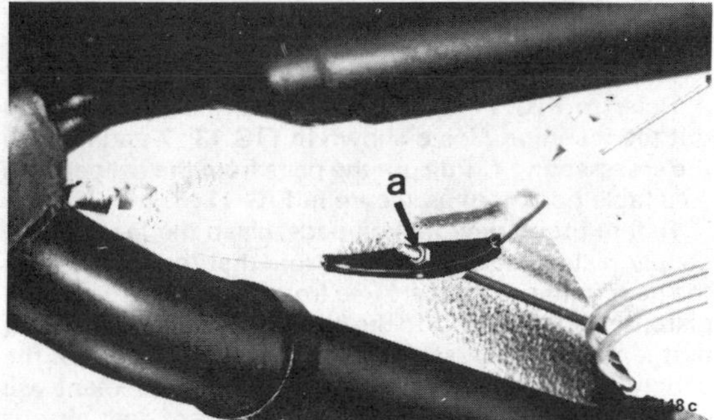

FIG 11:5   Handbrake cable adjustment

FIG 11:6   Removing the lock clips

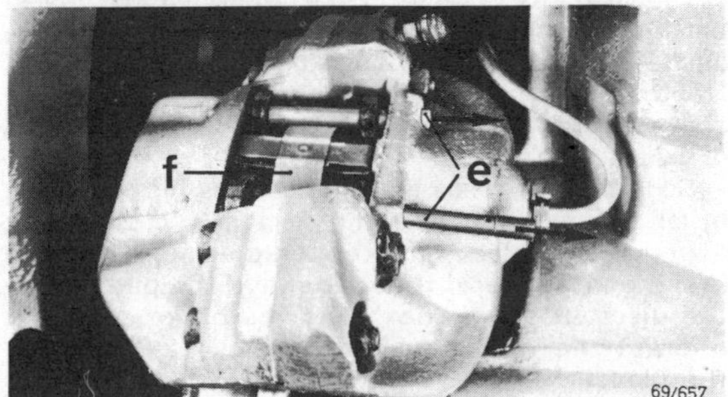

FIG 11:7   Pulling out the friction pad retaining pins

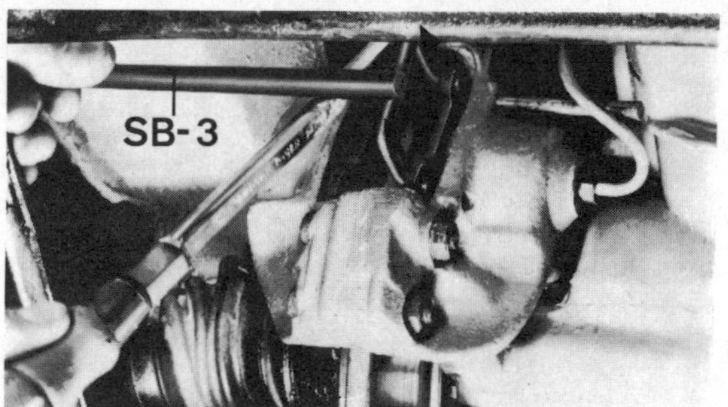

FIG 11:8   Removing the pads from the caliper

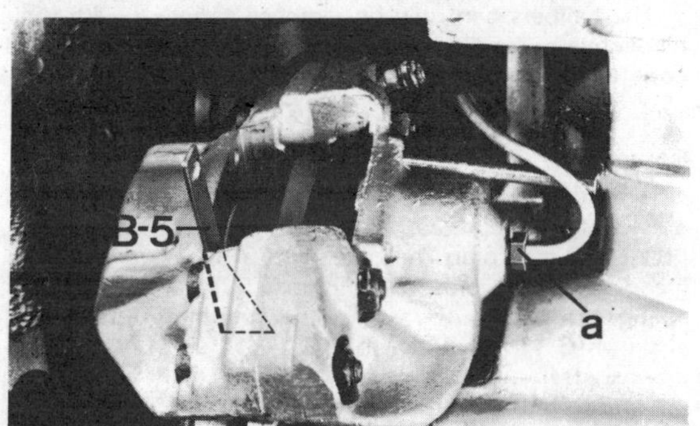

FIG 11:9   Checking the piston face angle with the special gauge

FIG 11:10   Removing the caliper mounting nuts

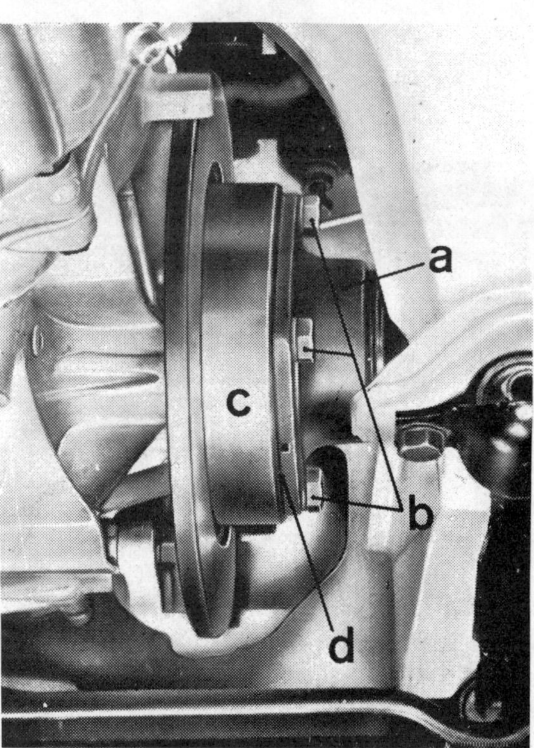

FIG 11:11   Removing the caliper and brake disc

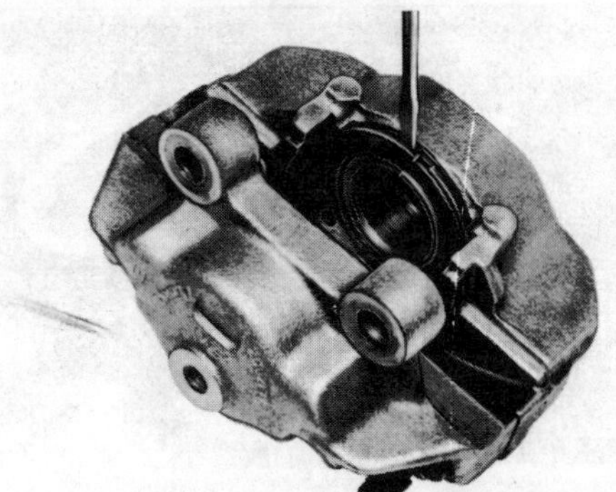

FIG 11:12   Levering off the clamp ring

FIG 11:13   Releasing a caliper piston

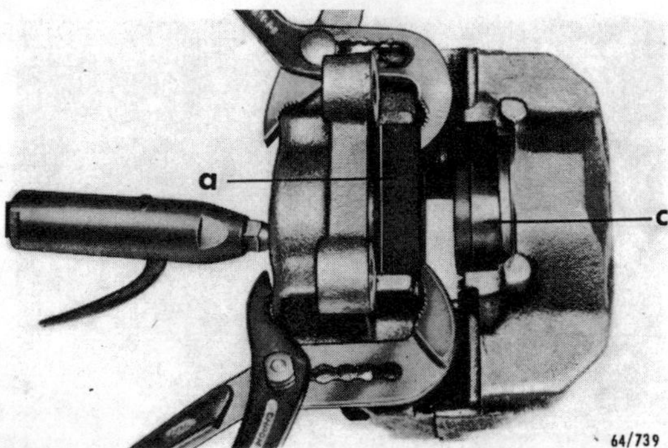

FIG 11:14   Removing the piston

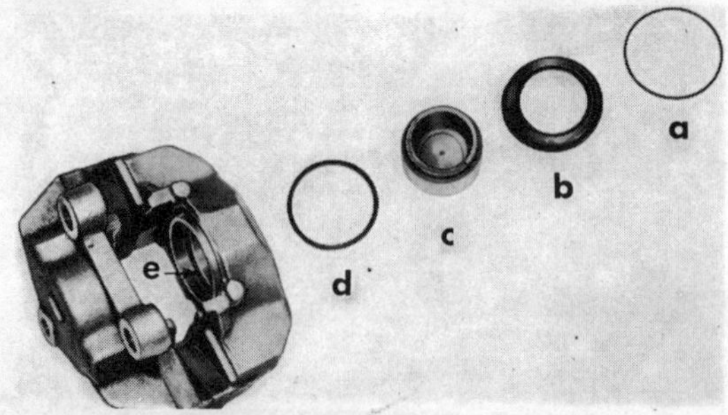

FIG 11:15   Caliper piston and seals

Key to Fig 11:15   **a** Clamping ring   **b** Cap   **C** Piston
d Seal   **e** Groove (for seal **d**)

11:3 Disc brakes

Renewing friction pads:

Refer to **FIG 11:6** and extract the lock clips **d**. Pull out the retaining pins **e** shown in **FIG 11:7** and remove the cross-spring **f**. Pull out the pads from the caliper with a suitable hook tool as shown in **FIG 11:8**.

Before fitting new friction pads, clean the faces of the caliper pistons carefully and ensure that the recesses for the pads in the calipers are free from dirt or rust. Push both pistons simultaneously to the bottom of their bores, noting that it may be necessary to syphon some fluid out of the supply tank when doing so, as piston displacement will cause the level to rise. Check the positions of both pistons in their bores. The machined face of the piston must be in alignment with the 20 deg. angle on special gauge B-5 as shown in **FIG 11:9**. If not, the pistons must be rotated until in the correct position. Check the metal backplates on the new pads for burrs, removing any found with a fine file. Under no circumstances must the brake pad extend above the brake disc, if necessary rework the outer surface of the pad with a file.

Slide the new pads into the recesses in the caliper. Install the retaining pins and fit a new cross-spring. Always use new lock clips. **On completion, pump the brake pedal several times to move the pads up to the discs. If this is not done the brakes will not operate the first time they are used. Check the fluid level.**

Removing and dismantling a caliper and disc:

The calipers can only be removed together with their respective brake discs and vice versa. Allow the brakes to cool fully before removal.

Removal:

Remove the friction pads from the caliper as described previously. Disconnect the brake pipe shown at **a** in **FIG 11:9** and plug the pipe with a dust cap from the bleed screw to prevent fluid loss. Use a thin 19 mm spanner to remove the two caliper retaining nuts shown at **a** in **FIG 11:10**. Refer to **FIG 11:11** and unscrew the drive shaft flange **a**. Slide back the drive shaft and push it upwards. Remove the brake disc and caliper, noting the insulator **d** between the flange and the brake disc.

Refitting:

This is the reverse of the removal procedure. Make sure that the caliper is installed with the bleed screw on top. Tighten the drive shaft flange fixings to 74 lb ft and the caliper mounting nuts to 68 lb ft. On completion, bleed the brakes as described in **Section 11:6**.

Dismantling:

The pistons and seals in the caliper should only be removed if absolutely necessary. The caliper must never be separated into two halves as the internal passages are sealed at the factory and must not be broken. All servicing is carried out with the two halves of the caliper bolted together.

Thoroughly clean the outside of the caliper, using hot water and detergent only. Do not use solvents such as

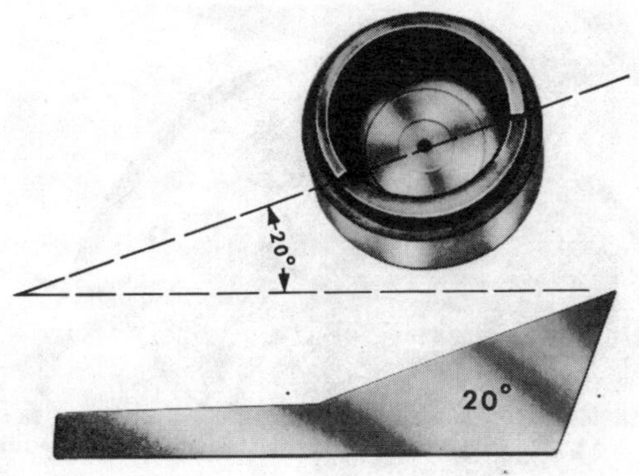

FIG 11:16   Installing the caliper pistons

FIG 11:17   Removing the grease cap

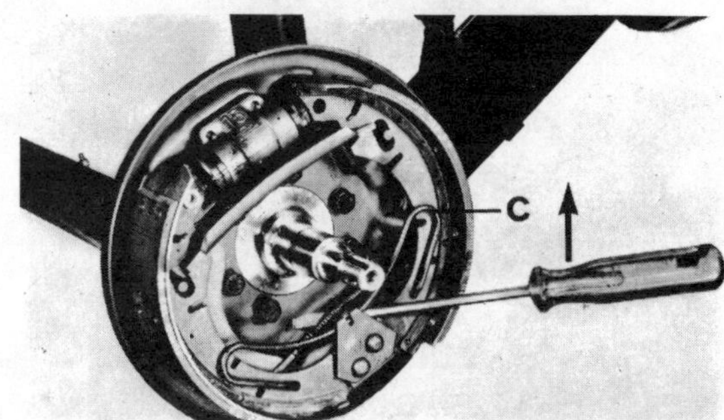

FIG 11:18   Removing the retaining spring

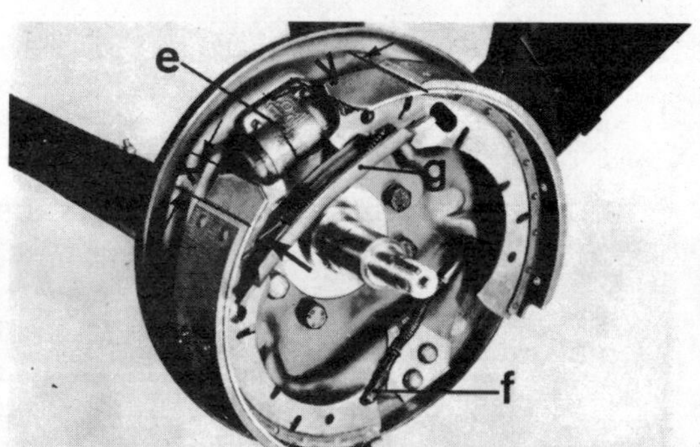

FIG 11:19   Removing the brake shoes

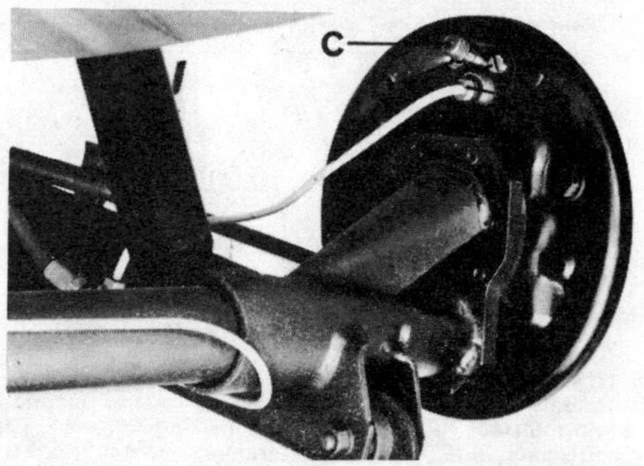

FIG 11:20   Removing a rear wheel cylinder

petrol for this purpose. Plug the brake line hole during cleaning. Lever off the clamp ring as shown in **FIG 11:12** and pull off the cap by hand. Refer to **FIG 11:13**. Place an old friction pad **a** and a suitably shaped piece of plywood **b** into position as shown. Apply compressed air at the brake pipe connection to blow the piston **c** out of the cylinder. Use care during this operation as the piston may exit with considerable force. Now remove the plywood and clamp the friction pad as shown in **FIG 11:14** so that the piston can be blown completely clear and removed. When the first piston assembly has been serviced, it is refitted and the second piston removed in similar fashion. Use only an old friction pad for piston removal. **On no account must a pad be used which is to be fitted to the caliper.**

Refer to **FIG 11:15**. Remove the seal **d** from groove **e** with a wooden or plastic pointed tool. Do not use any tool which may scratch the cylinder bore. Thoroughly clean all internal parts with brake fluid or methylated spirits. Fit new rubber seals, caps and clamping rings. Coat all parts with clean brake fluid during assembly. Use the fingers only to install the rubber seals in the grooves of the caliper bore to prevent damage. When fitting the piston to the caliper bore, make sure that the machined face is at an angle of 20 deg. as shown in **FIG 11:16**, using tool B-5 to check. The second piston and seals can now be removed from the caliper in the same manner as the first.

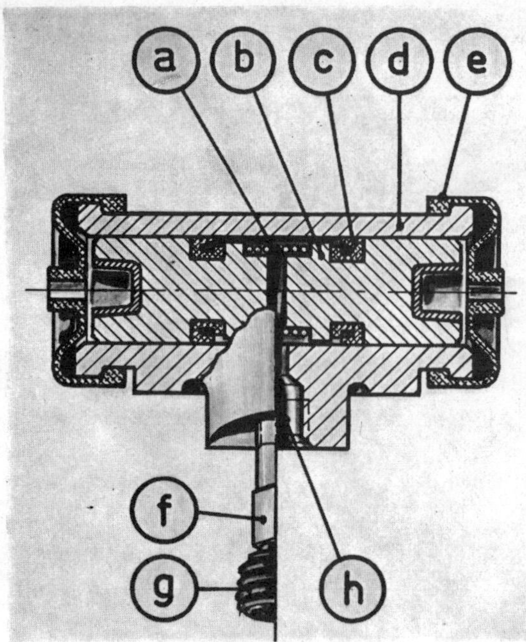

FIG 11:21   Section through a wheel cylinder

Key to Fig 11:21   **a** Spring   **b** Piston   **c** Grooved cup
d Wheel brake cylinder   **e** Cap   **f** Bleeder valve
g Dust cap   **h** 2 m kg (14.46 ft lb) maximum torque for
connection

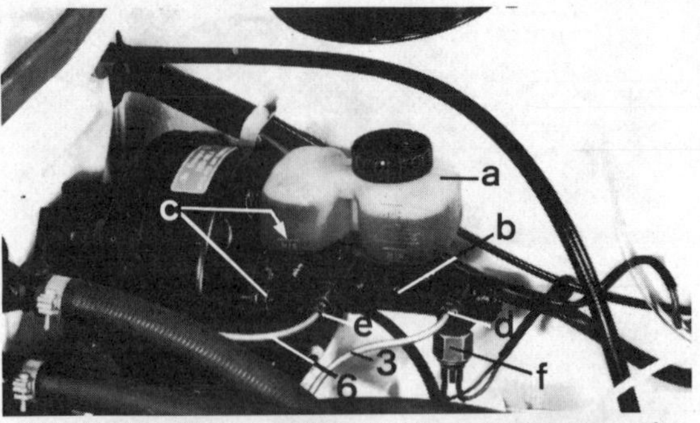

FIG 11:22   Master cylinder with vacuum servo unit

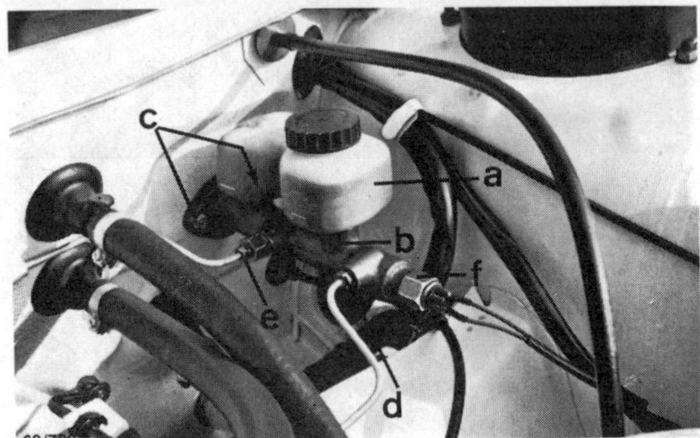

FIG 11:23   Master cylinder without vacuum servo unit

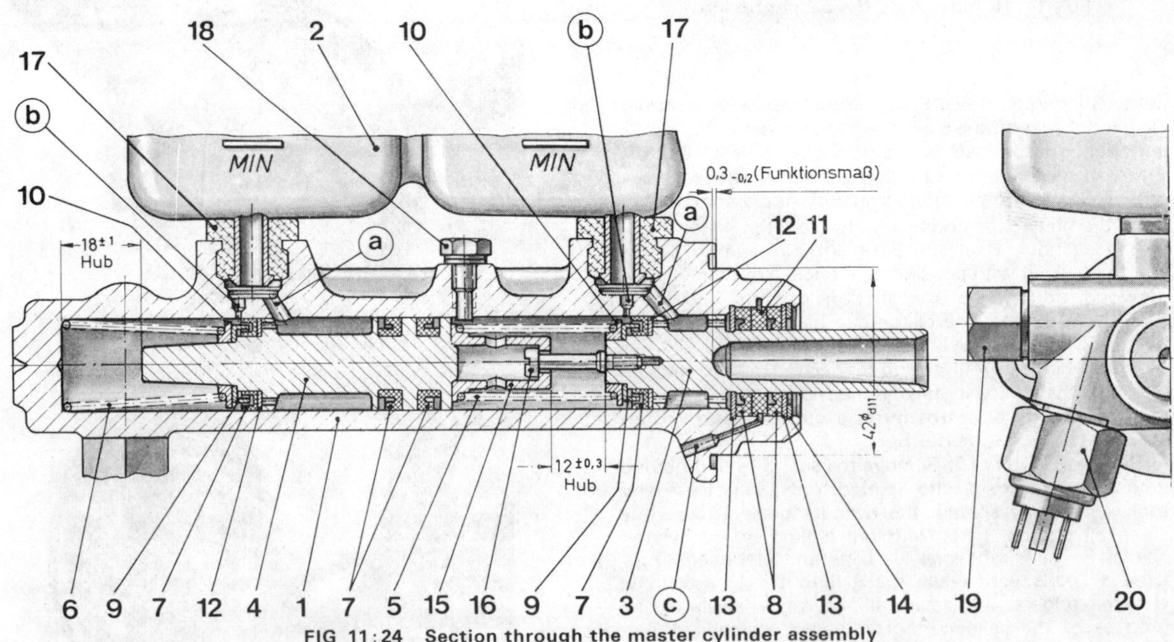

FIG 11:24   Section through the master cylinder assembly

Key to Figs 11:24, 11:25 and 11:26   1 Brake master cylinder   2 Brake fluid container   3 Primary piston
4 Secondary piston   5 Primary spring   6 Secondary spring   7 Primary boot   8 Secondary boot   9 Support ring
10 Spring retainer   11 Intermediate ring   12 Filler disc   13 Stop disc   14 Circlip 25 x 1.2   15 Stop sleeve
16 Stop screw, inner   17 Container plug   18 Stop screw, outer   19 Pressure valve   20 Brake light switch
a Filling bore   **b** Compensating bore   **c** Air compensating bore

11:4 Drum brakes

Removing the brake shoes:

Chock the front wheels, jack up the rear of the car, remove the road wheels and release the handbrake. Lever off the grease cap **a** shown in **FIG 11:17**. Pull the cotterpin from the centre nut and remove the nut. Pull off the brake drum **b** by hand, noting that it may be necessary to slacken the adjustment slightly as described in **Section 11:2** if the shoes bind on the drum. Make sure that the washer and front taper roller bearing do not fall out as the drum is removed. Remove the retaining screw **c** in **FIG 11:18**, being careful as the spring could snap out suddenly. Remove the brake shoes as shown in **FIG 11:19**. First disconnect the spring at the bottom, then disconnect the shoes from the wheel cylinder **e** and disconnect the handbrake cable **f**.

Refitting:

This is the reverse of the removal instructions, noting the following points: Make sure that the retaining clip **g** is installed correctly. The long end of the spring should be located on the brake shoe and handbrake lever as shown by the arrows in **FIG 11:19**. Pay attention to the distances **x** and **y** on the leading and trailing shoes. When fitting the brake shoes make sure that the groove in the wheel cylinder piston is vertical, turning it with a screwdriver if necessary. Fit the brake cable guide so that the projection engages in the notch of the brake plate as this prevents the brake cable from turning. If new shoes have been fitted, it will be necessary to slacken the adjusters as described in **Section 11:2** before refitting the hub. Adjust the wheel bearing free play as described in **Chapter 9, Section 9:12** and adjust the brakes as described in **Section 11:2**.

Relining brake shoes:

If the linings are worn down to the rivets renewal is necessary. It is not recommended that owners attempt to reline brake shoes themselves. It is important that the linings should be properly bedded to the shoes and ground for concentricity. For this reason it is best to obtain sets of replacement shoes on an exchange basis, or have the relining carried out by a service station. **Do not allow grease, oil or brake fluid to contact brake linings. If the linings become contaminated in any way they must be renewed as they cannot be successfully cleaned. If any lining is worn or contaminated, all four linings must be renewed. Do not renew linings singly.**

Servicing a wheel cylinder:

Remove the rear brake shoes as just described. Refer to **FIG 11:20** and disconnect the brake line at the union **a**, plugging the pipe to prevent fluid loss with cap **c** taken from the bleed screw. Take out the two screws **b** and remove the wheel cylinder.

The wheel cylinder components are shown in **FIG 11:21**. Clean the outside of the cylinder, remove caps **e** and withdraw the internal parts. Thoroughly clean all the parts in methylated spirits or brake fluid. Dry with compressed air, making sure that the bores and fluid passages are clear. Discard all rubber caps and seals. Inspect the pistons and the cylinder bores for signs of scoring or rust marks which would dictate renewal. If the pistons do not slide freely in the cylinder, carefully polish the cylinder sliding surfaces.

Reassembly is a reversal of the dismantling procedure, using new rubber parts. Coat all parts with clean brake fluid and assemble them wet, using the fingers only to fit rubber seals and caps to prevent damage. Refit the cylinder to the brake plate and install the brake shoes and drum as described previously. On completion, bleed the brakes as described in **Section 11:6**.

11:5 The master cylinder

Removal, Audi 100S, 100LS and 100GL:

The master cylinder for these models is shown in **FIG 11:22**, in unit with the vacuum servo unit which is a standard fitting. Unscrew joint **e** and catch the fluid which will drain from the supply tank in a clean container. Remove joint **d**. When removing brake lines 3 and 6 place rags underneath to prevent brake fluid from dripping onto the paintwork. Do not bend the pipelines. Pull off the brake light switch cable at **f**. Unscrew the nuts **c** and remove the master cylinder from the servo unit, paying attention to the ring between the two components.

Refitting:

This is the reverse of the removal instructions. On completion, bleed the brakes as described in **Section 11:6**.

Removal, Audi 100:

The master cylinder for this model is shown in **FIG 11:23**, no vacuum servo unit being fitted. Unscrew joint **e** and **d** and catch the fluid which will drain from the supply tank in a clean container. Pull off the brake light switch cable at **f**, remove nuts **c** and remove the master cylinder assembly.

Refitting:

This is the reverse of the removal instructions. On completion, bleed the brakes as described in **Section 11:6**.

Master cylinder servicing:

Clean the outside of the master cylinder. The components of the assembly are shown in **FIGS 11:24** and **11:25**. Remove the supply tank 2, unscrew the brake light switch 20, remove circlip 14 and dismantle the internal components. Note that it is necessary to remove or partially unscrew the stop screw 18 when removing the secondary piston 4. Thoroughly clean all parts in methylated spirits or brake fluid. Discard all rubber parts and inspect the remaining components for wear or damage. Make sure that the compensating bores **b** are clear. Check the pistons and cylinder bore for scoring or rust marks which would dictate renewal. Always renew any part if its serviceability is doubtful.

Coat all parts with clean brake fluid and assemble them wet. Preassemble and install the piston as shown in **FIG 11:26**, making sure that the new rubber boots are installed correctly and without damage. Check the pistons for smooth operation. After pressing in the pistons they should return quickly to the stop screw 18 or stop disc 13.

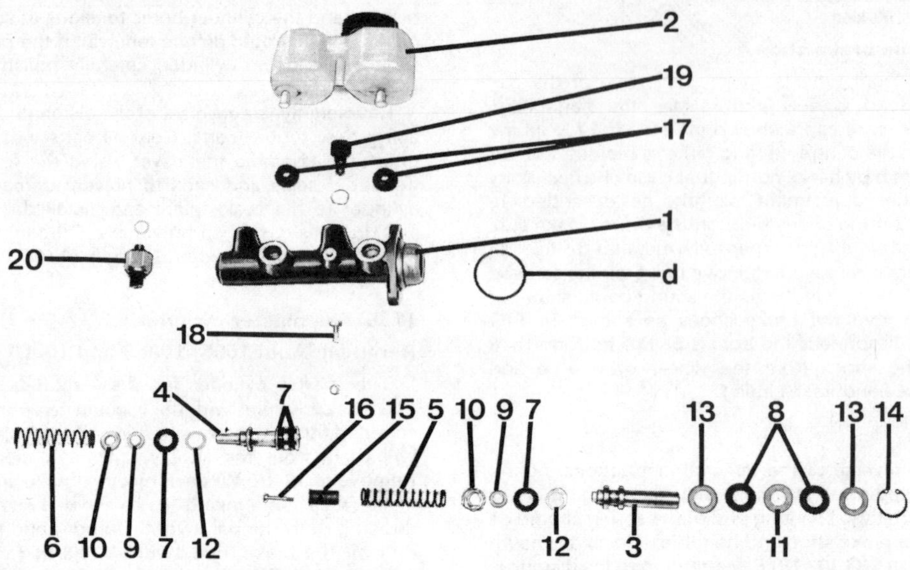

FIG 11:25 Master cylinder components

Repeat the test several times and, if the pistons do not slide smoothly, remove them and carefully polish the cylinder bores. Complete reassembly in the reverse order of dismantling.

Audi 100 models:

The master cylinder for these models is serviced as just described, but note that the piston 3 is slightly different to that shown. The piston is equipped with only one secondary boot 8 and there is no compensating bore **c**. The location of the brake light switch 20 is different and the master cylinder contains a rubber cap as seen in the piston rod direction.

11:6 Bleeding the system

This is not routine maintenance and is only necessary if air has entered the system due to parts being dismantled, or because the fluid level in the master cylinder supply tank has dropped too low. The need for bleeding is indicated by a spongy feeling of the brake pedal accompanied by poor braking performance. This must not be confused with the sharp drop in brake efficiency accompanied by greater pedal travel which indicates that one of the dual-circuits has failed. This latter condition must be investigated immediately and the fault rectified.

Bleeding must be carried out in the following sequence: left rear wheel, right rear wheel, right front caliper, left front caliper. **Do not bleed the brakes with any drum or caliper removed, or with any brake line disconnected.** The bleed screw **a** and bleed hose **b** is shown in **FIG 11:27** for rear drum brakes and in **FIG 11:28** for front disc brakes. On automatic transmission models, the caliper type shown in **FIG 11:29** is fitted. This contains three bleed screws. Bleeding must be carried out at a total of eight bleed screws in the following sequence for this type of caliper. 1 right upper, 2 left upper, 3 right lower outer, 4 right lower inner, 5 left lower outer, 6 left lower inner, 7 rear wheel left, 6 rear wheel right.

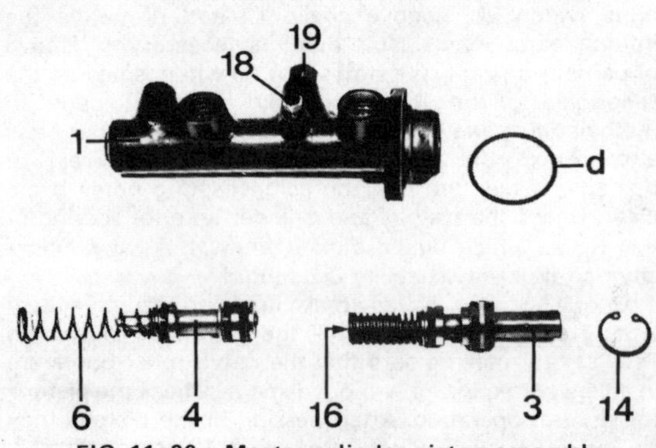

FIG 11:26 Master cylinder piston assembly

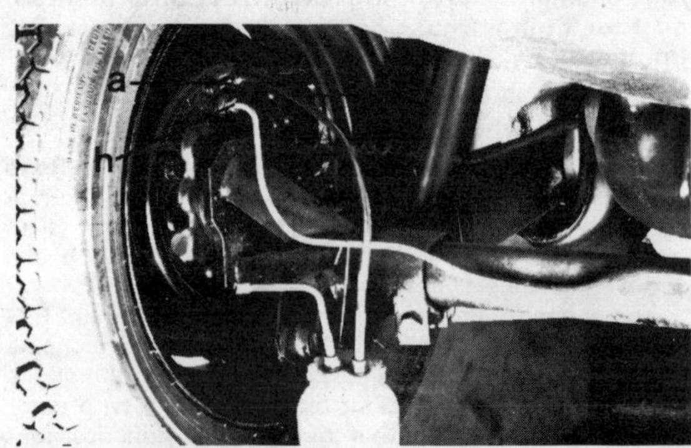

FIG 11:27 Bleeding rear drum brakes

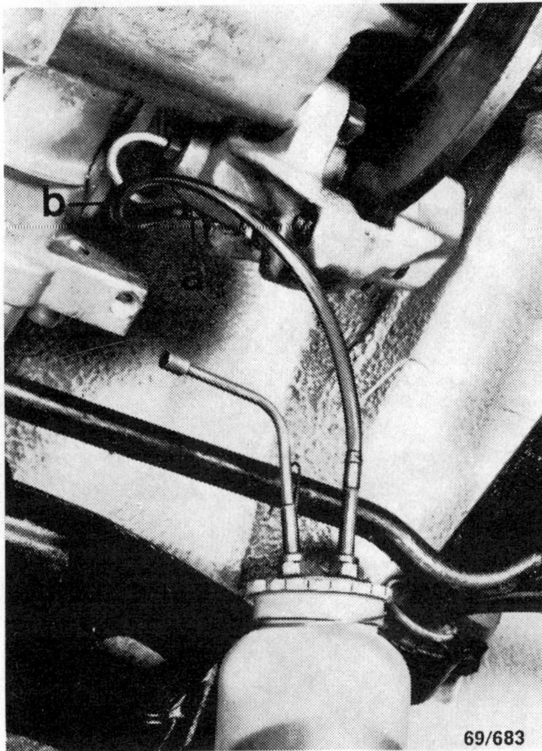

FIG 11:28 Bleeding front disc brakes

FIG 11:29 Caliper bleed screws on automatic transmission models

Check the fluid level in the master cylinder supply tank
and refill if necessary up to the 'MAX' mark on the tank.
Clean all dirt from around the appropriate bleed screw
and remove the dust cap.

Attach a length of rubber or plastic tube to the bleed
screw and lead the free end of the tube into a clean jar.
Get an assistant to apply pressure to the brake pedal, then
loosen the bleed screw to allow fluid to flow out of the
system. When the brake pedal reaches the floor, tighten
the bleed screw before allowing the pedal to return.
Repeat the operation until the fluid flowing into the jar is
free from air bubbles. Check and top up the brake fluid in
the supply tank during the operation to ensure that the
level does not drop too low. If the port in the master
cylinder is uncovered, air will be drawn into the system
and the bleeding operation will have to be restarted.

On completion, top up the fluid to the correct level.
Discard all fluid bled from the system.

11:7 Vacuum servo unit

The vacuum servo unit is bolted to the master cylinder
and operates to assist the pressure applied at the brake
pedal. The vacuum cylinder in the servo is connected to
the engine intake manifold by a hose which houses a
vacuum control valve. If the vacuum servo unit or the
control valve are defective exchange units must be fitted,
as no repairs are possible. The vacuum servo air filter
should be renewed every 30,000 miles, or more often if
the car is operated in dusty conditions. The filter is
located under the rubber boot **n** shown in **FIG 11:31**.

If the vacuum servo unit fails the braking system will
still function with full efficiency, albeit with the need for
greater than usual pressure on the brake pedal.

To test the servo unit, switch off the engine and depress
the brake pedal several times to clear all the vacuum from
the unit. Hold a steady light pressure on the brake pedal
and start the engine. If the servo is working correctly, the
brake pedal will move further downward without further
foot pressure, due to the build up of vacuum in the system.
If the servo does not operate as described, check the
condition of the servo air filter as a clogged filter can stop
a vacuum forming by preventing the entry of air on the
pressure side of the system. If the fault still persists,
check the control valve. The valve must pass air in one
direction only and must be fitted the right way round.
If the fault cannot be traced to either of these causes, the
defective component must be renewed. All hose connections in the system must be leakproof.

Removing vacuum servo:

Remove the master cylinder from the servo unit as
described in **Section 11:5**. Loosen the clip and pull the
vacuum hose from the servo unit. Remove the left and
right knee protector pads as well as the instrument panel
trim from inside the car. Refer to **FIG 11:30** and loosen
and remove pin **g** from swivel joint **h**. Remove the nuts **i**
and their washers and remove the servo unit from the
bulkhead. **FIG 11:31** shows the components of the
vacuum servo unit.

FIG 11:30   Removing the vacuum servo unit

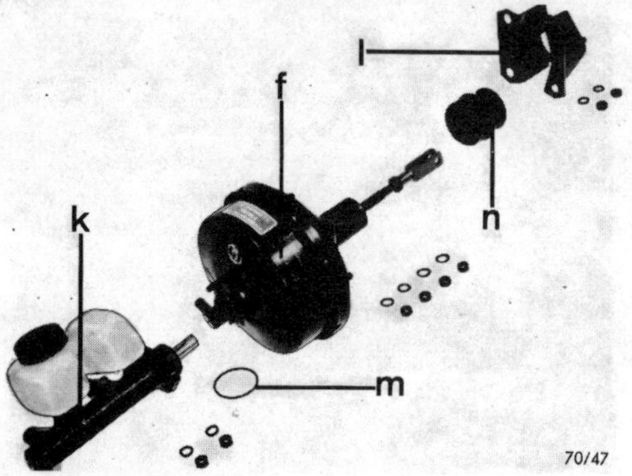

FIG 11:31   Vacuum servo components

FIG 11:32   Removing the handbrake cable from the mounting bracket

FIG 11:33   Removing the handbrake cable assembly

Refitting is a reversal of the removal instructions. On completion, check the master cylinder pushrod play as described in **Section 11:2**.

11:8 The handbrake

Normally, adjustment of the rear brake shoes will take up excessive handbrake free movement, as described in **Section 11:2**. If not, check the rear brake shoe linings and reline them if badly worn. Handbrake cable adjustment is described in the section mentioned.

Removing and refitting handbrake cable:

Jack up the car and remove the rear wheels and brake shoes as described in **Section 11:4**. Loosen the handbrake lever. Loosen the screw **h** shown in **FIG 11:32** and pull the cable **i** from the mounting plate **k**. Refer to **FIG 11:33**. Unscrew nut **a** from pushrod **b** and remove the metal holder **c**. Pry out the plastic bushes **d** from the left and right sides of the mounting plates. Pull off rubber caps **e** and pull the cable **i** out of the mount **g** in the direction of the arrow. Remove the cable from the slot in the mount by pulling downwards.

Refitting is a reversal of the removal procedure. When installing a cable in the brake holder **l**, make sure that the cable projection engages properly. Afterwards connect the cable to mounting plate **k**.

11:9 Fault diagnosis

(a) 'Spongy' pedal

1 Leak in the system
2 Worn master cylinder
3 Leaking wheel cylinders
4 Air in the fluid system
5 Gaps between brake shoes and undersides of linings

(b) Excessive pedal movement

1 Check 1 and 4 in (a)
2 Excessive lining or pad wear
3 Very low fluid level in supply tank
4 Too much free movement of pedal

(c) Brakes grab or pull to one side

1 Distorted discs or drums
2 Wet or oily pads or linings
3 Loose backplate or caliper
4 Disc loose on hub
5 Worn suspension or steering connections
6 Mixed linings of different grades
7 Uneven tyre pressures
8 Broken shoe return springs
9 Seized handbrake cable
10 Seized wheel cylinder piston

CHAPTER 12

THE ELECTRICAL SYSTEM

12:1 Description
12:2 The battery
12:3 The alternator
12:4 The starter
12:5 Fuse box, relay and flasher unit

12:6 Instrument cluster
12:7 Windscreen wipers
12:8 Headlamps
12:9 Lighting circuits
12:10 Fault diagnosis

12:1 Description

All models covered by this manual have 12-volt electrical systems in which the negative battery terminal is earthed to the car bodywork.

There are wiring diagrams in **Technical Data** at the end of this manual which will enable those with electrical experience to trace and correct faults.

With modern precision electrical equipment, it is not practical to attempt to dismantle and repair defective components. If after a long service life an electrical component should develop an internal fault, the procedure is to remove the unit and obtain and fit a factory reconditioned unit on an exchange basis.

12:2 The battery

The battery is located under the rear seat, access being by lifting the front edge of the seat as shown by the arrow in **FIG 12:1**. When refitting the seat, first place the front edge of the seat in position so that the pins **a** engage in holes **b** then press down the rear of the seat along the back-rest. The carpet **c** in **FIG 12:2** and plastic cap **d** cover the battery terminals, a breather hose **f** being attached to connection **e** so that battery gases are ducted out of the passenger compartment.

To maintain the performance of the battery it is essential to carry out the following operations, particularly in winter when heavy current demands must be met.

Keep the top and surrounding parts of the battery clean and dry as dampness can cause current leakage. Clean off corrosion from the metal parts of the battery mounted with diluted ammonia and coat them with anti-sulphuric paint. Clean the terminal posts and smear them with petroleum jelly after remaking the connections and tightening the terminal clamps securely. High electrical resistance due to corrosion at the terminals can be responsible for a lack of sufficient current to operate the starter motor.

Test the condition of the cells with an hydrometer as shown in **FIG 12:3**, after topping up the electrical level with distilled water as shown in **FIG 12:4** and running the engine for a while so that the charging of the battery mixes the distilled water properly. Never overfill the battery or it will tend to boil over under charge, resulting in a loss of electrolyte. **Never add neat acid. If it is necessary to prepare new electrolyte due to loss**

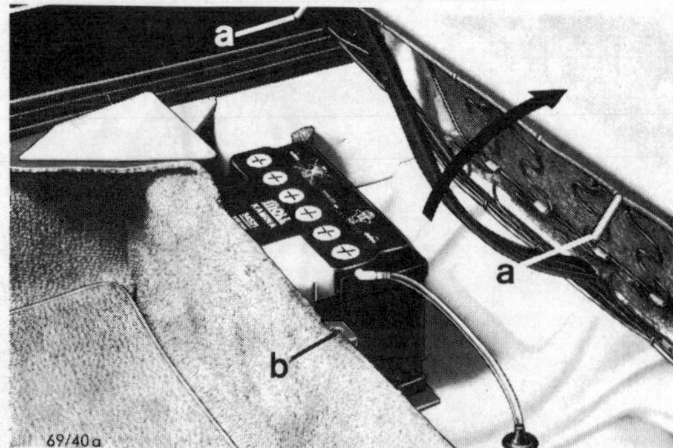

FIG 12:1   Battery location

FIG 12:2   Battery terminals and breather hose

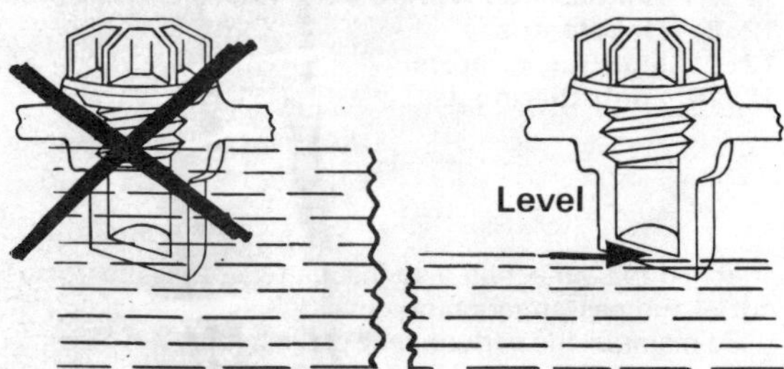

FIG 12:4   Topping up the battery to the correct level

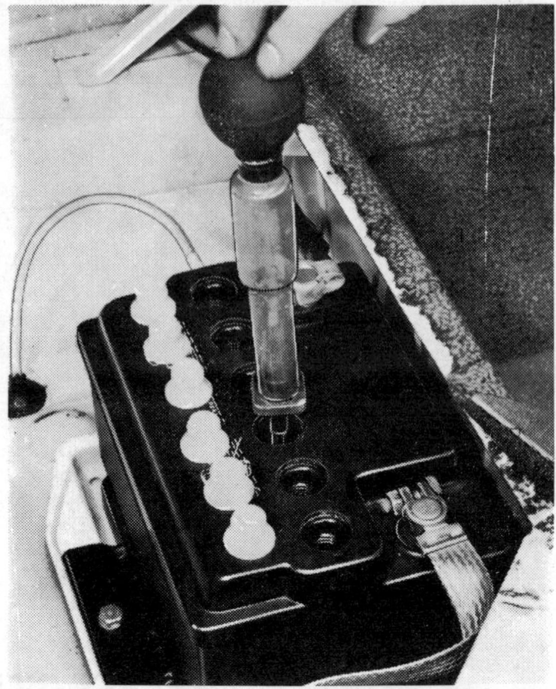

FIG 12:3   Testing the battery cells

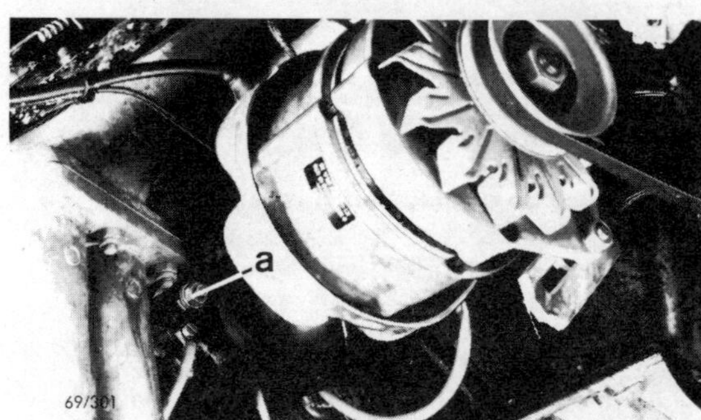

FIG 12:5   The red lead connection at the starter terminal screw

or spillage, add sulphuric acid to distilled water. **It is highly dangerous to add water to acid.**

The indications from readings of the specific gravity are as follows:

For climates below 27°C or 80°F:

Cell fully charged ..	Specific gravity 1.270 to 1.290
Cell half discharged ..	Specific gravity 1.190 to 1.210
Cell discharged ..	Specific gravity 1.110 to 1.130

For climates above 27°C or 80°F:

Cell fully charged ..	Specific gravity 1.210 to 1.230
Cell half discharged ..	Specific gravity 1.130 to 1.150
Cell discharged ..	Specific gravity 1.050 to 1.070

These figures assume an electrolyte temperature of 60°F or 16°C. If the temperature of the electrolyte exceeds this, add .002 to the readings for each 5°F or 3°C rise. Subtract .002 for any corresponding drop below 60°F or 16°C.

All cells should read approximately the same. If one differs radically from the others it may be due to an internal fault or to spillage or leakage of the electrolyte.

If the battery is in a low state of charge, take the car for a long daylight run or put the battery on a charger at 5 amps with the vent plugs removed, until it gases freely. Do not use a naked light near the battery as the gas is inflammable. If the battery is to stand unused for long periods, give a refreshing charge every month. It will be ruined if it is left uncharged.

12:3 The alternator

The alternator provides current for the various items of electrical equipment and to charge the battery, and operates at all engine speeds. The current produced is alternate, this being rectified to a direct current supply by diodes mounted in the alternator casing. Alternator drive

FIG 12:6 Removing the cable strap and tensioning screw

FIG 12:7 Removing the alternator

is by belt from a pulley on the crankshaft. Very little maintenance is needed, apart from the occasional check on drive belt tension as described later. The alternator must never be run with the battery disconnected, nor must the battery cables be reversed at any time. Test connections must be carefully made, and the battery and alternator wiring must be completely disconnected before any electric welding is carried out on any part of the car. These warnings must be observed, otherwise extensive damage to the alternator components, particularly the diodes, can result.

Testing when the alternator is not charging:

Check the drive belt tension as described later to make sure that a loose drive belt is not the cause of the trouble. Switch off all the lights and accessories and connect an ammeter in series with the control box and battery. Start the engine, increase the engine speed and observe the ammeter reading. The output should be 30 amps minimum at 2500 rev/min. If the alternator is in order, check the continuity of the cables to the control box. If the fault persists, have the control box tested by an Auto-electrical service station.

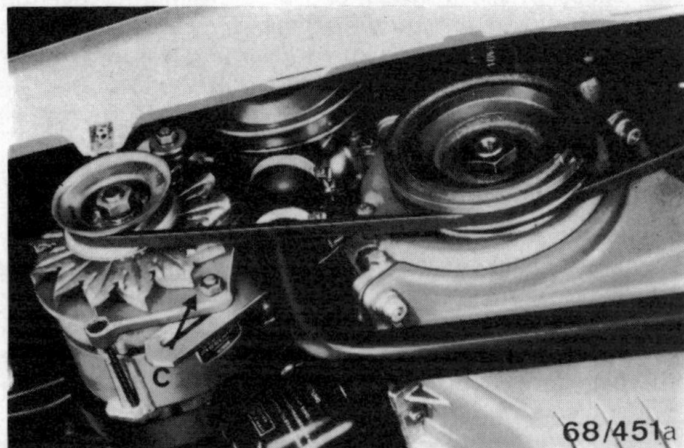

FIG 12:8 Tensioning the drive belt

FIG 12:9 Disconnecting the starter leads

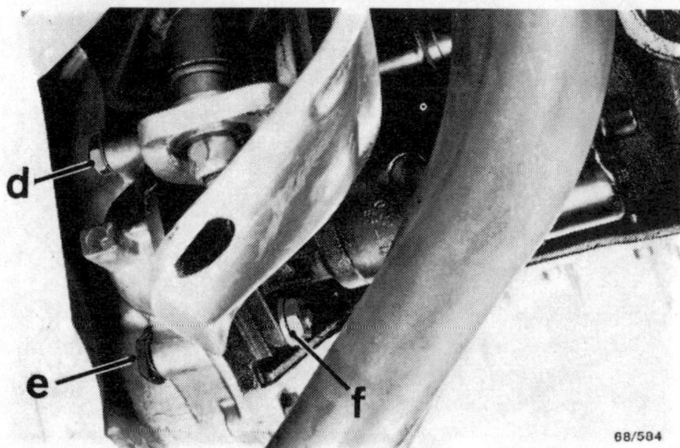

FIG 12:10 Removing the starter

FIG 12:11 Starter fitted with extra terminal 16

FIG 12:12 The fuse box

FIG 12:13 The flasher unit and the relays mounted on the fuse box

Removing the alternator:

Disconnect the battery lead. Disconnect the red lead 4 at the starter as shown at **a** in **FIG 12:5**. Disconnect the triple point plug from the control box and the flat plug connection (light blue lead) from the triple point plug. Refer to **FIG 12:6** and remove the cable strap **b** and the tensioning screw **c**. Swing the alternator over and remove the drive belt.

Unscrew the earth lead **d** shown in **FIG 12:7**. Loosen the nut **f** and pull out screw **e**, then lift off the alternator paying attention to the washers and sleeves.

Refit in the reverse order and adjust the drive belt tension as follows.

Checking drive belt tension:

FIG 12:8 shows the arrangement of the alternator and drive belt. The belt tension should be such that, when the belt is pressed with a load of 22 lb at the point midway between the pulleys, it deflects approximately half-an-inch. If the belt is too tight, excessive wear will occur on the alternator bearings. If it is too loose, it will slip and fail to turn the alternator fast enough, resulting in a drop in current supply. This condition can usually be detected by a squealing noise made by the belt slipping on the pulleys as engine speed is increased.

To adjust the belt, loosen the nut shown at **c** in **FIG 12:8** and swing the alternator in the required direction to tighten or loosen the belt. Tighten the nut and recheck the adjustment.

12:4 The starter

The starter is a brush-type series wound motor equipped with an overrunning clutch and operated by a solenoid. The armature shaft is supported in sintered bronze bushes which are factory packed with lubricant and require no servicing. When the starter is operated from the ignition switch, an engagement lever moves the pinion into mesh with the flywheel ring gear. When the pinion meshes with the ring gear teeth, the solenoid contact disc closes the circuit and the starter motor operates to turn the engine over. When the engine starts, the speed of the flywheel causes the pinion to overrun the clutch and armature. The pinion continues to be engaged until the engagement lever is released, when it returns under spring action.

Tests for a starter which does not operate:

Check that the battery is in good condition and fully charged, and that its connections are clean and tight. Switch on the headlamps and operate the starter switch. Current is reaching the starter if the lights go dim when the switch is operated, in which case it will be necessary to remove and service the starter. If the lights do not go dim, switch them off and operate the starter switch while listening for a clicking sound at the starter motor which will indicate that the solenoid is operating.

If no sound can be heard at the starter when the switch is operated, check the wiring and connections between the battery and the starter switch and between the switch

FIG 12:14 Removing the instrument panel padding

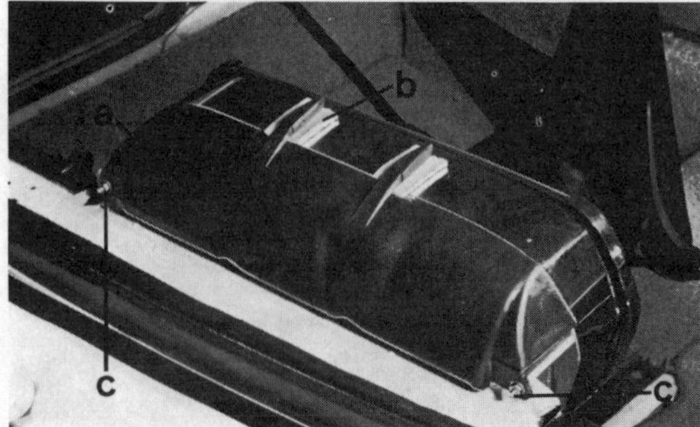

FIG 12:15 Removing the instrument cluster cover

and the solenoid. If the solenoid can be heard operating when the starter switch is operated, check the wiring and connections between the battery and the main starter motor terminals, taking care not to accidentally earth the battery to starter motor lead. If the wiring is not the cause of the trouble, the fault is internal and the starter motor must be removed and serviced.

Starter motor servicing must be carried out by a qualified auto-electrical service station, or, alternatively, an exchange unit obtained and fitted.

Removing the starter:

Disconnect the battery earth cable. Unscrew the oil filter canister and remove it, catching the oil in a suitable clean container so that it can be returned to the engine when work is completed. Refer to **FIG 12:9** and disconnect both leads from terminal **a**. Disconnect the lead from terminal **b** by slackening the screw a little and pulling off the spade connector. Unscrew the nuts **d** and **e** in **FIG 12:10** and remove the washers. Remove the starter towards the front.

Refitting is a reversal of the removal instructions, making sure that the lead connections are clean and tight. Thoroughly clean the seal and oil filter sealing surface and smear both lightly with engine oil. Tighten the filter canister gently to a torque of approximately 15 lb ft. Add the oil collected during removal, start the engine and check the filter for leaks.

Starter with terminal 16 added:

Starter motors may be fitted with an additional terminal 16 as shown in **FIG 12:11**. Removal and refitting instructions are as just described, disconnecting this additional terminal when doing so.

12:5 Fuse box, relay and flasher unit

The fuse box, containing nine fuses, is located in the passenger compartment below the instrument panel as shown in **FIG 12:12**. The fuses, their part numbers and the electrical circuits that they protect are as follows:

1 8 amp, Part No. 15.B1. Turn signal and emergency warning light systems.
2 16 amp, Part No. 15. Motor and slow-action relay for windscreen washer, blower motor, horn, temperature gauge, fuel gauge, oil pressure warning light and reversing lights.
3 16 amp, Part No. 30a. Windscreen wiper motor, brake lights, number plate lights, instrument illumination, cigarette lighter, clock and interior light.
4 8 amp, Part No. 58R. Overnight light and right tail light, parking light.
5 8 amp, Part No. 56a. High beam left.
6 8 amp, Part No. 56a. High beam right and high beam warning light.
7 8 amp, Part No. 56b. Dipped beam left.
8 8 amp, Part No. 56b. Dipped beam right.
9 8 amp, Part No. 58L. Overnight light and tail light left, parking light.

When fitting a new fuse, always check that it makes contact. If a break in any circuit is suspected, check the fuse contacts and fuse first. If a fuse blows, it may be due to a temporary overload, in which case renewal of the fuse is all that is required. However, the circuits protected

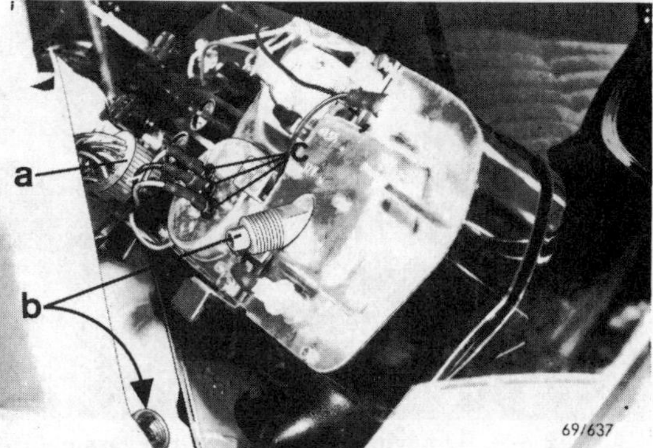
FIG 12:16   Removing the instrument cluster

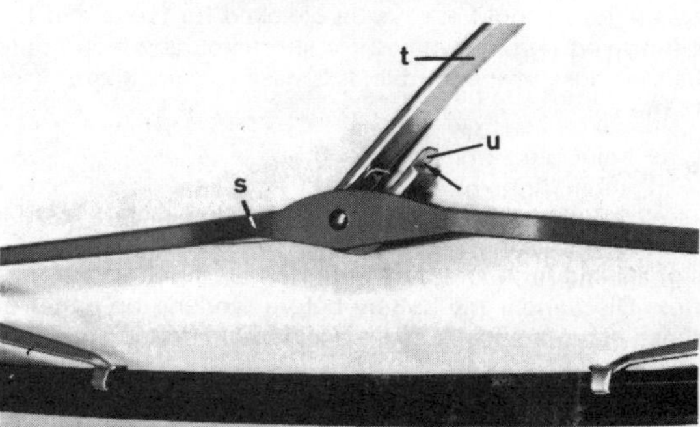
FIG 12:17   Removing a wiper blade

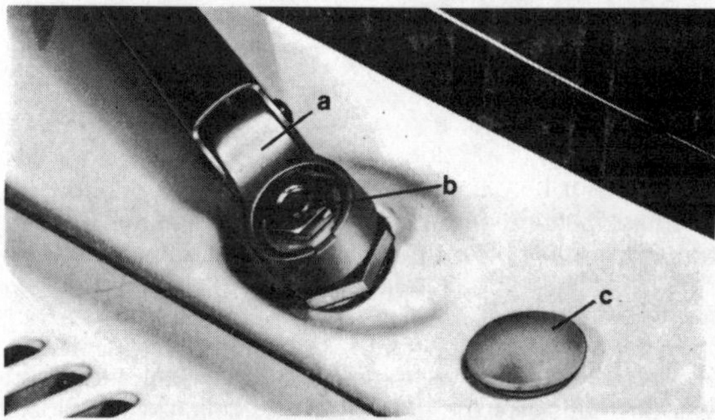
FIG 12:18   Removing the wiper arms

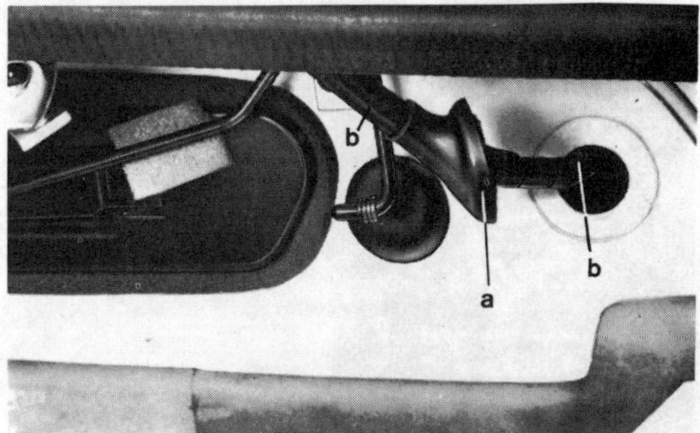
FIG 12:19   Freeing the wiper motor harness

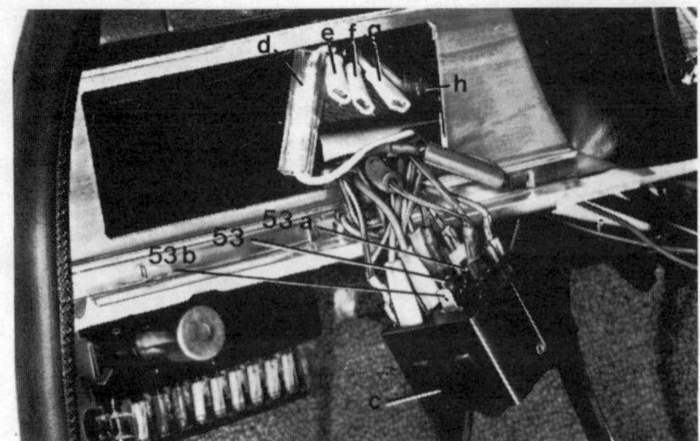
FIG 12:20   Removing the wiper switch assembly

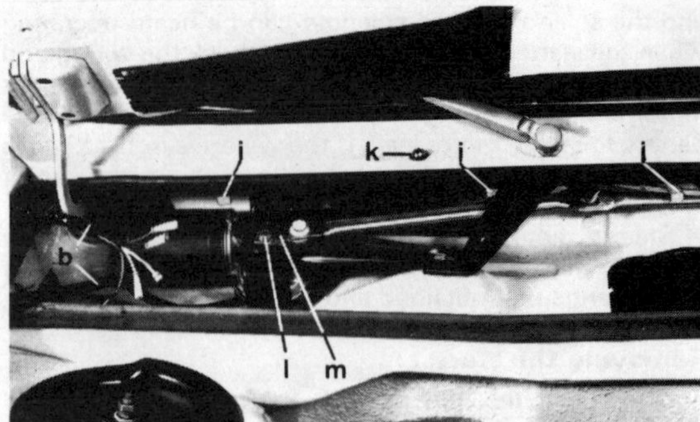
FIG 12:21   Disconnecting the harness and linkage from the motor

by the fuse should always be checked for faults and the wiring and units examined for shortcircuits which could be the cause of the trouble. It is wise to carry spare fuses in the car.

Relays:

As can be seen in **FIG 12:13**, the slow-action relay **a** for the windscreen washer and the relay **c** for the turn signals and high and dipped beams are fitted to the fuse box. Disconnect the battery before working on either of these components to avoid accidental shortcircuits. The complete fuse box can be removed by sliding in the direction of the arrow in **FIG 12:13** and carefully pulling off. Disconnect the flat plug connections at the rear to free the fuse box from the wiring. Refer to the wiring diagrams in the **Appendix** for the cable colour codes. The slow-action relay **a** may be removed separately by releasing the spring clip at **d**, pressing upwards in the direction of the arrow.

Flasher unit:

The flasher unit, in which a switch is operated by alternate heating and cooling of an actuating wire, is housed in a small cylindrical container shown at **b** in **FIG 12:13**. A small relay to flash the pilot light is incorporated.

In case of trouble check the bulbs and the main fuses. If one bulb is defective, the other bulb and the pilot light will flash at twice the normal speed, which will indicate this fault. If the flasher unit is defective, it must be renewed. Removal is by pulling the unit from its mounting. When refitting, make sure that the asymmetrical flat plug connections are correctly aligned before pressing into position. Make sure that replacement units have 1 to 4 x 21 watt capacity and a flashing frequency of 90 at 12.6 volts.

Traffic hazard warning system:

This system operates in conjunction with the flashing direction indicator lights. When the hazard warning light is switched on, all four flasher lights operate simultaneously through the flasher unit. As the system is meant as a warning to other traffic of a stationary vehicle, the hazard warning should not be switched on when the car is moving.

12:6 Instrument cluster
Removal:

Disconnect the battery earth cable. Remove the four screws shown at **a** in **FIG 12:14** plus one extra screw not shown at the other side of the steering wheel, then carefully remove the instrument panel padding. Refer to **FIG 12:15** and remove the nuts **c** and take off cover **a**, paying attention to the washers and foam rubber strips when doing so. Pull out the instrument cluster away from the dashboard as shown in **FIG 12:16**. Pull off the multiple plug **a** and cable **c**. Disconnect the speedometer cable threaded connection **b** and remove the instrument cluster.

Refitting is a reversal of the removal instructions.

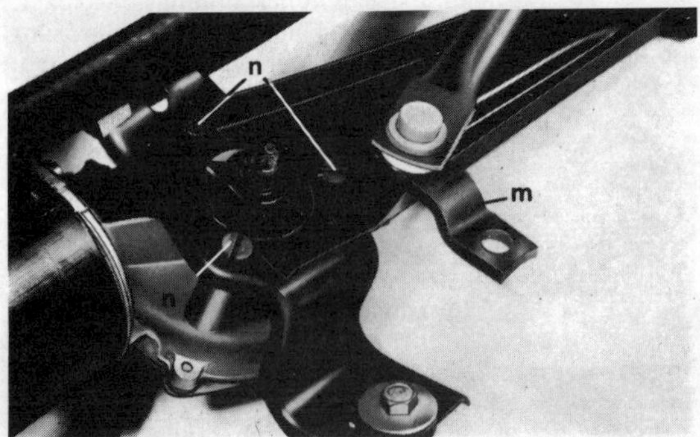
FIG 12:22   Removing the wiper motor

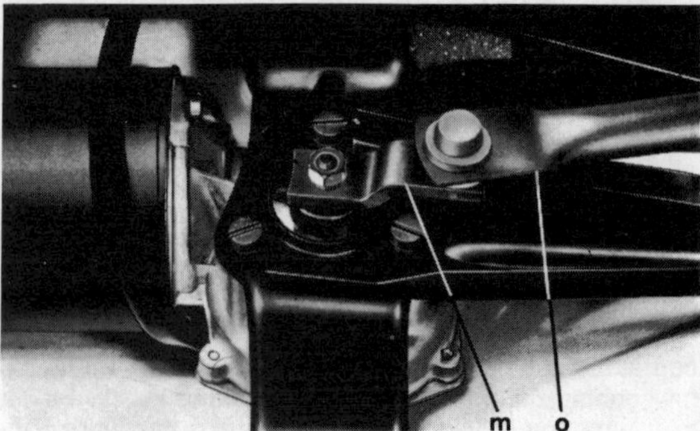
FIG 12:23   Refitting the lever on the motor linkage

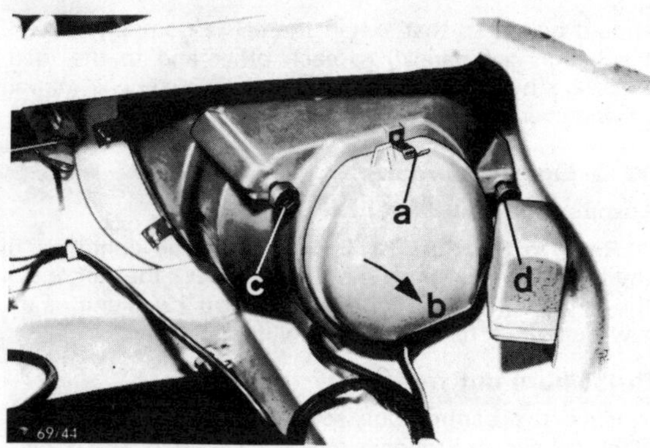

FIG 12:24 Removing the cap from the rear of the
headlamp unit

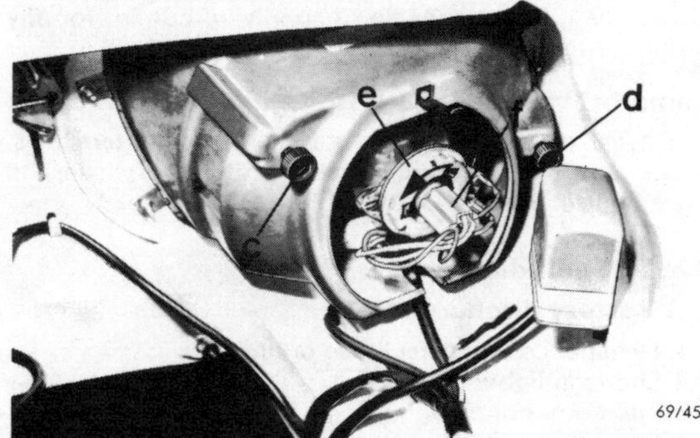

FIG 12:25 Removing the bulb holder

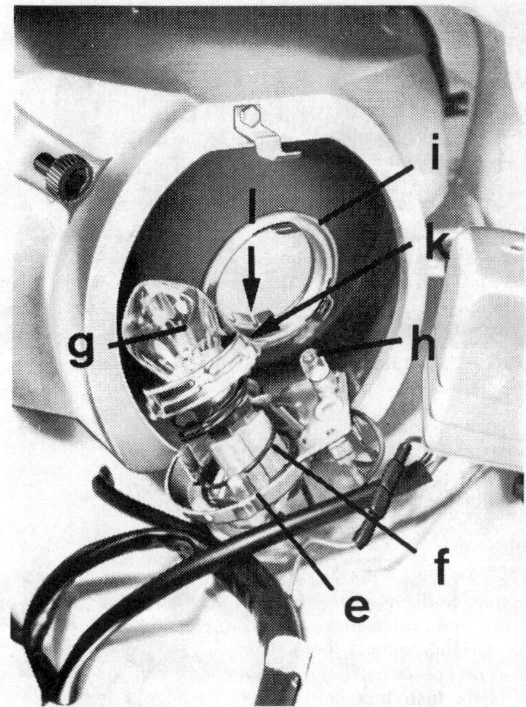

FIG 12:26 The bulb holder and connections

Key to Fig 12:26   **e** Tightening ring   **f** Plug (3-pole)
g Double filament bulb   **h** Parking light bulb   **i** Guide
ring in reflector   **k** Projection (must engage in guide ring
cut-out)   **l** Cut-out for **k**

Dismantling:

The bulbs and gauges can be removed from the instrument panel without difficulty. Note the positions of the
wiring connections and instrument fixings for correct
refitting. Bulb holders are removed by pressing them and
turning $\frac{1}{4}$ turn to the left, fitted by reversing this procedure.

12:7 Windscreen wipers

The windscreen wipers are powered by an electric
motor that drives the wiper arms through a crank and
linkage system. The motor uses self-lubricating bearings
and the gear housing is factory packed with grease and
sealed, so no regular lubrication is required. If, after a long
service life, the wiper motor becomes defective, an
exchange unit should be obtained and fitted. In the event
of failure, check the fuse and wiring first.

Removing wiper blades:

To ensure clear vision through the screen at all times,
wiper blades should be renewed at six monthly intervals,
regardless of mileage. Press the spring **u** in the direction
of the arrow in **FIG 12:17** and pull off the blade. Refit in
the reverse order.

Removing wiper arms:

Lever off the plastic cap **c**, unscrew the nut **b** and lift
off the arm, as shown in **FIG 12:18**. Refit in the reverse
order.

Removing the wiper motor:

Disconnect the battery negative cable. Remove the left
and right knee protector panels from the car interior.
Refer to **FIG 12:19** and, working from the engine
compartment side, pull out rubber grommet **a** somewhat
to free harness **b**. Press out the wiper switch as shown in
FIG 12:20 and pull off leads **d**, **e**, **f**, **g** and **h**, noting
their locations for correct refitting. Refer to **FIG 12:21**
and pull out the harness **b**. The harness runs below the
spray jets **k** together with the spray jet line and is connected
to metal tabs **i**. Bend open these tabs. Remove nut 1 and
disconnect the lever **m**. Remove the screws **n** shown in
FIG 12:22 and remove the motor and harness.

Refit in the reverse order, making sure that the lever **m**
is fitted in such a manner that it is approximately 90 deg.
to the driving direction, as shown in **FIG 12:23**.

12:8 Headlamps
Removing bulbs and headlamp units:

Disconnect the battery earth cable. Open the car
bonnet and refer to **FIG 12:24**. Lift spring **a** and remove
cap **b**. Press the tightening ring **e** together a little and
remove it together with the bulb, after turning it to the
left as shown in **FIG 12:25**. To renew the bulb, pull off
plug **f**. Do not touch the bulb with anything but a clean
cloth, as heat, grease or perspiration could affect the
quality of the reflector. When fitting the dual-filament

FIG 12:27 Headlamp cover ring upper and lower holders

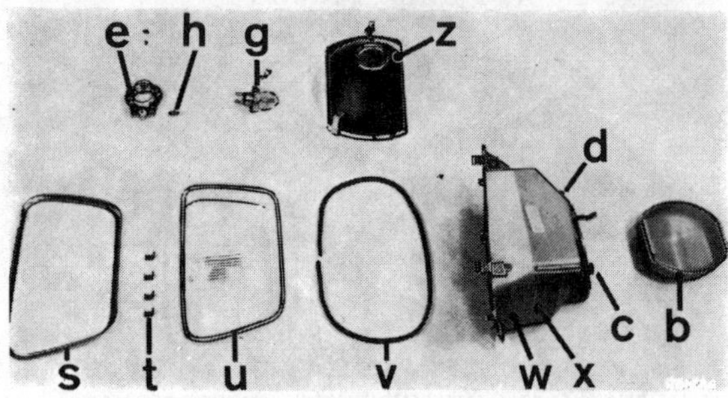

FIG 12:28 Headlamp components

Key to Fig 12:28 **b** Cap **c** Adjusting screw (vertical)
d Adjusting screw (horizontal) **e** Tightening ring
g Double filament bulb **h** Parking light bulb **s** Cover ring
t Clips (4 to mount lens in housing) **u** Lens **v** Seal
w Housing **x** Rubber plug (reflector mount) **z** Reflector

bulb, projection **k** must engage in the guide ring cutout 1, as shown in **FIG 12:26**.

To remove the headlamp unit, press the cover ring downwards in the direction of the arrows on the holders **m** and **n** in **FIG 12:27**, then press the cover ring upwards at **o** and **p** and remove it. Take out the three retaining screws and carefully remove the headlamp unit forwards. Pry off the clips **t** in **FIG 12:28** with a screwdriver and remove the lens and seal. If necessary, remove the reflector as follows:

The reflector is fitted in the housing on a pendulum in the form of a rubber plug **x** and is held in its proper position by the adjusting screws **c** and **d**. Loosen the adjusting screws until it is possible to remove the reflector from the housing. In doing so, slight pressure must be used to slide it over the rubber plug **x**. **Do not remove the rubber plug from the housing unless it is to be renewed.** If a new plug is to be fitted it must be dipped in soapy water for lubrication before being pressed into the housing. Do not touch the inside of the reflector or the surface will be dulled.

Refitting is a reversal of the removal procedure.

Beam setting:

The headlamp beam adjusting screws are accessible from the engine compartment, as shown in **FIG 12:24**. Screw **c** allows vertical adjustments to be made, screw **d** allows for horizontal adjustments. Headlamp main beams should be set so that, when the car is normally loaded, the beams are parallel to each other and to the road. Accurate beam setting is best left to a service station having special equipment for this purpose.

12:9 Lighting circuits

Lamps give insufficient light:

Refer to **Section 12:2** and check the condition of the battery, recharging if necessary. Check the settings of the headlamps as described in **Section 12:8** and renew any bulbs that have darkened with age.

Bulbs burn out frequently:

Have the control box setting checked at an auto-electrical service station.

Lamps light when switched on but gradually fade:

Refer to **Section 12:2** and check the condition of the battery as it is not capable of supplying current for any length of time.

Lamp brilliance varies with the speed of the car:

Check the condition of the battery and its terminals. Make sure that the terminal connections are clean and tight and renew any faulty cables.

12:10 Fault diagnosis

(a) Battery discharged

1 Terminal connections loose or dirty
2 Shorts in lighting circuit
3 Alternator not charging
4 Control box faulty
5 Battery internally defective

(b) Insufficient charge rate

1 Check 1 and 4 in (a)
2 Drive belt slipping

(c) Battery will not hold charge

1 Low electrolyte level
2 Battery plates sulphated
3 Electrolyte leakage from cracked case
4 Battery plate separators defective

(d) Battery overcharged

1 Control box needs adjusting

(e) Alternator output low or nil

1 Belt broken or slipping
2 Control box out of adjustment
3 Brushes sticking, springs weak or broken
4 Defective rotor or stator windings
5 Defective diode(s)

(f) Starter motor lacks power or will not turn

1 Battery discharged, loose cable connections
2 Starter pinion jammed in flywheel ring gear
3 Starter switch or solenoid faulty
4 Brushes worn or sticking, leads detached or shorting
5 Commutator dirty or worn
6 Starter shaft bent
7 Engine abnormally stiff, perhaps due to rebore

(g) Starter runs but does not turn engine

1 Pinion engagement mechanism faulty
2 Broken teeth on pinion or flywheel gears

(h) Noisy starter when engine is running

1 Pinion return mechanism faulty

(j) Starter motor inoperative

1 Check 1 and 4 in (f)
2 Armature or field coils faulty

(k) Starter motor rough or noisy

1 Mounting bolts loose
2 Damaged pinion or flywheel teeth
3 Pinion engagement mechanism faulty

(l) Lamps inoperative or erratic

1 Battery low, bulbs burned out
2 Faulty earthing of lamps or battery
3 Lighting switch faulty, loose or broken connections

(m) Wiper motor sluggish, taking high current

1 Wiper motor defective internally
2 Lack of lubrication
3 Linkage worn or binding
4 Wiper motor fixing bolts loose

(n) Wiper motor runs but does not drive arms

1 Wiper linkage faulty
2 Wiper transmission components worn

(o) Fuel or temperature gauge does not work

1 Check wiring for continuity
2 Check instruments and transmitters for continuity

CHAPTER 13

THE BODYWORK

13:1 Bodywork finish
13:2 Removing door trim
13:3 Door locks and handles
13:4 Removing window regulator mechanism

13:5 Removing and installing doors
13:6 Windscreen and backlight glasses
13:7 The heater

13:1 Bodywork finish

Large scale repairs to body panels are best left to expert panel beaters. Even small dents can be tricky, as too much hammering will stretch the metal and make things worse instead of better. If panel beating is to be attempted, use a dolly on the opposite side of the panel. The head of a large hammer will suffice for small dents, but for large dents a block of metal will be necessary. Use light hammer blows to reshape the panel, pressing the dolly against the opposite side of the panel to absorb the blows. If this method is used to reduce the depth of dents, final smoothing with suitable filler will be easier, although it may be better to avoid hammering minor dents and just use the filler.

Clean the area to be filled, making sure that it is free of paint, rust and grease, then roughen the area with emerycloth to ensure a good bond. Use a proprietary fibreglass filler paste mixed according to the recommendations and press it into the dent with a putty knife. Allow the filler to stand proud of the surrounding area to allow for rubbing down after hardening. Use a file and emerycloth or a disc sander to blend the repaired area to the surrounding bodywork, using finer grade abrasives as the work nears completion. Apply a coat of primer surfacer and, when it is dry, rub down with 'Wet or Dry' paper lubricated with soapy water, finishing with 400 grade. Apply more primer and repeat the operation until the surface is perfectly smooth. Take time on achieving the best finish possible at this stage as it will control the final effect.

The touching up of paintwork can be carried out with self-spraying cans of paint, these being available in a wide range of colours. Use a piece of newspaper or board as a test panel to practice on first, so that the action of the spray will be familiar when it is used on the panel. Before spraying the panel, remove all traces of wax polish. Mask off large areas such as windows with newspaper and masking tape. Small areas such as trim strips or door handles can be wrapped with masking tape or carefully coated with grease or vaseline. Apply the touching up paint, spraying with short bursts and keeping the spray moving. Do not attempt to cover the area in one coat, applying several successive coats with a few minutes drying time between each. If too much paint is applied at one time, runs may develop. If so, do not try to remove the run by wiping, but wait until it is dry and rub it down as before.

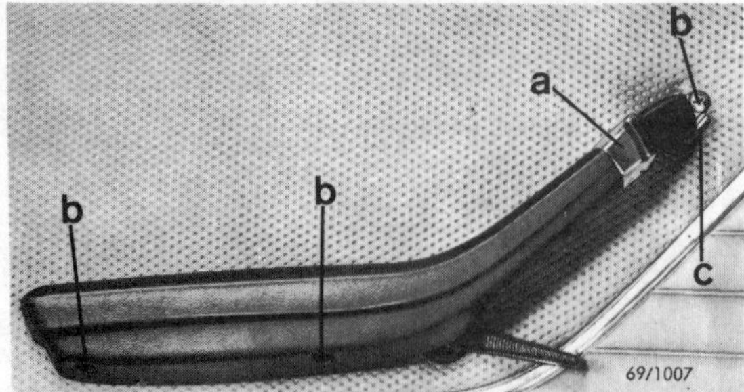

FIG 13:1   Removing the front door arm-rest

FIG 13:2   Removing window winder and inside door handle

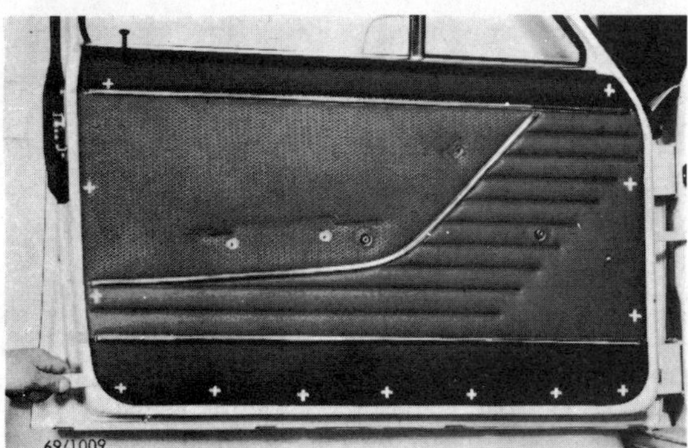

FIG 13:3   Levering off the front door trim

FIG 13:4   Removing the rear door arm-rest

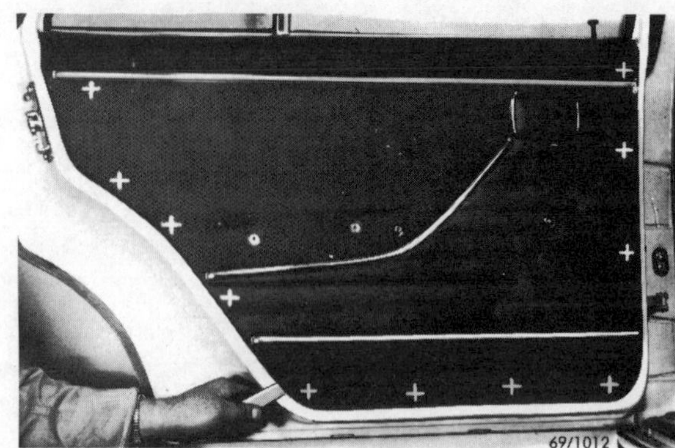

FIG 13:5   Levering off the rear door trim

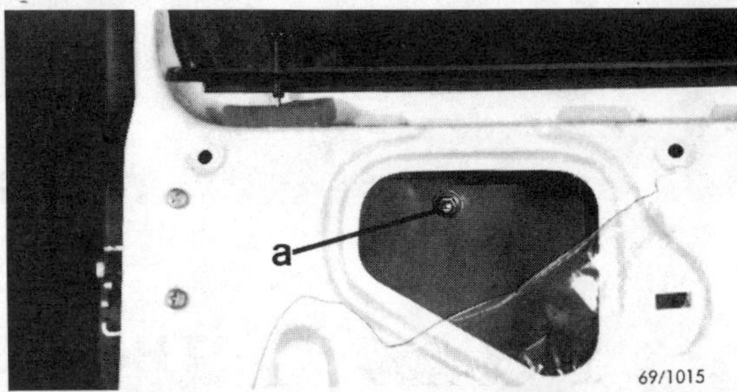

FIG 13:6   Front door handle attaching nut

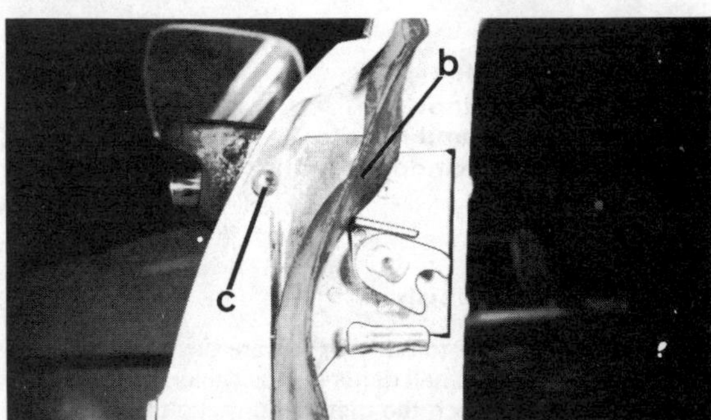

FIG 13:7   Pulling off the door seal

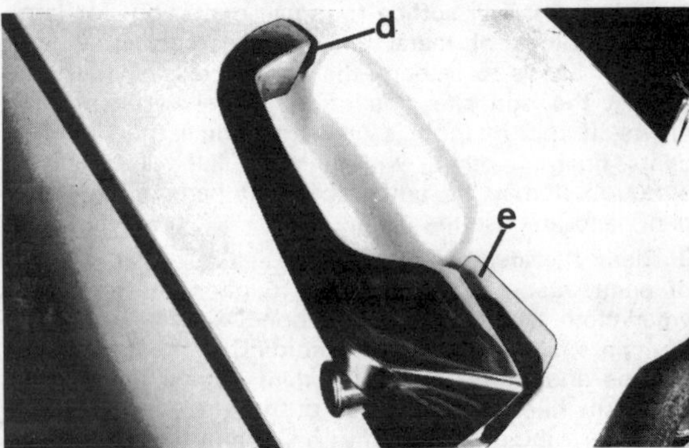

FIG 13:8   Plastic bases in position beneath the front door handle

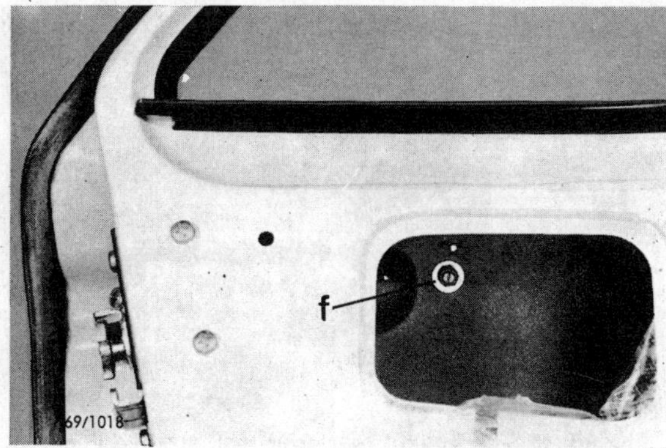
FIG 13:9 Rear door handle attaching nut

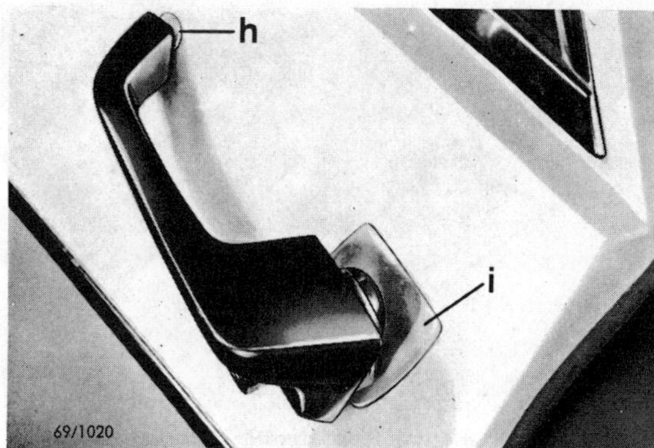
FIG 13:11 Plastic bases in position beneath the rear door handle

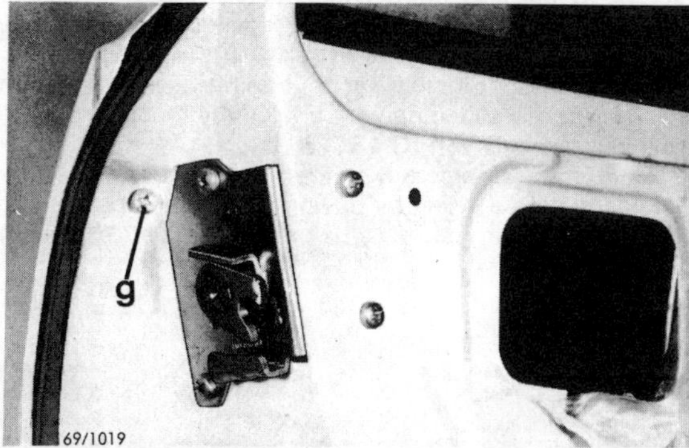
FIG 13:10 Removing the retaining screw and the rear door handle

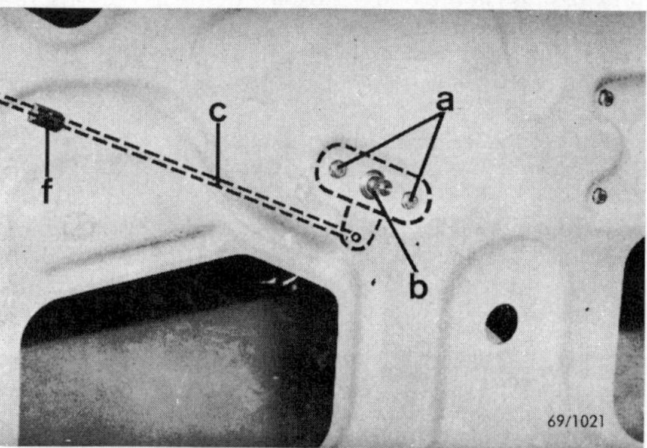
FIG 13:12 Disconnecting the front door lock mechanism

After the final coat is applied, allow a few hours of drying time before blending the new finish to the old with a cutting compound, buffing with a light, circular motion. Finish with the application of a good quality polish.

13:2 Removing door trim

Front door:

Refer to **FIG 13:1** and lever off the chrome cap **a** with a suitable blunt tool. Remove the three screws **b** and take off the armrest and mounting plate **c**. Remove the plastic cover **d** shown in **FIG 13:2** from the window winder. Take out the screw **e** and remove the winder and its base. Remove the screw **f** and the inside door handle **g**. Using a suitable blunt instrument inserted behind the panel, lever off the trim panel at the clip positions marked in **FIG 13:3**. Refitting is the reverse of the removal procedure.

Rear door:

Refer to **FIG 13:4** and take out the two screws shown to remove the armrest. Remove the window winder and inside door handle in the manner just described for front door components. Using a suitable blunt instrument inserted behind the panel, lever off the trim panel at the clip positions shown in **FIG 13:5**. Refit in the reverse order of removal.

13:3 Door locks and handles

Front door handle removal:

Remove the door trim as described in **Section 13:2**. Use a socket spanner to loosen the nut **a** shown in **FIG 13:6**, then remove the nut together with the plain and lock washers. Pull off the door seal material in the area of the door lock, as shown at **b** in **FIG 13:7**, then remove the screw **c** and the outside door handle assembly.

Refitting is a reversal of the removal procedure, making sure that the plastic bases sgown in **FIG 13:8** are correctly positioned beneath the handle.

Rear door handle removal:

Remove the door trim as described in **Section 13:2**. Use a socket spanner to loosen the nut **f** shown in **FIG 13:9**, then remove the nut together with the plain and lock washers. Remove the screw **g** shown in **FIG 13:10** and remove the outside door handle assembly.

Refitting is a reversal of the removal procedure, making sure that the plastic bases shown in **FIG 13:11** are correctly positioned beneath the handle.

Front door lock removal:

Remove the door trim and the outside door handle as described previously. Refer to **FIG 13:12**. Remove screws **a** and disconnect the remote control rod **c** at auxiliary

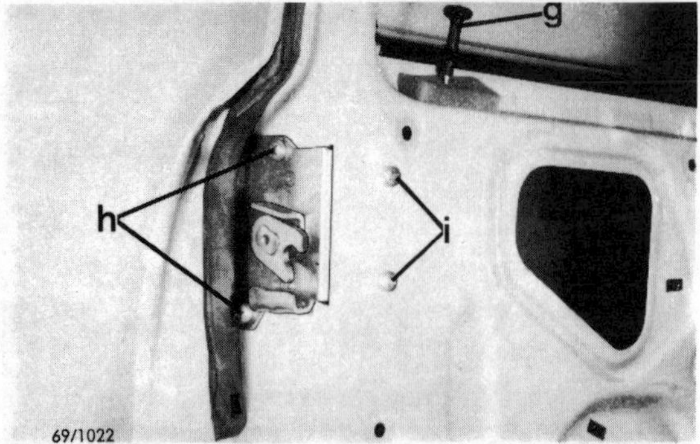

FIG 13:13   Removing front door lock retaining screws

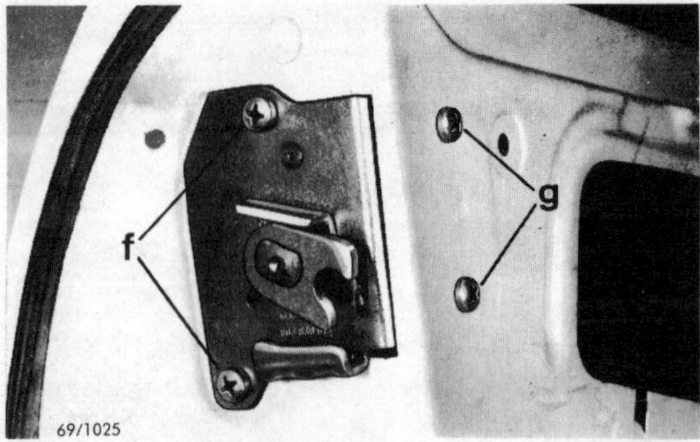

FIG 13:16   Removing rear door lock retaining screws

lock **b**. Press in the rubber holder **f** of the rod **c**. Unscrew button **g** shown in **FIG 13:13**, then remove screws **h** and **i**. Pull the door lock **k**, locking rods **l** and **m** and the remote control rod **n** out of the door opening, as shown in **FIG 13:14**.

Refit in the reverse order of removal.

Rear door lock removal:

Remove the door trim and the outside door handle as described previously. Refer to **FIG 13:15**. Remove the

screws **b** and disconnect the remote control rod **d** at auxiliary lock **c**. Press in the rubber holder **e** of the rod **d**. Remove the retaining screws **f** and **g** shown in **FIG 13:16**. Pull out the door lock as far as possible and use a 7 mm socket wrench to remove nut **k** from the locking cable 1, this being shown in **FIG 13:17**.

Refit in the reverse order of removal. The lock must be unlocked before fitting by pulling the button upward and the operating pawl **m** must be pressed inwards as shown in **FIG 13:18**.

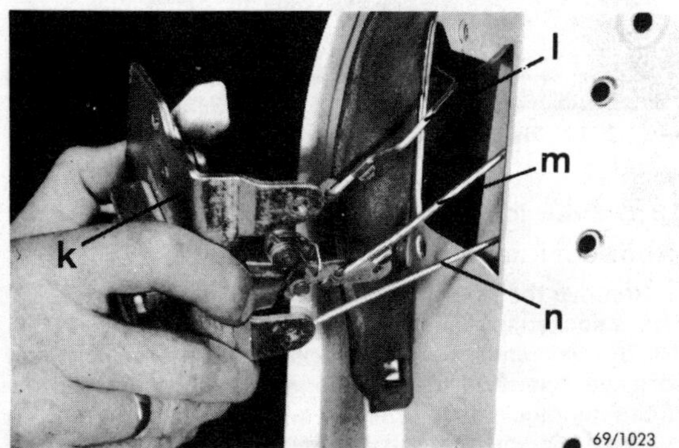

FIG 13:14   Removing the front door lock assembly

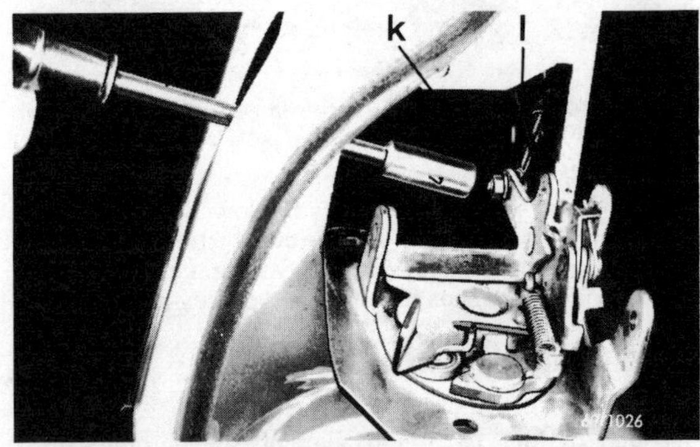

FIG 13:17   Disconnecting the rear door locking cable

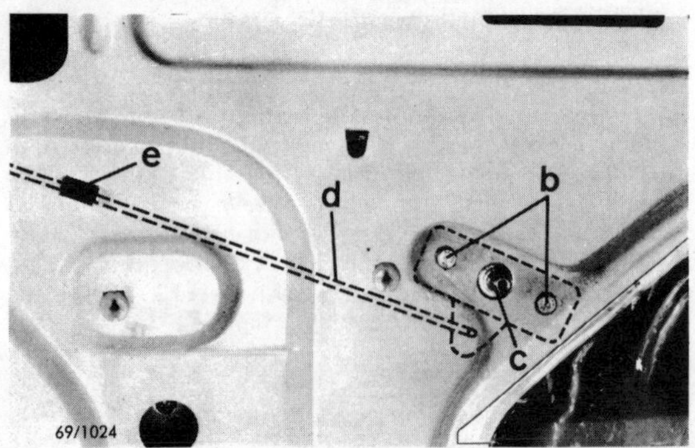

FIG 13:15   Disconnecting the rear door lock mechanism

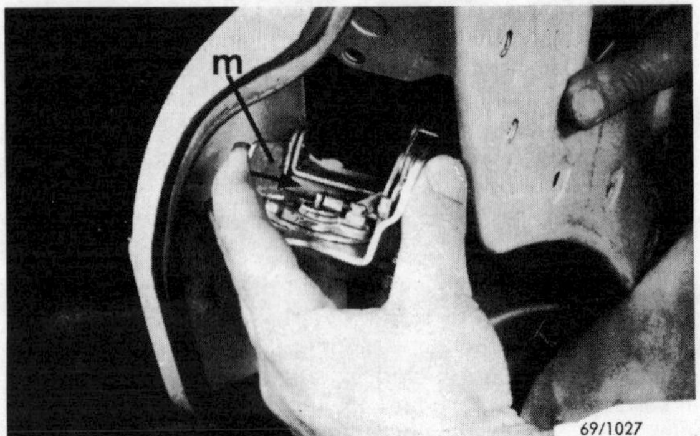

FIG 13:18   Refitting a rear door lock

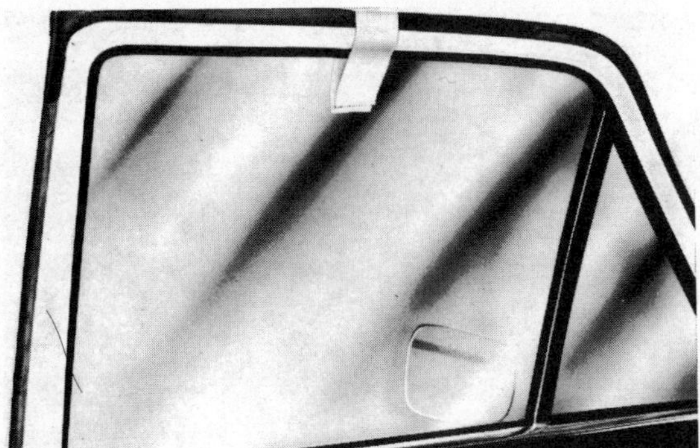

FIG 13:19 Taping the front door window to retain it fully closed, four-door model

13:4 Removing window regulator mechanism

Front door (4 door model):

Close the window completely and tape the glass as shown in **FIG 13:19** to secure it in this position. Remove the door trim as described previously. Refer to **FIG 13:20**. Remove the four screws **a** and pull the regulator arm **b** out of guide rail **c** towards the hinge side, as indicated by the arrow. Remove the regulator assembly through opening **d**.

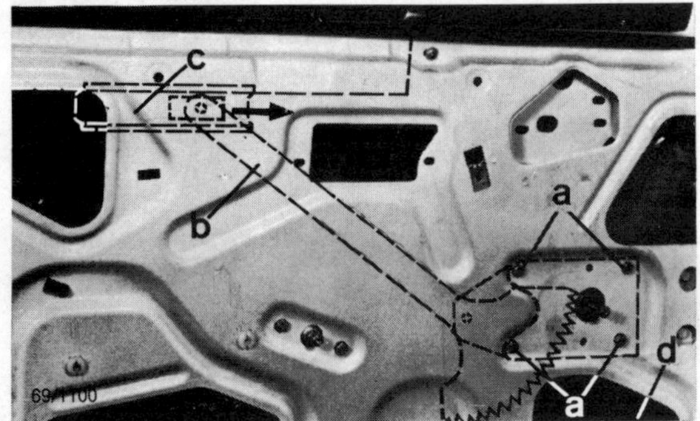

FIG 13:20 Front door window regulator details, four-door model

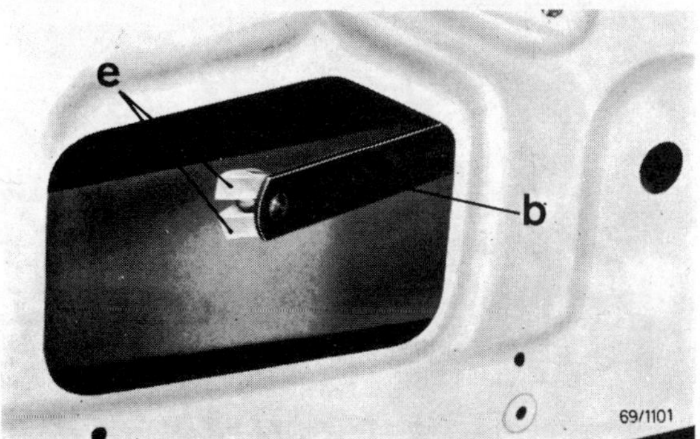

FIG 13:21 Regulator ball pin slides

FIG 13:22 Front door window regulator details, two-door model

Refit in the reverse order of removal, being sure to fit the slides **e** on the regulator ball pin as shown in **FIG 13:21**.

Front door (2 door model):

Lower the window completely, then remove the door trim as described previously. Refer to **FIG 13:22**. Remove the mounting screws **f** and pull the regulator arm **g** out of guide rail **h** towards the outside of the door as shown by the arrow. Raise the window completely and tape the

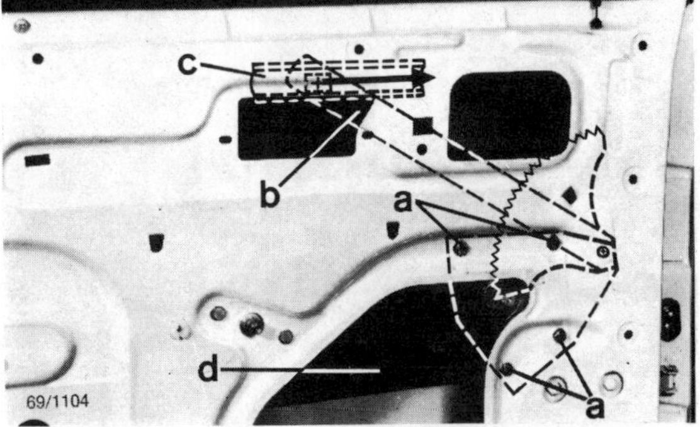

FIG 13:23 Removing the regulator assembly

FIG 13:24 Rear door window regulator details

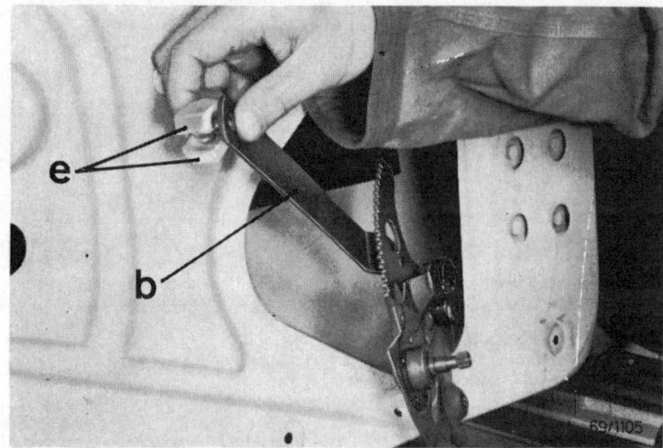

FIG 13:25   Regulator ball pin slides, rear door

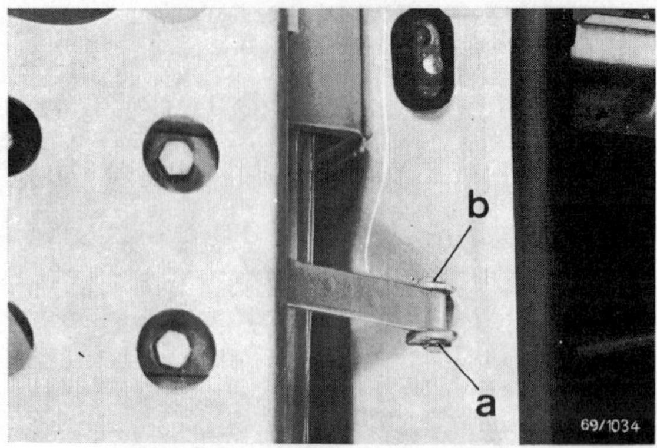

FIG 13:26   Releasing front door check strap

glass in the manner shown in **FIG 13:19** to secure it in position. Remove the regulator assembly from the door as shown in **FIG 13:23**.

Rear door:

Close the window completely and tape the glass in the manner shown in **FIG 13:19** to secure it in position. Remove the door trim as described previously. Refer to **FIG 13:24**. Remove the four screws **a** and pull the regulator arm **b** out of the guide rail **c** towards the hinge

side as shown by the arrow, then remove the regulator assembly through opening **d**.

Refit in the reverse order of removal, being sure to fit the slides **e** on the ballpin **b** as shown in **FIG 13:25**.

13:5 Removing and installing doors

Front doors:

Remove the door trim as described previously. Mark the position of the hinges on the door panel by scribing around them. This will ensure correct alignment when

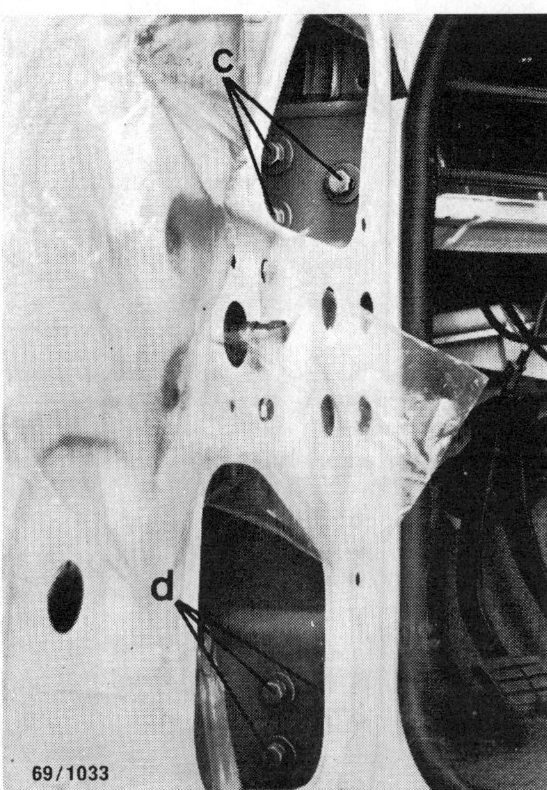

FIG 13:27   Removing the front door retaining screws

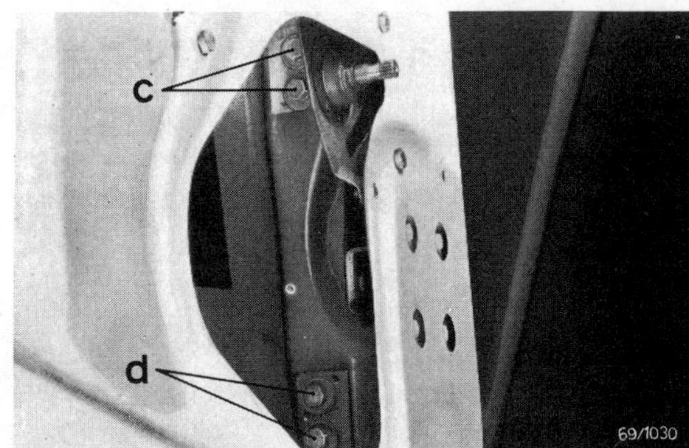

FIG 13:28   Removing the rear door retaining screws

FIG 13:29   Removing the windscreen

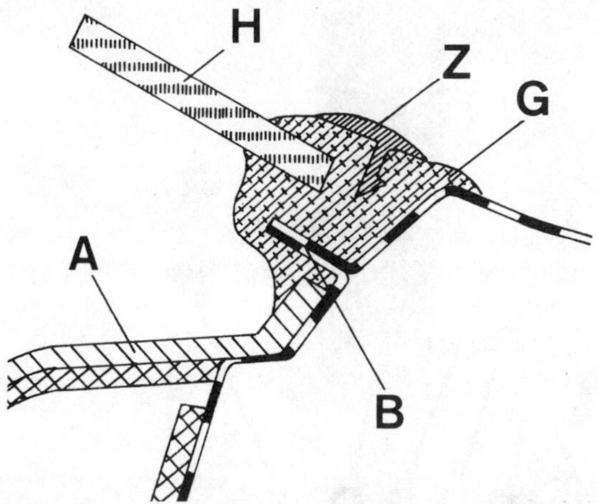

FIG 13:30   Cross-section through the windscreen seal

Key to Fig 13:30   **B** Edge of body   **G** Rubber frame
S Instrument panel padding   **W** Windshield   **Z** Chrome strip

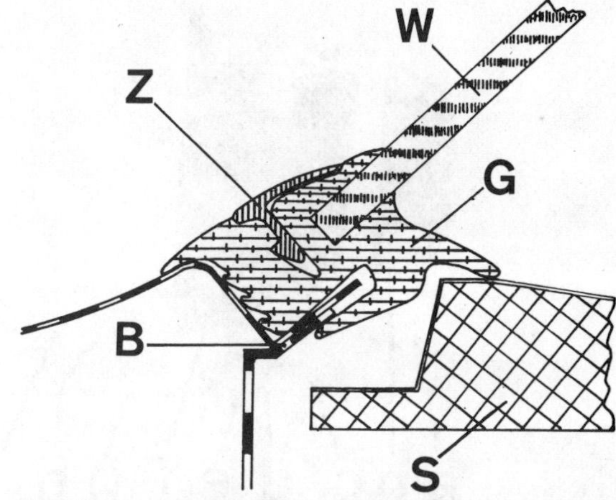

FIG 13:31   Cross-section through the backlight seal

Key to Fig 13:31   **A** Hat rack   **B** Edge of body
G Rubber frame   **H** Rear window   **Z** Chrome strip

refitting. Lever off the snap ring **a** shown in **FIG 13:26** and remove pin **b** by hammering out upwards. Take out three each screws **c** and **d** shown in **FIG 13:27** and lift off the door.

Refit in the reverse order of removal, using the scribe marks for alignment.

Rear doors:

Remove the door trim as described previously, then scribe mark around the hinge fixings on the door panel to ensure correct alignment when refitting. Lever off the snap ring and hammer out the pin in the manner described for front door check straps. Remove two each screws **c** and **d** shown in **FIG 13:28** and lift off the door.

Refit in the reverse order of removal, using the scribe marks for alignment.

13:6 Windscreen and backlight glasses

The removal and refitting instructions given in this section concern the windscreen glass. The instructions apply equally to the backlight glass.

Removal:

Remove the windscreen by pressing out as shown in **FIG 13:29**. When multi-layer safety windscreens are fitted, loosen the inner rubber lip with a knife blade before pressing out the screen. Have an assistant ready to steady the screen as it frees from the surround to avoid damage. Clean the aperture flange of all old sealer and made sure there are no particles of glass in the sealing rubber channels.

Fitting:

Apply a thin coat of glycerine or soapy water solution around the grooves of the rubber channel. Place the channel around the windscreen and press on the chrome strips around the complete circumference by hand.

FIG 13:30 shows a cross-section through the windscreen seal, **FIG 13:30** that for backlight seals. Fit a length of strong blind cord around the outside of the assembly, in the groove for the body edge **b**. Cross the ends of the cord at the bottom of the windscreen. Fit the screen correctly in the centre of the aperture with the

FIG 13:32   Fitting a windscreen glass

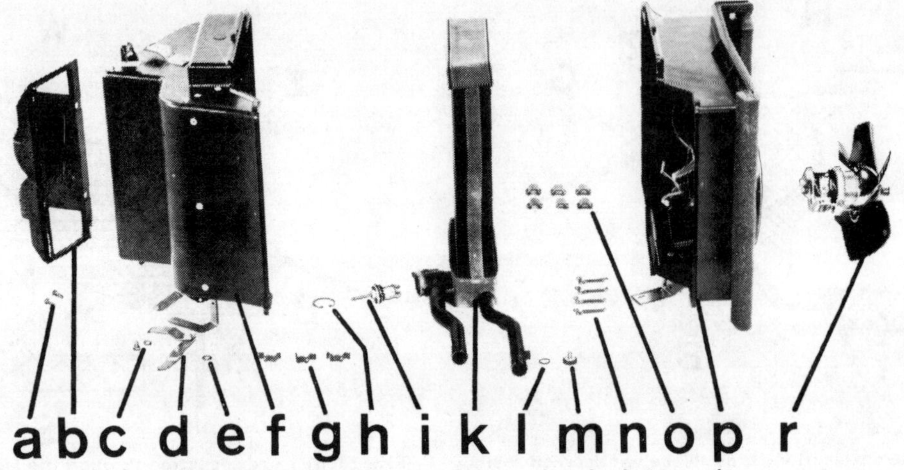

FIG 13:33 Components of the car interior heater unit

Key to Fig 13:33   **a** Self-tapping screw   **b** Foot area nozzle   **c** Hexagonal head screw   **d** Adjusting lever   **e** Nut 5
f Housing lower section   **g** Spring clip, Bowden cable   **h** Circlip 25 x 1.2   **i** Plunger   **k** Heater body (heat converter)
l Seal   **m** Breather screw   **n** Spring, blower motor   **o** Clip, housing halves   **p** Housing upper section   **r** Motor and fan

ends of the cord inside the car. Have an assistant apply steady hand pressure to the outside of the screen, while the cord is pulled out to lip the seal over the flange. Work equally on both sides of the screen. **Do not fit one end first then try to fit the other end.** The fitting method is shown in **FIG 13:32**. Use a pressure gun to inject sealing compound between the glass and the rubber and between the rubber and the aperture flange. Remove excess compound with a rag and white spirit. Do not use thinners as this could damage the paintwork.

13:7 The heater

FIG 13:33 shows the components of the car interior heater unit. Access to the heater unit is by removing the knee protector panels and the instrument panel trim. Heater unit removal is carried out from the interior of the car, after disconnecting the hoses and connections in the engine compartment. Always disconnect the battery and drain the cooling system before work is started. On completion, refill and bleed the cooling system as described in **Chapter 4, Section 4:2**.

APPENDIX

TECHNICAL DATA

      Engine   Fuel system   Cooling system   Ignition system
      Clutch   Transmission   Suspension   Steering   Brakes
      Electrical equipment   Capacities   Torque wrench settings

WIRING DIAGRAMS

      FIG 14:1   First version
      FIG 14:2   First version with combined flasher, dip beams and number plate light
      FIG 14:3   Second version
      FIG 14:4   Second version with combined flasher, dip beams and number
                  plate light
      FIG 14:5   Third version with series resistor between ignition lock and
                  ignition coil
      FIG 14:6   Third version with combined flasher, dip beams and number plate light
                  and with series resistor between ignition lock and ignition coil
      FIG 14:7   Fourth version, June 1969
      FIG 14:8   USA export version

HINTS ON MAINTENANCE AND OVERHAUL

GLOSSARY OF TERMS

INDEX

TECHNICAL DATA

Measurements are in inches unless otherwise stated

ENGINE

Engine:

Capacity	1760 cc
Bore and stroke	81.5 x 84.4 mm
Compression ratio and output (DIN)	9.1:1 80 bhp at 5000
	10.2:1 90 bhp at 5500
	10.2:1 100 bhp at 5500
Capacity	1871 cc
Bore and stroke	84 x 84.4 mm
Compression ratio and output (DIN)	8.2:1 95 bhp at 5200
	10.2:1 112 bhp at 5600

Crankshaft:

Material	Forged tempered steel
Main bearings	Five, tri-metal shell type
Thrust taken by	Centre main bearing

Connecting rods:

Type	I-section tempered steel forgings
Bigend bearings	Tri-metal shell type
Small-end bearings	Lead/bronze coated steel bushes

Pistons:

Material	Light alloy with steel inserts
Clearance	.00012

Piston rings:

Fitted gap	1 mm maximum
Clearance in piston groove	.015 mm maximum

Camshaft:

Bearings	Babbit, shell type
End float	.004

Valves:

Seat angle, inlet and exhaust	90 deg. plus 30 min.

Valve clearances:

Inlet	.006 warm
Exhaust	.015 warm

For initial setting only:

Inlet	.004 cold
Exhaust	.014 cold

Oil pump:

Type	Gear
Oil filter	Fullflow with renewable element

FUEL SYSTEM

Carburetter type:

Audi 100 and 100S	Solex 35.PDSIT.5 downdraught
Audi 100LS	Solex 32.TDID downdraught twin-stage
Audi 100 GL	Solex 32/35 TDID
Audi 100 Coupé S (1971)	Solex 32/35 TDID Twin

	35.PDSIT.5	32.TDID Stage 1	32.TDID Stage 2
Venturi	27	24	27
Main jet	X147.5	X125	X145
Air correction jet	70	160	100

Idle jet g55 g55 50
Idle air jet bore 160 140 100
Injection rate per stroke ... ... 1.25 ±.15 cc 1.8 ±.15 cc
Choke gap ... ... .13 ±.004 .09 ±.006
Throttle gap ... ... .067 ±.004 .063 ±.004
Bi-metallic spring ... ... 10 x .38 x 470 mm 8 x .38 x 470 mm
Float needle valve ... ... 1.75 (with ball) 2.0
Seal, float needle valve ... ... .5 mm 2 mm
Float weight ... ... 7.3 g 7.3 g
Fuel level ... ... .45 to .53 —
Float location ... ... — .61 to .67

	32/35 TDID		Twin 32/35 TDID	
Venturi ...	24	28	24	28
Main jet ...	X127.5	X135	X120	X130
Air correction jet ...	140	110	120	100
Idle jet ...	g50	50	50	50
Idle jet air bore ...	190	100	140	100
Choke gap ...	.138±.006		.098±.006	
Throttle gap ...	.043±.001		.025±.001	

Fuel pump:

Type ... ... Mechanical
Delivery rate ... ... 43 litres/hr at 2000 strokes/min
Maximum delivery pressure ... ... .25 kg/sq cm (3.55 lb/sq in)

COOLING SYSTEM

Cooling system:

Type ... ... Pressurized
Thermostat opens at ... ... 83°C (181°F)
Radiator pressure cap opens at ... ... 12.8 lb/sq in

IGNITION SYSTEM

Sparking plugs:

Audi 100 (up to 1971) ... ... Champion N4 or equivalent
Audi 100S, 100LS ... ... Champion N7Y
Audi 100GL, Coupé S ... ... Champion N6Y
Audi 100 (1972) ... ... Champion N8Y
Timing ... ... See **Section 3:5**
Electrode gap ... ... .020 to .024 → 72 change to .035 – .040
Distributor:

Type JFUR.4
Capacitor ... ... .23 to .35 microfarad
Contact points gap ... ... .016
Firing order 1–3–4–2

CLUTCH

Clutch:

Type ... ... Single dry plate
Pressure plate ... ... F & S MF.215
Driven plate ... ... 15.PSD with torsion damper
Pedal free travel ... ... .59 to .78

TRANSMISSION

Gearbox:

Number of forward speeds ... ... Four
Synchromesh ... ... All four forward gears

Drive ratios:

	Audi 72, 75, 80, 100S and 100LS	Audi 60 and 100	Audi Super 90
First gear	3.4:1	3.4:1	3.4:1
Second gear	1.95:1	1.95:1	1.95:1
Third gear	1.36:1	1.36:1	1.36:1
Top gear	.966:1	.966:1	.933:1
Reverse gear	3.1:1	3.1:1	3.1:1
Final drive ratio	3.9:1	4.1:1	3.9:1

AUTOMATIC TRANSMISSION

Gearbox:

Number of forward speeds ... ... Three

Gear ratios:

First gear 2.65:1
Second gear 1.59:1
Top gear 1.0:1
Reverse gear 1.8:1
Final drive ratio 3.73:1
Transmission fluid ... ... Dexron B.10.378

SUSPENSION

Front suspension:

Type ... ... Independent, by wishbones and
telescopic coil spring dampers

Rear suspension:

Type ... ... Tube axle, with torsion bar springs,
telescopic hydraulic dampers and
transverse rod

STEERING

Steering:

Type ... ... Rack and pinion
Ratio 21.6:1
Steering wheel turns, lock to lock 3.88

Steering angles:

	Coupé	Others
Castor	30'±20'	6'±20'
Camber	9'±20'	11'±20'
Toe-out	0 to .079	0 to .079

BRAKES

Brakes:

Type ... ... Disc front, drum rear
Operation ... ... Hydraulic, dual circuit system
Servo assistance ... ... Audi 100S and 100LS models
Brake disc diameter 11.02
Brake drum diameter 7.87
Disc pad linings ... ... Jurid 215
Drum brake linings ... ... Jurid 132 (K3)
Brake fluid SAE.70.R3

<h1 style="text-align:center">ELECTRICAL EQUIPMENT</h1>

Battery:

Type	12-volt 45 amp/hr	
Alternator	K1.14V35A20	
Control box	AD1/14-volt	
Regulating voltage	13.5 to 14.8	

Starter:

Type	12-volt .8 HP

<h1 style="text-align:center">CAPACITIES</h1>

Engine	7 Imp pints	8.5 US pints	4 litres
Gearbox	3.5 Imp pints	4.2 US pints	2 litres
Automatic transmission final drive ...	.3 Imp galls	.4 US galls	1.4 litres
Automatic transmission fluid	1.3 Imp galls	1.6 US galls	6 litres
Amount for fluid change	.7 Imp galls	.8 US galls	3 litres
Cooling system	6.6 Imp quarts	8 US quarts	7.5 litres
Fuel tank	12.3 Imp galls	15.3 US galls	58 litres

<h1 style="text-align:center">TORQUE WRENCH SETTINGS</h1>

Engine:	Thread	kgm	lb ft
Exhaust manifold end plate	M8	2.0	14.5
Starter to engine block	M12	6.0	43.5
Exhaust manifold to cylinder head	M8	2.4	17.5
Fuel pump to engine block	M8	2.0	19.5
Thermostat cover	M6	1.0	7.2
Oil pump (engine block oil line)	M6	1.0	7.2
Valve tappet clearance adjustment nut (installed with Molykote)	M12	1.5 to 5.0	11 to 36
Heater flange to cylinder head	M8	2.0	14.5
Camshaft guide flange	M8	2.5	18
Transmission to engine	M12	7.5	54
Transmission to engine	M10	4.5	33
Transmission to engine	M8	2.5	18
Guide rail to engine block	M6	1.2	8.7
Timing chain tensioner	M6	1.2	8.7
Rocker lever mounting screw in cylinder head ...	M12	max. 10.0	140
Distributor clamping lever to engine block ...	M8	2.0	14.5
Clamping screw	M6	.3 to .5	2.2 to 3.6
Thermostat to cylinder head	M8	2.0	14.5
Clutch coverplate to flywheel	M8	3.2	24
Bearing cap No. 5 to engine block	M8	3.2	24
Bearing cap to engine block	M12	8.0	58
Alternator to holder, holder to engine block ...	M8	2.5 to 3.0	18 to 22
Fan to hub	M8	1.0	7.2
Air guide ring to fan support	M8	2.0 to 2.5	14.5 to 18
Fan support to engine block	M10	4.5	33
Camshaft sprocket to camshaft	M12	8.0	58
Oil filter	¾ inch UNF	2.5 to 3.5	18 to 25
Oil pressure switch	M10	1.5	11
Oil pump upper section to lower section ...	M6	1.0	7.2
Oil pump to engine block	M8	2.0	14.5
Oil check valve	M18	2.5 to 3.5	18 to 25
Oil pan to engine block	M6	.8	6
Oil pan to engine block	M8	1.5	11
Oil pan plug	M26	4.0	29

	Thread	kg m	lb ft
Connecting rod bolt	M10	3.5 to 4.3	25 to 31
Pulley to crankshaft	M20	18.0 to 25.0	130 to 180
Pulley to water pump	M8	2.0	14.5
Intake manifold to cylinder head	M8	2.4	17.5
Intake manifold support	M8	2.0	14.5
Flywheel to crankshaft	M12	9.0	65
Timing housing cover	M6	.8 to 1.0	6 to 7.2
Heater element	M10	1.0	7.2

Engine mountings:

	Thread	kg m	lb ft
Stop to front crossmember	M8	2.5	18
Engine support to engine block	M10	4.2	30
Engine mount to console	M10	3.0	22
Engine support to engine mount	M12	6.0	43
Counter nut to left engine mount	M12	9.5	69
Rear engine mount to transmission	M12	3.0	22
Rear crossmember to rear engine mount	M10	4.2	30
Rear crossmember to body	M8	2.5	18
Carburetter to intake manifold	M8	2.0	14.5
Oil passage plug, front	M16	3.0	22
Oil passage plug, rear	M16	4.5	33
Cylinder head plug	M26	8.0	58
Timing chain tensioner plug	M6	.5 to 1	3.6 to 7.2
Water pump to engine block	M8	2.0	14.5
Water pump to engine block	M6	1.2	8.7
Spark plug	M14	3.0	22
Cylinder head to engine block; in steps	M12	4, 6, 8 (9 warm)	29, 43, 58 (65)
Cylinder head cover to cylinder head	M8	1.3	9.4

Manual transmission:

	Thread	kg m	lb ft
Stub axle	M8	2.5 to 3.3	18.0 to 23.8
Differential flange	M8	2.5 to 3.3	18.0 to 23.8
Transmission cover	M8	2.5 to 3.3	18.0 to 23.8
End cover	M8	2.5 to 3.3	18.0 to 23.8
Shift rod cover	M6	.8 to 1.0	5.78 to 7.23
Reverse operating lever	M10	3.0 to 4.0	21.7 to 28.9
Crownwheel—differential housing	M10	7.0	50.6
Drive pinion	M24	10.0 to 11.0	72.3 to 79.5
Caliper	M16	4.0 to 5.0	28.9 to 36.1
Oil inlet	Screw	3.0 to 3.5	21.7 to 25.3
Oil drain	Screw	3.0 to 3.5	21.7 to 25.3
Main shaft needle bearing	M6	.4 to .6	2.9 to 4.3
Speedometer bushing		3.5 to 4.0	25.3 to 28.9
Reverse switch		3.5 to 4.0	25.3 to 28.9
Clutch release shaft	Setscrew	1.0 to 1.5	7.23 to 10.85
Steering lock	Plug	.6 to .9	4.3 to 6.5

Front wheel drive unit:

	Thread	kg m	lb ft
Wishbone, upper, to body	M8	2.2	15.91
Wishbone, upper, assembly	M12	5.0	36.17
Wishbone, lower, to body, front	M10	4.2	30.38
Wishbone, lower, to body, rear	M8	2.2	15.91
Wishbone, lower, assembly	M10	4.2	30.38
Wishbone, lower, assembly	M12	5.0	36.17
Joint plate assembly	M30	12.0	86.8
Stabilizer to wishbone, lower	M8	2.2	15.91
Mounting, wishbone, lower/upper to steering knuckle	M10	4.2	30.38
Drive shaft to stub axle	M12	10.2	73.78

	Thread	kg m	lb ft
Spring leg to wishbone, upper	M12	9.0	65.1
Spring leg to body	M8	1.8	13.02
Assembly shock absorber to spring retainer	M10 x 1	3.0	21.7

Steering:

	Thread	kg m	lb ft
Track rod to track rod lever	M10	3.6	26.04
Track rod to rack	M14	7.0	50.63
Mounting, front ball and socket joint/track rod	M8	1.4	10.13
Mount to steering gear	M8	2.5	18.08
Steering gear to body	M8	1.1	7.96
Steering column to steering joint	M8	1.1	7.96
Hardy disc	M8	1.75 ±.25	10.85 ±1.81
Steering column to pinion	M8	2.5	18.08
Steering outer tube to body	M8	2.5	18.08
Steering wheel	M18	5.0	36.17

Rear axle assembly:

	Thread	kg m	lb ft
Damper to body	M10	3	21.7
Damper to rear axle	M12	7	50.6
Suspension arm to rear axle	M10	4.2	30.4
Suspension arm to rear axle	M10	4.2	30.4
Panhard rod to rear axle	M10	6.5	47.0
Panhard rod to rear axle	M10	6.5	47.0
Panhard rod to cross-tube	M12	4	28.9
Suspension arm to cross-tube	M8	2.2	15.9
Cross-tube to body	M10	4.2	30.4
Brake backplate	M8	2.2	15.9
Rear axle, outer	M8	2.2	15.9

Brakes:

	kg m	lb ft
Caliper to transmission	9.5 +1	68.7 +7.23
Drive shaft to transmission	10.2 ±.5	73.75 ±3.6
Brake pipeline joints	1.1 ±10%	7.96 ±.79

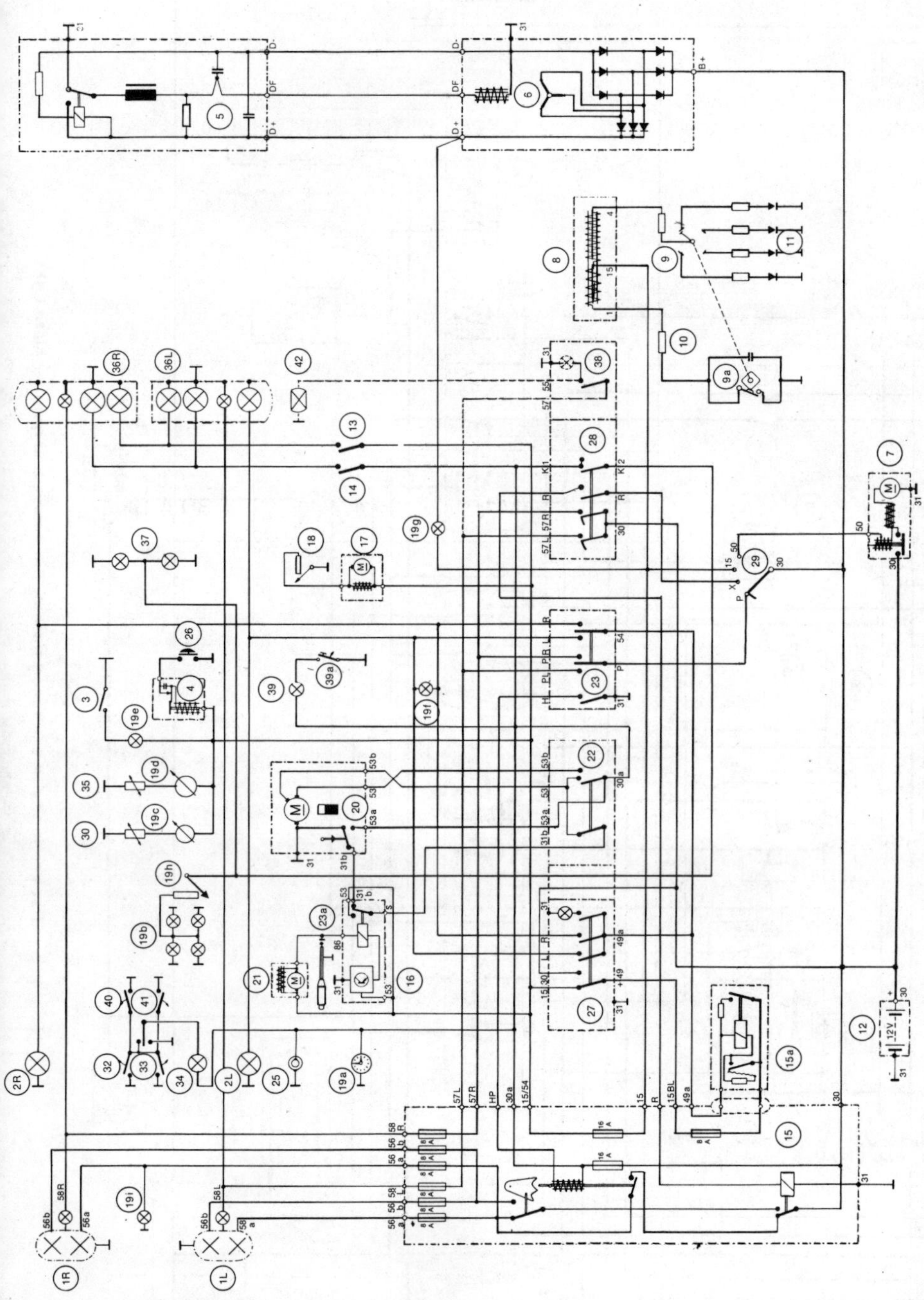

Key to Figs 14:1 to Fig 14:8

1R Headlight, right 1L Headlight, left 2R Turn signal, right 2L Turn signal, left 3 Oil pressure switch 4 Horn 5 Governor 6 Alternator 7 Starter
8 Ignition coil 9 Distributor 9a Contact breaker 10 Series resistor for position 8 11 Spark plugs 12 Battery 13 Reverse light switch 14 Brake light switch
15 Combination relay 15a Flasher unit 16 Relay, windshield washer 17 Blower motor 18 Series resistor for position 17 19a Clock 19b Instrument illumination
19c Temperature gauge 19d Fuel gauge 19e Oil warning lamp 19f Turn signal warning lamp 19g Battery warning lamp 19h Regulating resistor for position 19b
19i High beam warning lamp 20 Wiper motor 21 Washer motor 22 Wiper switch 23 Turn signal—dip beam switch 23a Washer impulse tracer 24 Multi-connector
25 Cigarette lighter 26 Horn button 27 Emergency warning light switch 28 Light switch 29 Steering-ignition lock 30 Temperature transmitter
32 Door contact switch, front, right 33 Door contact switch, front, left 34 Interior light and switch 35 Fuel tank gauge 36R Tail light, right 36L Tail light, left
37 License plate light 38 Switch, tail fog light 39 Glove compartment light 39a Switch for position 39 40 Door contact switch, rear, right 41 Door contact switch, rear, left 42 Tail fog light (optional extra)
19k Twin-circuit brake warning lamp* 24 Switching relay for position 4* 31 Twin-circuit braking system* 44 Audible buzzer* 45 Door contact switch for position 44 46L Side marker lights* 46R Side marker lights* 52 Additional turn signal, right** 53 Additional turn signal, left**

*For USA only   **For Italy only

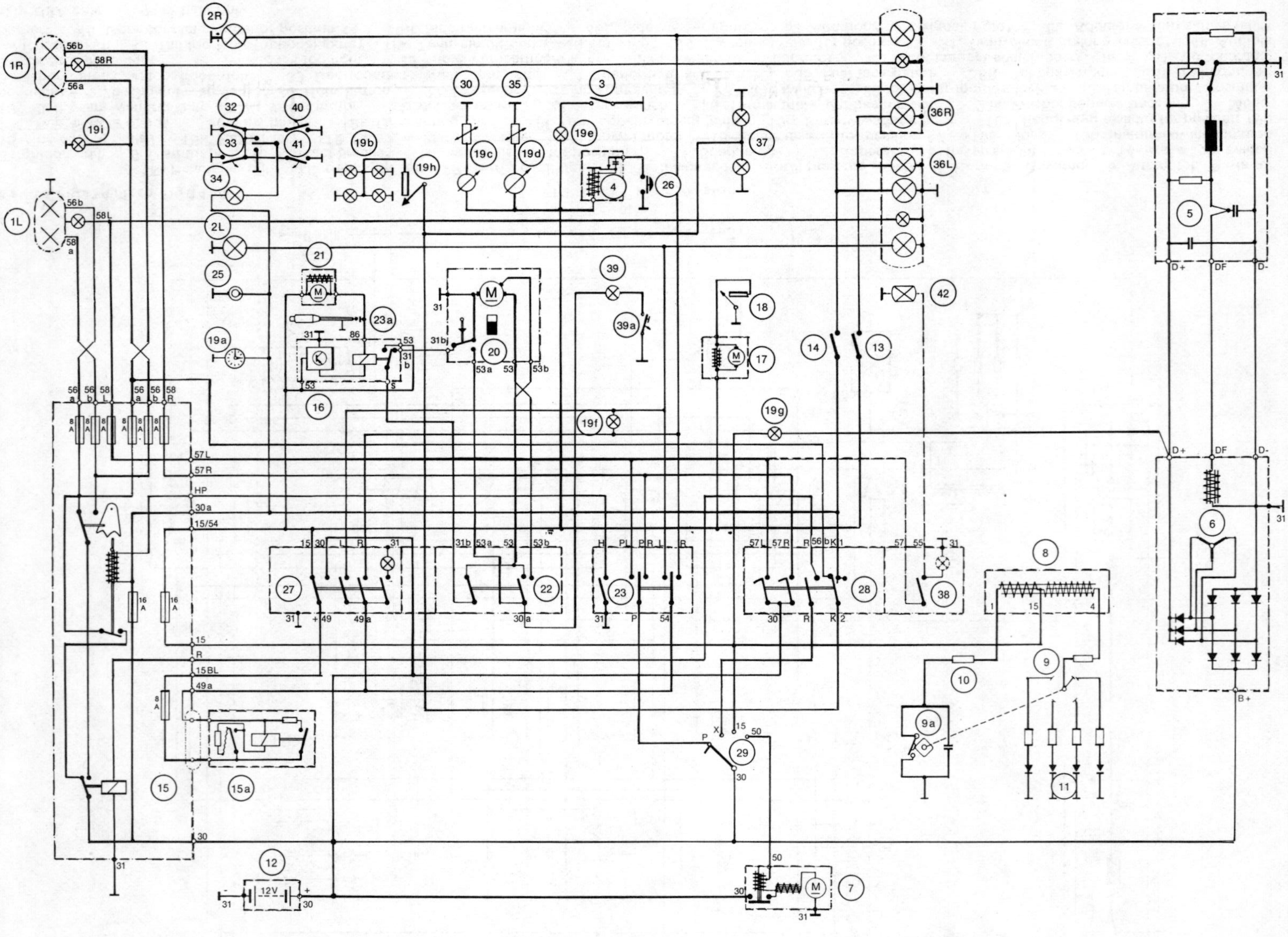

FIG 4:2   First version with combined flasher, dip beams and number plate light

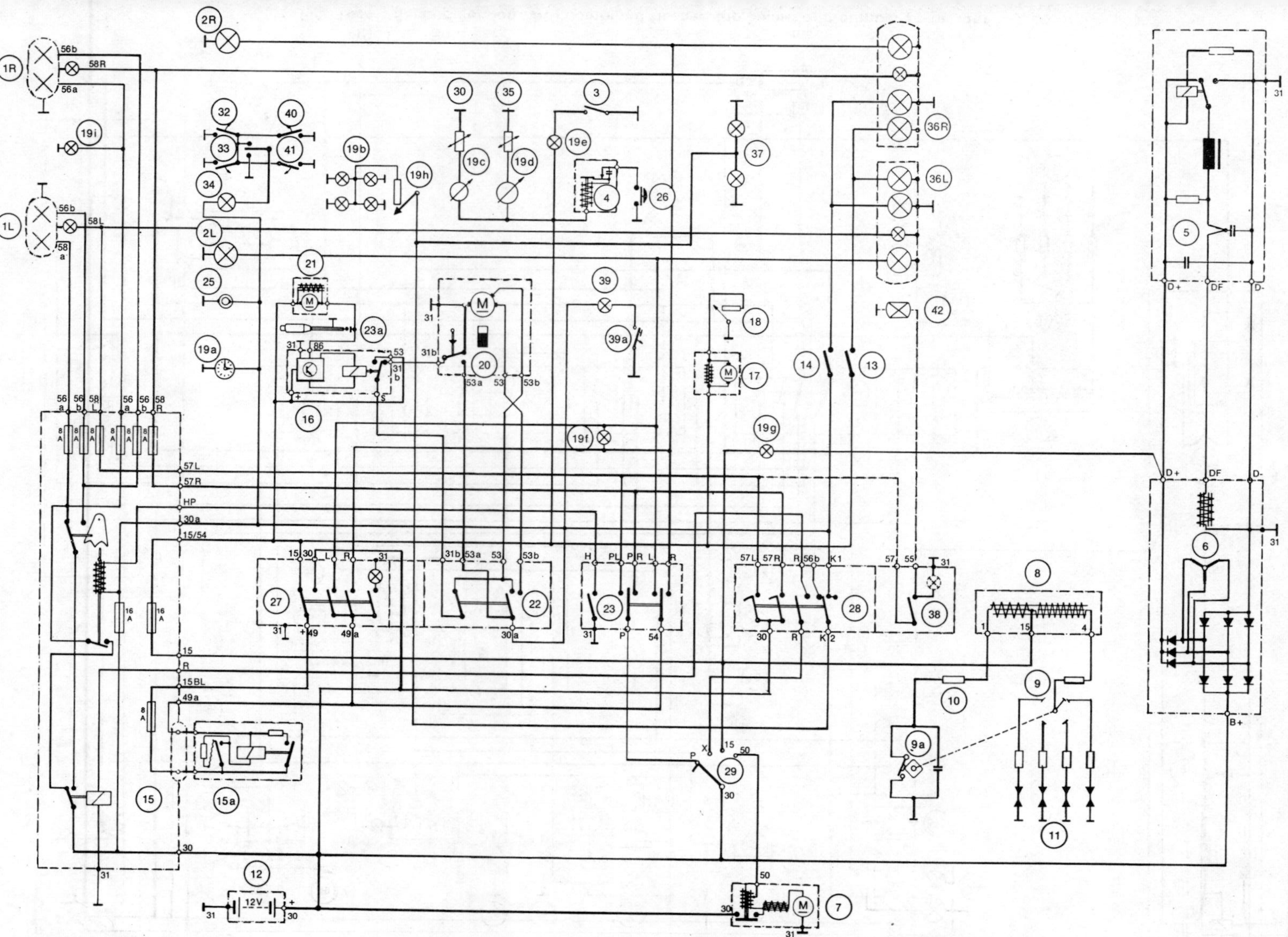

FIG 14:3 Second version

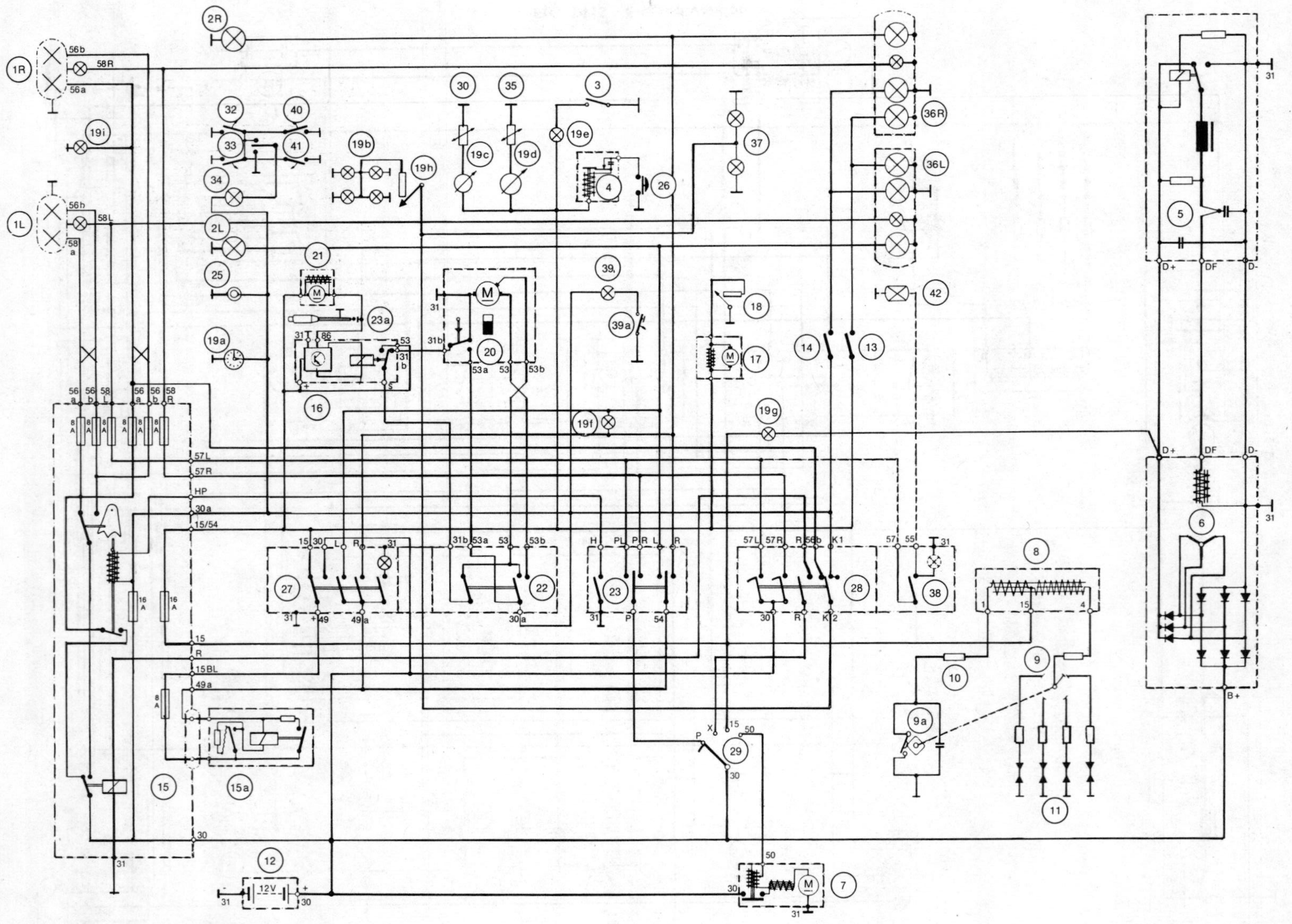

FIG 14:4 Second version with combined flasher, dip beams and number plate light

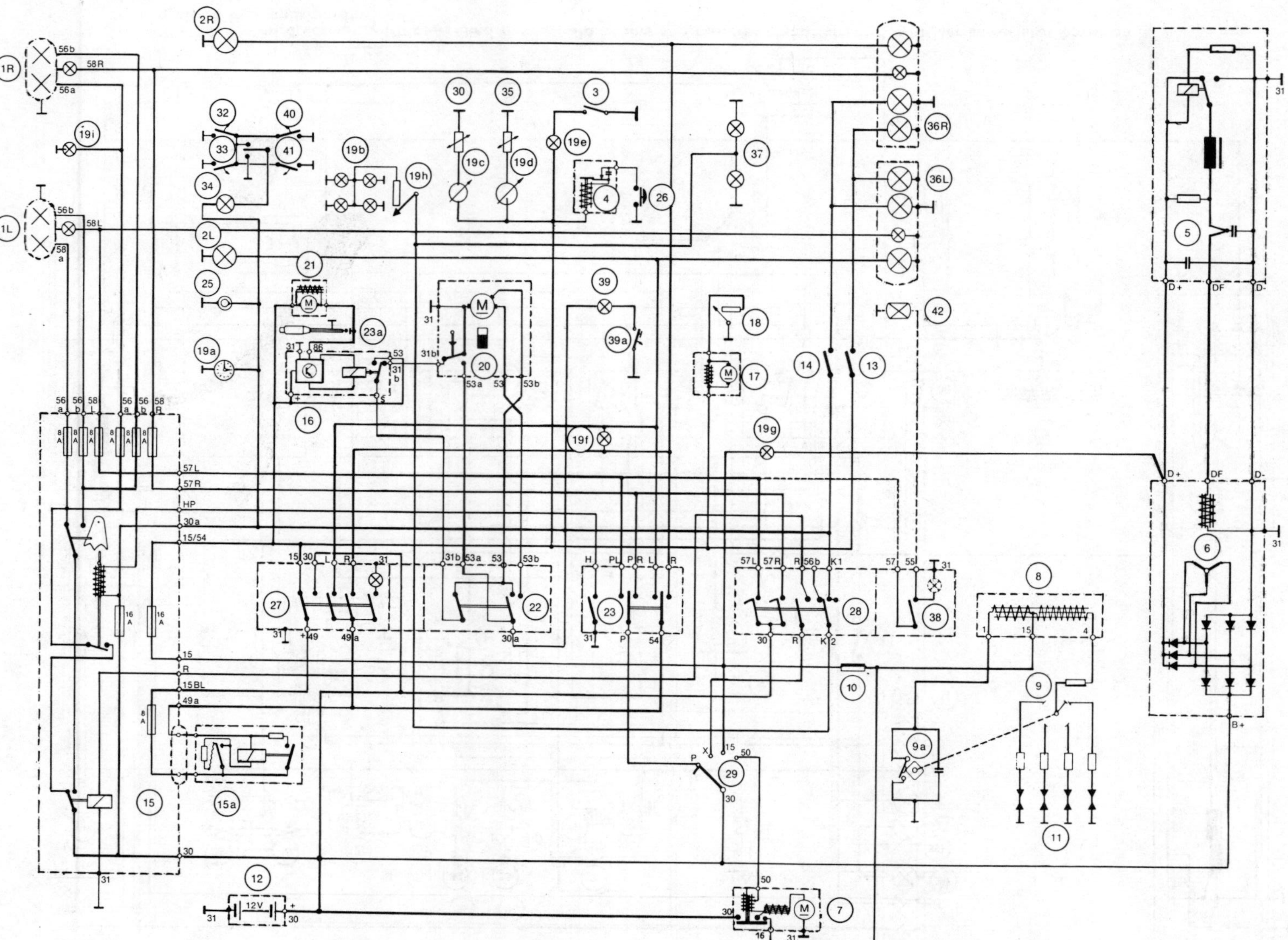

FIG 14:5 Third version with series resistor between ignition lock and ignition coil

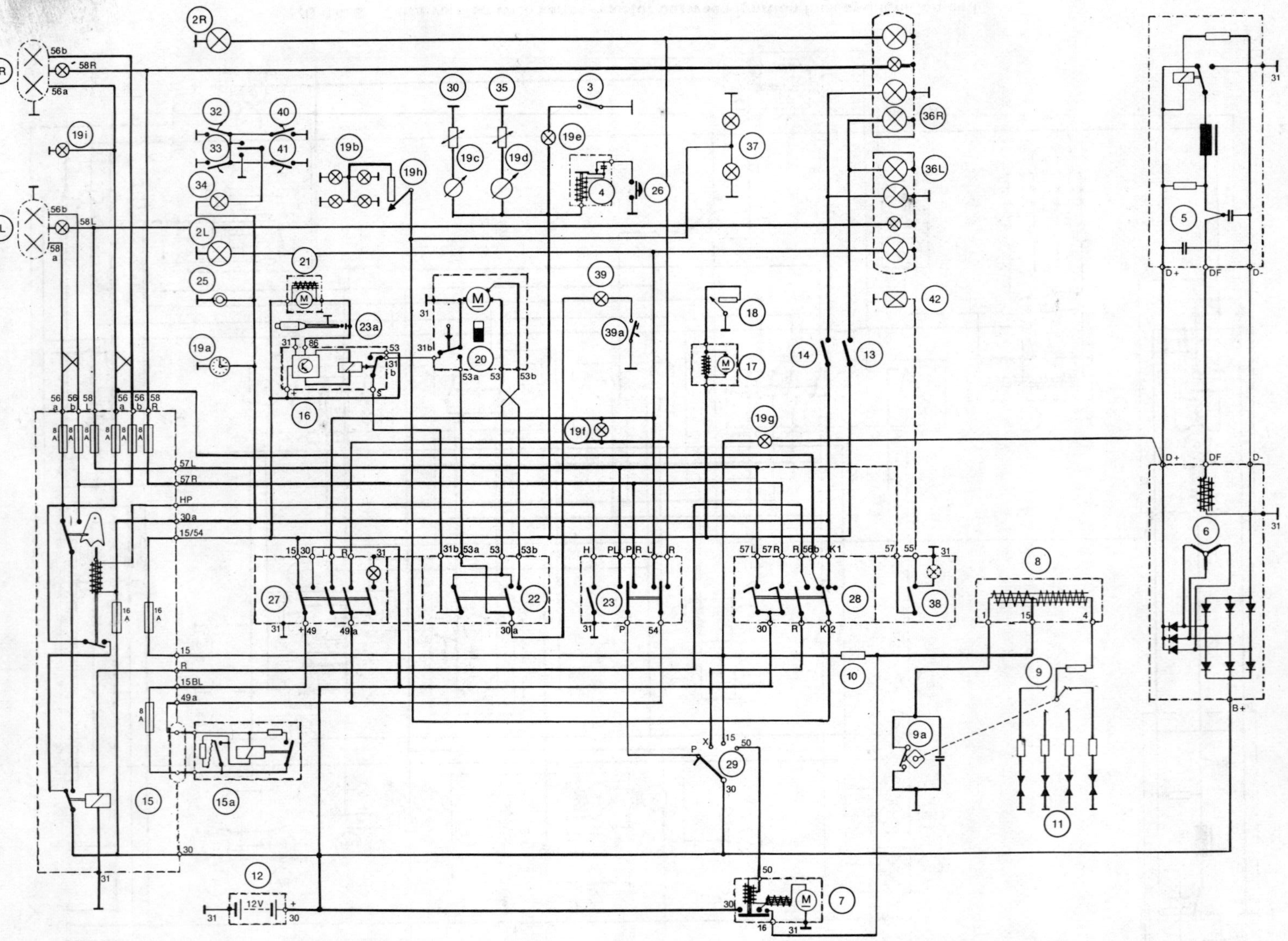

FIG 14:6 Third version with combined flasher, dip beams and number plate light and with series resistor between ignition lock and ignition coil

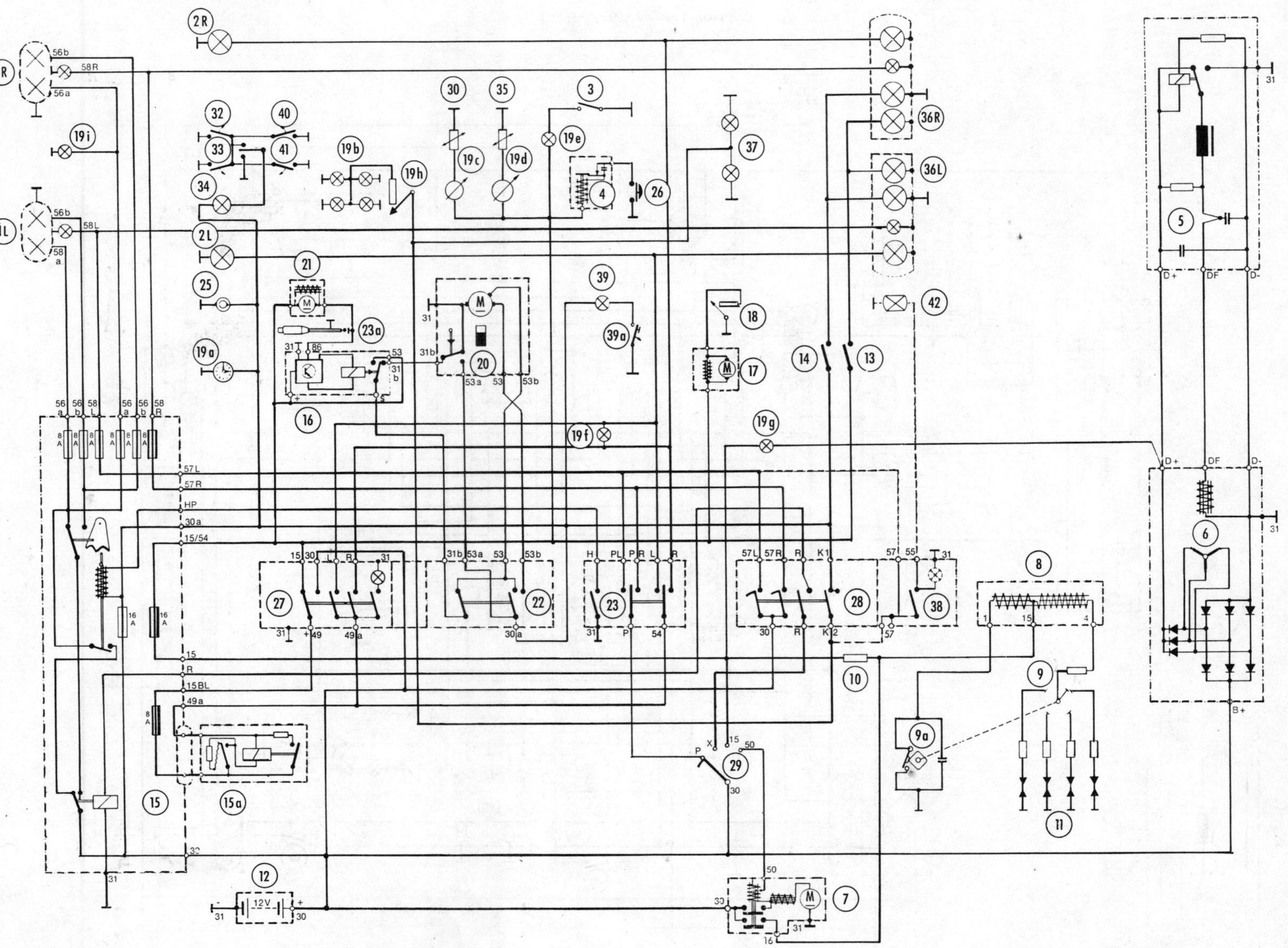

FIG 14:7 Fourth version, June 1969

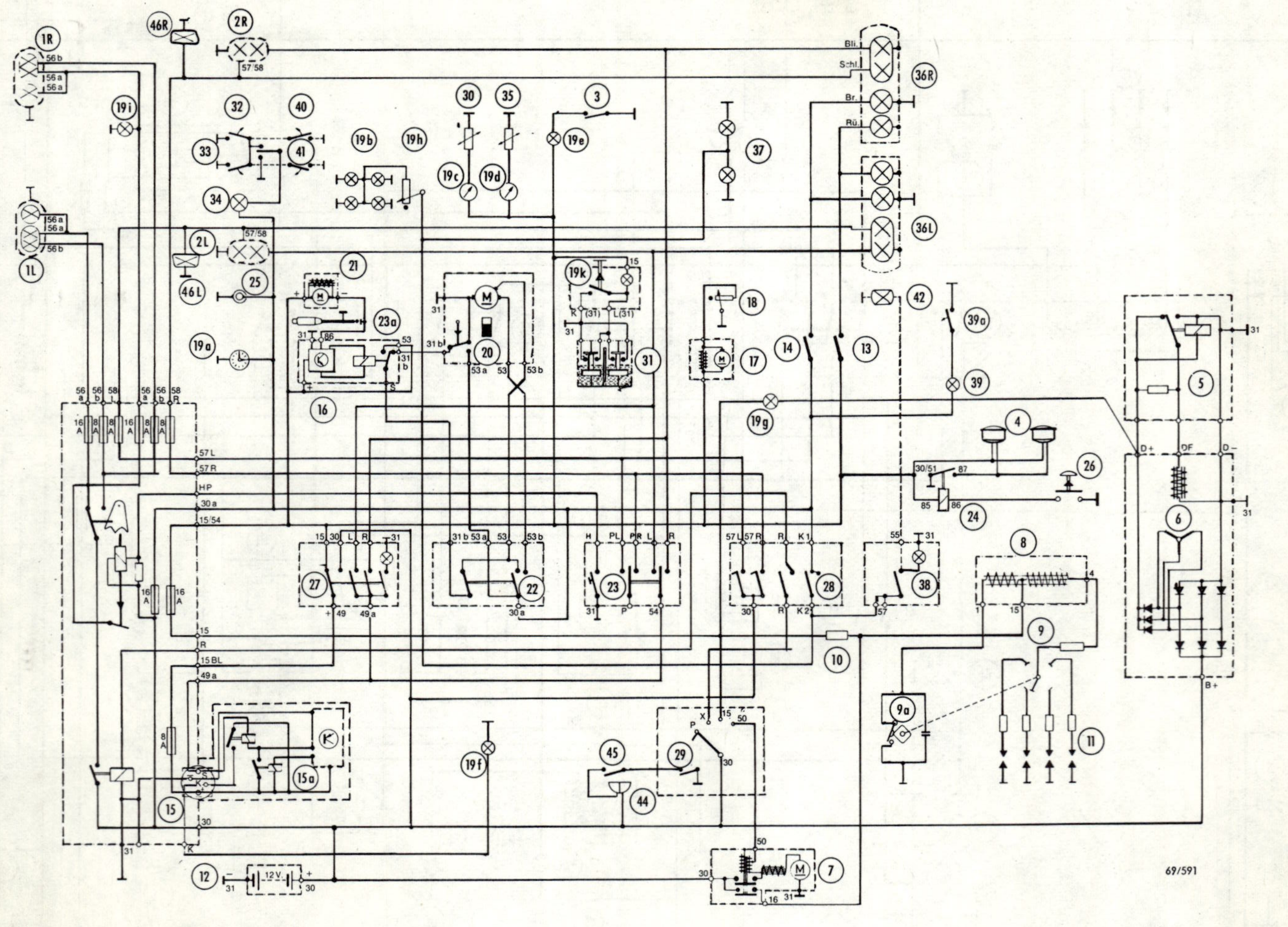

FIG 14:8   USA export version

Inches	Decimals	Milli-metres	Inches to Millimetres		Millimetres to Inches	
			Inches	mm	mm	Inches
$\frac{1}{64}$	.015625	.3969	.001	.0254	.01	.00039
$\frac{1}{32}$	.03125	.7937	.002	.0508	.02	.00079
$\frac{3}{64}$	.046875	1.1906	.003	.0762	.03	.00118
$\frac{1}{16}$	.0625	1.5875	.004	.1016	.04	.00157
$\frac{5}{64}$	.078125	1.9844	.005	.1270	.05	.00197
$\frac{3}{32}$	.09375	2.3812	.006	.1524	.06	.00236
$\frac{7}{64}$	.109375	2.7781	.007	.1778	.07	.00276
$\frac{1}{8}$	.125	3.1750	.008	.2032	.08	.00315
$\frac{9}{64}$	.140625	3.5719	.009	.2286	.09	.00354
$\frac{5}{32}$	.15625	3.9687	.01	.254	.1	.00394
$\frac{11}{64}$	.171875	4.3656	.02	.508	.2	.00787
$\frac{3}{16}$	.1875	4.7625	.03	.762	.3	.01181
$\frac{13}{64}$	.203125	5.1594	.04	1.016	.4	.01575
$\frac{7}{32}$	.21875	5.5562	.05	1.270	.5	.01969
$\frac{15}{64}$	.234375	5.9531	.06	1.524	.6	.02362
$\frac{1}{4}$	.25	6.3500	.07	1.778	.7	.02756
$\frac{17}{64}$	.265625	6.7469	.08	2.032	.8	.03150
$\frac{9}{32}$	.28125	7.1437	.09	2.286	.9	.03543
$\frac{19}{64}$	.296875	7.5406	.1	2.54	1	.03937
$\frac{5}{16}$	.3125	7.9375	.2	5.08	2	.07874
$\frac{21}{64}$	.328125	8.3344	.3	7.62	3	.11811
$\frac{11}{32}$	.34375	8.7312	.4	10.16	4	.15748
$\frac{23}{64}$	.359375	9.1281	.5	12.70	5	.19685
$\frac{3}{8}$	.375	9.5250	.6	15.24	6	.23622
$\frac{25}{64}$	.390625	9.9219	.7	17.78	7	.27559
$\frac{13}{32}$	.40625	10.3187	.8	20.32	8	.31496
$\frac{27}{64}$	.421875	10.7156	.9	22.86	9	.35433
$\frac{7}{16}$	.4375	11.1125	1	25.4	10	.39370
$\frac{29}{64}$	.453125	11.5094	2	50.8	11	.43307
$\frac{15}{32}$	.46875	11.9062	3	76.2	12	.47244
$\frac{31}{64}$	.484375	12.3031	4	101.6	13	.51181
$\frac{1}{2}$	.5	12.7000	5	127.0	14	.55118
$\frac{33}{64}$	.515625	13.0969	6	152.4	15	.59055
$\frac{17}{32}$	.53125	13.4937	7	177.8	16	.62992
$\frac{35}{64}$	.546875	13.8906	8	203.2	17	.66929
$\frac{9}{16}$	.5625	14.2875	9	228.6	18	.70866
$\frac{37}{64}$	.578125	14.6844	10	254.0	19	.74803
$\frac{19}{32}$	.59375	15.0812	11	279.4	20	.78740
$\frac{39}{64}$	.609375	15.4781	12	304.8	21	.82677
$\frac{5}{8}$	.625	15.8750	13	330.2	22	.86614
$\frac{41}{64}$	.640625	16.2719	14	355.6	23	.90551
$\frac{21}{32}$	.65625	16.6687	15	381.0	24	.94488
$\frac{43}{64}$	.671875	17.0656	16	406.4	25	.98425
$\frac{11}{16}$	.6875	17.4625	17	431.8	26	1.02362
$\frac{45}{64}$	.703125	17.8594	18	457.2	27	1.06299
$\frac{23}{32}$	.71875	18.2562	19	482.6	28	1.10236
$\frac{47}{64}$	.734375	18.6531	20	508.0	29	1.14173
$\frac{3}{4}$	.75	19.0500	21	533.4	30	1.18110
$\frac{49}{64}$	.765625	19.4469	22	558.8	31	1.22047
$\frac{25}{32}$	.78125	19.8437	23	584.2	32	1.25984
$\frac{51}{64}$	.796875	20.2406	24	609.6	33	1.29921
$\frac{13}{16}$	.8125	20.6375	25	635.0	34	1.33858
$\frac{53}{64}$	.828125	21.0344	26	660.4	35	1.37795
$\frac{27}{32}$	.84375	21.4312	27	685.8	36	1.41732
$\frac{55}{64}$	.859375	21.8281	28	711.2	37	1.4567
$\frac{7}{8}$	.875	22.2250	29	736.6	38	1.4961
$\frac{57}{64}$	.890625	22.6219	30	762.0	39	1.5354
$\frac{29}{32}$	.90625	23.0187	31	787.4	40	1.5748
$\frac{59}{64}$	.921875	23.4156	32	812.8	41	1.6142
$\frac{15}{16}$	.9375	23.8125	33	838.2	42	1.6535
$\frac{61}{64}$	.953125	24.2094	34	863.6	43	1.6929
$\frac{31}{32}$	.96875	24.6062	35	889.0	44	1.7323
$\frac{63}{64}$	.984375	25.0031	36	914.4	45	1.7717

UNITS	Pints to Litres	Gallons to Litres	Litres to Pints	Litres to Gallons	Miles to Kilometres	Kilometres to Miles	Lbs. per sq. In. to Kg. per sq. Cm.	Kg. per sq. Cm. to Lbs. per sq. In.
1	.57	4.55	1.76	.22	1.61	.62	.07	14.22
2	1.14	9.09	3.52	.44	3.22	1.24	.14	28.50
3	1.70	13.64	5.28	.66	4.83	1.86	.21	42.67
4	2.27	18.18	7.04	.88	6.44	2.49	.28	56.89
5	2.84	22.73	8.80	1.10	8.05	3.11	.35	71.12
6	3.41	27.28	10.56	1.32	9.66	3.73	.42	85.34
7	3.98	31.82	12.32	1.54	11.27	4.35	.49	99.56
8	4.55	36.37	14.08	1.76	12.88	4.97	.56	113.79
9		40.91	15.84	1.98	14.48	5.59	.63	128.00
10		45.46	17.60	2.20	16.09	6.21	.70	142.23
20				4.40	32.19	12.43	1.41	284.47
30				6.60	48.28	18.64	2.11	426.70
40				8.80	64.37	24.85		
50					80.47	31.07		
60					96.56	37.28		
70					112.65	43.50		
80					128.75	49.71		
90					144.84	55.92		
100					160.93	62.14		

UNITS	Lb ft to kgm	Kgm to lb ft	UNITS	Lb ft to kgm	Kgm to lb ft
1	.138	7.233	7	.967	50.631
2	.276	14.466	8	1.106	57.864
3	.414	21.699	9	1.244	65.097
4	.553	28.932	10	1.382	72.330
5	.691	36.165	20	2.765	144.660
6	.829	43.398	30	4.147	216.990

AUDI 100

HINTS ON MAINTENANCE AND OVERHAUL

There are few things more rewarding than the restoration of a vehicle's original peak of efficiency and smooth performance.

The following notes are intended to help the owner to reach that state of perfection. Providing that he possesses the basic manual skills he should have no difficulty in performing most of the operations detailed in this manual. It must be stressed, however, that where recommended in the manual, highly-skilled operations ought to be entrusted to experts, who have the necessary equipment, to carry out the work satisfactorily.

Quality of workmanship:

The hazardous driving conditions on the roads to-day demand that vehicles should be as nearly perfect, mechanically, as possible. It is therefore most important that amateur work be carried out with care, bearing in mind the often inadequate working conditions, and also the inferior tools which may have to be used. It is easy to counsel perfection in all things, and we recognize that it may be setting an impossibly high standard. We do, however, suggest that every care should be taken to ensure that a vehicle is as safe to take on the road as it is humanly possible to make it.

Safe working conditions:

Even though a vehicle may be stationary, it is still potentially dangerous if certain sensible precautions are not taken when working on it while it is supported on jacks or blocks. It is indeed preferable not to use jacks alone, but to supplement them with carefully placed blocks, so that there will be plenty of support if the car rolls off the jacks during a strenuous manoeuvre. Axle stands are an excellent way of providing a rigid base which is not readily disturbed. Piles of bricks are a dangerous substitute. Be careful not to get under heavy loads on lifting tackle, the load could fall. It is preferable not to work alone when lifting an engine, or when working underneath a vehicle which is supported well off the ground. To be trapped, particularly under the vehicle, may have unpleasant results if help is not quickly forthcoming. Make some provision, however humble, to deal with fires. Always disconnect a battery if there is a likelihood of electrical shorts. These may start a fire if there is leaking fuel about. This applies particularly to leads which can carry a heavy current, like those in the starter circuit. While on the subject of electricity, we must also stress the danger of using equipment which is run off the mains and which has no earth or has faulty wiring or connections. So many workshops have damp floors, and electrical shocks are of such a nature that it is sometimes impossible to let go of a live lead or piece of equipment due to the muscular spasms which take place.

Work demanding special care:

This involves the servicing of braking, steering and suspension systems. On the road, failure of the braking system may be disastrous. Make quite sure that there can be no possibility of failure through the bursting of rusty brake pipes or rotten hoses, nor to a sudden loss of pressure due to defective seals or valves.

Problems:

The chief problems which may face an operator are:
1 External dirt.
2 Difficulty in undoing tight fixings.
3 Dismantling unfamiliar mechanisms.
4 Deciding in what respect parts are defective.
5 Confusion about the correct order for reassembly.
6 Adjusting running clearance.
7 Road testing.
8 Final tuning.

Practical suggestions to solve the problems:

1 Preliminary cleaning of large parts—engines, transmissions, steering, suspensions, etc.,—should be carried out before removal from the car. Where road dirt and mud alone are present, wash clean with a high-pressure water jet, brushing to remove stubborn adhesions, and allow to drain and dry. Where oil or grease is also present, wash down with a proprietary compound (Gunk, Teepol etc.,) applying with a stiff brush—an old paint brush is suitable—into all crevices. Cover the distributor and ignition coils with a polythene bag and then apply a strong water jet to clear the loosened deposits. Allow to drain and dry. The assemblies will then be sufficiently clean to remove and transfer to the bench for the next stage.

On the bench, further cleaning can be carried out, first wiping the parts as free as possible from grease with old newspaper. Avoid using rag or cotton waste which can leave clogging fibres behind. Any remaining grease can be removed with a brush dipped in paraffin. If necessary, traces of paraffin can be removed by carbon tetrachloride. Avoid using paraffin or petrol in large quantities for cleaning in enclosed areas, such as garages, on account of the high fire risk.

When all exteriors have been cleaned, and not before, dismantling can be commenced. This ensures that dirt will not enter into interiors and orifices revealed by dismantling. In the next phases, where components have to be cleaned, use carbon tetrachloride in preference to petrol and keep the containers covered except when in use. After the components have been cleaned, plug small holes with tapered hard wood plugs cut to size and blank off larger orifices with grease-proof paper and masking tape. Do not use soft wood plugs or matchsticks as they may break.

2 It is not advisable to hammer on the end of a screw thread, but if it must be done, first screw on a nut to protect the thread, and use a lead hammer. This applies particularly to the removal of tapered cotters. Nuts and bolts seem to 'grow' together, especially in exhaust systems. If penetrating oil does not work, try the judicious application of heat, but be careful of starting a fire. Asbestos sheet or cloth is useful to isolate heat.

Tight bushes or pieces of tail-pipe rusted into a silencer can be removed by splitting them with an open-ended hacksaw. Tight screws can sometimes be started by a tap from a hammer on the end of a suitable screwdriver. Many tight fittings will yield to the judicious use of a hammer, but it must be a soft-faced hammer if damage is to be avoided, use a heavy block on the opposite side to absorb shock. Any parts of the steering system which have been damaged should be renewed, as attempts to repair them may lead to cracking and subsequent failure, and steering ball joints should be disconnected using a recommended tool to prevent damage.

3 It often happens that an owner is baffled when trying to dismantle an unfamiliar piece of equipment. So many modern devices are pressed together or assembled by spinning-over flanges, that they must be sawn apart. The intention is that the whole assembly must be renewed. However, parts which appear to be in one piece to the naked eye, may reveal close-fitting joint lines when inspected with a magnifying glass, and, this may provide the necessary clue to dismantling. Left-handed screw threads are used where rotational forces would tend to unscrew a right-handed screw thread.

Be very careful when dismantling mechanisms which may come apart suddenly. Work in an enclosed space where the parts will be contained, and drape a piece of cloth over the device if springs are likely to fly in all directions. Mark everything which might be reassembled in the wrong position, scratched symbols may be used on unstressed parts, or a sequence of tiny dots from a centre punch can be useful. Stressed parts should never be scratched or centre-popped as this may lead to cracking under working conditions. Store parts which look alike in the correct order for reassembly. Never rely upon memory to assist in the assembly of complicated mechanisms, especially when they will be dismantled for a long time, but make notes, and drawings to supplement the diagrams in the manual, and put labels on detached wires. Rust stains may indicate unlubricated wear. This can sometimes be seen round the outside edge of a bearing cup in a universal joint. Look for bright rubbing marks on parts which normally should not make heavy contact. These might prove that something is bent or running out of truth. For example, there might be bright marks on one side of a piston, at the top near the ring grooves, and others at the bottom of the skirt on the other side. This could well be the clue to a bent connecting rod. Suspected cracks can be proved by heating the component in a light oil to approximately 100°C, removing, drying off, and dusting with french chalk, if a crack is present the oil retained in the crack will stain the french chalk.

4 In determining wear, and the degree, against the permissible limits set in the manual, accurate measurement can only be achieved by the use of a micrometer. In many cases, the wear is given to the fourth place of decimals; that is in ten-thousandths of an inch. This can be read by the vernier scale on the barrel of a good micrometer. Bore diameters are more difficult to determine. If, however, the matching shaft is accurately measured, the degree of play in the bore can be felt as a guide to its suitability. In other cases, the shank of a twist drill of known diameter is a handy check.

Many methods have been devised for determining the clearance between bearing surfaces. To-day the best and simplest is by the use of Plastigage, obtainable from most garages. A thin plastic thread is laid between the two surfaces and the bearing is tightened, flattening the thread. On removal, the width of the thread is compared with a scale supplied with the thread and the clearance is read off directly. Sometimes joint faces leak persistently, even after gasket renewal. The fault will then be traceable to distortion, dirt or burrs. Studs which are screwed into soft metal frequently raise burrs at the point of entry. A quick cure for this is to chamfer the edge of the hole in the part which fits over the stud.

5 **Always check a replacement part with the original one before it is fitted.**

If parts are not marked, and the order for reassembly is not known, a little detective work will help. Look for marks which are due to wear to see if they can be mated. Joint faces may not be identical due to manufacturing errors, and parts which overlap may be stained, giving a clue to the correct position. Most fixings leave identifying marks especially if they were painted over on assembly. It is then easier to decide whether a nut, for instance, has a plain, a spring, or a shakeproof washer under it. All running surfaces become 'bedded' together after long spells of work and tiny imperfections on one part will be found to have left corresponding marks on the other. This is particularly true of shafts and bearings and even a score on a cylinder wall will show on the piston.

6 Checking end float or rocker clearances by feeler gauge may not always give accurate results because of wear. For instance, the rocker tip which bears on a valve stem may be deeply pitted, in which case the feeler will simply be bridging a depression. Thrust washers may also wear depressions in opposing faces to make accurate measurement difficult. End float is then easier to check by using a dial gauge. It is common practice to adjust end play in bearing assemblies, like front hubs with taper rollers, by doing up the axle nut until the hub becomes stiff to turn and then backing it off a little. Do not use this method with ballbearing hubs as the assembly is often preloaded by tightening the axle nut to its fullest extent. If the splitpin hole will not line up, file the base of the nut a little.

Steering assemblies often wear in the straight-ahead position. If any part is adjusted, make sure that it remains free when moved from lock to lock. Do not be surprised if an assembly like a steering gearbox, which is known to be carefully adjusted outside the car, becomes stiff when it is bolted in place. This will be due to distortion of the case by the pull of the mounting bolts, particularly if the mounting points are not all touching together. This problem may be met in other equipment and is cured by careful attention to the alignment of mounting points.

When a spanner is stamped with a size and A/F it means that the dimension is the width between the jaws and has no connection with ANF, which is the designation for the American National Fine thread. Coarse threads like Whitworth are rarely used on cars to-day except for studs which screw into soft aluminium or cast iron. For this reason it might be found that the top end of a cylinder head stud has a fine thread and the lower end a coarse thread to screw into the cylinder block. If the car has mainly UNF threads then it is likely that any coarse threads will be UNC, which are not the same as Whitworth. Small sizes have the same number of threads in Whitworth and UNC, but in the ½ inch size for example, there are twelve threads to the inch in the former and thirteen in the latter.

7   After a major overhaul, particularly if a great deal of work has been done on the braking, steering and suspension systems, it is advisable to approach the problem of testing with care. If the braking system has been overhauled, apply heavy pressure to the brake pedal and get a second operator to check every possible source of leakage. The brakes may work extremely well, but a leak could cause complete failure after a few miles.

Do not fit the hub caps until every wheel nut has been checked for tightness, and make sure the tyre pressures are correct. Check the levels of coolant, lubricants and hydraulic fluids. Being satisfied that all is well, take the car on the road and test the brakes at once. Check the steering and the action of the handbrake. Do all this at moderate speeds on quiet roads, and make sure there is no other vehicle behind you when you try a rapid stop.

Finally, remember that many parts settle down after a time, so check for tightness of all fixings after the car has been on the road for a hundred miles or so.

8   It is useless to tune an engine which has not reached its normal running temperature. In the same way, the tune of an engine which is stiff after a rebore will be different when the engine is again running free. Remember too, that rocker clearances on pushrod operated valve gear will change when the cylinder head nuts are tightened after an initial period of running with a new head gasket.

Trouble may not always be due to what seems the obvious cause. Ignition, carburation and mechanical condition are interdependent and spitting back through the carburetter, which might be attributed to a weak mixture, can be caused by a sticking inlet valve.

For one final hint on tuning, never adjust more than one thing at a time or it will be impossible to tell which adjustment produced the desired result.

GLOSSARY OF TERMS

Allen key — Cranked wrench of hexagonal section for use with socket head screws.

Alternator — Electrical generator producing alternating current. Rectified to direct current for battery charging.

Ambient temperature — Surrounding atmospheric temperature.

Annulus — Used in engineering to indicate the outer ring gear of an epicyclic gear train.

Armature — The shaft carrying the windings, which rotates in the magnetic field of a generator or starter motor. That part of a solenoid or relay which is activated by the magnetic field.

Axial — In line with, or pertaining to, an axis.

Backlash — Play in meshing gears.

Balance lever — A bar where force applied at the centre is equally divided between connections at the ends.

Banjo axle — Axle casing with large diameter housing for the crownwheel and differential.

Bendix pinion — A self-engaging and self-disengaging drive on a starter motor shaft.

Bevel pinion — A conical shaped gearwheel, designed to mesh with a similar gear with an axis usually at 90 deg. to its own.

bhp — Brake horse power, measured on a dynamometer.

bmep — Brake mean effective pressure. Average pressure on a piston during the working stroke.

Brake cylinder — Cylinder with hydraulically operated piston(s) acting on brake shoes or pad(s).

Brake regulator — Control valve fitted in hydraulic braking system which limits brake pressure to rear brakes during heavy braking to prevent rear wheel locking.

Camber — Angle at which a wheel is tilted from the vertical.

Capacitor — Modern term for an electrical condenser. Part of distributor assembly, connected across contact breaker points, acts as an interference suppressor.

Castellated — Top face of a nut, slotted across the flats, to take a locking splitpin.

Castor — Angle at which the kingpin or swivel pin is tilted when viewed from the side.

cc — Cubic centimetres. Engine capacity is arrived at by multiplying the area of the bore in sq cm by the stroke in cm by the number of cylinders.

Clevis — U-shaped forked connector used with a clevis pin, usually at handbrake connections.

Collet — A type of collar, usually split and located in a groove in a shaft, and held in place by a retainer. The arrangement used to retain the spring(s) on a valve stem in most cases.

Commutator — Rotating segmented current distributor between armature windings and brushes in generator or motor.

Compression — The ratio, or quantitative relation, of the total volume (piston at bottom of stroke) to the unswept volume (piston at top of stroke) in an engine cylinder.

Condenser — See capacitor.

Core plug — Plug for blanking off a manufacturing hole in a casting.

Crownwheel — Large bevel gear in rear axle, driven by a bevel pinion attached to the propeller shaft. Sometimes called a 'ring wheel'.

'C'-spanner — Like a 'C' with a handle. For use on screwed collars without flats, but with slots or holes.

Damper — Modern term for shock-absorber, used in vehicle suspension systems to damp out spring oscillations.

Depression — The lowering of atmospheric pressure as in the inlet manifold and carburetter.

Dowel — Close tolerance pin, peg, tube, or bolt, which accurately locates mating parts.

Drag link — Rod connecting steering box drop arm (pitman arm) to nearest front wheel steering arm in certain types of steering systems.

Dry liner — Thinwall tube pressed into cylinder bore

Dry sump — Lubrication system where all oil is scavenged from the sump, and returned to a separate tank.

Dynamo — See Generator.

Electrode — Terminal, part of an electrical component, such as the points or 'Electrodes' of a sparking plug.

Electrolyte — In lead-acid car batteries a solution of sulphuric acid and distilled water.

End float — The axial movement between associated parts, end play.

EP — Extreme pressure. In lubricants, special grades for heavily loaded bearing surfaces, such as gear teeth in a gearbox, or crownwheel and pinion in a rear axle.

Fade	Of brakes. Reduced efficiency due to overheating.
Field coils	Windings on the polepieces of motors and generators.
Fillets	Narrow finishing strips usually applied to interior bodywork.
First motion shaft	Input shaft from clutch to gearbox.
Fullflow filter	Filters in which all the oil is pumped to the engine. If the element becomes clogged, a bypass valve operates to pass unfiltered oil to the engine.
FWD	Front wheel drive.
Gear pump	Two meshing gears in a close fitting casing. Oil is carried from the inlet round the outside of both gears in the spaces between the gear teeth and casing to the outlet, the meshing gear teeth prevent oil passing back to the inlet, and the oil is forced through the outlet port.
Generator	Modern term for 'Dynamo'. When rotated produces electrical current.
Grommet	A ring of protective or sealing material. Can be used to protect pipes or leads passing through bulkheads.
Grubscrew	Fully threaded headless screw with screwdriver slot. Used for locking, or alignment purposes.
Gudgeon pin	Shaft which connects a piston to its connecting rod. Sometimes called 'wrist pin', or 'piston pin'.
Halfshaft	One of a pair transmitting drive from the differential.
Helical	In spiral form. The teeth of helical gears are cut at a spiral angle to the side faces of the gearwheel.
Hot spot	Hot area that assists vapourisation of fuel on its way to cylinders. Often provided by close contact between inlet and exhaust manifolds.
HT	High Tension. Applied to electrical current produced by the ignition coil for the sparking plugs.
Hydrometer	A device for checking specific gravity of liquids. Used to check specific gravity of electrolyte.
Hypoid bevel gears	A form of bevel gear used in the rear axle drive gears. The bevel pinion meshes below the centre line of the crownwheel, giving a lower propeller shaft line.
Idler	A device for passing on movement. A free running gear between driving and driven gears. A lever transmitting track rod movement to a side rod in steering gear.
Impeller	A centrifugal pumping element. Used in water pumps to stimulate flow.
Journals	Those parts of a shaft that are in contact with the bearings.
Kingpin	The main vertical pin which carries the front wheel spindle, and permits steering movement. May be called 'steering pin' or 'swivel pin'.
Layshaft	The shaft which carries the laygear in the gearbox. The laygear is driven by the first motion shaft and drives the third motion shaft according to the gear selected. Sometimes called the 'countershaft' or 'second motion shaft.'
lb ft	A measure of twist or torque. A pull of 10 lb at a radius of 1 ft is a torque of 10 lb ft.
lb/sq in	Pounds per square inch.
Little-end	The small, or piston end of a connecting rod. Sometimes called the 'small-end'.
LT	Low Tension. The current output from the battery.
Mandrel	Accurately manufactured bar or rod used for test or centring purposes.
Manifold	A pipe, duct, or chamber, with several branches.
Needle rollers	Bearing rollers with a length many times their diameter.
Oil bath	Reservoir which lubricates parts by immersion. In air filters, a separate oil supply for wetting a wire mesh element to hold the dust.
Oil wetted	In air filters, a wire mesh element lightly oiled to trap and hold airborne dust.
Overlap	Period during which inlet and exhaust valves are open together.
Panhard rod	Bar connected between fixed point on chassis and another on axle to control sideways movement.
Pawl	Pivoted catch which engages in the teeth of a ratchet to permit movement in one direction only.
Peg spanner	Tool with pegs, or pins, to engage in holes or slots in the part to be turned.
Pendant pedals	Pedals with levers that are pivoted at the top end.
Phillips screwdriver	A cross-point screwdriver for use with the cross-slotted heads of Phillips screws.'
Pinion	A small gear, usually in relation to another gear.
Piston-type damper	Shock absorber in which damping is controlled by a piston working in a closed oil-filled cylinder.
Preloading	Preset static pressure on ball or roller bearings not due to working loads.
Radial	Radiating from a centre, like the spokes of a wheel.

Radius rod	Pivoted arm confining movement of a part to an arc of fixed radius.
Ratchet	Toothed wheel or rack which can move in one direction only, movement in the other being prevented by a pawl.
Ring gear	A gear tooth ring attached to outer periphery of flywheel. Starter pinion engages with it during starting.
Runout	Amount by which rotating part is out of true.
Semi-floating axle	Outer end of rear axle halfshaft is carried on bearing inside axle casing. Wheel hub is secured to end of shaft.
Servo	A hydraulic or pneumatic system for assisting, or augmenting a physical effort. See 'Vacuum Servo'.
Setscrew	One which is threaded for the full length of the shank.
Shackle	A coupling link, used in the form of two parallel pins connected by side plates to secure the end of the master suspension spring and absorb the effects of deflection.
Shell bearing	Thinwalled steel shell lined with anti-friction metal. Usually semi-circular and used in pairs for main and big-end bearings.
Shock absorber	See 'Damper'.
Silentbloc	Rubber bush bonded to inner and outer metal sleeves.
Socket-head screw	Screw with hexagonal socket for an Allen key.
Solenoid	A coil of wire creating a magnetic field when electric current passes through it. Used with a soft iron core to operate contacts or a mechanical device.
Spur gear	A gear with teeth cut axially across the periphery.
Stub axle	Short axle fixed at one end only.
Tachometer	An instrument for accurate measurement of rotating speed. Usually indicates in revolutions per minute.
TDC	Top Dead Centre. The highest point reached by a piston in a cylinder, with the crank and connecting rod in line.
Thermostat	Automatic device for regulating temperature. Used in vehicle coolant systems to open a valve which restricts circulation at low temperature.
Third motion shaft	Output shaft of gearbox.
Threequarter floating axle	Outer end of rear axle halfshaft flanged and bolted to wheel hub, which runs on bearing mounted on outside of axle casing. Vehicle weight is not carried by the axle shaft.
Thrust bearing or washer	Used to reduce friction in rotating parts subject to axial loads.
Torque	Turning or twisting effort. See 'lb ft'.
Track rod	The bar(s) across the vehicle which connect the steering arms and maintain the front wheels in their correct alignment.
UJ	Universal joint. A coupling between shafts which permits angular movement.
UNF	Unified National Fine screw thread.
Vacuum servo	Device used in brake system, using difference between atmospheric pressure and inlet manifold depression to operate a piston which acts to augment brake pressure as required. See 'Servo'.
Venturi	A restriction or 'choke' in a tube, as in a carburetter, used to increase velocity to obtain a reduction in pressure.
Vernier	A sliding scale for obtaining fractional readings of the graduations of an adjacent scale.
Welch plug	A domed thin metal disc which is partially flattened to lock in a recess. Used to plug core holes in castings.
Wet liner	Removable cylinder barrel, sealed against coolant leakage, where the coolant is in direct contact with the outer surface.
Wet sump	A reservoir attached to the crankcase to hold the lubricating oil.

INDEX

A

Air cleaner	41
Alternator refitment	134
Alternator removal	134
Alternator servicing	133
Alternator testing	133
Antifreeze solutions	53
Anti-roll bar	105
Automatic transmission, description	81
Automatic transmission, fault diagnosis	89
Automatic transmission, power flow	85
Automatic transmission, ratios	153
Automatic transmission, removal	91
Axle removal, rear	109

B

Backlight replacement	147
Battery maintenance	131
Beam-setting, headlamps	138
Belt tensioning	50, 134
Big-end bearings	19, 21
Bleeding brake system	128
Bodywork renovation	141
Brake calipers	124
Brake disc removal	124
Brake drum removal	127
Brake fluid level	121
Brake linings	127
Brake maintenance	121
Brake master cylinder	127
Brake pads	124
Brake vacuum servo	129

C

Calipers	124
Camber angle	109
Camshaft bearings	20
Camshaft chain tensioner	22
Camshaft drive	22
Camshaft end float	21
Camshaft refitment	21
Camshaft removal	20
Capacities	154
Capacitor, distributor	46
Carburetter adjustment, 35.PDSIT	29
Carburetter adjustment, 32.TDID	35
Carburetter adjustment, 32/32.TDID	39
Carburetter dismantling, 35.PDSIT	29
Carburetter dismantling, 32.TDID	33
Carburetter dismantling, 32/32.TDID	39
Carburetter fuel level	29, 35
Carburetter jet cleaning	29, 33
Carburetter removal and refitment	28, 32, 39
Castor angle	109
Clutch adjustment	55
Clutch description	55
Clutch dismantling	57
Clutch pedal clearance	55
Clutch reassembly and refitment	58
Clutch release bearing	57

Clutch removal (cont.)

Clutch removal	57
Clutch spring	57
Condenser (capacitor), distributor	46
Connecting rod removal	19
Connecting rod replacement	22
Contact breaker adjustment	43
Control box (electrical)	133
Cooling system	49
Crankcase breather	23
Crankshaft bearings	21
Crankshaft regrind undersizes	21
Crankshaft thrust bearing	9
Current regulator adjustment	133
Cylinder head nut sequence	13
Cylinder head refitment	13
Cylinder head removal	12
Cylinder head servicing	14

D

Dampers, suspension	97
Decarbonizing	15
Differential dismantling	93
Differential pinion settings	95
Differential reassembly	95
Distributor drive shaft	46
Distributor reassembly	46
Distributor refitment	46
Distributor removal	46
Door trim	143
Draining cooling system	49
Drive shafts, transmission	97

E

Electrical equipment	131
Electrolyte, battery	131
Engine description	9
Engine description, USA	23
Engine reassembly	21
Engine removal	11

F

Fan removal	50
Filter element, fuel	27
Filter element, oil	23
Firing order	152
Flasher unit	136
Flywheel removal	19
Friction linings, clutch	57
Friction linings, drum brakes	127
Friction pads, disc brakes	122, 124
Front brakes	124
Front suspension description	97
Front suspension dismantling	97
Front suspension setting angles	109
Fuel pump removal and dismantling	27
Fuel pump servicing	27
Fuel pump testing	25
Fuel system	25
Fuel system, sealed	41

G

Gasket, head 13
Gauges 136
Gearbox ratios 152
Glossary 171
Grinding-in valves 15
Gudgeon pins 20
Guides, pushrod 17
Guides, valve 14

H

Handbrake adjustment 122
Handbrake cable 130
Headlamp beam-setting 138
Head nut tightening sequence 13
Head servicing 14
Hints on maintenance and overhaul ... 167
Hydraulic brake system 121
Hydrometer test of electrolyte 131

I

Idling adjustment, 35.PDSIT carburetter ... 29
Idling adjustment, 32.TDID carburetter ... 35
Idling adjustment, 32/32.TDID carburetter ... 39
Ignition faults 44
Ignition system 43
Ignition testing 45
Ignition timing 47
Instruments 136

J

Jet cleaning... ... ... 29, 33
Jet sizes 151

L

Lighting circuits 138
Locks, door 143
Low-tension circuit tests, ignition 45

M

Main bearing refitment 21
Main bearing removal 20
Master cylinder, brake 127
Mountings, engine 11

N

Needle valve, carburetter float 29, 33

O

Oil filter description... 23
Oil filter servicing 23
Oil pressure relief valve 20
Oil pump 22
Oil seal, crankshaft 20

P

Pedal clearance, clutch 55
Piston removal 19
Piston ring gaps 20
Piston rings 20
Pistons and connecting rods 20
Pump, fuel 27
Pump, oil 22
Pump, water 52

R

Rack and pinion, steering 119
Radiator flushing and refilling 49
Radiator removal 50
Rear axle 110
Rear brakes 127
Rear hubs 110
Rear suspension description 97
Rear suspension refitment 110
Rear suspension removal 110
Rear window 147
Regulator, voltage 133

S

Sealed fuel system 41
Solenoid, starter motor 134
Spark plug gap 47
Spark plugs and leads 48
Starter motor refitment 135
Starter motor removal 135
Starter motor servicing 135
Starter motor testing 134
Steering ball joints 119
Steering column 114
Steering description... 113
Steering linkage 119
Steering lubrication 120
Steering wheel removal 113
Sump 18
Suspension, front 97
Suspension, rear 97

T

Technical data 151
Thermostat, cooling system 52
Timing the ignition 47
Timing, valve 21
Toe-in adjustments 120
Tracking front wheels 120
Traffic hazard warning unit 136
Transmission description 51
Transmission dismantling and reassembly ... 59
Transmission removal 59
Transmission servicing 59
Trim removal, door 143

U

Universal joints, steering column 115
Universal joints, transmission 97

V

Vacuum servo 129
Valve clearances 17
Valve grinding 15
Valve guides 14
Valves, fuel pump 27
Valve springs 14
Valve timing 21
Voltage regulator adjustment 133

W

Water circulation system 49
Water pump removal 52
Window winding mechanism 145
Windscreen glass replacement 147
Windscreen wipers and motor 137
Wiring diagrams 157

THE AUTOBOOK SERIES OF WORKSHOP MANUALS

Alfa Romeo Giulia 1962 on

Aston Martin 1921-58

Audi 100 1969 on

(Austin, Morris etc.)
1100 Mk. 1 1962-67

(Austin, Morris etc.) 1100 Mk. 2,
1300 Mk. 1, 2, America 1968 on

Austin A30, A35, A40 Farina

Austin A55 Mk. 2, A60 1958-69

Austin A99, A110 1959-68

Austin J4 1960 on

Austin Maxi 1969 on

Austin, Morris 1800 1964 on

BMC 3 (Austin A50, A55 Mk. 1
Morris Oxford 2, 3 1954-59)

Austin Healey 100/6, 3000
1956-68

(Austin Healey, MG) Sprite,
Midget 1958 on

BMW 1600 1964 on

BMW 1800 1964-68

BMW 2000, 2002 1966 on

Chrysler Valiant Straight Six
1966-70

Citroen DS 19, ID 19 1955-66

Citroen ID 19, DS 19, 20, 21
1966-70

Datsun 1200 1970 on

Datsun 1300, 1600 1968 on

Datsun 240Z Sport 1970 on

De Dion Bouton 1899-1907

Fiat 124 1966 on

Fiat 124 Sport 1966 on

Fiat 125 1967 on

Fiat 500 1957-69

Fiat 600, 600D 1955-69

Fiat 850 1964 on

Fiat 1100 1957-69

Fiat 1300, 1500 1961-67

Ford Anglia Prefect 100E 1953-62

Ford Anglia 105E, Prefect 107E
1959-67

Ford Capri 1300, 1600 1968 on

Ford Capri 2000 GT, 3000 GT
1969 on

Ford Classic, Capri 1961-64

Ford Consul, Zephyr, Zodiac, 1, 2
1950-62

Ford Corsair Straight Four
1963-65

Ford Corsair V4 1965-68

Ford Corsair V4 1969 on

Ford Cortina 1962-66

Ford Cortina 1967-68

Ford Cortina 1969-70

Ford Cortina Mk. 3 1970 on

Ford Escort 1967 on

Ford Falcon V8 1964-69

Ford Thames 10, 12, 15 cwt
1957-65

Ford Transit 1965-72

Ford Zephyr Zodiac Mk. 3
1962-66

Ford Zephyr V4, V6, Zodiac
1966 on

Hillman Avenger 1970 on

Hillman Hunter 1966 on

Hillman Imp 1963-68

Hillman Imp 1969 on

Hillman Minx 1 to 5 1956-65

Hillman Minx 1965-67

Hillman Minx 1966-70

Hillman Super Minx 1961-65

Holden Straight Six 1948-66

Holden Straight Six 1966 on

Jaguar XK120, 140, 150,
Mk. 7, 8, 9 1948-61

Jaguar 2.4, 3.4, 3.8 Mk. 1, 2
1955-69

Jaguar 'E' Type 1961-69

Jaguar 'S' Type 420 1963-68

Jaguar XJ6 1968 on

Jowett Javelin Jupiter 1947-53

Landrover 1, 2 1948-61

Landrover 2, 2a 1959-71

Mercedes-Benz 190b, 190c
200 1959-68

Mercedes-Benz 220 1959-65

Mercedes-Benz 220/8 1968 on

Mercedes-Benz 230 1963-68

Mercedes-Benz 250 1965-67

Mercedes-Benz 250/8 1968 on

Mercedes-Benz 280/8 1968 on

MG TA to TF 1936-55

MGA MGB 1955-68

MG MGB 1969 on

Mini 1959 on

Mini Cooper 1961 on

Morgan 1936-69

Morris Marina 1971 on

Morris Minor 2, 1000 1952-71

Morris Oxford 5, 6 1959-71

NSU 1000 1963 on

NSU Prinz 1 to 4 1957 on

Opel Ascona, Manta 1970 on

Opel G.T. 1900 1968-72

Opel Kadett, Olympia 993cc,
1078cc 1962 on

Opel Kadett, Olympia 1492,
1698, 1897cc 1967 on

Opel Rekord C 1966 on

Peugeot 204 1965-72

Peugeot 404 1960-69

Peugeot 504 1968-70

Porsche 356a, 356b, 356c
1957-65

Porsche 911 1964-69

Porsche 912 1965-69

Reliant Regal 1962-70

Renault R4, R4L, 4 1961 on

Renault 6 1968 on

Renault 8, 10, 1100 1962 on

Renault 12 1969-71

Renault R16 1965 on

Renault Dauphine
Floride 1957-67

Renault Caravelle 1962-68

Rover 60 to 110 1953-64

Rover 2000 1963 on

Rover 3 Litre 1958-67

Rover 3500, 3500S 1968 on

Saab 95, 96, Sport 1960-68

Saab 99 1969 on

Saab V4 1966 on

Simca 1000 1961 on

Simca 1100 1967 on

Simca 1300, 1301, 1500, 1501
1963 on

Skoda One (440, 445, 450)
1957-69

Sunbeam Rapier Alpine 1955-65

Toyota Corolla 1100 1967 on

Toyota Corona 1500 Mk. 1
1965-70

Toyota Corona 1900 Mk. 2
1969 on

Triumph TR2, TR3, TR3A
1952-62

Triumph TR4, TR4A 1961-67

Triumph TR5, TR250, TR6
1967 on

Triumph 1300, 1500 1965 on

Triumph 2000 Mk. 1, 2.5 PI
Mk. 1 1963-69

Triumph 2000 Mk. 2, 2.5
PI Mk. 2 1969 on

Triumph Herald 1959-68

Triumph Herald 1969-71

Triumph Spitfire Vitesse
1962-68

Triumph Spitfire Mk. 3 1969-70

Triumph GT6, Vitesse 2 Litre
1969 on

Vauxhall Velox, Cresta 1957-69

Vauxhall Victor 1, 2, FB
1957-64

Vauxhall Victor 101 1964-67

Vauxhall Victor FD 1600, 2000
1967 on

Vauxhall Viva HA 1963-66

Vauxhall Viva HB 1966-70

Vauxhall Viva, HC Firenza
1971 on

Vauxhall Victor 3300, Ventura
1968 on

Volkswagen Beetle 1954-67

Volkswagen Beetle 1968 on

Volkswagen 1500 1961-66

Volkswagen 1600 Fastback
1965 on

Volkswagen Transporter
1954-67

Volkswagen Transporter
1968 on

Volvo P120 1961-70

Volvo P140 1966 on

Volvo 1800 1961 on